TWENTIETH-CENTURY RUSSIAN LITERARY CRITICISM

TWENTIETH-CENTURY RUSSIAN LITERARY CRITICISM

Edited by Victor Erlich

NEW HAVEN AND LONDON
YALE UNIVERSITY PRESS
1975

Published with assistance from
the Kingsley Trust Association Publication
Fund established by the Scroll and Key Society
of Yale College.

Designed by Sally Sullivan
and set in Caledonia type.
Printed in the United States of America by
The Murray Printing Co., Forge Village, Mass.

Published in Great Britain, Europe, and Africa by
Yale University Press, Ltd., London.
Distributed in Latin America by Kaiman & Polon, Inc., New York City;
in India by UBS Publishers' Distributors Pvt.,
Ltd., Delhi; in Japan by John Weatherhill, Inc., Tokyo.

Roman Jakobson's "On a Generation That Squandered Its Poets" is printed
here by permission of the author. It originally appeared in *Smert Vladimira Maja-
kovskogo* [Death of Vladimir Majakovskij] copyright 1931, Petropolis-Verlag
(Berlin, 1931).

Contents

PART 4: EMIGRÉ CRITICS

PART 5: THE RECENT SCENE

Preface

The seventeen essays presented in this volume range in date from 1909 to 1972. "Criticism" serves here as a generic term for the systematic discussion of literature, whether of the "academic" or of the "free-lance" variety. This broad definition includes, to be sure, both critical principles and assumptions (that is, literary theory) and interpretations of individual works. The introduction pays close attention to the former, but the selections themselves, whatever their larger methodological implications, fall into the latter category.

Therein lies the first difference between this anthology and an important collection, edited by Ladislav Matejka and Krystyna Pomorska, *Readings in Russian Poetics* (1971), whose main thrust is theoretical. Moreover, while the Matejka–Pomorska volume presents and explicates helpfully the formalist-structuralist tradition in Russian literary scholarship, the chief objective here has been to exemplify the diversity of twentieth-century Russian criticism by featuring several successive or concurrent critical perspectives, stances, and individual styles.

Primary concern with literary criticism as a mode distinguishes this work from another excellent compendium bearing on the study of Russian literature, *Major Soviet Writers* (1973) edited by Edward J. Brown, where the principle of selection is provided by the subject matter of the essays rather than by the overall contributions or intellectual orientations of their authors. This is not to say that Professor Brown's focus on modern Russian literary masters has no relevance to our endeavor. In order to render this volume accessible to the nonspecialist, it was necessary to restrict its thematic scope to major figures, be they Gogol or Dostoevsky, Tolstoy or Pushkin, Majakovskij or Mandelstam, and thus to exclude penetrating analyses of estimable Russian poets or fiction writers whose names would have meant little or nothing to the English-speaking reader.

In making a limited selection from a vast body of material the first consideration, naturally, was quality. Yet once this basic requirement was met, other factors came properly into play. In a volume that seeks to trace the complex path of twentieth-century Russian criticism such criteria as representativeness or relative historic importance could hardly be ignored. Thus, Aleksandr Voronskij's article on Isaac Babel, or Vladimir Lakshin's on

Bulgakov's *The Master and Margarita*, though vivid and credit-
able critical performances in their own right, owe their presence
in the volume at least as much to their commanding positions
within the modes or periods which they represent as to their intrinsic merits. This is especially true of Lakshin, whose warm
receptivity to Bulgakov's achievement epitomizes a memorable
episode in the history of recent Soviet criticism, an episode associated with the late Aleksandr Tvardovskij's liberal stewardship
of *Novyj mir*, where Lakshin's essay appeared. (Tvardovskij
helped make modern Russian literary history by publishing in the
November 1962 issue of *Novyj mir* Aleksandr Solzhenitsyn's *One
Day in the Life of Ivan Denisovich*.) By the same token, Georgij
Adamovich's assessment of Vladimir Nabokov is not one of the
most trenchant analyses of that writer, nor is it, arguably, one of
Adamovich's most satisfying essays. Yet the uneasy response of
the Russian emigration's leading critic to its most gifted novelist
was worth recording.

A deliberate effort was made to steer clear of material now
available, or shortly to be made available, in English-language
collections or monographs. The two initially contemplated exceptions were a fragment from Trotsky's *Literature and Revolution*
and an abbreviated version of Andrej Sinjavskij's "Poetry of Boris
Pasternak." In both instances overriding considerations were at
work. Trotsky's is by far the liveliest volume of criticism produced
by a Soviet Marxist, and Sinjavskij's essay is a towering landmark
in recent Russian criticism.

Subsequently another departure from the nonduplication principle proved imperative. Even though Roman Jakobson's "On a
Generation That Squandered Its Poets" has just appeared in
Brown's *Major Soviet Writers*, this was one of my first and firmest
selections, and I thought it too important, both as critical analysis
and as personal testimony, to be left out. (My disappointment at
not being the first to offer the full English text of Jakobson's "On a
Generation . . ." is largely offset by the pleasure of featuring it
here in Professor Brown's excellent translation.)

In other instances I have held the line, sometimes unhappily,
against further duplication. Having been apprised of the tables of
contents of a forthcoming anthology of Gogol criticism and of
another prospective volume bearing on the Gogol–Dostoevsky relationship, I have chosen not to include Boris Eikhenbaum's
path-breaking formalist essay "How Gogol's 'Overcoat' Is Made,"

the equally important "structuralist" analysis of the same tale by Dmitry Cizevsky, and an excerpt from M. M. Bakhtin's seminal book on Dostoevsky. The presentation of symbolist criticism has been affected too. Valerij Brjusov's perceptive and lucid reevaluation of Gogol, "Burned to Ashes," slated for publication elsewhere, was regretfully omitted only to be replaced by Andrej Belyj's "Gogol," an essay of at least equal importance but, I fear, of a more dubious translatability.

Some of the above choices were admittedly arbitrary, and some of the "tradeoffs" precarious. Yet all the essays here are of considerable inherent interest, and I would like to believe that, in spite of necessary omissions, this volume will offer the reader a sense of the vitality and variety of modern Russian criticism.

I wish to thank the following persons whose translations I have used: John Fred Beebe, Edward J. Brown, Henry Gifford, Irene Etkin Goldman, Sona Hoisington, James M. Holquist, James Karambelas, Carol A. Palmer, Stephen Rudy, and Elizabeth Trahan. Whenever no other translator is named in the essay's first unnumbered footnote, the translation is my own. Footnotes not ascribed to either author or translator are mine. Generally, the translations seek to render the letter as well as the spirit of the originals. On occasion, when the text seemed prolix or too arcane for the nonspecialist, some deletions have been made.

Victor Erlich

New Haven
July 1974

Introduction

Modern Russian Criticism from Andrej Belyj to Andrej Sinjavskij: Trends, Issues, Personalities

VICTOR ERLICH

One of the salient features of modern literary criticism is the proliferation of schools, approaches, methodologies. In his cross-cultural survey made in 1961, René Wellek was able to distinguish six "main trends" especially characteristic of our era: "Marxist criticism, psychoanalytic criticism, linguistic and stylistic criticism, a new organistic formalism, myth criticism . . . , and what amounts to a new philosophical criticism inspired by existentialism and kindred world views."[1]

For reasons that have as much to do with political pressures and stringencies as with national traditions and culturally determined habits of mind, Russian twentieth-century criticism has been at the same time a distinctive and an integral part of the process outlined by Wellek. While some of the trends listed above were prominent, indeed preeminent, in Russia, others have been marginal if not altogether absent. The discrepancies between the Russian and the Western—or, more specifically, Anglo-American—situations have been chronological as well as substantive. For example, "new formalism" and "linguistic and stylistic criticism" did not come into their own in England or the United States until the late 1930s. In Russia these positions, which could be said to converge in the Russian formalist movement, were fully articulated by 1920. In fact, by the time Anglo-American New Criticism hit its stride, Russian formalism had been driven from the scene by Stalin's cultural henchmen. Similarly, the methodological pluralism adumbrated above was forcibly eliminated in Russia around 1930 in favor of the accredited version of Marxist criticism. For at least two subsequent decades the intellectual quarantine clamped down on Russian culture effectively isolated Soviet study of literature from the mainstream of modern critical thought.

1. "The Main Trends of Twentieth-Century Criticism," *Concepts of Criticism* (New Haven, 1963), pp. 345–46.

This is not to say that all observable gaps in twentieth-century Russian criticism can be laid at the door of bureaucratic constraints. One of the major strands in Western literary criticism of the last two centuries that is drastically underrepresented in modern Russian critical discourse is the psychological approach, whose most influential recent variant has been psychoanalytic. It is a matter of record that after a few psychoanalytic forays into Russian classics (Pushkin and Gogol,[2] for example) in the early 1920s, depth-psychology, whether of the orthodox Freudian or of the Jungian variety, was firmly discouraged in the Soviet Union. Yet the dearth of such studies in Russia cannot be fully accounted for by invoking official Soviet taboos.[3] A tendency to slight psychological dynamics for the sake of social issues has long been a potent force in Russian literary culture.

The political conditions that prevailed in nineteenth-century Russia generated among the intelligentsia a keen sense of social urgency and of social guilt. Consequently, the view of literature as a mirror of society or preferably as a vehicle for social change enjoyed a distinct advantage over both the detached psychological curiosity and a systematic concern with the writer's psyche. The key figure in mid-nineteenth-century French criticism was Charles Augustin Sainte-Beuve (1804–69), whose voluminous studies combined vivid historicism with a keen sense of personality. The most influential Russian critic of the period was Vissarion Belinskij (1811–48), the "father of the Russian intelligentsia," the epitome of a passionate, indeed frenzied *engagement*.

The plight of imaginative literature in the nineteenth-century and the concomitant social burden of the Russian writer and critic have been frequently commented upon. Because stringent censorship often made explicit criticism of the regime almost impossible, the tasks of championing individual rights and exposing social evils fell largely to the creative writer. The literary artist had at his disposal numerous devices of literary indirection prone to elude a literal-minded censor. But poetic ambiguity is a double-edged weapon. The elliptic "Aesopian language" used by the writer not infrequently impaired the effectiveness of the "subversive" mes-

2. See especially Ivan Ermakov, *Ocherki po analizu tvorchestva N. V. Gogolja* (Moscow, 1924).

3. Recent Russian criticism produced outside the Soviet Union paid relatively little heed to the Freudian concepts. The only eminent Russian émigré critic who was visibly influenced by them was Alfred Bem (see p. 25 below).

sage; a subtle hint that bypassed the censor was likely to go un-
noticed by the reader as well. Whenever the political atmosphere
temporarily allowed a measure of plain speaking, the poetic para-
ble had to be deciphered, the half-concealed idea had to be stated
more explicitly. This was clearly the responsibility of the literary
critic, more specifically of the student of modern Russian literature. It was thus that the ideological exegesis of nineteenth-
century Russian poetry, drama, and fiction became the paramount
concern of a number of social critics, whether of the publicist or
academic variety. Viktor Shklovskij, an irreverent twentieth-
century man of letters whose name will recur in these pages, was
to accuse these enlightened commentators of confounding the history of Russian literature with the history of Russian liberalism.

This single-minded preoccupation with the writer's actual or
alleged "message" exacted a heavy toll. To be sure, the point can
be easily overstated and overgeneralized. To speak without major
qualifications about the traditional anti-aesthetic bias of Russian
criticism is grossly to oversimplify the matter. For one thing, the
situation was never monolithic. Even at the time when "advanced" journals tended to scorn aesthetic values, there were
imaginative mavericks of a more or less conservative persuasion,
such as Nikolaj Strakhov or Konstantin Leontiev, who dealt per-
ceptively with the problems of style and genre. For another thing,
the pioneer of Russian social criticism, Vissarion Belinskij, was
not at all immune to literary considerations. Whatever the short-
comings of this erratic but gifted critic, he was not guilty of the
grimly didactic approach to literature that has been on occasion
attributed to him. His ideological frenzy was tempered by a
genuine delight in what he was able to recognize as great poetry.
By the same token, his mounting urge to view literature as a
reflection of society or as a battleground of ideas was held in
check by his residual belief in the autonomy of art as a distinct
cultural activity. Yet this is more than can be said of his immediate
heirs—Nikolaj Chernyshevskij (1828–89), Nikolaj Dobroljubov
(1836–61), Dmitrij Pisarev (1840–68), and the lesser lights of Russian radical criticism in the third quarter of the last century. These
high-minded doctrinaires tended to look at the creative writer
with the stern, distrustful eye of a prosecutor. The defendant had
to prove his innocence or, more exactly, justify his existence by
meeting a recognizable social need, by offering a timely and progressive message.

The compulsion of Nikolaj Dobroljubov to treat a contemporary play, novel, or short story as a springboard for a sociopolitical tract had obvious pitfalls. Clearly, the cost of this procedure varied, depending on the nature of the work under discussion. When the occasion was Ivan Goncharov's *Oblomov*, Dobroljubov's emphasis on social types was not altogether inappropriate. While his disquisition about "Oblomovitis" as a social disease lost sight of the novel's psychological dimension—its main attraction to the modern critic—it was quite in line with the author's overt intent, notably one of sounding a warning against the seedy paternalism and lethargy of traditional Russian gentry. Yet whenever the tenor of the work failed to minister to the critic's ideological needs, his response was apt to be either a facile condemnation or a wishful misreading. Thus D. Pisarev, the enfant terrible of Russian radical criticism, dismissed *Eugene Onegin* as an irrelevant and frivolous poem—a judgment that rested on the embarrassingly crude error of equating the author with his admittedly flawed hero.

A classic example of the other, more benign fallacy was the treatment of Nikolaj Gogol. For both better and worse, Belinskij's role was crucial here. He was the first influential critic to recognize Gogol's greatness. Yet he also bears a large share of responsibility for widespread misjudgment of the essential nature of his art by proclaiming the bizarre, demon-ridden, and politically timid author of *The Inspector General* and *Dead Souls* the father of social realism in Russia, a bold challenger of a reactionary and obsolete system. Next came the interpretation of Gogol's famous tale "The Overcoat," a masterfully uncanny blend of tomfoolery and pathos, as a straightforward plea for the little man pushed around by the powers-that-be.

This image of Gogol, though sharply called into question by an uncommonly astute contemporary, the critic–poet Apollon Grigor'ev,[4] was not seriously challenged until the end of the century. The new perspective on the strange genius was opened by a major shift in Russian literary sensibility that is associated with the advent of the symbolist movement.

---

4. See his unfinished essay, "F. Dostoevskij i shkola santimentalnogo naturalizma" [F. Dostoevsky and the school of sentimental naturalism], *N. V. Gogol-Materialy i issledovanija* [Materials and investigations] (Moscow and Leningrad, 1936).

The Symbolists

By the 1890s Russian criticism had felt the full impact of the fin-de-siècle crisis in European thought and creativity. In Russia as in the West, the philosophical assumptions and the artistic currents that dominated the scene at midcentury were receding under the impact of an acute malaise, an intense if often inchoate metaphysical quest. The chief literary vehicle of the new stirrings was symbolism, which set out to use the vaunted "music," the fluid auditory and visual imagery at the poet's disposal, to enhance the emotional suggestiveness and the associative wealth of the poetic idiom.

In Moscow and St. Petersburg this all-European cultural upheaval meant, in addition, a resurgence of poetic values held back for several decades by bleak social utilitarianism. Lyric poetry, neglected by influential critics and overshadowed since the 1840s by prose fiction, staged a triumphant comeback. The mellifluously monotonous verse of the second-string "civic" poets gave way to Valerij Brjusov's "Parnassian" mastery of form, to Konstantin Balmont's lush euphony, and above all to the haunting verbal magic of Aleksandr Blok, the "tragic tenor of the era" (Anna Akhmatova). And in the wake of this poetic revival came a renascence of verse study and a concerted effort to attack the problems of poetic craft in categories of symbolist aesthetics.

The organic connection between poetry and poetics, so characteristic of the symbolist era, was often a matter of a personal union. With few exceptions the most influential literary critics and theoreticians of that fertile era were also its leading poets and novelists, be they the maitre of the Moscow symbolists, Valerij Brjusov (1873–1924), the dazzling and versatile Andrej Belyj (1880–1934), the erudite and hieratic Vjacheslav Ivanov (1886–1949), or the remarkable poet–essayist–scholar Innokentij Annenskij (1856–1909).

Russian symbolism was both a resurgence of poetic craft and a quest for a transpoetic epiphany, an esoteric truth that poetry was uniquely capable of conveying or hinting at. If the former emphasis encouraged intricate, indeed technical studies in versification, the latter fostered interest in the philosophical, or, if one will, mythic dimension of imaginative literature. Dostoevsky's major fiction, often underestimated and not infrequently deplored by the publicists who in his lifetime dominated the Russian critical opinion, was now subjected to sympathetic and imaginative, if at times somewhat loaded, scrutiny. In Dmitrij Merezhkovskij's *Tolstoy and Dostoevsky* (1901–02), a study whose insights and images have reverberated well into recent Western criticism, the two masters of the Russian novel were discussed in terms of the eternal struggle between Christ and Antichrist, spirit and flesh. This obtrusive antithesis—obviously the central theme of Merezhkovskij's voluminous oeuvre—lends undue schematicism to an otherwise deftly drawn and illuminating parallel. Another characteristic symbolist contribution to Dostoevsky criticism, Vjacheslav Ivanov's *Freedom and the Tragic Life*,[5] was saved from danger of metaphysical ponderousness by the critic's keen sense of the formal underpinnings of Dostoevsky's fictional universe, an awareness encapsulated in the seminal phrase "novel-tragedy."

A no less significant achievement of symbolist criticism was a dramatic reinterpretation of Gogol. This time the master had to be rescued not from neglect or hostility but from friendly, indeed enthusiastic, misreading. Valerij Brjusov and Andrej Belyj used the occasion of the one hundredth anniversary of Gogol's death (1909) to "turn around," in Shklovskij's phrase,[6] the traditional view of the great spellbinder. In their seminal lecture–essays the two leading Russian symbolists punctured the notion of Gogol's realism by portraying him eloquently and persuasively as a master of the grotesque hyperbole.[7] If the two messages were alike, the speakers' styles differed appreciably. Brjusov traced the motif of grotesque exaggeration through Gogol's life and work in a vivid but essentially sober argument. Belyj's breathless, rhapsodic prose—a string of glittering Gogolian metaphors, some of which are actually Gogol's—enacts as well as illuminates its subject.

If the Brjusov–Belyj emphasis on Gogolian demonology was elaborated on by Merezhkovskij in his *Gogol and the Devil*,[8] the subhuman, freakish, "soulless" quality of Gogolian humanity is evoked in Innokentij Annenskij's "The Aesthetics of Gogol's *Dead*

---

5. The title of a 1952 Noonday Press volume that incorporates several studies of Ivanov's, most notably, "Dostoevskij i roman-tragedija" [Dostoevsky and the novel-tragedy], *Borozdy i mezhi* [Furrows and hedges] (Moscow, 1916), pp. 5–72.

6. See p. 63 below.

7. A. Belyj, "Gogol" and V. Brjusov, "Ispepelennyj" [Burned to ashes], *Vesy* 4 (Moscow, 1909).

8. *Gogol i chёrt* (St. Petersburg, 1906).

Souls and Its Legacy" (1910).[9] Another note sounded in this suggestive and intensely personal essay is stubborn insistence on the aesthetic enchantment of the Gogolian universe. The poet in Annenskij is properly and richly alive to the creative exuberance of Gogol's art, to the paradoxical quality of aesthetic joy, so clearly at odds with the essential hopelessness of the writer's moral vision.

Annenskij's impressionistic manner has its pitfalls. His habit of drifting in and out of the viscous prose of *Dead Souls* without actually quoting can be disconcerting to a layman. Nor is Annenskij above being willfully wrongheaded on occasion: his view of Chekhov as a melancholy and feeble writer is utterly misguided. Yet he has an imaginative grip on an essential and rarely acknowledged aspect of Gogol and manages to convey it arrestingly, if at times idiosyncratically.

It can be argued that the symbolists' interpretations of Gogol were in their own way no less self-serving than those urged by Belinskij or Chernyshevskij. Doubtless, in both instances the concept of the master is visibly affected by the critic's ideological preconceptions and/or temperamental proclivities. Granted, too, that the full truth about Gogol is more complex or heterogeneous than either set of interpretations would allow. Still I would maintain that the symbolists, as well as their immediate precursor, the brilliant turn-of-the-century maverick Vasilij Rozanov,[10] came closer to grasping that truth than did the social critics, and that they did so not simply because their critical gifts and literary sensibilities were superior to Chernyshevskij's or Belinskij's, but because they were better attuned to Gogol's grotesque imagination. This is especially true of Andrej Belyj. His brilliantly nightmarish *St. Petersburg* (1910), possibly the greatest twentieth-century Rus-

9. Annenskij's essay published posthumously in the influential literary and art journal *Apollon* was preceded by two volumes of criticism, *Kniga otrazhenij* [A book of reflections] (St. Petersburg, 1906). In the preface Annenskij calls attention to the personal cast of his essays: "Ordinarily a critic stands outside the work as he analyzes and evaluates it. He is not only outside of it, but somewhere above it. As for me, I wrote about things that gripped me, things that led me on and claimed my allegiance, things I sought to preserve within myself by making them a part of myself" (1:3).

10. An original and heterodox thinker, V. V. Rozanov (1856–1919), challenged the *idées reçues* about Gogol in two brief but important essays appended to a celebrated commentary on *The Brothers Karamazov*, *The Legend of the Grand Inquisitor* (1890). The burden of Rozanov's message was that Gogol's vision brilliantly distorted reality and reduced man to a homunculus.

sian novel, belongs squarely in the Gogolian tradition. Some
twenty years after his path-breaking essay, Belyj acknowledged
this debt explicitly in an unfinished but richly rewarding study,
Gogol's Craftsmanship (1934). The final section of this book, devoted to what Annenskij had called the legacy of Gogol's aesthetics, includes quite appropriately an amply documented chapter on Gogol and Belyj.

It is imaginative breakthroughs such as these that place the best
of symbolist-inspired essays and studies among the landmarks of
twentieth-century Russian critical thought. Yet by the second decade of the century, even as the preeminence of symbolism in
lyric poetry was being challenged, tenets of symbolist aesthetics
were increasingly called into question. To some of the budding
literary scholars the heady mixture of partisan poetics with
metaphysical speculation and intuitive "appreciation" appeared
both too esoteric and too arbitrary. In their quest of methodological rigor and in their determination to establish literary studies as
an autonomous and integrated intellectual discipline they gravitated toward a close analysis of the literary craft. As one of their
eminent teachers at the Petersburg university recalled a few years
later, "They applied themselves with astounding zeal to style,
rhythm and other problems of the outward shape of poetry."[11] In
doing so they kept pace, often unknowingly, with kindred developments in Western European countries.

In France influential teachers and historians of literature, such
as Gustave Lanson, evolved a method of "explication de textes" as
a technique fostering "the habit of close reading and precise
interpretation."[12] In Germany art historians such as Wölfflin
placed style rather than the artist's creative personality at the
center of the scholar's concern as he urged somewhat extravagantly a "history of art without names," where the "heroes" would
be not individual masters but successive suprapersonal schools or
styles, for example the Gothic, the Renaissance, the baroque.[13]

In Russia the preoccupation with the structure of the work of art
found its main expression in the literary studies. It was triggered

11. From a retrospective article by S. A. Vengerov, an eminent professor
of Russian literature at the University of St. Petersburg, in *Pushkinist* [The
Pushkin scholar] (Petrograd, 1916).
12. Gustave Lanson, "La méthode dans l'histoire littèraire," reprinted in
Etudes Françaises (Paris, 1925), vol. 1.
13. Heinrich Wölfflin, *Kunstgeschichtliche Grundbegriffe* (Berlin, 1917).

at once by new departures in Russian linguistics, which under the aegis of such innovators as J. Baudouin de Courtenay fostered a functional approach to language, and by the spirit of experimentation, of intoxication with "the self-valuable word," that informed the post-symbolist Russian poetic avant garde. In early Russian futurism the medium, dramatized or "laid bare" by untrammeled verbal play, was often the only message. By 1915–16 the methodological ferment in Russian literary criticism crystallized into an organized movement that became known as "Russian formalism."

Formalists and Near-Formalists

It is worth noting that the "formalist" label was applied to the new school by its opponents rather than by its adherents. The latter tended to favor such abstruse or unwieldy self-definitions as the "morphological" approach or "specifiers" (*spetsifikatory*). No wonder these designations didn't "take."[14]

Subsequently the term formalism has been used so loosely as to degenerate into an intellectual expletive, a "meaningless noise meaning disapproval" (S. I. Hayakawa), with ominous implications of cultural sabotage or counter-revolution or more narrowly, of an unhealthy responsiveness to Western influences or undue preoccupation with "mere" form. What can be legitimately referred to as "Russian formalism"—allowing for the inadequacy of the label—is a school in Russian literary scholarship that originated in the second decade of this century, flourished in the 1920s and was forcibly suppressed in 1930. Its leading exponents were unorthodox linguists and literary historians such as Boris Eikhenbaum (1886–1959), Roman Jakobson (1895–), Viktor Shklovskij (1893–), Boris Tomashevskij (1890–1957), and Jurij Tynjanov (1894–1943). As the formalist movement got under way it drew into its orbit form-oriented literary scholars who could not be described as full-fledged formalists and, in fact, had some vocal disagreements with the movement, for example Viktor Vinogradov (1895–1969) and Viktor Zhirmunskij (1891–1971).

14. See especially Boris Eikhenbaum, "Vokrug voprosa o formalistakh" [Around the problem of the formalists], *Pechat' i revoljutsija* [The press and the revolution] 5 (Moscow, 1924): 3.

The formalists viewed literature as a distinct field of human endeavor, as a verbal art rather than as a reflection of society or a battleground of ideas. In attempting to delimit literary studies from contiguous fields such as psychology, sociology, or cultural history, the formalist theoreticians were quick to focus on "distinguishing features" of literature. "The subject of literary scholarship," said Roman Jakobson in an early study, "is not literature in its totality but literariness, i.e. that which makes of a given work a work of literature."[15]

In their quest for the differentia the formalists tried to steer clear of traditional answers and pat solutions. They had little use for such notions as "intuition," "imagination" or "genius," locating the peculiarly literary in the poet rather than the poem. The situs of literariness was to be sought not in the author's or the reader's psyche, but in the work itself, more specifically in the artistic devices peculiar to imaginative writing, whereby the creative writer reshapes his subject matter, or "material"—reality— and manipulates his medium—language.

To Jakobson and Shklovskij, imaginative literature is a unique mode of discourse characterized by the "orientation toward the medium" or the "perceptibility of the mode of expression."[16] In literary art, it was argued, especially in poetry, language is not simply a vehicle of communication. From a mere tag, a proxy for an object, the word becomes here an object in its own right, an autonomous source of pleasure, as multiple devices at the poet's disposal—rhythm, meter, euphony, imagery—converge upon the verbal sign to reveal its complex texture. Artistic prose, concede the formalists, lacks the tight organization of language that characterizes verse; it works in larger verbal blocks. Yet the difference here is not one of kind but of degree. Narrative fiction has its own intricate pattern of tension and balance, its own parallels and contrasts.[17] The events or motifs that constitute the basic story material or, in formalist parlance, add up to the "fable," are not

15. *Novejshaja russkaja poezija* [Recent Russian poetry] (Prague, 1921), p. 11.
16. Ibid., p. 10; N. I. Efimov, "Formalizm v russkom literaturovedenii" [Formalism in Russian literary scholarship], *Nauchnye izvestija Smolenskogo Gosudarstvennogo Universiteta* [Scholarly bulletin of the Smolensk State University] 5 (1929); pt. 3, p. 70.
17. See especially Viktor Shklovskij, *Teorija prozy* (Moscow–Leningrad, 1925); *Khod konja* [A knight's move] (Moscow–Berlin, 1923). An essay from *Khod konja* appears on pp. 81–85 below.

simply related; they are mediated through narrative devices and organized into a "plot" for maximum aesthetic effect.

These basic assumptions were tested in acute if occasionally rather abstruse studies of rhythm, style, and composition, as well as in numerous forays into literary history and practical criticism. In the latter realms the formalists sought to eschew explicit value judgments and supplant them by "historic estimates," that is, assessments of an author's role in the literary process. In reality, the studies of Jakobson and Shklovskij, of Eikhenbaum or Tynjanov reveal a pronounced aesthetic bias, a fairly coherent set of preferences. Not unlike the New Critics, with whom they had a great deal in common but whose antihistoricism they did not share, the formalists set less store by such qualities as directness of expression, sincerity, high seriousness, correspondence with reality, than they did by inner coherence, density of texture, and form-consciousness. But where their Anglo-American counterparts celebrated irony and paradox, the Russians were fascinated by parody as a means of dislodging a specific set of conventions or of pointing up the essential conventionality of literary art. Tynjanov showed that in Dostoevsky's novel *The Friend of the Family* the author was parodying the ponderous rhetoric of Gogol's ill-fated tract *Selected Passages from a Correspondence with Friends* and used this important and amply documented thesis as a springboard toward a general proposition about parody as a catalyst of literary change.[18] Shklovskij, whose sweeping generalizations and clever bons mots helped shape the Russian formalist approach to narrative fiction, in a characteristic overstatement proclaimed the archetypal novel–parody, Lawrence Sterne's *Tristram Shandy*, "the most typical novel in world literature."[19] The most typical, presumably, because the most literary, the most keenly aware of itself as a novel and of the inherent conventions of the genre.

No wonder Shklovskij was so eager to identify the elements of literary parody and pastiche in Pushkin's narrative masterpiece. His provocative essay "Pushkin and Sterne: *Eugene Onegin*" couched in the staccato style that was his trademark, was a welcome antidote to the traditional notions of *Eugene Onegin* as an

18. See Tynjanov, *Dostoevskij i Gogol: K teorii parodii* (Petrograd, 1921). A slightly abbreviated version of p. 2 of this study appears on pp. 102–16 below.
19. Shklovskij, *Teorija prozy*, p. 161.

"encyclopedia of Russian life"[20] and of the poem's hero as a recognizable social type, let alone to the moralistic disquisitions on whether Tatjana should or should not have rebuffed Evgenij in chapter 8. Yet, not uncharacteristically, Shklovskij's breezy argument overshoots the mark.

Eugene Onegin is indeed one of the most literary works in the language. It is also one of the most elusive and difficult to label. While it bears considerable resemblance to Byron's freewheeling and satirical *Don Juan*—avowedly "a narrative not meant for narration"—Pushkin's more protean performance manages to combine a magnificent display of what Byron dubbed "conversational facility" with a story that should be neither pondered nor dismissed out of hand. To put it differently, *Eugene Onegin* is a consummate play with various potential attitudes toward the action, including empathy and seriousness. That is why "parody" ultimately is too confining a generic term here and why Shklovskij's query "Did Pushkin weep over Tatjana or was he making light of her?" (see p. 75 below) is a trifle simplistic.

Shklovskij's spiritedly lopsided discussion of Pushkin's novel in verse was one of the many shifts effected by formalist-oriented criticism. Through the good offices of Boris Eikhenbaum and Jurij Tynjanov, Pushkin's place in the evolutionary scheme of Russian literature was significantly altered. Seen this time from the standpoint of style and genre rather than from that of theme and world view, the great poet appeared not as a demiurge of nineteenth-century Russian poetry but as an heir to the pioneering efforts of the classicist era.[21] Under the pen of Eikhenbaum, Gogol's "Overcoat" became "an apotheosis of the grotesque," an intricate piece of expressive stylization. To the same resourceful and perceptive literary historian who was to develop into the leading Tolstoy scholar of our times, the moral crisis of the young Tolstoy ap-

20. This essay appears below. In an excellent recent discussion of *Eugene Onegin* an American Slavist observes: "Belinskij has called *Eugene Onegin* an encyclopedia of Russian life. One would be equally justified in calling *Eugene Onegin* a literary encyclopedia." S. Leon Stilman, "Problemy literaturnykh zhanrov i traditsij v 'Evgenii Onegine' [Problems of literary genres and traditions in *Eugene Onegin*], American Contributions to the 4th International Congress of Slavists (The Hague, 1958), p. 321.

21. See especially Tynjanov, "Arkhaisty i Pushkin" [The archaists and Pushkin], *Arkhaisty i novatory* [Archaists and innovators] (Leningrad, 1929); Eikhenbaum, "Problemy poètiki Pushkina" [Problems of Pushkin's poetics], *Skvoz' literaturu* [Across literature] (Leningrad, 1924). The latter appears as "Pushkin's Path to Prose" below.

peared primarily as a struggle for a new style, a challenge to romantic clichés grown stale.[22] A few years later a new perspective on the other giant of Russian fiction was offered by a gifted young scholar strongly influenced by, if not wholly committed to, the formalist methodology. M. M. Bakhtin (1895–) in his seminal study *Problems of Dostoevsky's Work* (1929) addressed himself to the structural characteristics of Dostoevsky's fiction only to arrive at the concept of the "polyphonic novel"—a novel of many voices, none of which is to be equated with the author's own.[23] One of the effects of this immensely influential phrase was to discourage the tendency endemic among the Dostoevsky critics to single out some of his characters as authorial mouthpieces and thus deduce from his oeuvre an unequivocal doctrine.

Many of these reinterpretations were as vulnerable as they were provocative. The essential one-sidedness of some of the original formalist assumptions was accentuated further by the strident polemical style that seemed de rigueur in the first years of the Revolution. In a strenuous effort to make themselves heard among the clatter of competing manifestos, the formalists found extravagant overstatement necessary. In their early studies Jakobson and Shklovskij played down the link between literature and society and denied the relevance of any extraliterary considerations. Eventually, in recognition of the inadequacy of their initial premises and in the face of the concerted attack on the part of the Marxist-Leninists, they made a last-minute attempt to combine rigorous formal analysis with some hasty sociologizing. But this makeshift synthesis came too late. By 1929–30 the methodological debate in the Soviet Union was abruptly discontinued. Formalism was suppressed as rank heresy and in curiously circular reasoning branded as "false because it was reactionary and reactionary because it was false."[24] Throughout the Stalin era "formalism" remained a multipurpose term of abuse. Yet, as recent developments clearly demonstrate (see pp. 27–28 below), the substantive influence

22. "Kak sdelana 'Shinel' Gogolja" [How Gogol's "Overcoat" is made], *Poetika* (Petrograd, 1919). See especially Eikhenbaum, *Molodoj Tolstoj* (Petrograd–Berlin, 1922), in English, *The Young Tolstoy* (Ann Arbor, Mich., 1972); "O krizisakh Tolstogo." *Skvoz' literaturu*, pp. 67–72, which appears as "On Tolstoy's Crises" below.
23. *Problemy tvorchestva Dostoevskogo* (Leningrad, 1929).
24. See M. Gelfand, "Deklaracija car'a Midasa ili chto sluchilos' s Viktorom Shklovskim?" [The declaration of King Midas or what happened to Viktor Shklovskij?], *Pechat' i revoljutsija* 2 (1930).

of formalist theorizing and historical–literary research on serious students of literature in Russia could not have been undone by a bureaucratic fiat.

If in Russia the maturation of the formalist movement was cut short by extraliterary pressures, a judicious restatement of the basic formalist tenets proved possible in another Slavic country. Dmitry Cizevsky, Roman Jakobson, Jan Mukarovsky, and René Wellek—the theorists of so-called Czech structuralism grouped around the Prague Linguistic Circle founded in 1926—sought to salvage the seminal insights of Russian formalism without canonizing its youthful excesses. This time the watchword was, in Jakobson's phrase, "autonomy of the aesthetic function rather than separatism of art."[25] Within the modified, structuralist framework, "literariness" was no longer the only pertinent aspect of literature—nor for that matter merely one of its many components—but a strategic property informing and permeating the entire work, a principle of dynamic integration, a *Gestaltqualitaet*, to borrow a term from another field. By the same token the work of literature was not simply a "sum-total of devices employed in it,"[26] as Shklovskij had mechanistically phrased it, but a multidimensional verbal structure held together by the aesthetic purpose.

Thus to a pure formalist such as the early Shklovskij, *Crime and Punishment* was a mystery story "complicated by philosophical problems." To a structuralist student of Dostoevsky, the theological confrontation between Ivan and Alësha in *The Brothers Karamazov* was neither a foreign body in Dostoevsky's fictional universe nor, notwithstanding Shklovskij, a suspense-building device, but an organic part of the novel's structure. The structuralist's main concern, however, would be not with the intrinsic validity of the Grand Inquisitor's argument, but rather with a demonstration of how Ivan's metaphysical despair embodied in the Legend contributes to the plot, how it helps to trigger the disaster.

The advantages of the new approach are evident in Jakobson's and Mukarovsky's explorations of Czech romantic poetry and in Dmitry Cizevsky's illuminating encounter with that touchstone of

---

25. "Co je poesie?" [What is poetry?], *Volne smery* [Free currents] (Prague, 1933–34), pp. 229–39; in French, "Que c'est que la poésie?", *Questions de poétique* (Paris, 1973), p. 123.

26. Viktor Shklovskij, *Rozanov* (Petrograd, 1921), p. 15.

Russian criticism—Gogol's "Overcoat."[27] Though Cizevsky's essay cannot boast the pioneering status of Eikhenbaum's "How
Gogol's 'Overcoat' Is Made," it transcends the limitations of the
earlier study by forging a plausible link between the story's verbal
texture and its moral universe. Unfortunately Czech structuralism
was allotted little time for testing its hypotheses. The intellectual
climate in postwar Czechoslovakia was less than hospitable to any
departure from Marxism-Leninism. Viewed as a set of methodological guidelines, as a sophisticated awareness of context,
function, and pattern, Prague structuralism in its literary aspect is
essentially an outgrowth of Russian formalist theorizing. By the
same token the present-day neostructuralist vogue in the West,
especially on the Left Bank, owes a great deal to the formalist
impulse. But this clearly is quite another story. It is high time that
we return to the Russian scene.

As the turbulent twenties recede into the past, the ad hoc quality of some of its critical generalizations is becoming increasingly
apparent. The tenor of the early formalist manifestos was visibly
colored by their authors' determination to be, in Arthur Rimbaud's
phrase, "absolument moderne." This ultramodernist bias was a
mixed blessing. The movement's close alliance with the literary
avant-garde lent a blatantly partisan quality to some of the formalist theories of literature. Not infrequently the new "defense of
poesie" would at close range turn out to be an ingenious brief for
the kind of poetry that the critic's friends and associates were
currently producing. At the same time, the sense of commitment
to the creative ferment of one's era, often bolstered by enduring
personal friendships, enriched and enlivened many formalist and
near-formalist writings. It is excitement of participation that is felt
in Shklovskij's and Tynjanov's responses to the contemporary
scene, in Zhirmunskij's discerning and affectionate study of Aleksandr Blok,[28] and, last but certainly not least, in Jakobson's brilliant essay on Majakovskij, where analytical prowess blends with
vividness and poignancy of eyewitness testimony (see "On a Generation" below).

If in one's final assessment of the formalist heritage the impatience with its excesses and occasional aridities is apt to be offset by

27. "O 'Shineli' Gogolja" [On Gogol's "Overcoat"] *Sovremennye zapiski*
[Contemporary annals] 67 (Paris, 1938): 172–95.

28. *Poezija Aleksandra Bloka* (Petrograd, 1921). A section of this study
appears below as "The Passion of Aleksandr Blok."

an enduring sense of intellectual gratitude, this fact is due only in part to the relevance and fertility of the formalist concepts. It is also and in no small measure, a tribute to the impressive concentration of sheer critical talent within the ranks of the formalist movement. Few serious students of Russian literature, whatever their methodological persuasion, will fail to place Tynjanov's *Dostoevsky and Gogol*, Eikhenbaum's *Young Tolstoy*, and Jakobson's "On a Generation That Squandered Its Poets" among the finest achievements of modern Russian criticism.

Early Soviet Marxists

Needless to say, Russian formalism was not the only school of early Soviet criticism to be victimized by the totalitarian streamlining of Russian culture. In fact it can be argued that in some sense the chief casualty of this process was its ostensible benefactor—Marxism-Leninism. Nothing can be more crippling to an "ism" than its enjoying an administratively enforced monopoly position, especially when the doctrine in question is as precarious and fragmentary as Marxian aesthetics. To be sure, Marxism-Leninism enjoyed a privileged status ever since 1917. Yet during the first decade of the Soviet regime, when some measure of intellectual freedom still prevailed, it was not impossible to disagree openly on some fundamentals. A lively, if not unrestricted, discussion of critical principles and criteria would reveal time and again significant cleavages within what purported to be a monolithic camp.

As a general theory of social evolution Marxism did not solve, nor could it be expected to solve, the specific problems of individual humanistic disciplines. While it postulated the ultimate causal dependence of such "ideological" phenomena as art, science, and religion on the economic process, the Marxist doctrine in its original form neither precluded nor specifically encouraged inquiry into the forces operating within a particular cultural realm. In an often quoted letter to the pioneer of German Marxist criticism Franz Mehring, Friedrich Engels candidly admitted a significant gap in Marxist thought: "Marx and I placed and had to place the chief weight upon the [fact of the] *derivation* of political, legal, and other ideological notions . . . from fundamental economic facts. In consequence we neglected the formal side, i.e. the way in which these ideas arose . . . the nature of the connection between "base" and the "superstructure." To borrow an apt metaphor from Alfred Kazin, dialectical materialism became a vast filing cabinet, the particular compartments of which were still waiting to be filled with appropriate studies.[29] The state of the compartments reserved for the study of literature hinged largely on the individual Marxist critic's resourcefulness and acumen, on the degree of flexibility and common sense with which he applied the Marxian tenets to imaginative writing, and not least on his regard for the autonomy of literary values.

Within the Soviet setting this latter attitude was undermined not only by socioeconomic reductionism against which Engels had explicitly cautioned, but also by Lenin's relentless political instrumentalism, the Bolshevik proclivity for treating art as a weapon. Both pitfalls are very much in evidence in the theory and practice of the more doctrinaire Soviet Marxist critics. In their pronouncements, sociological analysis of literature was all too often supplanted by ideological label-mongering and partisan vituperation. G. Lelevich, a spokesman for the ultra-orthodox faction On Guard, defined art as an "instrument of emotional infection, a means of organizing the reader's psyche in conformity with the interests of a given class." In line with this formula—a curious blend of Lenin with the Tolstoy of *What Is Art?*—Anna Akhmatova was accused of "organizing the reader's psyche toward clerical-feudal-bourgeois restoration" and Andrej Belyj, who sought frantically to come to terms with post-1917 realities, was labeled "not only an anti-Soviet element but an anti-social one as well."[30] Diatribes such as these harked back to the ideological stridency of the Russian radical criticism of the 1860s. In spite of a thick overlay of Marxist lingo, they owed more to Dmitrij Pisarev than to Karl Marx.

Within the On Guard framework the writer's class allegiance became the chief criterion. The predictable consequence of this position was a demand that all voices except those of "proletarian," or orthodox, writers be silenced, a ban that was to include all "halfhearted" sympathizers, or in Trotsky's phrase, "fellow travelers" of the Revolution in whose ranks, incidentally,

29. Quoted in Alfred Kazin, *On Native Grounds* (New York, 1942), p. 413.
30. Lelevich, *Proletariat i literatura* (Leningrad, 1925), p. 85, quoted in Victor Erlich, "Soviet Literary Criticism: Past and Present," *Russia under Khrushchev*, ed. A. Brumberg (New York, 1962), p. 348.

were found practically all the truly gifted Soviet writers of the
1920s. The On Guardist logic was impeccable: if a writer always
fulfills his "unwritten" "social command"—that of infecting his
audience with the attitudes of his class—the "petty bourgeois"
interlopers could not be tolerated. They were liable to poison the
trusting Soviet reader with socially alien bacilli.

A more flexible and humane brand of Marxist criticism was
championed by Aleksandr Voronskij (1884–1943), an influential
critic and editor. He combined political orthodoxy with a strong
personal commitment to literature, a commitment underpinned by
an aesthetic which, though not incompatible with Marxism, could
be easily construed within the Soviet Marxist framework as a
"bourgeois-idealistic" heresy. To Voronskij art was not primarily a
matter of mobilizing or manipulating group emotions on behalf of
a class-determined world view. It was a distinctive form of cognition, a largely intuitive mode of apprehending reality. As a Marxist
Voronskij had to concede that the way in which the artist perceived the world and the extent to which he was apt to gain an
insight into reality were significantly affected by his social environment. But a great writer, insisted Voronskij, manages time and
again to rise above the limitàtions of his class and of its political
spokesmen. In fact, a true artist, armed by intuition and creative
integrity, cannot help seeing and embodying in his work certain
truths that run counter to his conscious bias and to the interests of
his class. This assumption was invoked in support of the thesis
that a non-Party writer of talent and integrity can be not only
aesthetically but also politically more valuable than a mediocre
proletarian, since the former's writings can yield a more accurate
sense of new social realities and thus provide a safer guide to
political action.

As a result, Voronskij gave active support to such gifted and
"ideologically confused" writers as Boris Pilnjak, Konstantin
Fedin, Vsevolod Ivanov, and Leonid Leonov, authors who sym-
pathized with the new Russia but steered clear of a total political
commitment. No wonder *Red Virgin Soil*, a literary journal edited
by Voronskij, became one of the most vital and readable Russian
periodicals in the 1920s.

Significantly Voronskij was one of the few Party critics to recognize the remarkable gifts of Isaac Babel and to hail him as "a very
great hope of contemporary Russian literature" (see p. 197 below).
Now Babel, a bespectacled Jewish intellectual from Odessa who

somewhat incongruously served as a political commissar in the Cossack Division in 1920, was hardly a "fellow traveler." Yet his brilliantly compact civil war vignettes shot through with irony and ambivalence—qualities that after 1930 turned him, in his own phrase, into "a past master of the art of silence"—were a far cry from straightforward, edifying Communist prose.[31] Voronskij does not begrudge Babel the absence of explicitness, of revolutionary didacticism, in *Red Cavalry* and waxes enthusiastic over the young writer's mastery of form and his unquestionable literary "culture." Yet Voronskij's critical tools are too blunt, his own prose too diffuse and imprecise to do justice to Babel's idiosyncratic brilliance. "He speaks simply, without unnecessary verbiage" is a singularly inadequate description of an artful, at times near-baroque, compression. Voronskij's is one of the most generous Marxist assessments of the finest Soviet prose writer, but it is by no means one of the best essays on the subject. It does not come nearly as close to "placing" Babel as a literary artist as do Shklovskij's perceptive aperçus.[32] Nor was Voronskij capable of the acumen and critical detachment with which Lionel Trilling discusses the dilemma of the narrator in Babel's *Red Cavalry* (see note 31).

One might add that Voronskij's tolerance had easily definable limits. While he tolerated, indeed encouraged, vacillating but potentially right-minded non-Party writers, he showed little patience with the militant nonconformism of Evgenij Zamjatin, author of the boldly antitotalitarian satire *We*.

Broad-mindedness is clearly a relative notion. Viewed against the background of his era, Voronskij's performance inspires respect not only because of the accuracy of some of his judgments, but, more importantly, because of his refusal to surrender literary criteria, to disregard the autonomy of art. Whatever the rigidities of his ideological commitment, it did not quite succeed in dampening his genuine delight in creativity or in dulling his impatience with right-minded mediocrity. It is not surprising that Voronskij's was among the first heads to roll when by 1930 the

31. The phrase is drawn from a richly ambiguous speech that Babel delivered in 1939 at the First Writers' Congress in Moscow; see Lionel Trilling's introduction to Isaac Babel, *Collected Stories* (London, 1957), p. 13.

32. For an English rendition of Shklovskij's 1924 essay see "Isaac Babel: A Critical Romance," *Modern Soviet Writers*, ed. Edward J. Brown (New York, 1973), pp. 295–300.

doctrinaires and zealots whom he had fought so steadfastly gained
the upper hand in Soviet letters.

In his increasingly strenuous battle against ultra-orthodox
simplifiers Voronskij found an effective ally in no less a figure
than Leon Trotsky, who in 1924 took some time out of his hectic
schedule to produce a collection of essays on literary subjects,
Literature and Revolution. It is a tribute to the intellectual ver-
satility and polemical skill of the Communist chieftain that this
foray into literary criticism should make a more lively and provocative volume than do the writings of so many full-time Soviet
Marxist critics. Judged outside of that rather bleak context, *Literature and Revolution* appears to be a vigorous and at times brilliant
exhibition of both the strengths and the weaknesses of Trotsky the
literary critic. His spirited polemic with what he inaccurately dubs
"the Formalist School in poetry" shows him to be amateurishly
imprecise in handling the problems of poetic technique. At the
same time he scores debating points in puncturing holes in
Shklovskij's hasty raid on sociological criticism.[33] While rejecting
the formalist Weltanschauung as sterile and reactionary, Trotsky
grudgingly admits the usefulness of some formalist research. His
reluctance to dismiss the formalist contribution as a mere "aesthetic gourmandise" must have stemmed in part from his recognition of the inner dynamism of literature. Artistic creation, he avers,
is a "deflection, a transformation of reality in accordance with the
peculiar laws of art." While Marxism alone can explain why and
how a given tendency in art originated in a given period of history, historical materialism per se fails to "provide the basis for
aesthetic judgment." Hence the conclusion: "A work of art should
in the first place be judged by its own law, that is by the law of
art."[34]

Trotsky's discussion of Aleksandr Blok's "The Twelve," the
most powerful poem to emerge from the revolutionary turmoil of
1917, is not only sympathetic but on the whole remarkably astute.
Trotsky's apt phrase, whose punning effect is inevitably lost in
translation—"he flung himself toward us but in doing so he broke
down"—remains to this day one of the best and pithiest state-

33. In a breezy essay that appeared in his 1923 collection *Khod konja*
[A knight's move], Shklovskij tried to demolish the sociological interpretation
of literature in five clipped aphorisms.

34. *Literatura i revoljutsija* (Moscow, 1924) pp. 175, 178.

ments of Blok's predicament.[35] Yet in the same essay Trotsky could pour savage scorn on an intelligent free-lance critic, Kornej Chukovskij for implying, quite sensibly, that what Blok flung himself toward was less likely the actual Bolshevik Revolution than the revolution he saw in his fevered dreams.

Trotsky's tone in "Majakovskij and Russian Futurism" (below) is somewhat priggish. I cannot help feeling that he begrudges Majakovskij's early Soviet poetry its unabashed euphoria, its irrepressible sense of fun. (The Revolution, he implies in a highly critical discussion of Majakovskij's bumptious proletarian epic "150,000,000," is not a Bohemian picnic.) But his diagnoses of the essentially individualistic nature of Majakovskij's revolutionary *engagement* and of the poet's ineluctably narcissistic ("Majakomorphic") world view have shrewdness, wit, and aptness of phrasing, qualities that were in short supply in Soviet Marxist criticism.

A few years later, with Marxist-Leninist criticism whipped into uniformity, Voronskij's philosophy of art stood convicted of such deadly sins as "Bergsonian idealism." Soviet letters were moving inexorably toward the single aesthetic canon of "socialist realism," an increasingly meaningless concept subject to endless bureaucratic manipulation rather than a genuine basis for literary judgment. (A Polish wag defined socialist realism as "that brand of naturalism which is currently favored by the Central Committee.")

If during the Stalin era literary theorizing became increasingly a matter of intellectual shadowboxing—of timid exegeses on insipid or ambiguous pronouncements—literary-historical research was often quite useful and practical criticism was not uniformly bleak. Essays by G. Goffensheffer or Isaj Lezhnëv on Mikhail Sholokhov, J. U. Juzovskij's studies on Maxim Gorky, or Vladimir Grib's on Balzac were relatively unhackneyed and occasionally perceptive. Unfortunately Vladimir Ermilov's slick manipulation of the nineteenth-century Russian masters in service of a shifting party line were more representative.[36] This is not to suggest that Ermilov, who started his career in the 1920s as a spokesman of the

---

35. The original phrase is "No on rvanulsja k nam. Rvanuvshis', nadorvalsja" (ibid., p. 90).

36. See Ermilov, *Protiv reaktsionnykh idej v tvorchestve F. M. Dostoevskogo* [Against reactionary ideas in F. M. Dostoevsky] (Moscow, 1948); *Nash Pushkin* [Our Pushkin] (Moscow, 1949); *A. P. Chekhov* (Moscow, 1951); *N. V. Gogol* (Moscow, 1952).

diehard On Guard faction, should be considered a victim of
Stalinist thought control. A more relevant measure of its crippling
impact was a temporary deterioration of Viktor Shklovskij. His
Notes on the Prose of the Russian Masters (1953) was an appall-
ingly timid rehash of official clichés bolstered time and again by
quotations from the nineteenth-century social critics (Belinskij,
Chernyshevskij, and Dobroljubov) for whom the early Shklovskij
had precious little use.

Emigré Critics

It is a fact not sufficiently appreciated in the West that some of
the most vital Russian criticism of the 1930s was produced outside
Russia by essayists and scholars who in the early years of Soviet
power chose exile.

The morning after the November Revolution found many Russian literary intellectuals apprehensive or hostile. Some of them
subsequently came around or withdrew into what Trotsky dis-
paragingly called "internal emigration." Some others were allowed to leave for Berlin, Paris, Prague, Belgrade, or Sofia as the
new regime was taking hold. Among them were established, often
eminent, poets and fiction writers, notably Konstantin Balmont,
Ivan Bunin, Zinaida Gippius, Vjacheslav Ivanov, Dmitrij Merezhkovskij, Aleksej Remisov, Boris Zajtsev, as well as young men and
women of letters who did not come into their own until after the
Revolution, such as Vladislav Khodasevich, Georgij Ivanov,
Marina Tsvetaeva, and Irina Odoevtseva.

The full story of Russian émigré literature between 1920 and
1939 is yet to be told. An auspicious beginning was made by Gleb
Struve in his *Russian Literature in Exile* (New York, 1956). One of
the salient facts that emerge from this informative and judicious
account is the relative prominence in Russian émigré literary culture of such nonfictional modes as "criticism, the essay, philosophical prose, high-level journalism, and memoir literature."[37]
Some of the leading Russian émigré essayists, such as Fëdor Ste-
pun (1884–1965). and Georgij Fedotov (1886–1951), shuttled re-
wardingly between literary criticism and philosophical polemics
or intellectual history. Others, quite in line with the Silver Age

37. *Russkaja literatura v izgnanii* (New York; Chekhov Publishing House
1956), p. 371.

tradition, combined creative accomplishments with analytical prowess. Mark Aldanov (pseudonym of Mark Aleksandrovich Landau, 1886–1957) is primarily known as a prolific and urbane historical novelist. Yet his *Tolstoy's Enigma*, written apparently before the Revolution but published in 1923 in Berlin, remains to this day one of the most perceptive treatments of the great writer's obtrusive dilemmas. It is no reflection on the originality and brilliance of Isaiah Berlin's justly acclaimed essay on Tolstoy's philosophy of history, *The Hedgehog and the Fox*, to suggest that Berlin's insight into Tolstoy's tragic inner contradictions was in part anticipated by Aldanov.

Another "hybrid" career was that of Vladislav Khodasevich, probably the most accomplished Russian émigré poet. He was also one of the most astute commentators on the state of Russian literature in exile as well as a fine Pushkin scholar.

The scholarly or academic strain in Russian émigré criticism was represented by such figures as Alfred Bem (d. 1945), Pëtr Bitsilli (1879–1953), and Konstantin Mochulskij (1892–1950). The latter is best known in the West as author of a valuable study of Dostoevsky.[38] Bem and Bitsilli were active and erudite literary historians. Though they registered many a sensitive response to the contemporary literary scene, they will be best remembered, I believe, for their perceptive studies in Pushkin, Dostoevsky, and Chekhov.[39] Both were keenly interested in problems of style and composition and visibly influenced by some formalist concepts and emphases, though neither, as Struve correctly remarks, could be considered a full-fledged formalist.[40]

Concern with poetics, especially with the complex interplay between sound and meaning in poetry, has been one of the many themes in the remarkably wide-ranging oeuvre of Vladimir Weidlé (1895–), a distinguished art historian as well as a resourceful literary critic. Weidlé's studies and essays are informed by a fine and

38. *Dostoevskij: Zhizn' i tvorchestvo* [Life and work] (Paris, 1947). Recently translated into English.

39. P. M. Bitsilli, *Etjudy o russkoj poèzii* [Studies in Russian poetry] (Prague, 1926); "K voprosu o vnutrennej forme romana Dostoevskogo" [On the inner form of the Dostoevsky novel], Sofia University Yearbook 42 (1945–46); *Tvorchestvo Chekhova: Opyt stilisticheskogo analiza* [Chekhov's art: Attempt at a stylistic analysis] (Sofia, 1942). A brief section of this study appears as "From Chekhonte to Chekhov" below. A. L. Bem, *Dostoevskij: Psikhoanaliticheskie etjudy* [Psychonanalytic studies] (Berlin, 1938); *O Pushkine* (Uzhorod, 1937).

40. *Russian Literature in Exile*, p. 375.

truly cosmopolitan sensibility that is equally at home in the Italian Renaissance and in early twentieth-century literary Petersburg. But perhaps the most influential and in a certain sense most representative Russian émigré critic is Georgij Adamovich (1894–1972). Let me hasten to add that "representative" is not meant to imply typicality or spokesmanship in the usual sense of the word. Throughout his controversy-ridden career, Adamovich was always his own man. Though for a number of years the leading critic of a prestigious Russian daily in Paris, he often acted as a maverick, ever-ready to take an unpopular position, to swim against the current. This paradoxically was one of the reasons for Adamovich's resonance within a somewhat claustrophobic, faction-ridden milieu. Another and probably a more crucial reason was his willingness to serve as a monitor of Russian émigré culture, to speak with directness and candor about the plight of the Russian writer-in-exile who gained untrammeled freedom of expression at the cost of marginal existence and of mounting isolation from his natural constituency. (Characteristically, the title of a major collection of essays by Adamovich is *Freedom and Loneliness*.)

The stature of Adamovich as a literary critic has on occasion been called into question. Much has been made of the arbitrariness and capriciousness of some of his judgments, of his numerous inconsistencies, and of the inadequacy or naïveté of his overt aesthetics. These strictures are not altogether unwarranted. Because of a strong neoclassical bias, Adamovich grossly underestimated the achievement of one of the most exciting modern Russian poets, Marina Tsvetaeva. Since he felt committed to Tolstoy, he at times appeared unfair to Dostoevsky. Arguably, he was less appreciative than he might have been of a most gifted young émigré man of letters who was later to become the most celebrated bilingual writer of our times, Vladimir Nabokov. Yet if his responses to the current literary scene or his reassessments of the classics could be wrongheaded and willful, they were never dull or derivative, hackneyed or perfunctory. His legacy is admittedly spotty, but at its best it has the immediacy, the acuteness, and the centrality that are the earmarks of a major critic.

What ultimately makes Adamovich so distinctive and a characteristically Russian phenomenon is the rare combination of a freewheeling impressionistic manner with an underlying moral seriousness that never degenerates into mere didacticism. It is thus that this poet–essayist, who steered clear of doctrinal entanglements and whose sole commitment was to the literary imagination, could warm up to a second-rate *engagé* versifier, Evgenij Evtushenko, simply because, rightly or wrongly, he sensed in him some of the moral élan of great Russian literature. It is thus that, chilled as well as dazzled by Vladimir Nabokov's virtuosity, he was moved to join some of his fellow émigré reviewers in questioning that "exceptionally talented writer's" citizenship in the republic of Russian letters (see p. 226 below).

The Recent Scene

Whatever the blind spots and the built-in limitations of the Russian émigré critics, theirs were the only truly free Russian voices that spoke about Russian and world literature in the blighted period of 1930–53. In the wake of the autocrat's death, as brutal persecution of independent-minded Soviet intellectuals gave way to the somewhat more permissive cultural climate, nonaccredited approaches and relatively heterodox emphases were afforded more latitude. Though formalism remained a pejorative term, it was now increasingly viewed as a regrettable fallacy rather than as a punishable offense. The erstwhile formalist spokesmen who, like Shklovskij, had been cowed into conformism, or, like Eikhenbaum and Tomashevskij, confined themselves to low-profile participation in the academic editions of Russian classics managed to recapture some of the vitality of their earlier writings. Bakhtin brought out an expanded version of his seminal study of Dostoevsky and a provocative book on François Rabelais. Perhaps even more important of late has been the activity of younger scholars such as Vjacheslav Ivanov, Jurij Lotman, and Boris Uspenskij.[41] Their sophisticated and often highly technical studies

---

41. See Viktor Shklovskij, *Za i protiv: Zametki o Dostoevskom* [Pro and contra: Notes on Dostoevsky] (Moscow, 1957); *Khudozhestvennaja proza: Razmyshlenija i razbory* [Artistic prose: Meditations and analyses] (Moscow, 1969). Boris Eikhenbaum, *Lev Tolstoj, 70-e gody* [The 70's] (Leningrad, 1960); *Stat'i o Lermontove* [Articles about Lermontov] (Moscow–Leningrad, 1961); Boris Tomashevskij, *Pushkin*, vol. 1, 1813–1824 (Moscow–Leningrad, 1956); vol. 2 (unfinished), 1824–1837 (Moscow–Leningrad, 1961). Bakhtin, *Problemy poètiki Dostoevskogo* (Moscow, 1963); *Tvorchestvo Fransua Rable i narodnaja kultura srednevekov'ja i renessansa* [Rabelais and the folk culture of the Middle Ages and the Renaissance] (Moscow, 1965); English translation, *Rabelais and His*

in structural poetics hark back to the creative symbiosis of linguistics and literary theory that characterized both Russian formalism and Prague structuralism, even as they take note of recent Western developments in semiotics. In fact, what has been dubbed "Soviet neostructuralism" may well turn out to be one of the most rigorous intellectual manifestations of the current structuralist trend in literary studies.

Systematic concern with poetics and critical awareness of the Slavic formalist–structuralist heritage inform the work of two eminent Leningraders who have tended to avoid doctrinal commitments, Efim G. Ètkind, and Lidija J. Ginzburg. The former, a wide-ranging and gifted comparatist is best known as an authority on the art of translation. His *Poetry and Translation* has already become a classic in the field;[42] his scholarly and readable introduction to poetics is yet unpublished. If Ètkind entered literary scholarship under the aegis of the judicious and erudite Viktor Zhirmunskij, Lidija Ginzburg is a worthy heir to Jurij Tynjanov. Both in her collection of essays on Russian lyric poets and in her more recent study of psychological prose,[43] she achieves the felicitous synthesis of a richly textured historical sense with structural sophistication, a synthesis that owes a great deal to the Tynjanov legacy. Her article "The Poetics of Osip Mandelstam" (below) is the most illuminating assessment of Mandelstam to emerge recently from the Soviet Union; in fact, it is one of the best discussions of his poetic craft in any language.

It is no reflection on the intellectual distinction of Ginzburg's probing analysis to suggest that its importance rests in large measure on the centrality of its subject. Informed responsiveness to the major achievements of modern Russian literature, hitherto neglected or suppressed, marks some of the most memorable and appealing moments in recent Soviet criticism. The best of Vladimir Lakshin's sensitive and humane essays tend to fall into this category. His article "Friends and Enemies of Ivan Den-

---

World (Cambridge, Mass., 1968). Jurij M. Lotman, *Leksii po strukturalnoj poètike* (reprint, Providence, R.I., 1968); *Struktura khudozhestvennogo teksta* [Structure of the artistic text] (Moscow, 1970); Boris Uspenskij, *Poètika kompozitsii* (Moscow, 1970); English translation, *A Poetics of Composition* (Berkeley and Los Angeles, 1973).

42. Ètkind, *Poèzija i perevod* (Moscow, 1963).

43. Ginzburg, *O lirike*, (Moscow, 1964); 2d enl. ed., 1973); *O psikhologicheskoj proze* (Leningrad, 1971).

isovich"[44] is a forthright and sympathetic reaction to Aleksandr Solzhenitsyn's momentous debut. His encompassing and vivid, if occasionally hortatory and consistently prolix, discussion of M. Bulgakov's brilliant *The Master and Margarita* (below) was an uncommonly open-minded and appreciative treatment of an explosive novel that enjoyed in the Soviet Union a precarious, semilegal status. (Even the drastically censored version of *The Master and Margarita* which had been serialized in a Soviet journal *Moskva* is yet to appear in Russia in book form.)

Significantly, it was another master of the modern Russian imagination who provided an occasion for what is, without any doubt, one of the high points of post-Stalin Russian criticism. In "The Poetry of Pasternak" by Andrej Sinjavskij we witness an encounter between a major poet and a first-class critical intelligence.[45] Not unlike Andrej Belyj, Innokentij Annenskij, or Mark Aldanov, Sinjavskij represents a hybrid, or dual, strain in Russian criticism. His "underground" alter ego Abram Tertz, the author of *The Trial Begins* and *The Fantastic Stories*, was primarily a fiction writer. Sinjavskij-Tertz is a resourceful, versatile, and uncommonly gifted man of letters. But for all the uncanny power of some of his satirical nightmares, his chief strength may well lie in the discursive mode. His much discussed essay "On Socialist Realism"—a brilliantly subversive exercise in irony and a trenchant commentary on the crushing weight of the Soviet aesthetic and political dogma—is a remarkable cultural diagnosis.[46] His delicate reconstruction of Pasternak's poetic universe, a blend of affection and acumen, is literary criticism of the highest order.

The fate of Andrej Sinjavskij is part of the public record. In February 1966, shortly after the identity of Abram Tertz was discovered by the authorities, the writer was arraigned and sen-

---

44. "Ivan Denisovich, ego druz'ja i nedrugi," *Novyj mir* (January 1964); 223–45.

45. This study appeared in 1965 as an introduction to a collection of Pasternak verse (Boris Pasternak, *Stikhotvorenija i poèmy* [Moscow, 1965]). As soon as the identity of Tertz was established, the edition was hastily withdrawn; the subsequent edition featured another introductory essay. A drastically abbreviated version of Sinjavskij's "Poèzija Pasternaka," in a fine translation by Henry Gifford, appears as "On Boris Pasternak" below.

46. The essay "Chto takoe sotsialisticheskij realizm?" [What is socialist realism?] written in 1958 and first published anonymously in the French journal *Esprit* in Paris in February 1959. It is available in English as *On Socialist Realism* (New York, 1960).

tenced to seven years' imprisonment in a trial widely described as a partial throwback to the Stalinist age of darkness. Today he is an exile in Paris. To the student of modern Russian culture the Sinjavskij story can be said to carry a double message. If his achievement as a critic is testimony to the resilience of the Russian literary sensibility, his plight is a sobering reminder that even in post-Stalin Russia the cost of a heterodox vision can be exorbitantly high.

1
The Symbolists

Gogol

ANDREJ BELYJ

I

A song so familiar, so close to our hearts and entrancing our souls, and yet distant and still undeciphered—that is Gogol's song. . . .

And a horrible, heart-gripping laughter that sounds like laughter from a graveyard, and nevertheless troubles us as if we too were dead men—a dead man's laughter—that is Gogol's laughter!

"A song struck up in the distance, the distant tolling of a bell, which fades away . . . the endless horizon . . . Russia, Russia!" And a line earlier—on the "boundless plain" "a soldier on horseback, carrying a green box with leaden grapeshot and the insignia of a certain artillery battery" (*Dead Souls*). Two visions, two ideas, but also two creative aspirations. Here is one of them: "To clothe it [this drama][1] in the wondrous moonlit night and its silvery shimmer, and in the warm luxurious breath of the South. To pour over it a glittering stream of the sun's bright rays, and to let it be filled with unbearable brilliance." (Meditation *pro domo sua* concerning an unwritten play.) And the other wish is to "dash off" a multivolume history of the Ukraine, without any qualifications for this task.[2]

"Eyes . . . invading the soul with singing" ("Viy"): the image of a horseman "echoing" instead of being reflected in the waters ("A Terrible Vengeance"). "The midnight moonlight . . . steamed over

This essay, translated here by Elizabeth Trahan and John Fred Beebe, was first published in the symbolist journal *Vesy* [Scales], Moscow, 1909. An earlier version of the translation appeared in *Russian Literature Triquarterly*, no. 4 (Fall 1972): 131–43, copyright © 1972 by Ardis Publishers. Reprinted by permission. Most of the departures from the *RLT* text were agreed to by Dr. Trahan, whose cooperation is gratefully acknowledged.

1. Translators' interpolation. The rhapsodic sequence that follows is drawn from "Notes toward a Drama from Ukrainian History," written in 1838 or 1839. The "Notes" were first published in the journal *Osnova* [Foundation] in 1861.

2. In a letter to a friend in 1834, Gogol speaks of a plan to "dash off" a history of the Ukraine in six small or four large volumes.

the ground." "The rubies of her lips . . . burning into his heart"
("Viy"). "The glittering song of the nightingale" ("A May Night").
"Hair like light-gray mist." "The Maiden shining through the
water, as through a shift of glass." "Pincers are coming out of your
eyes" ("A Terrible Vengeance"). "Girls . . . in shifts, white as a
meadow bedecked with lilies of the valley" and with bodies
"carved out of clouds" so that the moon shone through them ("A
May Night"). Perhaps, in a moment, the lily-of-the-valley white-
ness of their shifts will become glass water, and trickle down in a
stream, and the stream will go up in smoke, or break over a rock
and turn into water dust, just as the water gushes as gray dust in
"A Terrible Vengeance," to glimmer then like silvery wolf hair or
to flash out from under the oars "like sparks from a flint."

What kind of images are these? From what impossibilities have
they been spun? Everything is jumbled together in them: colors,
smells, sounds. Where can you find bolder comparisons, where is
artistic truth more improbable? Poor symbolists! To this day they
are being rebuked by the critics for their "sky-blue sounds"; but
find me an image in Verlaine, Rimbaud, Baudelaire that would be
as improbable in its boldness as Gogol's. No, you cannot find it,
and meanwhile people read Gogol and they fail to see, even
today, that we have no word in our dictionary with which to label
Gogol; we still have no way to gauge all the possibilities that he
exhausted. We still do not know what Gogol is, and although we
do not see the real Gogol, his creations, even when reduced by
our limited perception, are closer to us than all other Russian
writers of the nineteenth century.

What style!

He has eyes invading the soul with singing, or else coming out
like pincers, hair spreading like light-gray mist, water turning into
dust, or else water that becomes a glass smock, trimmed with
wolf-hair—with moonlight. Every page, nearly every sentence
crosses into some kind of new world, springing out of the soul in
"oceans of fragrance" ("A May Night"), in "floods of joy and
light," in a "gale of gaiety" ("Viy"). And it was from these gales,
floods, and oceans, when trees murmur their "drunken mumble"
("The Lost Letter"), when man flies in ecstasy like a bird—"and it
seemed . . . would fly right out of the world" ("A Terrible
Vengeance")—that Gogol's songs were born. Then he would wish
to "clothe" his song "in the wondrous moonlit night. . . . To pour
over it a glittering stream of the sun's bright rays, and to let it be

filled with unbearable brilliance." And then he would begin to
erect his universe: in the depths of his soul a new expanse was
being born such as we have not known. In floods of bliss, in gales
of emotion there erupted the lava of creativity that hardened into
"high-peaked" mountains, blossoming with forests and meadows,
sparkling with ponds. And these mountains are not mountains: "Is
it not some mischievous sea that has overrun its shores, tossed its
monstrous waves like a whirlwind and, petrified, they have remained motionless in the air?" "These forests are not forests: . . .
they are hair growing on a wood demon's shaggy head." "These
meadows are not meadows . . . but a green belt girding the sky"
("A Terrible Vengeance"); and that pond is not a pond: "like a
feeble old man it held the distant, dark sky in its cold embrace,
covering the fiery stars with icy kisses" ("A May Night"). That is
the kind of earth Gogol sees, where forests are a wood demon's
beard, where meadows are a belt encircling the sky, where mountains are congealed waves, and where a pond is a feeble old man
embracing the sky. And the sky? In "A Terrible Vengeance"
Gogol has the sky filling the sorcerer's room when he calls up
Katerina's soul; the sky itself emanates from the sorcerer like a
magic current. Such is Gogol's sky: it is a sorcerer's sky. And in
that kind of sky originates his earth, a sorcerer's earth: that is why
a forest turns out to be a wood demon's head, and even a chimney
"turns into a rector." The children of this earth, too, are horrible:
they are sorcerers, a Viy, or a Pannochka;[3] their bodies are transparent, carved out of clouds; even pigs, in this strange land, "roll
their eyes." That earth is not our earth; it is a cloud ridge pierced
by moonlight. Begin to daydream . . . and your dream will at your
desire change the cloud outline into a mermaid, or a devil, or a
new city, which, for all you know, may even look like St. Petersburg.

   Gogol's song is a song of unbearable brilliance, and the light of
this song has created for him a new, better earth where a dream is
not a dream but a new life. His song is moonlight, which "like a
transparent veil, fell lightly" ("Viy") upon the earth that Gogol
walked. "With precious damask muslin white as snow" ("A Terrible Vengeance") Gogol has shrouded from us, and from himself,

---

   3. Viy, is the ghoulish chief of gnomes whose gaze strikes dead a hapless
Kiev seminarian in a remarkable horror story by Gogol under the same title.
Pannochka, the Ukrainian word for "a young lady," is a witch in "Viy."

the real earth; and the folds of this muslin gave birth to the
transfigured bodies of flying maidens, apparently carved out of
clouds. In Gogol's early period, reality often appears under a
romantic veil of moonlight, for Gogol's reality is like the lady
whose face one can bear only when it is veiled. But suddenly
Gogol tears the veil off his lady. Here is what Gogol turns reality
into: "The cowherd let out such a laugh that it was as if two bulls
were bellowing at each other simultaneously" ("Viy"). "Ivan
Ivanovich's head resembles a radish with the tail down; Ivan
Nikiforovich's head resembles a radish with the tail up". . . "Ivan
Ivanovich has snuff-colored eyes, and a mouth . . . somewhat like
the letter V; Ivan Nikiforovich has . . . a nose shaped like a ripe
plum" ("The Two Ivans"). "And now the whole lower part of our
assessor's face is a sheep's snout, as it were. . . . Yet all because of
a perfectly trivial incident: when his deceased mother was in
labor it so happened that a sheep stuck its head through the window and the devil put it into its head to let out a bleat" ("A
Litigation").[4]

That's reality for you! First shapes carved out of cloud glitter,
then sheep snouts crawl in bellowing at us like two bulls, and
radishes crawl out with tails up and tails down, with snuff-colored
eyes. They all begin not to walk but to scuttle, mince about, sidle.
And what is most horrible of all is that Gogol makes them express
themselves in a refined manner. These "radishes" wink with their
snuff-colored little eyes, sprinkle their speech with such phrases
as "if you please," and Gogol reports on them not in a straightforward way but with a strange, desperate sort of joviality. The lower
part of the assessor's face is not simply a sheep's snout, but "a
sheep's snout, as it were"; "as it were" for the most trifling reason:
because at the moment of the assessor's birth a sheep walked up
to the window—a horrible "as it were." It is customary to call
Gogol a realist, but, by all that's holy, where is reality here? What
we face is not humanity but prehumanity; the earth is populated
here not by men, but by radishes. In any case, this world whose
fortunes are affected by sheep sticking their heads through the
window, or by a black cat that disappears ("Old-World Land-

4. "A Litigation" is a dramatic fragment of four short scenes composed about
1840 and apparently based on material from the unfinished comedy on which
Gogol got "hung up" in 1833, "The Order of Vladimir of the Third Class " —
Trans.

owners"), or by calling someone "a gander,"[5] is not a world of
men, but of animals.

And all these mincing, shuffling busybodies, these Perepenkos,
Golopupenkos, Dovgochkhuns, and Shpon'kas are not men, but
radishes.[6] Men like that simply do not exist. Yet as the crowning
horror, Gogol makes this menagerie or turnip patch—I don't know
what to call it—dance the mazurka, take snuff from each other and,
worse still, experience mystical ecstasies. Thus one of his
radishes—Shpon'ka[7]—experiences ecstasy while contemplating a
sunset. Worse than that, Gogol has amphibians and reptiles buy-
ing human souls. But under just what skies does the life of these
creatures take place? "If . . . it hadn't turned as dark in the field as
it is underneath a sheepskin coat," Gogol remarks somewhere.
"It's as dark and desolate [at night] as in a wine cellar" ("The Lost
Letter"). Gogol knew how to open up the sky in the rapture of his
soul and even perceived something beyond the sky, for his heroes
were about to take a leap out of the world; yet Gogol also knew
another sky, one that is like a sheepskin coat and like the trapdoor
of a wine cellar. And behold, no sooner does he remove the muslin of his fancies from the world than you are no longer in the
clouds, but right here on earth, and this "here" of the earth turns
into something beneath a sheepskin coat, and you yourself into a
bedbug or a flea, or, worse yet, into a radish, stored in the cellar.

And thus another of Gogol's fairy tales begins, the reverse of the
first. Gogol did not know people. He knew giants and dwarfs.
Neither did Gogol know the earth—he knew a mist "carved out"
of moonlight, or a black cellar. And when he combined the cellar
with the seething white foam of clouds, or a radish with creatures
flying in the air, he arrived at some sort of strange semblance of
the earth and its people. This earth is not our earth: the ground
suddenly begins to vanish from under our feet, or it turns out to be
a coffin in which we, corpses, are suffocating. And these people
are not the people we know: a Cossack is dancing, and suddenly a

---

5. Reference to the preposterous feud between Ivan Ivanovich and Ivan
Nikiforovich, set off by the latter's calling the former "a gander" ("The Two
Ivans").

6. All these names, which occur in *Evenings on a Farm near Dikanka or* in
Mirgorod, are comic: in Ukrainian they mean roughly "split-too-far," "bare
navel," "long sneezer," and "collar button." —*Trans.*

7. A sheepish young squire who appears in Gogol's early story, "Ivan
Fëdorovich Shpon'ka and His Aunt."

fang protrudes from his mouth. An old woman is gulping down dumplings, next thing she has flown up the chimney. An official is walking along Nevsky Prospect, and starts: his own nose is walking toward him.[8] Small wonder that recent criticism did not hesitate to turn Chichikov, that most "realistic" of all of Gogol's heroes, into the devil! Now we see Chichikov and now we don't—instead there is a little "German" with a pig's snout, and up in the sky. He is hunting stars and has already crept up on the moon.[9] Gogol has lost contact with what we call reality. Someone has jerked the earth out from under his feet. All that remains is the memory of the earth. The earth of humanity has decomposed into ether and manure; and all the creatures inhabiting the earth have been transformed into disembodied souls, seeking new bodies for themselves. Their bodies are not our bodies. They are a cloud mist, pierced by moonlight, or they have become radishes in human shape, growing in the manure. And all the best human emotions (such as love, compassion, joy) have gone off into the ether. It is significant that we do not know what woman Gogol loved, or whether he loved at all. When he describes a woman, she is either a vision or a cold statue with breasts "lusterless, like unglazed porcelain," or a lewd woman, mincing in the night toward a seminary student. Is it possible that woman does not exist except as an old hag or a mermaid with porcelain breasts carved out of clouds?

When he teaches about human emotions, he moralizes and, worse, reminds the department heads that he is, as it were, an official of the Department of Heaven. For the Russia of his time he envisions the grandeur of "a new city descending from heaven to earth."

Does Gogol rejoice? No, Gogol's face grows dark with the years, and Gogol dies from fear.

His emotions are inexpressible, ineffable: in his love fantasies there is no longer room for love. There is some kind of cosmic, but disembodied ecstasy. On the other hand, ordinary human emo-

8. The incidents referred to above occur respectively in "A Night before Christmas," "A Terrible Vengeance" (*Evenings on a Farm near Dikanka*), and the Petersburg tale "The Nose."

9. By "recent criticism" Belyj probably means such studies of Gogol as Merezhkovskij's *Gogol and the Devil*, where Chichikov is construed as an emissary of the Fiend. As for "a little German with a pig's snout up in the sky," that is how the devil, cast this time in the role of a relatively innocuous prankster, appears in the spirited Ukrainian tale, "A Night before Christmas."

tions are for him the emotions of collar buttons and radishes winking at each other. And everyday life is a madhouse. "I am sick and tired of the play [*The Inspector General*]," Gogol wrote to a journalist. "I would like to run away right now." And in "A Madman's Diary" the hero cries, "Save me! Give me a *troika* as swift as the whirlwind! Mount, coachman . . . wing your way up, horses, and carry me out of this world! On and on till nothing is seen of it—nothing."

Should not Gogol, in this world of radishes and pumpkins glittering in the sunlight, with Dovgochkhun[10] seated solemnly among them, exclaim together with his madman: "On and on till nothing is seen of it—nothing"?

II

I do not know what Gogol is: a realist, a symbolist, a romantic, or a classicist. Yes, he saw all the dust motes on Ivan Ivanovich's coat so distinctly that he turned Ivan Ivanovich himself into a dusty cloak. The only thing he did not see in Ivan Ivanovich was his human face. Yes, he saw real aspirations, human emotions; so clearly did he perceive the deep inexpressible roots of these emotions that they became emotions no longer of human beings but of some sort of as yet bodiless creatures. The flying witch and the dirty old woman, Shpon'ka the vegetable and Shpon'ka experiencing ecstasy as incompatible; the distant past of humanity (bestiality) and the distant future (angelhood) were located by Gogol in the present. But the present decomposed in Gogol. He is not yet a saint, no longer a human being. The seer of the future and of the past sketched the present but put into it some kind of mysterious soul. And the present became the prototype of something. But of what?

Some say Gogol is a realist. They are right. Some say he is a symbolist. They are right too. His forests are not forests; his mountains are not mountains. He has mermaids with bodies of clouds. Like the romantics, he was attracted to devils and witches and, like Hoffmann and Poe, he introduced the fantastic into reality. If you wish, Gogol is a romantic; but has not Gogol's epic also been compared to Homer?

10. Dovgochkhun is the last name of the bumptious Ivan Nikiforovich, one of the quarrelsome squires in "The Two Ivans."

Gogol is a genius whom you cannot possibly approach through academic labels. I have a predilection for symbolism. Consequently it is easier for me to see the features of Gogol's symbolism. The romantic will see in him a romantic; the realist will see a realist.

But we are not talking about literary schools. We are talking about Gogol's soul. The sufferings, torments, and raptures of this soul reach such human or rather superhuman heights that it would be blasphemous to measure them with our yardsticks. And indeed, does one use a yardstick to measure the altitude of towering peaks and the morass of bottomless marshes? Gogol is the morass and the peak, the mud and the snow; but Gogol is no longer the earth. Gogol had a score to settle with the earth. The earth had wreaked its terrible vengeance upon him. Our normal emotions are not Gogol's emotions: his love is not love; his gaiety is anything but gaiety. Laughter—what kind of laughter do we find here? It is simply a roar at Ivan Ivanovich's cloak, and at that, a roar that sounds "as if two bulls were bellowing at each other simultaneously." Gogol's laughter changes into a tragic roar, and some kind of darkness falls heavily upon us out of that roar: "And in that day they shall roar against them like the roaring of the sea; and if one look unto the land, behold darkness and sorrow, and the light is darkened in the heavens" (Isa. 5:30). Gogol had come up to a brink of life beyond which he hears a roar; and this roar he turned into laughter. But Gogol's is a sorcerer's laughter; Gogol takes a look at the earth, bursts out laughing—"and, behold, darkness and sorrow," although the sun is shining, "rows of fruit trees, drowned in the crimson of the cherries and in the sapphire sea of plums, covered by a lead coating." That's how Gogol arranges the earth's surface with fairy-tale magnificence in his realistic stories (for example, in "The Old-World Landowners"). But beyond this magnificence, as under some golden carpet thrown over an abyss of horror, the abyss, in the words of the prophet Habakkuk, "gave forth its voice, lifted its arms on high" (Hab. 3:10). And right after the description of the dead life of Afanasij Ivanovich and Pulkherja Ivanovna—a description in which, it would seem, there is nothing mysterious, a description where everything is as clear as day, where their life is illuminated with idyllic splendor, just as their orchard is inundated by the "crimson of the cherries" and by the "sapphire sea of plums"—even during this golden noon splendor Gogol is visited by an abyss of fear, just as Pulkherja

Ivanovna is visited by the abyss in the form of a black cat. And at that very moment, cutting short the idyll, Gogol confesses:

> You doubtless have chanced to hear a voice calling you by name, which uneducated folk explain as a soul pining for a human being . . . I remember that in childhood I often heard it . . . . The day, just then, would be especially bright and sunny. Not a single leaf would be stirring in the orchard. There would be a dead silence, even the grasshoppers would stop chirping. Not a soul would be in the orchard. But I confess that if the wildest and stormiest night with all the hell of the elements had caught me alone in the middle of an impenetrable forest, I would not have been as frightened as of this horrible silence in the middle of a cloudless day. ["The Old-World Landowners"]

This fear of midday, when the earthly distinctness of phenomena appears with special clarity, was called by the ancients "panic terror"; this terror is noted in the Bible: "Save us from the midday devil." Great Pan or the devil (I do not know which) from out of the underbrush of the soul would raise up his countenance against Gogol and, terrified by this countenance, Gogol would grow faint in the midday silence among the sapphire plums, melons, radishes, and Dovgochkhuns. In each Dovgochkhun Gogol would see a Basavrjuk,[11] and it would be precisely in the daytime and not at night that each civil servant would turn for Gogol into some object or animal.

But why? The daytime drawing near of the abyss of the spirit toward the surfaces of daytime consciousness, the roaring of the abyss ("and in that day they shall roar against them like the roaring of the sea") in sunlit silence, is the normal state of the highly adept mystic. In antiquity, all mystery cults began with fear (the abyss opened under the feet of the one being initiated into the mystery rites of Egypt; the abyss emitted men who had been changed into animals with dogs' heads, before the initiation of the *epoptai* at the greater Eleusinian mysteries), and this fear changed into ecstasy, into a state that reveals the world as perfect and that Dostoevsky calls the "moment of eternal harmony"—the moment at which you experience the rebirth of the body's soul; it culminates in true transfiguration (the Seraphim), true madness (Nietzsche), or true death (Gogol).

---

11. A personified devil in an early tale, "St. John's Eve." —*Trans.*

Yes, in his images, in his relationship to the earth, Gogol transcended the limits of art. He was wandering in the garden of his soul, and blundered into a place where the garden is no longer a garden and the soul is not a soul. As his artistic vision deepened, Gogol reached beyond the limits of his self. Yet, instead of utilizing this expansion of his personality for artistic goals, he threw himself into the abyss of his alter ego—he set out on paths that one must not travel without a carefully mapped out occult route, without an experienced guide. Instead of merging his empirical self with the world-self, Gogol broke the bond between the two selves—and a black abyss yawned between them. One self would be horrified by the contemplation of collar buttons and radishes, the other self would fly out there beyond the heavenly vault. Between the two selves lay the world's space and time in billions of miles and billions of years. And then, when the soul's call would come ("You doubtless have chanced to hear a voice calling you by name, which uneducated folk explain as a soul pining for a human being")—when this call would come, the black abyss of space and years separating Gogol's two selves would tear asunder before him the veil of the phenomena—and he would hear a roar, "the roaring of the furious sea." "I confess that if the wildest and stormiest night with all the hell of the elements had caught me alone in the middle of a . . . forest, I would not have been as frightened," sighs Gogol. That was why he dashed about hopelessly seeking someone initiated into the mysteries who could save him. And he ran into Father Matthew. What could Father Matthew do? He could not understand Gogol. The meekest and best-intentioned man who did not see what Gogol saw could only destroy him.[12] Gogol rose on the wings of ecstasy, and even flew out of this world, like his mad Pani Katerina who "was flying . . . and it seemed . . . would fly right out of the world." She flew out, and went out of her mind, as Gogol had already flown out when he cried in the words of his madman: "Carry me out of this world! On and on till nothing is seen of it—nothing." On and on—in the words of Isaiah: "And, behold, darkness and sorrow, and the light is darkened in the Heavens."

12. Father Matthew, or Matvej Konstantinovskij, Gogol's father confessor during the last seven or eight years of his life, was according to eyewitness testimony a fiercely narrow-minded priest and was actually not known for meekness.

Gogol should have made a pilgrimage to the tomes of Boehme,[13] to the ancient manuscripts of the Orient. Gogol should have understood first of all that there were explanations for his predicament. Then he would have realized that perhaps there existed people who could cure the horrible dislocation of his soul. But Gogol did not have the patience to study, and as a result he sought a guide in just the wrong place. Gogol had not studied Oriental mystical literature—in general, he had not studied anything; did he not want to "dash off" the history of the Ukraine in some sixteen volumes?[14] Thales and Plato, on the other hand, had traveled to Egypt; hence Plato's teachings about ideas and the soul—that soul which, longing for a body, calls a human being (that was the call Gogol heard). The soul pined for Gogol; Gogol pined for his soul, but the abyss lay between them. And the light had grown dim for Gogol. Gogol knew the mysteries of rapture, he also knew the mysteries of horror. But he did not know the mystery of love. The initiates knew it; but this fact Gogol did not know either; he did not know that he was peering into the sanctuary.

His rapture is a wild rapture; and the sweetness of his inspirations is a wild sweetness; his lips do not smile but "leer in a laugh of bliss." The Cossack dances and suddenly "a fang protrudes from his mouth" ("A Terrible Vengeance"). "The rubies of her lips are burning into his heart" (this is not love but some kind of vampirism!). In all the ecstasy that transfigures both Gogol and the world ("the grass seemed to be the bottom of some kind of clear . . . sea,")—in all this ecstasy there is "an excruciating, unpleasant, and at the same time sweet sensation," or a "piercing, agonizing sweet delight"—in a word, a "devilishly sweet" ("Viy"), but not a divinely sweet sensation. And therefore the transfigured brilliance of Nature begins tò frighten and the "Dnieper" begins to glitter like "silvery wolf hair" (why wolf hair?). And when the earth is transfigured so that distances change (just outside Kiev "appeared the blue waters of the Liman,[15] beyond the Liman . . . the Black Sea . . . . The Galician land could be seen"), why "does one's hair stand on end" and why does the "devilishly sweet" sensation culminate in the horse's turning his head, and "marvel-

13. Jakob Boehme (1575–1624), a German mystic who exerted a profound influence on some romantic philosophers.
14. Not unlike Gogol, Belyj had a penchant for hyperbole: as indicated above, Gogol spoke of six small or four large volumes.
15. A large bay at the mouth of the Dnieper. —*Trans.*

ous to relate, laughing aloud?" Gogol's ecstasy culminates not in the mystery of love but in a wild dance; everything is transfigured—not by love but by a dance of madness; truly—Gogol is in a bewitched spot: "The old man went . . . whirling in a dance all over the clearing . . . from behind someone laughed. He looked around; no melon patch, no wagon drivers, nothing . . . all around were deep pits; under his feet a bottomless precipice; above his head towered a mountain . . . behind it, an ugly face was blinking" ("A Bewitched Spot"). The soul had called a human being. There was rapture and dancing. And the offshoot of all this is a bottomless precipice and an ugly face. That is how it always is with Gogol: Khoma Brut sets off with the Pannochka on his back. Then comes the roar, "Bring Viy," and Viy, the spirit of the earth whom Gogol had slandered, points at him—"There he is"; and the people who have been turned by Gogol into fiends rush at Khoma-Gogol and kill him.[16] This was because Gogol had a vision; he saw the Countenance, but he had not transfigured himself so as to be able to look upon the Countenance with impunity, to hear the call of the beloved Soul, whose voice, in the words of Revelation, "is like the sound of many waters." This sound became for Gogol a "roar," the brilliance of transfiguration became the glitter of "wolf hair" and the soul a "witch." Hecate and the bewitched animals did not touch those who were being initiated into the mystery rites, when they left the Eleusinian temple. But they gnawed at Gogol, as the dead man gnawed at the sorcerer. And the Countenance seen by Gogol did not save him. This Countenance became for him the "horsemen in the Carpathians." And from him Gogol fled. "In the cloud before him shone someone's wondrous face. Unbidden, uninvited it had come to pay him a visit. . . . And though, seemingly, there was nothing terrible about it, an overwhelming horror took hold of him" ("A Terrible Vengeance"). And on a clear, sunny day Gogol trembled because it seemed to him that "someone's long shadow was flashing, though the sky was clear and no clouds were passing along it" ("A Terrible Vengeance"). It was the shadow of the wondrous face that, in spite of being wondrous, terrified Gogol all his life. This was because the

16. Khoma Brut, an *homme moyen sensuel* who has stumbled into the abyss, was fated to be ridden by the witch and then to ride her to death. He is overpowered by Viy and his henchmen during an anxious night vigil over Pannochka's body.

bridge of love, which transfigures the earth, had collapsed for Gogol, and between the Heavenly Countenance and him had formed a black, roaring abyss, which Gogol covered with a curtain of laughter. That is why the laughter turned into a roar, "as if two bulls were bellowing at each other simultaneously." Gogol feared the abyss, but he dimly remembered (not consciously, of course) that beyond this abyss (beyond billions of miles and years) there was a dear voice calling him. Gogol could not refrain from stepping forth to answer that call: he went—and fell into the abyss. The bridge of love had collapsed for him, and Gogol could not fly across the abyss; he flew into it when he flew out of the world (as neophytes, being tested, might fly into the abyss). Gogol is oppressed by something in the past, by some betrayal of the earth——by the sin of love (it is not by chance that we know nothing of the infatuations of Gogol, whose nature was passionate to the point of perversion). "Save me! . . . And carry me out of this world! On and on till nothing is seen of it—nothing." Nothing, neither collar buttons, nor the earth, nor the Countenance.

"Divine night! Enchanting night! . . . Do you know the Ukrainian night? Oh, you don't know the Ukrainian night," exclaims Gogol rapturously in "A May Night." And, truly, are there many who know such nights where water is turned into glittering wolf hair, and grass seems to be "the bottom of some kind of clear . . . sea?" Nevertheless it seems to us that this rapture and this joy were ominous; all such nights ended badly for Gogol. Finally, Gogol no longer wanted either "days with a call" or nights "with wolf hair," and he cried out: "On and on till nothing is seen of it—nothing."

Gogol loves Russia, his native country. He loves her as a lover does his beloved. "Russia! What do you want from me? What inscrutable bond is there between us?" (*Dead Souls*). Gogol loves a Russia that no one else knows. Gogol loves Russia with an ancient love. His relation to her is like the sorcerer's relation to his daughter Katerina; Gogol uses sorcery on her: "Why do you look at me like that? . . . My eyes are alight with unnatural power." What a tone, what jealous imperiousness! Gogol is putting a sorcerer's spell on Russia: she is for him throughout a mysterious figure, and at the same time his mistress. Do not Gogol's eyes shine with the same power as the eyes of the old father in "A Terrible Vengeance"? "The strange brilliance of his eyes seemed

uncanny to her" (Katerina or Russia?). . . . "See how I look at
you," says the sorcerer, appearing to his daughter in a dream. "See
how I look at you with my eyes," Gogol seems to say, appearing to
us in the dream of Russian life (Russian life is the most amazing
dream): "Dreams reveal much truth" ("A Terrible Vengeance").
And with a kind of prophetic truth, barely discernible in a dream,
Gogol addresses the Russian land, which has been asleep to this
day. "Russia! . . . But just what is the inscrutable, imperious power
that draws me to you? . . . What inscrutable bond is there between
us? . . . My eyes are alight with unnatural power." Gogol, perhaps
more than any other Russian writer, is inscrutably, unnaturally
bound to Russia, and he is bound by no means to the Russia of the
past, but to today's Russia, and even more to tomorrow's.

Is not everything that is happening to us, to our land, to our
nation, a dream? Just recently our native land was illumined by a
strange brilliance, so that from Moscow there became visible the
Liman and the Black Sea and a mysterious horseman. And now,
even on a sunny day, when there are no clouds, someone's terrible
shadow flashes: a shadow of horrible provocation coming from the
depths of the soul, from the depths of the earth. Everything has
become strange and unintelligible; and our country is gripped by
a deadly longing; both here and there a wild dance of strange
gaiety, of strange oblivion goes on. And like the Carpathian Mountains, the storm clouds of disaster hover over us: on those mountains stands an unknown avenger. And a strange wail arises from
the depths of our soul: Russia! What do you want of us? What calls
and sobs and clutches at our hearts? We do not know. And something calls and sobs—and clutches at our hearts.

We are standing before the veil of the future like neophytes
facing the temple: soon the veil of the temple will be rent in
two—what will gaze out at us: Hecate and the ghosts? Or the soul
of our nation, the soul of the people wrapped in a shroud?

Gogol was the first to approach this mystery rite, and a dead
man rose up before him. Gogol died.

And now we stand before the same vision—the vision of death.
That is why Gogol's vision is closer to us than anything that has
been said about our country. We must remember that the veil of
death will fall away only when we cleanse our souls for the great
mystery rite. This mystery rite is the service of our country, not
only in form, but in spirit and truth. Then the shroud will fall
away and our soul, our country will be revealed to us.

III

In speaking about Gogol, however briefly, it is impossible not to say at least a few words about his style. One could write voluminous studies on the subject. Just as Gogol's "realism" consists of two fairy tales—one about the prehuman, the other about the superhuman earth—so is also the natural flow of his style compounded of two kinds of unnaturalness. It consists of a jeweler's verbal workmanship, so fine that one keeps wondering how Gogol could, while piling technical marvel upon marvel—indeed, turning the fabric of his language into a succession of tours de force —how Gogol could precisely by means of these tricks express the ecstasy of a living soul. Yet this aspect of Gogol's stylistics is obtruded upon time and again by crude—even ungrammatical —turns of speech, by clumsy, incongruous, or banal locations. Such meaningless epithets as "wondrous," "splendid," or "enchanting" decorate Gogol's style, and in themselves express nothing; but in combination with the most intricate similes and metaphors they impart a particular charm to Gogol's style. Who does not remember the striking "Tale of Captain Kopejkin"?[17] But observe, if you please, the technical trick of the core of this narrative: a completely banal account of the misadventures of the unfortunate captain is interrupted literally after every other word by expressions such as "don't you see," "so to say," and so on.

Precisely through this crude device Gogol achieves dazzling expressiveness. Gogol's style manages to be both substandard and superior in virtuosity not only to Wilde's, Rimbaud's, and Sologub's, but often even to Nietzsche's.

All the devices that characterize the best stylists of our time (and mark them precisely as stylists of our time) are present in Gogol.

First, the abundant use of alliteration, in "Viy" for example: *Svetlyj serp svetil* [the shining sickle shone]. *Vikhr' veselja* [a gale of gaiety]. *Usmekhnut'sja smekhom* [to leer in a laugh] (here the alliteration is combined with an intensification of the verb *usmekhnut'sja* by the noun *smekhom*). *V eë chertakh nichego ne bylo* tusk*logo*, mut*nogo*, umer*shego* [in her features there was no-

---

17. This rather long anecdote, found in chap. 10, p. 1 of *Dead Souls* and ramblingly told by the postmaster at a gathering of local notables, is a remarkable example of a style aiming at producing the illusion of oral narration.

thing that was wan, dull, or dead] (here we have *tu, ut*, and simultaneously *mu, um*). *Kak klokotanie kipjashchej smoly* [like the bubbling of boiling tar]. *Kruglyj krepkij stan* [round and firm waist]. *Kostjanye kogti* [bony claws]. And in "A Terrible Vengeance": *Ostrye ochi ne otryvalis* [the sharp eyes would not let go], and so on.

Second, the masterful use of word order:

1. The noun was separated from its adjective by the insertion of additional words. Some naive critics have charged such a fine stylist as Sologub[18] with using this allegedly modernistic device. But here are random examples from Gogol: "Meadows, by the darkness of night swallowed up." "There shone the golden cupolas in the distance of the Kiev churches." "He couldn't refrain, as he went out, from looking" (all from "Viy"). "Horrible torments, obviously, he was suffering" ("A Terrible Vengeance"), and so on.

2. Compound epithets were also copiously used by Gogol: "the white-transparent sky," "golden-essensed brocade," "long-necked goose," or "high-topped mountains."

3. Sometimes these epithets are exceedingly daring: "deafened walls," "a self-contradicting [*poperechivajushchee sebe*] emotion," "spring-water coolness," and so on.

4. Especially characteristic is Gogol's use of verbs; it is indicative of an unabashed impressionism: From "Viy": "breasts shown through," "the moonlight steamed," "words . . . were sobbing," "the water is tumbling down," "the cold cut into the Cossack's veins," "there is a bustle and an uproar in a quarter of Kiev [*shumit, gremit*]," "mountain after mountain . . . they shackle the earth," "the eyes are swindling his soul out," "the quail thunders," "the flame . . . snatched itself away," and so on.

5. I have not even mentioned Gogol's similes. Sometimes he describes for pages whatever the object is being compared to, without that object being described at all. Suffice it to cite one sentence: "A noise was heard [what kind of noise?] . . . like the wind"; but not simply the wind; it is "the wind in a quiet hour of the evening." Now this wind "was playing chords, whirling, on the mirror of the waters" and not simply "the wind was playing chords, whirling," but also "bending the silvery willows still

18.   Fëdor Sologub (1863–1927) was a Russian symbolist poet and novelist.

lower into the water." At one pole of the comparison merely a
"noise," at the other the minutest analysis. No one since Gogol
has used such elaborate similes. Characteristic of Gogol is an
equation composed of three parts: "Those meadows [1] are not
meadows [2]; they are a green belt [3]" and so on.

6. The piling up of verbs, nouns, and adjectives is characteristic
of Sologub. The same holds true for Gogol: "The steppe grows
red, blue, burns with colors." Or, "Quails, bustards, gulls, grass-
hoppers, thousands of insects, and from them a whistling, buzzing,
creaking, screaming, and suddenly a harmonious choir" ("Ivan
Fëdorovich Shpon'ka"). "And again on both sides of the highway
began a new succession of mileposts, station-masters, water-wells,
and strings of wagons, and drab villages with their samovars and
peasant women." "Little wretched towns . . . with their little
shops, flour barrels, twisted loaves . . . strips of green, yellow, and
freshly furrowed black" (*Dead Souls*).

7. No less characteristic of Gogol are repetitions of the same
word, parallelisms, and semiparallelisms (often disguised). From
"A Terrible Vengeance": "In the old days they liked to have a
good meal, they liked still better to have a drink, and best of all
they liked to make merry." "They feasted till early morn, and they
feasted as no one feasts any more." "From behind the woods
loomed an earthen rampart, from behind the rampart rose an old
castle" (here the parallelism is maintained to the end). "Under the
ceiling bats flash by . . . and their shadow flashes along the walls"
(disguised parallelism).

8. Sometimes the word order or parallelism attains unusual
finesse: "The day dawned, but it was not sunny: the sky was
overcast and a fine rain fell on the fields and on the wide Dnieper.
Katerina awoke, but she was not happy; her eyes were tear-stained
and she was troubled and restless." Here we have a double parallelism of form and sense: a parallel in the sentence structure and
simultaneously a parallel between the weather and Katerina's
state of mind: "The day dawned"—"Katerina awoke"; "but it was
not sunny"—"but she was not happy"; "the sky was overcast"—"her eyes were tear-stained"; "and a fine rain fell"—
"and she was troubled."

9. Sometimes parallelism is only implied: "and from the window distantly shine the mountains and the Dnieper; beyond the
Dnieper loom the blue forests. . . . But it is not the distant sky and
not the blue forest that Sir Danilo is admiring" (figure of

intensification). "He is watching the protruding cape" ("A Terrible Vengeance").

10. At times when Gogol's artistry reaches its limits, he bangs on our nerves with intentionally banal rhetoric: "Divine night! Enchanting night!" Yet it is precisely this rhetoric that, coming in the wake of the subtlest color schemes and the deftest turns of phrases, acquires the brilliance of perfection and creates the impression that nothing is simpler and more natural than Gogol's prose. But that is an illusion.

I cannot begin to mention here even a fraction of all the contrivances consciously utilized in Gogol's stylistics. But I know one thing: his stylistics reflects the finest sensibility of the nineteenth century. Gogol's superhuman torments were reflected in superhuman images; and these images brought forth a superhuman formal achievement.

Perhaps Nietzsche and Gogol are the greatest stylists in all of European art, if by style is understood not only the use of words, but also the verbal embodiment of the soul's life rhythms.

The Aesthetics of Gogol's *Dead Souls* and Its Legacy

INNOKENTIJ ANNENSKIJ

An emaciated man in a dressing gown sits in a deep, low chair. His white nightshirt, pathetically crumpled around his thin neck, still bears the traces of a night ordeal. He sits, slightly bent forward, and looks straight ahead. Something about his posture suggests that intent, almost rapacious curiosity of which only Gogol was capable.

Yes, this is Gogol. These are his anxiously sharpened features and the familiar lock glistening over the ear. The seated man faces an expanse of fire made to look like a luxuriant tropical plant.

At Gogol's feet by the fire crouches a young servant boy waiting for further orders. He has already consigned to flames without daring to look a small bundle. Another bundle and a notebook crinkled up by proximity to the fire are awaiting their turn . . .[1]

I have indicated here some elements of the moving and naïve drawing made in the year of Gogol's death. Yes, the myth of Gogol originated as early as that. I suggest, however, that we look at this drawing a little differently than one customarily does.

For a moment we shall leave tragedies behind. Let Gogol experience here for the last time—all his ailments, fears, and apprehensions notwithstanding—the sheer excitement of being "on the road";[2] an excitement that magically blends Gogol the fantasist with Gogol the realist, the Gogol of meditation with the Gogol of laughter, Gogol the hawk with Gogol the sentimentalist.

Instead of the scroll containing a treasure forever lost to us, let us watch once again burst into flame the one and only poet who knew how to merge in his love of existence—not of life, mind you, but precisely of existence—a dusty box with nails and sulphur and

---

This essay was first published in *Apollon*, no. 8 (1911): 50–58.

1. Reference is to the burning of a large portion of Part Two of *Dead Souls*, which occurred on the eve of Gogol's death.

2. The last chapter of Part One of *Dead Souls* contains a grandiloquent eulogy that begins: "How much of the strange and of the alluring and of that which carries you away, and of the wonderful there is in the word 'the road'!" (*Dead Souls* [New York: Rinehart, 1948], pt. 1, p. 271; this is the edition cited in subsequent notes).

the golden strip in the East, and in whose world the transparent
and flaming maple leaf, even as it shone out of a dense darkness,
did not dare lord it over a speckled roadside post.[3]

Let us think of the man sitting in front of the fire as the Gogol of
old who for the last time passes in review the scenes he has conjured up, now sunny, now hazy, now silvery. Here is a godfor-
saken hamlet all bathed in moonlight. And there—a crossing at an
eerily misty dawn, or a garden luxuriating indolently at noon.[4]
Once again the writer relives that voluptuous alternation of falling
asleep in the bracing coolness of the night—Gogol had cherished
these moments ever since his childhood!—and the languid
awakenings under the sun's relentless rays. It is precisely there,
on the road, or, to be exact, in the memories of the road that the
most exciting colors of the Gogolian canvases and the most brilliant of his creative syntheses originate. Even his vaunted Russia
("Russia, what wouldst thou of me?"), was she not a half-childish
mirage in the Italian panorama of remembrance?[5] And was it not
that Gogolian road with its expansive vistas, its marvelous gaudi-
ness, its mournful call, and its irresistible lure of the distant, the
unknown, was it not that same road that vouchsafed both the
grandeur of the novelist's design and the inexorability of his
penance?

Let us be clear about this, gentlemen. *Dead Souls* is truly an
oppressive book, indeed a terrifying one, and it is so not only to its
author. The novel's very title is a sneer. But we may as well face
another disturbing fact: never was what is called *poshlost'*,[6] so
compelling, so attractive as it is in *Dead Souls*. And there is no
point here in talking about a horse ridden to death, about the
alleged overexploitation of the virtuous hero.[7] Nor is it necessary
to drag in Father Matvej.[8]

---

3. The imagery of this passage is drawn from Part One of *Dead Souls*.

4. The passages referred to occur in such early tales of Gogol as "The
Sorochintsy Fair" and "A May Night."

5. Reference to one of the two lyrical apostrophes to Russia found in Part
One of *Dead Souls* (p. 270). The bulk of the novel was written abroad, chiefly
in Italy, which accounts for the opening phrase of the famous passage: "Russia,
Russia, I behold thee, from my alien, far-off place do I behold thee."

6. This Russian noun, whose essential untranslatability is celebrated by
Vladimir Nabokov in his study of Gogol, denotes a cluster of qualities such as
shoddiness, vulgarity, grossness, and satisfied mediocrity. Allegedly, Pushkin
thought Gogol singularly adept at portraying this disreputable syndrome.

7. Again a reference to a digressive sequence in *Dead Souls*. Justifying the
choice of a shady operator as the hero of his novel, Gogol maintains that his
predecessors have overworked the man of virtue. "And so let us harness a
scoundrel" (p. 274).

8. Matvej Konstantinovskij (see n. 12 of preceding essay) on a number of

The truth of the matter is that every one of us is two persons: one is a tangible being, a voice, a color, a gesture, a laughter. The other is enigmatic, secret. It is the murky, indivisible, incommunicable essence of each one of us. But that is precisely what makes us alive; without it the world would sometimes seem a devilish mockery. The former seeks to become a type, is in fact lost without typicality, but only the latter creates a personality.

The first one eats, sleeps, shaves, breathes, and ceases to breathe. The first can be put in jail and placed in a coffin. But only the second one can feel God, only he can be loved, only on him can one make moral demands.

Gogol forcibly separated the two persons fused by life. He made the former so vividly typical, his characters proved so stunningly physical, that the second man was virtually rubbed out. He became downright expendable, as the first and tangible one took it upon himself to speak for them both. And, a newcomer to literature, he began to reign merrily, raucously.

Do you recall Chichikov in a brand-new frock coat "of the smoke and flame of Navarino,"[9] reeking of eau de cologne, kissing the boots of an official who outranks him?[10] Will you bring yourself to say that this is, don't you see, the penalty for greed, acquisitiveness, and baseness? Will you attempt, be it for a moment, to define thus the core of Gogol's artistic vision? Or can you ever conceive of the following scene? The old Korobochka[11] lies in bed; her thin gray braids are loose. An aged priest approaches her bed with the last sacraments, and suddenly some passionate impulse of a thousand-year-old faith lifts the petty soul out of its coils to a height that many a philosopher would not dare to scale. . . . Gogol's "typical" physicality, relegated the twilight man to the background; it swelled monstrously at his expense. It cluttered up and overwhelmed the universe. Thus, Sobakevich is surrounded,

---

occasions urged Gogol to abandon literature. Some biographers held this zealously devout priest largely responsible for the ascetic-religious bent in the late Gogol and specifically for the fateful auto-da-fé.

9. Presumably, a smoke-gray frock coat with red flecks. The flamboyant designation seems to be derived from the battle of Navarino—an 1827 naval encounter between the British–French–Russian force and the Egyptian–Turkish vessels.

10. Reference to an episode that occurs in Part Two of *Dead Souls*.

11. Korobochka, a tightwad old landlady, is one of the figures in the *Dead Souls* freak gallery.

indeed smothered by fellow Sobakeviches. Peasants, huts, even
the peasants' names, dishes served, chairs, the thrush, the dress
coat, the portraits on the walls—they were all Sobakeviches.[12] If
the Werthers or the Hamlets colored the world poetically in
elegiac hues, here the impact is more tangible, material—and
more terrifying: by turning everything into a replica of himself,
this central Sobakevich was inevitably reduced to the status of a
mere object, and his typicality to that of a nightmarish caricature.
As for Nozdrëv,[13] his corporeality could be called creative.
Nozdrëv is not simply a liar; in fact, he is not simply Nozdrëv. He
is a kind of irrepressible, mad abundance, a gay insouciance of
nature itself.

Abundance is writ large here in everything: in his cheeks on
which hair sprouts like grass in spring, in his eating habits, his
language, his wild yarns, his gamblers' tricks, his brawls. When
Nozdrëv was in luck, he would buy indiscriminately horse sad-
dles, kerchiefs for the nanny, stallions, raisins, pistols, herring,
paintings. Do not the fertility of Nozdrëv's glowing checks and his
passion for wheeling and dealing, meddling, trading, brawling,
epitomize his passionate and inexhaustible imagination or, better
still, fancy? And Manilov?[14] Is not all of Manilov contained in his
smacking lips, his prolonged kiss? And these men-eyebrows,
men-smells, which give one the feeling that this is all a man
needs to have!

But is there anything more to be found in the Public Prosecutor
or Petrushka[15] than the former's eyebrows or the latter's smell, so
wondrously, so monstrously personified?

And is not Chichikov's character defined by his eating habits?
On the other hand, is it not Chichikov who injects harmony and
unitý into the world of *Dead Souls*, the monstrous world of glut-
tony and soullessness? Bliny at Korobochka's, the haggis at
Sobakevich's, a fish patty at Petukh's[16]—no, the whole fantasy of
Petukh with his sturgeon, red buntings, the boat with lanterns, the

12. Sobakevich, to be sure, is another major protagonist in *Dead Souls*.
We will recall that in the description of the Sobakevich household, "Every
object, every chair seemed to be saying, 'I, too, am Sobakevich!' " (p. 107).
13. The exuberant bully and irrepressible gambler who becomes Chichikov's
undoing.
14. The insipid Manilov is another Gogolian squire.
15. Chichikov's foul-smelling servant.
16. The extravagant glutton featured in Part Two, chapter 3 of *Dead Souls*.

singers, and even the dog that has overeaten. Then the piglet served in horseradish in an inn with a dark awning that rests upon slender wooden columns resembling church candlesticks; a mouth-watering puff paste always eager to please; and finally two hot buns that Chichikov hugs in his carriage—what is it all but Chichikov himself, his indestructible, acquisitive vigor, his gay bounce, his animal-like adaptability? No wonder Chichikov's day-dreaming is so akin to craving for food.

Though there is always something unsettling about the corporeality of the Gogolian universe, this quality is especially terrifying whenever Gogol willfully reduces men and nature to a common denominator and urges their repellent unity, their interchangeability, so demeaning to man. Here a colossal trunk of a birch tree that had been deprived of its crest by some tempest or thunderstorm rises up in the air like a dazzling marble column. Only twenty steps away you stumble into something old, ragged, supernumerary, and seedy, with a tobacco-stained, pointed chin. Outdoors the storm has raged, indoors the kiddies have done their best.[17] Actually, the garden and the old man have been in the throes of the same process—a process of growing wild, of going to seed.[18] And if as a result the garden becomes enchanting and Pljushkin tawdry and vile, this after all is no more than a trifle in the Gogolian universe—a world that makes it worthwhile to be an artist.

What would have become of our literature had he not assumed on our behalf that lonely burden, that anguish, and had he not plunged into the sea of materiality the still timid, even if blessedly airy, language of Pushkin?

Pushkin and Gogol. Our two-faced Janus. Two mirrors on the door that separates us from our past.

It is as if everything that existed in our land before Pushkin had been growing and reaching toward him—our not yet visible but eagerly awaited Sun.

Pushkin was the culmination of Old Russia. He gave form to this Russia, rejoicing in her slow, imperceptible maturation and inor-

17. Clearly, reference is to that seedy miser Pljushkin (see Part One, chapter 6 of *Dead Souls*). The narrator blames much of Pljushkin's deterioration on his thoughtless and profligate children.

18. The appearance of Pljushkin is preceded by a remarkable set-piece, the description of the old squire's tangled, overgrown garden.

dinately proud of the diamond on her forehead that had finally
emerged from under her fairy-tale tatters.

Not so Gogol. Full of fear and anguish over the future of Russian
literature, he stands before it as a genius illuminating its un-
fathomable path. Pushkin's perfection, though luminously remote,
smiled kindly and encouragingly upon the timid and the drab.
Gogol's beauty would thrust itself upon man, and he would recoil
from its dazzlingly terrifying proximity. People affected by Gogol
moved not toward him, but away from him; they scattered like a
distant glow. But as they were leaving behind the shrine of his art
and the radiance of his ordeal, these people carried along two of
Gogol's most essential thoughts: (1) I shall be myself; (2) I shall
love only the enigma under whose sign I was born, the enigma of
my native land.

There are many of these people. But let me name today just a
few. First, to be sure, there is Dostoevsky. True, his face, flat,
broad, with high cheekbones, forms a total contrast with Gogol's.

His native land is a bleak public hospital in Moscow.

Not for him the deviltry, the dark stormy nights, or the indolent
squiredom.

Instead—the tradition of a respectable bureaucratic family. And
where once Vij held sway[19]—a corpse that one approaches with a
scalpel and with one's glasses on.

For Dostoevsky the village is already no more than a summer
place. And his kind, affectionate peasant Marej does not know
how to tell tall tales. In fact, it is he, Marej, who ruined for Dostoevsky his only fairy tale—one about the "uncanny, ghastly
wolf."[20] We see before us not the steppe visionary of the
Evenings[21] but a sober woodsman. A fanatic, perhaps, but no
spinner of wild yarns.

Dostoevsky's first hero, Makar Alekseevich Devushkin, took it
very much amiss when Varen'ka Dobroselova[22] lent him, with a

19. See n. 3 of the preceding essay.

20. Reference to a story, "The Peasant Marej," found in the February 1876
section of Dostoevsky's *A Writer's Diary*. In this ostensibly autobiographical
fragment the narrator recalls gratefully having met, when a child of nine, a kind
peasant Marej, who assured the agitated boy that the wolf he thought was lurking
in the bushes was a figment of his overheated imagination.

21. Clearly, the chatty narrator of Gogol's first collection of stories, *Evenings
on a Farm near Dikanka* (1831–32).

22. Makar Devushkin and Varen'ka Dobroselova are characters in Dostoevsky's debut, an epistolary novel *Poor Folk* (1845).

purely literary cruelty, the tale about a stolen overcoat. Small wonder! This two-legged creature is my brother? So be it! At any rate, you and I were raised on the proposition that this is precisely what Gogol was trying to convey. But poor Makar Alekseevich's schooling was scanty. How could he be expected to see in his prototype anything but caricature, if not slander?[23]

Gogol still managed to read *Poor Folk*. But in 1846 Dostoevsky took a major step away from Gogol[24]—an irretrievable step, or so it seemed for a long time. That was the revenge of the enigmatic one whom Gogol had neglected: for nothing less than the human would satisfy the new arrival. He was to insist that amidst the most revolting filth, we remember having been created after the image of God—and be moved to tears by the likeness. Yet there is also the Gogol who wrote pastorals. He, too, had an interesting and robust offspring in Goncharov.

Though Goncharov was later to disown Gogol, Zakhar's existence cannot be gainsaid. And is not Oblomov a blood relation of Tentetnikov and of the Platonov family?[25]

Gogol splashed his paint on the canvas. His language served his genius most brilliantly when he got entangled in grandiloquence or clung to its glittering textures. Gogol snatched impressions with all he had—his eyes, ears, nose. He soaked life in through all the pores of his huge sensory apparatus.

Goncharov wrote correctly and orotundly; his artistic response to the world was purely visual. Moreover, what excited him were not colors but forms, and these were much more intricate than with Gogol. His chief concern was with the design of life's fabric, with the disentanglment of individual threads that lose their distinctive coloring as they interweave. Anything touched, however fleetingly, by Gogol's brush would immediately turn into an object, a type. Gogol multiplied these types beyond measure and reveled in their staggering freakishness. Goncharov wrote with a

23. Obviously, the tale at issue is Gogol's "Overcoat." Not unlike its unheroic hero Akakij Akakievich, Dostoevsky's Makar Devushkin is a lowly clerk. In contradistinction to a number of contemporary critics, he interprets Gogol's famous story as a slur on the "little man."

24. The year 1846 saw the appearance of Dostoevsky's second novel, *The Double*, a study of a split personality.

25. Zakhar is Oblomov's servant. Annenskij seems to imply that Zakhar's seediness is a throwback to Gogol's Petrushka. Tentetnikov and the Platonov brothers appear in Part Two of *Dead Souls*. These vaguely sensitive and lethargic young landowners may be said to foreshadow Oblomov.

fastidious selectivity. He dealt only in what he could call his own—in matters carefully considered, pondered, and long settled; in the sober, the workaday, the typical.

Nozdrëv is Gogol's creation, an invention of a poet of genius, but Oblomov had lived for ages. He had grown as slowly and imperceptibly as a tree or a bush. Within Goncharov himself Oblomov had gone through a long process of clarification until he was found lying on the couch, on Gorokhova Street, with a sty on his right eye.

Let us not disturb the recently troubled shade of Turgenev. He was a Pushkinian, perhaps the most orthodox of them all. Turgenev could create harmony only out of the old, amidst conventions dear to his heart. To Turgenev even the new is something that already was. Safeguarding the past, this artist harbored the illusion of communing with the eternal.

But Lev Tolstoy, Tolstoy the pantheist, is remarkably akin to Gogol. We might say that Tolstoy represents the quintessence of Gogol. It is Gogol stripped of his romanticism.

Gogol the sharp [hawkish] profile, Gogol the troubled genius of comedy, has been transmogrified into the sculptor-ironist of Jasnaja Poljana; Gogol the magus has become godlike Tolstoy. Poor Chartkov, the painter in "The Portrait,"[26] is still frantic, while Ivan Ilyich, who has already served his sentence, is calm: he knows that this, too, even this, is oh, only that? In Gogol life is not afraid of sparkling with all the absurdity of an anecdote. Conversely, in Tolstoy the most incongruous set of circumstances—in "The Power of Darkness,"[27] for example—is presented as necessary, as executed by nature according to the specifications of the Jasnaja Poljana wizard.

There are those whose chief business is to pull poisoned threads out of the Gogolian carpet. In the hands of the early Saltykov,[28] its fabric would turn into a limp rag as long as this late-blooming artist was busy castigating bureaucrats. Yet it was the mature Saltykov who by stripping the Gogolian universe of its harmony revealed its unmitigated horror. It was he who populated Gogol's Russia with tragedies. Themistocles turned out to be Porfirij Golovlëv.[29]

26. This luridly romantic tale by Gogol features the moral deterioration of a struggling painter, Chartkov.
27. "The Power of Darkness" (1887) is Tolstoy's best-known play.
28. Saltykov-Shchedrin (1826–89), a late nineteenth-century novelist and publicist, was a master of hard-hitting radical satire.
29. Themistocles is an eight-year-old son of the sugary Manilov (*Dead*

The 1880s produced its own Gogolian: Chekhov, frail and consumptive, painted only in pastel colors. In his works even mastery of life is tinged with anguish. His aesthetic detachment seemed timorously self-protective.

In Chekhov *poshlost'* ceased to be a threat. At most it would make feeble attempts to appear frightening. It developed a potential for meditation, for tenderness; it nearly became a dream.

Poshlost' a dream? Strange, but true. In Chekhov, Gogol's daydream about the road is essentially transformed. Gone are the wanderer, the fugitive, the warm traveling cloak, and the wonderful sleep in the carriage. And yet there remains here something that is restless and frantic, something that mocks distances. To Moscow . . . to Moscow . . . the Great Basmannaja Street. No, even in Chekhov Gogol's most vital legacy is the song of the open road . . .[30]

Yet the harshness and the chill of Gogol's sorrowful vision repelled Chekhov—a tender plant, though one thoroughly deprived of the sun; he was all nerves laid bare. The Chekhovian universe is a far cry from Gogol's magical, enchanting blend, from the world conjured up by name, be it Korobochka or Sobakevich. It is rather a deftly contrived mosaic of the "Peasants,"[31] or, to cite a still more accomplished variant, of the cherry orchard gone to seed.

And if Gogol was discovering life worthy of divine laughter in realms where another would have seen nothing but rot, Chekhov, in his own words, could turn any object, even an ashtray, into a story.

But in all fairness, gentlemen, is this a total loss? Has not Chekhov's literary professionalism shown up the hollowness of Manfred's heroic claims?[32] Let us praise, then, the achievement of the writer who demonstrated so graphically how terrifying and preposterous is mere literariness.

Gogol's influence did not cease with Chekhov. In fact, Gogol's

---

Souls). Porfirij Golovlëv is a character of Saltykov-Schedrin's savagely satirical novel *The Golovlëvs* and is one of the most repellent figures in Russian fiction.

30. Annenskij draws once again on the imagery and the plot of *Dead Souls*, more specifically, on the already mentioned eulogy of the road (see n. 2 above). The wanderer presumably is the narrator, the fugitive Chichikov.

31. "Peasants" (1897) is one of Chekhov's darker stories.

32. Reference to the hero of a verse drama by Byron and to his romantic posturing.

devil has never been as busy as he is today. Having shunted aside
all the mediators and reconcilers, Gogol the avatar has material-
ized in our midst. Hardly anyone has come so close to Gogol as
did Sologub. True, not that befuddled Sologub of the *Lure of
Death*, but the Sologub who has envisioned or encompassed the
life of the Petty Demon.[33] Granted, that Sologub's physicality
harbors an inborn temptation, and that his moon was actually
made in Hamburg.[34] What of it? Were not Sologub's protagonists, whom it would be ridiculous to denounce, but still more
absurd to love or even pity, were not these homunculi produced
in the laboratory of *Dead Souls*? Moreover, does Sologub's prose,
ragged yet glittering, have a closer kin than in Gogol's idiom?

Links between Gogol and our poets have always been more
tenuous. There has been no dearth in Russian poetry of either
exoticism or theatricality.

Only one parallel comes to mind, and not a recent one at that. A
quarter of a century after *Dead Souls*, another Russian "poem"
was cut short by the author's death.[35] I am speaking of Nekrasov's
"Who Is Happy in Russia?"[36]

The two poems differ widely in overall design and impact. The
creative personalities that begot them, the ethnic milieus from
which they sprang are strikingly disparate. And yet they share a
quality no foreigner can fathom—a thrust that is unmistakably and
recklessly our own. Nekrasov's later epic offers us an opportunity
not so much to take Gogol's measure as to shudder at the boundlessness of the universe that Gogol had so boldly set out to embody, that is, to contain within himself.

33.   See n. 18 of the preceding essay. *The Lure of Death* (*Nav'i chary*), one of
Sologub's early novels, is indeed undistinguished. His greatest success, *Petty
Demon* (*Melkij bes*, 1907) is one of the most remarkable works of early twentieth-
century Russian fiction.

34.   An echo from Gogol's "A Madman's Diary." In one of his last entries the
insane clerk maintains that the "moon is usually made in Hamburg—and very
badly at that."

35.   The sentence sounds puzzling until one realizes or recalls that the subtitle of *Dead Souls* was *A Poem*.

36.   Nikolaj Nekrasov (1821–77) was a major mid-nineteenth-century Russian
poet. "Who Is Happy in Russia?" is a broadly conceived social pageant—a cross
between a populist epic and a racy satire.

2
Formalists and Near-Formalists

Pushkin and Sterne: *Eugene Onegin*

VIKTOR SHKLOVSKIJ

The *Titanic* perished when it struck an iceberg that had tipped over beside it.

Icebergs don't overturn by chance, however. After an iceberg breaks away from some Greenland glacier, it floats off, driven by the wind; and so it sails on until it reaches the warm current. The iceberg, as it drifts on, is now enveloped by mist. It generates vapors from the surrounding atmosphere. But the warm current sucks and licks at the submerged part of the iceberg. It is finally undermined. The upper portion becomes heavier than the submerged base and tips over. It now presents a completely different picture: it is no longer pointed, but flat-topped, sturdier, more massive.

Literary works have a similar fate. Periodically their interpretations undergo violent shifts. What was comic is now tragic. What was once considered exquisite is now perceived as banal.

It is as if the work of art were written anew.

Thus the symbolists turned around the image of Gogol. Instead of Gogol's vaunted realism, they discovered in his work a fantastic universe. In his book *The Green Meadow* Andrej Belyj had this to say of that new Gogol:

> That's reality for you! First shapes carved out of cloud glitter, then sheep snouts crawl in bellowing at us like two bulls, and radishes crawl out with tails up and tails down, with snuff-colored eyes. They all begin not to walk but to scuttle, mince about, sidle. And what is most horrible of all is that Gogol makes them express themselves in a refined manner. These "radishes" wink with their snuff-colored little eyes, sprinkle their speech with such phrases as "if you please," and Gogol reports on them not in a straightforward way but with a strange, desperate sort of joviality. The lower part of the assessor's face is not simply a sheep's snout, but "a sheep's snout, as it were"; "as it were" for the most trifling reason: because at the moment

This essay, translated here by James M. Holquist, was first published in *Ocherki po poètike Pushkina* [Essays on Pushkin's poetics] (Berlin, 1923), pp. 199–220.

of the assessor's birth a sheep walked up to the window—a horrible "as it were." It is customary to call Gogol a realist, but, by all that's holy, where is reality here? What we face is not humanity but prehumanity; the earth is populated here not by men, but by radishes. In any case, this world whose fortunes are affected by sheep sticking their heads through the window, or by a black cat that disappears ("Old-World Landowners") or by calling someone "a gander," is not a world of men, but of animals.[1]

Shakespeare, too, has gone through many a transformation. He has been raised from oblivion to glory through [Dr.] Johnson's praise, plunged from glory to his nadir, epitomized by Voltaire's "drunken-savage" dictum, and raised again to an apotheosis at the hands of the romantics.

Of course each era has its own Shakespeare. Goethe even wanted to rewrite *Hamlet* (see *Wilhelm Meister*).[2] At the Folk Comedy Theater, Sergej Radlov presented *The Merry Wives of Windsor* in the style of a harlequinade.[3] He chose thereby to emphasize, rather than to tone down, the elements of tomfoolery that had been shamefacedly suppressed in yesterday's Shakespeare.

Another avant-garde theater that is unfortunately little known abroad, the Chamber (*Kamernyj*) Theater, interprets Shakespeare in the same way. Tairov[4] defines the style in which *Romeo and Juliet* should be played as one of sketch and harlequinade: "All members of the cast should refrain from creating psychologically lifelike and individualized characterizations that would make the sociohistorical setting credible. The characters should be neither

1. See pp. 36–37 above.
2. This cryptic reference is not entirely accurate. For one thing, the view of *Hamlet* alluded to is voiced by the hero rather than by the author. For another thing, what is urged here is not exactly a different version of the play, but an admittedly strained interpretation of its chief protagonist. Having been entrusted with the Prince's part, Wilhelm Meister finds it essential to evolve a concept of Hamlet's character that lays chief stress on knightly valor and dignity rather than on "melancholia" and inner strife. (See J. W. v. Goethe, *Wilhelm Meister's Apprenticeship* [New York, 1959], pp. 205–06.)
3. A short-lived Russian experimental theater (1920–22) that combined avant-garde techniques with motifs of the Russian folktale and urban folksong. Sergej Radlov, one of its two directors, had been previously an active associate of Vsevolod Meyerhold.
4. Aleksandr Tairov (1885–1950), head of the Kamernyj Theater, was one of the most inventive Russian stage directors in the 1920s.

young nor old; in fact, without detriment to the theatrical intention, one should replace men with women and vice versa."

Let us quote another section of the same article: "What is the scene he [Friar Laurence] acts out by Juliet's corpse if not a harlequinade? And is not the scene with musicians which Shakespeare mounted directly after the scene in which Paris and Juliet's relatives lament her death, also a harlequinade? This scene is usually cut. . . .

What then is *Romeo and Juliet* as the modern theater renders it? Let us not mince words.

It is a sketch.

Yes, a tragi-erotic sketch."

You must not think that Aleksandr Tairov is a man brutalized by Soviet conditions who willfully abuses Shakespeare. Art in Soviet Russia has not sunk to barbarism. Besides, Aleksandr Tairov, I am sorry to say, is immune to barbarism. The time has come simply for Shakespeare to "tip over" again.

The shifts in our perception of an author are accounted for by the law of literary history which decrees that each author is viewed by us not in isolation but against the backdrop of our own traditions. We measure an author by our own aesthetic standards. To please us a work does not need to meet our aesthetic standards, but the manner in which it violates these standards is of the essence.

The situation is akin to a well-known experiment in physiology: a person submerges one of his hands in cold water, and the other in hot, then proceeds to touch various objects. The same object will seem warm to one hand but cold or lacking temperature to the other.

It is the habitual that "lacks temperature," that is not experienced.

Hence another law: not a single artist has escaped oblivion (a period of indifference or nonperception) just after his death or often toward the end of his career.

So it was that Pushkin was denied recognition. At the very time he was writing *The Bronze Horseman* the general opinion was that he had written himself out. Even Belinskij was saying this politely. An author comes alive again when he is perceived by us in a new way. Literary revolutions not only create new aesthetic values but restore old ones. What results is less a reevaluation than a reversal.

Pushkin studies are currently flourishing in Russia. The activity of the Pushkin Institute, the revival of the Pushkin seminar at the [Moscow] University, the profound new works of Jurij Tynjanov on Pushkin's lexicon, Boris V. Tomashevskij's work on the nature of Pushkin's rhythms, Osip Brik's studies on the instrumentation of Pushkin's verse and careful reconstruction of the poet's manuscripts—all these might suggest that we are witnessing a Pushkin revival.[5] It seems to me, however, that something else is happening—Pushkin is fading away.

New wine has been poured into the Pushkinian bottles. The bottles are still serviceable since art itself does not age, but the wine has already turned sour. The new interpretation advanced by the symbolists, derived from Dostoevsky and Rozanov[6] and taken up by Andrej Belyj, has already become a cliché.

And the voice that first warned us that Pushkin was fading away was that of a symbolist. In 1921 at the House of Writers we were moved and troubled by the speech of Aleksandr Blok.[7] "On the Poet's Calling" was a speech not about Pushkin but about the destiny of the poet. Blok said: "Peace and freedom, the poet needs both if he is to liberate harmony, but even peace and freedom are being taken away from us:[8] not outward but creative peace; not childish willfulness nor license to play at being a liberal, but creative freedom—the *secret freedom*. The poet is dying because

5. By the mid-1920s Jurij Tynjanov emerged as one of the era's most vital Pushkin scholars. It is not quite clear to me which "profound new works on Pushkin's lexicon" Shklovskij has in mind here. Tomashevskij's analysis of Pushkin's iambic pentameter appeared alongside Shklovskij's "Pushkin and Sterne" in a 1923 symposium, *Studies in Pushkin's Poetics*. Four years earlier Osip Brik contributed to the formalist miscellany *Poetics* a paper on "Sound Repetitions," which deals primarily with alliterative patterns in Pushkin and Lermontov.

6. For Rozanov see n. 10 of the Introduction above. Actually, to speak of a single interpretation of Pushkin, common to Dostoevsky, Rozanov, and the symbolists, is a bit misleading. It would be more accurate to say that these otherwise somewhat disparate perspectives shared the tendency to read into the master's legacy a body of intuitive wisdom, "a great secret yet to be divined," as Dostoevsky put it in his famous "Pushkin speech," in 1880.

7. In February 1921 the Petrograd literary community turned the commemoration of the 84th anniversary of Pushkin's death into a major event. On February 11 Blok delivered at the House of Writers a memorable speech. On February 14 Vladislav Khodasevich (1886–1939), who was later to become the leading Russian émigré poet (see p. 25 above), read his essay "The Swaying Tripod" and Boris Eikhenbaum spoke on "Problems of Pushkin's Poetics." (The latter paper appears below as "Pushkin's Path to Prose.")

8. Reference to a line from a late Pushkin poem: "There is no happiness in this world/ But there is peace and freedom."

there is no more air for him to breathe—life has lost its meaning."

Shortly afterward we buried Blok . . .

But one year after these forebodings were voiced by Blok, who at the House of Writers fashioned from his anguish an homage to Pushkin, another symbolist poet, dry and bitter Khodasevich,[9] proclaimed the second eclipse of Pushkin.

> There was a moment in the history of Russian literature when Pisarev "abolished" Pushkin, having declared him superfluous and trivial [see p. 6 above]. But Pisarev's position found favor with few readers and was soon abandoned. Pisarev's name has subsequently aroused irritation, even anger, natural in lovers of literature but impossible for the historian, indifferently harking to good and evil.
>
> Those who supported Pisarev were men of little mind and meager aesthetic sensibility, but it cannot be said that they were evil-intentioned men, obscurantists, or hooligans. They sided with the best, not the worst, in the age-old rift in Russian society.
>
> This was the first eclipse of Pushkin's sun. It seems to me that the second is not far off. This time it will not appear in so crude a guise. Pushkin will be neither mocked nor abused, but there will be a growing coolness toward him.
>
> And not only among readers; this tendency can also be felt in modern Russian poetry.
>
> There is a good deal in Pushkin that is almost completely lost on some of our young poets. For one thing, they are not sufficiently acquainted with the Pushkin era; the spirit, the style of his age, is alien to them. They come too late to appreciate its legacy. The same must be said of his language. For all I know, they may be following Pushkin's precept "learn your Russian from Moscow's old baker women." But these old women no longer speak the same language themselves.
>
> Our most precious possession, our love for Pushkin, we throw into the flames of the tripod [caldron] like a handful of fragrant herbs.
>
> And it shall be consumed! ["The Swaying Tripod"]

9. As indicated above, Shklovskij's chronology is faulty. Khodasevich spoke three days rather than one year later. Also the description of Khodasevich as "another symbolist poet" is only partly valid. His poetry owes a great deal to the symbolist impulse, but his astringently neoclassical craft belongs both chronologically and substantively to the postsymbolist era.

We are losing our live feeling for Pushkin not because we are far removed from him in our daily life or in our language, but because the time has come to change the yardstick by which to measure Pushkin.

Pushkin is now slipping away from us into a cold mist, and the moment is fast approaching when our conception of him will undergo a radical shift.

The study of the literary tradition, the formal study of art, will be utterly senseless if it does not enable us to see the work anew.

Our ordinary perception glides like a carpenter's plane over a piece of wood. Stanislavskij, in his articles on the technique of acting, points out that certain actors are able to speak their parts "with feeling," yet at the same time, being ordinary people, are unable to relate them in their own words. They [their words] have been "planed smooth." The habitual words interweave to form habitual sentences, which in turn form habitual paragraphs, and all these roll along inexorably like a bulldozer down the hill.

The aim of the formalist method, or at least one of its aims, is not to explain the work, but to call attention to it, to restore that "orientation toward form" which is characteristic of a work of art.

In this essay I shall attempt·not so much to resolve the question of Laurence Sterne's influence on Pushkin as to emphasize the features that are common to both writers.

That Pushkin knew Sterne's work cannot be doubted:

> To his ancestral hall returning,
> Vladimir Lensky sought the plot
> Of his old neighbor's last sojourning
> And sighed in tribute to his lot.
> And long he mourned for the departed.
> "Poor Yorick!" quoth he, heavyhearted.[10]

Pushkin added here the following note: "Poor Yorick!—Hamlet's exclamation over the skull of the fool (see Shakespeare and Sterne)."

Yet it is only in *Eugene Onegin* that we are able to detect a

---

10. From *Eugene Onegin* by Pushkin, translated by Walter Arndt (p. 55). Copyright © 1963 by Walter Arndt. Reprinted by permission of the publishers, E. P. Dutton & Co., Inc. All the *Eugene Onegin* quotations that follow will be drawn from Walter Arndt's deft rendition of Pushkin's narrative masterpiece.

number of devices akin to those of the world's most paradoxical author, Sterne, the creator of *Tristram Shandy* and *A Sentimental Journey*.

I wish to stipulate once again that my further concern will be not so much with the question of literary evolution as with the coincidence of similar motifs. *Eugene Onegin*, like *Tristram Shandy*, is a parodistic novel; moreover, in both works the target of parody is neither the mores nor the social types of an age, but the technique of the novel itself, its very structure.

Let me briefly recapitulate the composition of *Tristram Shandy*.

Instead of the conventional pre-Sternean device of beginning a novel with a description of its hero or his situation, *Tristram Shandy* begins with an exclamation: *"Pray, my dear*, quoth my mother, *have you not forgot to wind up the clock?"*

We know neither the identity of the speaker nor what the clock is all about. It is only on page 9 of the novel that the query is clarified.[11]

Eugene Onegin begins similarly. The scene opens on the chronological midpoint of the novel, with a dialogue in which the identity of the speaker is held in abeyance. "Now that he is in grave condition, / My uncle, decorous old prune" etc.

The speaker is identified in the next stanza: "Thus a young good-for-nothing muses" (p. 5). There follows a description of the hero's upbringing. It is only in the fifty-second stanza of chapter 1 that we find a comprehensive clarification of the opening lines.

> And as he had anticipated,
> His uncle's steward soon sent news
> That the old man was quite prostrated
> And wished to say his last adieus.
> In answer to the grievous tiding,
> By rapid stage Eugene came riding
> Posthaste to honor his behest;
> Prepared, in view of the bequest,
> For boredom, sighs, and simulation,
> And stifling yawns well in advance
> (With this I opened my romance):
>
> [p. 27]

---

11. *The Life and Opinions of Tristram Shandy, Gentleman* (London, 1924). Actually the exclamation cited by Shklovskij is preceded by a rambling paragraph on the main character's birth and on life's vicissitudes.

Thus our attention is called to a rearrangement of the time sequence. In Sterne's *Tristram Shandy* separate parts of the novel are likewise reshuffled. The dedication, for instance, is found on pages 15–16. Moreover, the author remarks that such an arrangement violates three basic requirements, those of "matter, form, and place." The preface occurs in chapter 64 and runs from pages 170 to 179. In Pushkin the dedication appears in the fifty-fifth stanza of chapter 7:

> But here, with bows before this feather
> In Tanja's cap, we turn away,
> Lest we abandon altogether
> The one I sing, and go astray . . .
> Yes—let me quickly put on record:
> I sing of a young friend, his checkered
> Career in fortune's cruel coil.
> Your blessing on my earnest toil,
> O Epic Muse! About me hover,
> And even lend thy faithful wand,
> Lest I roam thither and beyond!
> That's all, and I am glad it's over,
> My debt to classicism is paid:
> Though late, the Invocation's made.

[p. 190]

The unusual structure of *Eugene Onegin* and the Sterne-like quality of Pushkin's devices have already impressed more than one critic. "In addition to all its other qualities, *Eugene Onegin* is characterized by a truly amazing method of composition that contradicts all the basic rules of writing," wrote Pavel V. Annenkov in his *Materials for the Biography of A. S. Pushkin*.[12]

It is a measure of how tradition-bound is our approach to Pushkin that we should have turned the novel's masterfully contrived muddle into a canon.

Similarly Arab scholars construed as norms all Mohammed's deviations from the standard language of his time. And today we eulogize Pushkin's serenity and classicism, even as he confronts us with turmoil.

---

12. A. S. Pushkin, *Materialy dla ego biografii i otsenki ego proizvedenij* (St. Petersburg, 1873). P. V. Annenkov (1813–87) was an engaging essayist and memoir writer.

Recognition always dulls the cutting edge.

The lyrical digressions in *Eugene Onegin* are yet another Sternean element. The novel's plot is remarkably simple. The epic retardation results from the fact that while Tatjana loves Onegin, Onegin does not love her; and when he does fall in love with her, Tatjana rejects him. The plot device wherein the two protagonists' intentions keep diverging can be motivated in literature in a number of ways. In Ariosto sorcery provides the motivation: a knight falls in love with a girl and pursues her; failing to overtake her, he camps overnight in an enchanted forest and drinks from a stream which has the ability to change emotions into their opposites. It so happens that the pursued maiden has also drunk from the same stream. The situation is now reversed; she is in love with him. He flees from her to China, and so forth. Later she drinks of this water again. In such an unfolding of the plot there is doubtless an element of parody. The same device is found in Shakespeare's *Midsummer Night's Dream*.

In Pushkin's *Ruslan and Ludmila*[13] Finn is in love with Naina, but Naina does not love him. Finn endeavors to win her love only to provoke Naina's well-known phrase, "Hero, I do not love thee." Finn practices sorcery, and thus captures Naina's love, but only after she has become a nag. Finn flees from her, she pursues him. The element of sorcery shrinks here, while "natural" motivation looms larger. By the same token, a short story built around a riddle has a motivation of greater validity than a fairy tale containing a riddle.

Pushkin was aware of the nature of his novel's basic plot and underscored its schematic quality by the use of symmetry. Tatjana writes a letter to Evgenij. He appears and lectures her. A corresponding movement occurs when Onegin sees Tatjana, writes her a letter, visits her—and she lectures him!

Tatjana's letter to Onegin and his to her, as well as their respective harangues, exhibit a number of parallels. Since I cannot list them all here, I shall content myself with citing only the concluding scenes:

Chapter 4, stanza 17:

> Quailing
> Tatjana listened to him preach;

13. Pushkin's first narrative poem—a cross between a poetic fairytale and a mock epic.

> From streaming tears her sight was failing;
> She scarcely breathed, bereft of speech.

[p. 94]

Chapter 8, stanza 48:

> She left. Eugene stood robbed of motion,
> Struck dumb as by a thunderbolt.
> Yet in his heart, what stormy ocean
> Of feelings seething in revolt!

[p. 220]

In both instances the stanzas that follow use the device of the poet's taking leave of his hero and usher in a digression.

Such is the less than intricate scheme of the novel.

But taking his cue from Sterne—most likely through the mediation of Byron, who had elaborated the same technique in verse—Pushkin rendered his novel extraordinarily complex by his use of digressions. These digressions cut into the body of the novel and push aside the events.

The true plot of *Eugene Onegin* is not the story of Onegin and Tatjana, but a playing with this story. The real content of the novel lies in its formal patterns, while the plot structure itself is used the way Picasso uses real objects in his paintings.

First we get, as in Sterne, an event from the middle of the plot; then a description of the hero's setting; the setting expands and crowds out the hero; the theme of "little feet" enters;[14] and finally the poet does return to his hero. "But what about Onegin?" (p. 20).

The same kind of return to the hero occurs in chapter 4, stanza 37 (p. 104): "Well, and Onegin? Brothers, patience!"

These exclamations remind us that we have once again forgotten the hero. The reminder occurs after a digression of sixteen stanzas.

Incidentally, the riddle of the omitted stanzas in *Eugene Onegin* might also be solved in light of Sterne's influence. As is well known, a number of stanzas in *Eugene Onegin* are omitted, notably 13, 14, 39, 40, and 41 of chapter 1. Most characteristic of all is the omission of stanzas 1–6 in chapter 4.

---

14. Reference to one of the many personal digressions in chapter 1 of *Eugene Onegin*—an eloquent tribute to the adorable "little feet" of various beauties the author has known.

In other words, the beginning of the chapter has been omitted!

Yet there is no break in the action. All Pushkin has done is to abandon Tatjana, underlining the conventionality of the device by a thoroughly Sternean gesture:

> But by your leave, I feel unequal
> Just now, dear friends, to adding more
> To all that has been said before,
> And tell this chance encounter's sequel;
> I need to rest and have some fun;
> Some other time I'll get it done!

[p. 84]

Likewise, the first movement of chapter 4 has to do not with action, but with Onegin's musings. The connection of these stanzas (7–9) with Evgenij is weak; what we find is authorial ruminations like those in stanza 11 of chapter 1.

A gap such as this concerns the digressions, not the action. (Note: The four stanzas that appeared in the *Moscow Herald*[15] in 1827, and are generally assumed to belong here, also featured the reflections of the poet rather than of the hero.)

We know that several of the "omitted stanzas" were never written. Once again, I feel, Pushkin is playing with the novel's plot. In a like manner Sterne "omitted" whole chapters of a prose work.

The fact that *Eugene Onegin* was never finished may also be accounted for by Sterne's influence. We will recall that *Tristram Shandy* ends as follows: "*L—d!* said my mother, *what is all this story about—A Cock and a Bull*, said Yorick—*And one of the best of its kind, I ever heard.* The End."

A *Sentimental Journey* ends thus: "So when I stretch'd out my hand, I caught hold of the Fille de Chambre's . . ."

Of course, biographers are convinced that death befell Sterne at the very moment he was stretching out his hand, but, since he could have died only once and has left us two unfinished novels, it may be handier to assume the use of a certain stylistic device.

The device Pushkin employed to conclude his story differs from the corresponding device in Sterne. Sterne will sometimes break off a story, offering as his reason the fact that the final portion of

---

15. *Moskovskij Vestnik* (The Moscow Herald) was a biweekly, launched in 1827 by a group of Moscow followers of the German romantic philosopher Schelling.

the manuscript has been lost (for example, the interpolated
novella in *A Sentimental Journey*). Gogol inherited the same device, justifying it on the same grounds.[16] Pushkin simply breaks
off his narrative, emphasizing the deliberateness of the interrup-
tion:

> Blest he who left in its full glory
> The feast of life, who could decline
> To drain the brimming cup of wine,
> Refused to read life's waning story,
> And with abrupt resolve withdrew,
> As I from my Onegin do.

[p. 222]

Of Pushkin's other works, the one more akin to *Eugene Onegin*
is "The Little House in Kolomna." I shall not analyze this work in
detail. Let me offer only one observation: the work is almost completely taken up with the description of the device employed in it.
It is a poem about a poem. It is an almost purely nonobjective,
medium-oriented composition. The plot, if we mean by it the
story, plays an even smaller role than in *Eugene Onegin*.

If in *Eugene Onegin* the basic story line is given as a fixed
standard for gauging the deviations—since it is impossible to de-
viate from nothing—in "The Little House in Kolomna" the plot
itself is a parody. Pushkin successfully parodies here all his prospective critics including Dostoevsky and Gershenzon[17] by insert-
ing into his nonobjective composition a flimsy vaudeville plot.
This plot mocks the conventional response to the work of art—the
standard question "What happened?"[18]

---

16. Shklovskij is referring here to an early Gogol story, "Ivan Fedorovich
Shpon'ka and His Aunt." In the preamble the garrulous editor–beekeeper blames
the absence of a chapter on his "old woman," who lined the baking tin with half
of the pages on which the story was written.

17. An eminent literary and intellectual historian M. Gershenzon was author
of a collection of essays *Mudrost' Pushkina* [Pushkin's Wisdom], 1919.

18. The "flimsy vaudeville plot" of "The Little House in Kolomna" is briefly
this: a winsome young girl Parasha and her aged mother lead a quiet life in a
suburb of St. Petersburg. Parasha runs the house but spends a fair amount of
time sighing and star-gazing. The old cook dies. A new cook, engaged by
Parasha, is a taciturn, tall girl, clearly unexperienced but cheap. When next
Sunday she does not show up at church, the old lady promptly runs home to check
if the new servant is up to some mischief only to find her shaving in front of
Parasha's mirror. Thus unmasked, the "cook" vanishes. Did Parasha blush? "I
know nothing more."

Can't you at least give us a moral?
No . . . or rather yes: bear with me for a while.

LV

Here's the moral: in my opinion
It is dangerous to hire a cook for nothing.
Besides, for one born a man
It is strange and futile to don a skirt.
Sooner or later he'll have to shave
his beard, which does not become a woman.
That's all that can be squeezed out of my tale.[19]

Well, quite a bit more was squeezed out of *Eugene Onegin*. Let
me raise an intriguing question: was *Eugene Onegin* meant to be
taken seriously at all? To put it crudely, did Pushkin weep over
Tatjana, or was he making light of her? Russian literature, with
Dostoevsky as its head, insists that Pushkin did indeed weep.

And yet *Eugene Onegin* is replete with parodistic devices. If its
plot does not collapse as does that of *Tristram Shandy*, this is most
readily explained by the fact that *Eugene Onegin* is not simply a
novel but a novel in verse—"a devil of a difference," as Pushkin
himself put it.[20]

Already Aristotle had urged the poet to pay special attention to
parts of the composition that are short on action. In general it
would seem that the amount of effort expended on the work is a
definable, or at any rate, a finite quantity. If one part of the work is
strengthened, another is apt to be weakened. In *Eugene Onegin*
the parodistic treatment of the plot is rendered less obtrusive by
an intricate stanzaic pattern with an abrupt break before the last
two lines, which are linked by rhyme and contain either a summa-
tion of the stanza or, more often, its pointed resolution. For example, "There I myself once used to be: / The North, though, dis-
agrees with me."[21]

The choice of words in *Eugene Onegin* is also highly parodistic.
We encounter at this level a plethora of barbarisms, arbitrarily
introduced and deliberately underscored:

19. Pushkin, "Domik v Kolomne," *Sochinenija* [Works] (Moscow, 1954),
2:226.

20. In this much-quoted letter to the poet–critic P. A. Vjazemskij (4 November
1823), Pushkin reports: "I am writing now a novel, but a novel in verse—a devil
of a difference."

21. A characteristic authorial wink at the audience. Pushkin is hinting here
at his enforced sojourn in the South in 1820–24.

Madame first watched him competently.
From her *Monsieur* received the child;
The boy was likeable, though wild.
Monsieur, a poor abbé from Paris, etc.

[p. 6]

. . . .

But *pantalons, gilet* and *frack*—
With such words Russian has no truck,
For as it is, I keep inviting
Your censure for the way I use ·
Outlandish words of many hues
To deck my humble style of writing,
Although I used to draw upon
The Academic Lexicon.

[p. 16]

By mentioning the Academy dictionary, Pushkin once again calls
attention to the exoticism of foreign words with which his text is
studded.

Pushkin's notes to *Eugene Onegin* in general smack of parody.
Onegin's phrase "Didelot himself now leaves me cold" is provided with the following gloss. "5. A trait of chilled sentiment
worthy of *Childe Harold*. Didelot's dances are marked by
sprightly imagination and extraordinary charm. One of our romantic writers found in them much more poetry than in all of French
literature." Note especially the parodistic sentence structure.[22]
Pushkin speaks of the name "Tatjana" as exotic. While in "Poltava" the historical name of Kochubej's daughter Matrëna was
changed to the conventionally romantic Marija,[23] the name "Tatjana" in Pushkin's time sounded more like a challenge than a
stylization.

Tatjana was her name . . . I grovel
That with such humble name I dare
to consecrate a tender novel.
What if it's fragrant with a peasant

22. Charles-Louis Didelot (1767–1837) was a French balletmaster and
choreographer associated with the early nineteenth-century Russian ballet.
Shklovskij may be alluding here to the contrast between the studied polish of
the note and the casualness of Onegin's shrug that occasions it.
23. Pushkin's "Poltava" (1828) is a historical poem which deals in part with a
resentful Ukrainian chieftain's rebellion against Peter the Great. Marija, the
daughter of the loyalist Kochubej, is in love with the somber rebel Mazepa.

>Antiqueness, if it does recall
>The servant quarters? . . .

>[p. 48]

Pushkin provided this passage with the following commentary: "The most euphonious Greek names such as Agathon, Philatus, Theodora, Thekla are used with us only among the common people." Pushkin had a special reason to mention the name "Agathon":

>. . . the girlish treble sounds
>more tearful than the reed-pipe's blowing.
>"What is your name?" He stares, and on
>He strides, replying: "Agathon."

>[p. 119]

Since the latter passage is less traditional, less quotable, as it were, than the passage about Tatjana's name, its odd, not to say, comic flavor is more readily apparent.

Rhymes in *Eugene Onegin* are frequently parodistic. Proper names are often rhymed: Ovid, Gris, Shakhovskoj, Cleopatra, Byzantium, Juvenal, Theocritus, [Adam] Smith, Kaverin, Knjazhnin, Terpsichore, Venus, Flora, Bentham, Diana, Apollo, Albion, Salgir. (All examples are drawn from chapter 1).

At times the rhyme underscores its own triteness:

>Oh dreams, my dreams, where is your sweetness?
>Oh youth's (the rhyme fair beckons) fleetness.

>[p. 106]

>. . . . .
>At last a crackling frost enfolded
>Fields silvered o'er with early snows:
>(All right—who am I to withhold it,
>The rhyme you knew was coming—*Rose*).

>[p. 159]

In *Eugene Onegin* similes, generally rare in Pushkin, also tend toward parody. Sometimes they are motivated by being assigned to a protagonist.

>. . . Olga's blended
>Of peach and cream, as round and soft
>As that insipid moon aloft
>On that insipid dome suspended.

>[p. 63]

This is a curious example of a "discarded" simile. The comparison is not made, only the slot for it is provided.

> The blissful and benignant juices
> Of Veuve Cliquot or of Moët
> Their effervescent froth and tinkle
> (Symbolical of what you will) . . .
>
> [p. 107]

This empty comparison is, it would seem, unique in poetry.

Thus, in a cursory survey in which even the digressions have scarcely been analyzed, it has been possible to indicate that elements of parody deeply inform the whole structure of Pushkin's novel in verse. It is true that Pushkin himself would appear to treat Tatjana in a grave and sympathetic manner:

> Tatjana, Tanja, whom I cherish!
> My tears now flow with yours; the sands
> Are running out, and you must perish
> At our modish tyrant's hands.
> . . . .
> But stay; I feel an urgent need
> To vary this unwholesome ration
> With taste of lovers' happiness;
> I am constrained, I will confess,
> My gentle readers, by compassion;
> So bear with me and let it be:
> My Tanja is so dear to me!
>
> [pp. 68, 97]

Yet the tone of these excerpts, just as the reference and the apostrophe to the critic in stanza 32 of the same chapter is pure Sterne; sentimental play and play with sentimentality.

Likewise, the following description of Tatjana with its blatantly archaic diction clearly verges on parody:

> And all the while the moon was shining
> And in its fallow gleam outlining
> Tatjana's cheek with sickly glare,
> The loose profusion of her hair.
>
> [p. 70]

It is likely that Pushkin parodied himself in "The Little House in Kolomna," simply bringing his irony out more explicitly:

> . . . pale Diana,
> Gazed long into the maid's window
> (No novel is complete without this,
> That's the rule.)[24]

Pushkin's sentimental treatment of Lenskij is also a singular instance of play. The motif of the city dweller's sorrow at the poet's grave is a recognizable stylistic convention, and the twice-repeated exclamation in stanzas 10 and 11 of chapter 7 seems to hark back directly to Sterne's cry, "Poor Yorick!"

Now, why is it that *Eugene Onegin* was cast in the form of a Sternean novel/parody? The appearance of *Tristram Shandy* was due to the petrification of the devices of the traditional *roman d'aventure*. All its techniques had become totally ineffectual. Parody was the only way to give them a new lease on life. *Eugene Onegin* was written, as Professor Eikhenbaum has pointed out,[25] on the eve of the rise of new prose. Poetic molds were cooling off. Pushkin was dreaming of writing a prose novel—rhyme bored him.

Eugene Onegin is like that "eccentric" who appears toward the end of a variety show and exposes all the tricks of the foregoing act. I will be told at this point that Onegin himself, whatever can be said of the novel's structure, is a recognizable social type.

Kljuchevskij even succeeded in precisely determining the historical origins of this social type in his article "Onegin's Ancestors."[26] He concluded that Evgenij Onegin was the younger brother of the Decembrists, the product of a society disenchanted with lofty ideals. This, of course, is not true.

Chapter 1 of *Eugene Onegin*, as everyone knows, was completed on 22, October 1823, that is, before the Decembrist uprising.

Pushkin himself, as we know from chapter 10, which he wrote in a secret code, considered Onegin a future Decembrist.[27]

---

24. "Domik v Kolomne," p. 220.
25. See "Pushkin's Path to Prose" below.
26. V. O. Kljuchevskij (1841–1911) was a distinguished Russian historian. The article, the exact title of which is "Eugene Onegin and His Ancestors," was first published in the journal *Russkaja mysl'* [Russian thought] in 1887. It deals with the sociohistorical antecedents of the Onegin syndrome and diagnoses the latter as a compound of disenchantment and moral confusion generated in the wake of the so-called "Decembrist" insurrection (see n. 27).
27. The main body of *Eugene Onegin* consists of eight chapters. There are,

Thus even so subtle a historian as Kljuchevskij made here a crude error. It might seem that the error was a matter of just a couple of years; the point is, though, that these years were crucial.

Kljuchevskij's error consists in regarding a "type" as a real-life entity, while in fact it is a stylistic phenomenon.

How should I end this article?

If it were a novel, I could end it with a wedding.

But articles are a more difficult affair.

It is imperative that we understand the "new Pushkin." He may turn out to be the real Pushkin.

One can honor a poet's memory not only by burning "fragrant herbs" but also by the gay work of destruction.

---

in addition, two fragments, "Onegin's Journey" and "Chapter 10," which is a matter of eighteen incomplete stanzas, arranged, as a contemporary scholar put it, in "deliberate disorder." They contain a number of epigrammatic and ambivalent references to the "Decembrist" movement—a "secret union of young noblemen opposed to tyranny and slavery" (Nabokov) who were to stage on 14 December 1825 an abortive insurrection against Nicholas I. Onegin is never mentioned here, but some Pushkinians assume that he was slated to join the ranks of the conspirators.

Parallels in Tolstoy

VIKTOR SHKLOVSKIJ

In order to make of an object an artistic fact, one must pry it loose of the facts of life. To do this it is necessary to "shake up" the thing the way Ivan the Terrible used to "shake up" his henchmen. It is necessary to tear it out of the context of habitual associations, to turn it like a log in a fire. The artist is always the instigator of a revolt of things. With poets, things mutiny, shuck off their old names; in assuming new ones they take on a new aspect. The poet uses images—tropes, similes. He calls fire a red flower, he attaches new epithets to old nouns. He will even, like Baudelaire, say that the carrion raised its legs like a woman inviting obscene caresses. In this way the poet effects a "semantic shift." He snatches a notion from the semantic plane at which it is usually found, and with the aid of a word (trope) he transfers it to a new semantic plane. We are struck by the novelty resulting from placing the object in a new ambience. A new word fits the object like a new dress. This is one way of converting an object into something palpable, something capable of becoming the material of art. Another method is to create a "staircase-like construction":[1] an object is bifurcated through the medium of reflections and juxtapositions.

This strategy is nearly universal. Many stylistic devices are based on it, notably parallelism: "Oh, little apple, where do you roll? / Oh, Mama, I have a yen for marriage."[2]

An object may at times split into two, or break down into its various components. In Alexander Blok the single word "railroad" breaks into "blues of the road, [blues] of the rail".[3]

This essay first appeared in *Khod konja* [The knight's move] (Moscow–Berlin, 1923), pp. 115–25. This is a slightly abbreviated version; some of Shklovskij's examples were not translatable in English.

1. The term *stupenchatoe postroenie* (staircase-like construction) was coined by Shklovskij and used previously by him in his early contribution to the theory of prose bearing the awkward title, "A Connection between Devices of Plot Construction and General Stylistic Devices," *Poètika* (Petrograd, 1919).

2. To be sure, the parallelism is more apparent in the original: "O, jablochko, kudy kotishsja?/ O, mamochka, za muzh khochetsja."

3. The Russian compound adjective is *zhelezno-dorozhnyj*; the line in question reads *toska dorozhnaja zheleznaja.*

In Leo Tolstoy's works, which are as formal as musical compositions, he employed the device of "making it strange" (not calling things by their usual names) as well as provided examples of a "staircase-like construction".

I have had occasion to write a good deal about "making it strange" in Tolstoy.[4] One variant of this device consists in bearing down, focusing on a certain detail in a picture, and distorting proportions thereby. Thus, in a battle scene, Tolstoy elaborates the motif of a moist, chewing mouth. By drawing attention to such details, a singular displacement is achieved. In his excellent book on Tolstoy, Konstantin Leontiev[5] failed to grasp this device. But the most common strategy in Tolstoy is one of refusing to recognize an object, of describing it as if it were seen for the first time. Thus a stage setting is called a "piece of painted cardboard" (*War and Peace*), the sacramental wafer a "bun." An assertion is therefore made that Christians eat their God.[6]

This Tolstoyan device can, I believe, be traced back to French literature, possibly to Voltaire's *L'Ingénu* or to the description of life at the French court offered by Chateaubriand's savage.[7] Be that as it may, Tolstoy "made strange" the works of Wagner, describing them as seen from the vantage point of a shrewd peasant, that is, one who like the French "savage" lacks habitual associaciations.[8] Incidentally, the same device of describing a city as seen by a rustic was employed in the ancient Greek novel (see Veselovskij).[9]

---

4. Shklovskij has chiefly in mind his programmatic essay, "Art as a Device" (1919), where the crucial concept of *ostranenie* ("making it strange") was first adumbrated.

5. A remarkable late nineteenth-century novelist and publicist (1831–91) whose long essay, "Analysis, Style and Ambience: On the Novels of Count L. N. Tolstoy," was one of the most perceptive contemporary assessments of Tolstoy's major fiction.

6. The passage from *War and Peace* quoted here occurs in the scene of Natasha Rostova's first visit to the opera. The balance of the paragraph is based on the description of the church service in Tolstoy's late novel *Resurrection*.

7. Reference, apparently, to the section of Chateaubriand's prose epic *Les Natchez* where the hero confronts in bafflement Paris of Louis XIV.

8. Clearly a reference to a passage in Tolstoy's tract *What Is Art?* where, after a lengthy debunking of Wagner's "The Ring of the Nibelungen" as "a model of counterfeit art" the author "pictures to himself the terrible perplexity" that a "respected, wise, educated, country laborer" would experience in the face of such an absurd and incoherent spectacle (*Chto takoe iskusstvo, Polnoe sobranie sochinenij* [Moscow, 1913] 30:137).

9. The foremost Russian authority on comparative literature and folklore

The other device, that of "staircase-like construction," has many interesting uses. I will not attempt to give even the most summary sketch of how Tolstoy employed this device in the process of creating his own singular poetics and will content myself with a few examples. The young Tolstoy used parallelism rather naïvely. Thus, in order to elaborate the theme of dying, to deploy it, he found it necessary to juxtapose three motifs—the death of a gentlewoman, the death of a serf, the death of a tree. I am speaking here about the story "Three Deaths." The various parts of the tale are linked together by a definite "motivation": the serf is coachman to the gentlewoman, the tree is cut down to make a coffin for the serf.

In "Kholstomer" the parallel between horse and man is drawn: "the dead body of Serpukhovskij, after having walked and eaten and drunk on this earth, was put away into the ground much later. Neither his skin, nor his bones [nor his meat] were of any use to anyone."[10] The connection made here rests on the fact that Serpukhovskij was at one time the horse's master. In "Two Hussars" the parallelism, announced in the very title of the story, pervades the incidents—love affairs, card games, friendships, and so on.[11]

The connection between the two terms of the parallel is provided by the kinship of the protagonists.

When one compares Tolstoy's craft to that of Maupassant, one finds that the French master tends to omit the second term of the parallel. In a Maupassant short story this element—be it the traditional short-story pattern or the conventional, French bourgeois outlook—is often implicit. In many of his stories Maupassant describes a peasant's death; he does so with great simplicity, yet he "makes it strange": the standard literary portrayal of a city dweller's death functions here, by implication, as a source of contrast, even though such a description does not actually appear in the story.

In this regard Tolstoy is, if one will, cruder than Maupassant;

(1838–1906); Veselovskij's path-breaking *Poetics of Plots* (1906) exerted a visible influence on Shklovskij's studies on the theory of narrative fiction.

10. The subtitle of "Kholstomer" (1861) translates "A Story of a Horse." The quoted sentence is preceded by a detailed description of the "hero's" death.

11. This, one of Tolstoy's early stories, offers a contrasting portrayal of two successive generations of the Russian *jeunesse dorée* as represented respectively by a rowdy father and a prudent son.

he needs an explicit parallel, for example, the contrast between kitchen and drawing room in "The Fruits of Enlightment."[12] This may be explained by the greater availability of the French literary tradition. The French reader feels a violation of the canon more keenly; he identifies the terms of the parallel more readily than our reader, whose conception of the norm is rather hazy.

Let me say, in passing, that when I speak of a literary tradition, I do not have in mind one author's borrowing from another. I see the writer's tradition as his dependence on an extant set of literary norms just as an inventor's tradition is the sum total of the currently available technical resources.

The juxtapositions of various protagonists or of two groups of protagonists are among the more complex instances of parallelism in Tolstoy's novels. In *War and Peace,* for example, one can clearly discern the following juxtapositions: Napoleon vs. Kutuzov and Pierre Bezukhov vs. Andrej Bolkonskij, with Nikolaj Rostov serving as an external point of reference for both parties. In *Anna Karenina* the Anna–Vronskij group is set off against the Lëvin–Kitty group. Their coexistence is "motivated" by kinship. This is the usual motivation in Tolstoy, and, perhaps, among novelists in general. Tolstoy himself wrote [in a letter][13] that he had made the "old" Bolkonskij father to a brilliant young man (Andrej), "since it is awkward to treat a character not related to someone else in the novel." Another method favored by English novelists whereby one and the same protagonist participates in various configurations was hardly ever used by Tolstoy; as a matter of fact he used it only in the Petrushka–Napoleon episode, where it was employed for the purpose of "making it strange."[14]

The actual link between the juxtaposed groups in *Anna Karenina* is so tenuous that the connection can only be conceived as having been motivated by artistic necessity.

12. "Plody prosveshchenija" (1890), a satirical play by Tolstoy; a mordant exposé of spiritualism and, more broadly, of the fatuousness of high society.
13. To Princess L. I. Volkonskaja (May 1865), in L. Tolstoy, *Polnoe sobranie sochinenij* (Moscow, 1958) 61:80.
14. Shklovskij must be referring here to the brief encounter between Napoleon and a captive Russian soldier, a sly Cossack Lavrushka, described in pt. 10 of *War and Peace.* It is not entirely clear what point is made here; presumably the other configuration in which Napoleon and Lavrushka appear was the account of this episode found in L. Thiers' *History of the Consulate and the Empire under Napoleon* (Philadelphia, 1861–63). Predictably, Tolstoy undercuts the "official" version by making Napoleon appear fatuous rather than benign.

Yet Tolstoy did use kinship in a highly interesting way—not to "motivate" a parallel but to create a "staircase-like construction." In the Rostov family we encounter two brothers and one sister. They seem to represent an unfolding of a single type. Tolstoy at times compares them to one another, as in the section preceding the death of Petja. Nikolaj Rostov is a simplified, "crude" version of Natasha. By the same token, Stiva Oblonskij reveals one side of Anna Karenina's inner makeup. The words "a wee bit," which she says with Stiva's intonation, are a throwback to the childhood home they shared. Stiva is a step below his sister. Here the connection between characters does not really stem from kinship. As we have seen, Tolstoy was not averse to making relatives of independently conceived characters. Kinship was needed in order to achieve a staircase-like construction. That literary conventions governing portrayal of relatives do not require characterological affinity is best shown by the traditional device of juxtaposing a noble brother with a wicked one.

Here everything, as always in art, is motivation of the artifice.

Pushkin's Path to Prose

BORIS EIKHENBAUM

Suddenly, though not unexpectedly, we have found ourselves in the midst of a Pushkin celebration.[1] Life moves through
a maze of contradictions. The very act of repudiating the past, of
challenging stable traditions, generates an urge to look back and
see which discarded and forgotten elements of the past have
proved congenial and essential. The question that haunts everyone is this: after all we have gone through in life and in art, is
Pushkin still living? And if he is, what does he mean to us? Have
we moved so far away that we barely perceive him, or is the distance that separates us from him precisely what we need in order
to grasp the whole without losing sight of the details, the kind of
perspective an artist requires to create a form?

Until recently Pushkin was too close to us and we saw him
dimly. We spoke of him in a hackneyed, lifeless language, repeating a thousand times the hasty and imprecise words of Belinskij.[2] By now all the hackneyed and lifeless words that can be
found in the Russian language have been learned by heart. The
limp and facile—because essentially noncommittal—word "genius" had been uttered and repeated time and again only to turn
Pushkin into a plaster statuette rather than a monument.

It is this pathetic statuette, this knickknack which decorated
boudoirs that the futurists were shouting about as they urged us
to "throw [it] overboard from the steamer of modern times."[3] Yes,
this Pushkin whom they used to dull our senses at school—and
will continue to do so!—this Pushkin whose name is invoked by
aesthetic reactionaries and illiterates, this impoverished Pushkin
with whom the spiritually idle cultural voyeurs busy themselves
—it is this generally accessible, endlessly serviceable, and no
longer read Pushkin that we must throw overboard.

This essay, translated here by Irene Etkin Goldman, first appeared as "Problemy
poètiki Pushkina" in Boris Eikhenbaum, *Skvoz' literaturu* [Across literature],
Voprosy poètiki (Leningrad, 1924), pp. 157–70.

1. See Shklovskij's "Pushkin and Sterne" above.
2. See Introduction, pp. 4–5 above.
3. Reference to a notorious futurist manifesto "A Slap in the Face of the
Public Taste" (1912), which among other things called for "throwing Pushkin,
Dostoevsky, Tolstoy et al. overboard from the steamer of modern times."

We are still so young that we don't know how to handle our own culture, our own literature. Tolstoy gave us a cue: he prompted us to view him as a sage, a "teacher of life." Clearly this would not do for Pushkin.

Those admirers of Pushkin who in an attempt to "raise the ante" proclaim his appearance in Russian poetry totally unexpected are palpably wrong. Pushkin is not the beginning but the end of a long path traversed by eighteenth-century Russian poetry. This is the process to which he owes his emergence. "Only of an erratic and totally undisciplined artist can one say that he is entirely self-generated. One can never say this of a genuine artist" (Goethe). Pushkin is a culmination, not a beginning. Having absorbed all the poetic traditions of the eighteenth-century—that hardworking, strenuous era of Russian art—Pushkin created a high canon, classical in its balance and apparent ease. He did not and could not have followers, since art cannot live by canons.

Art creates a norm in order to violate it. Russian poetry after Pushkin sought new paths in its attempt to violate the Pushkin, canon. It struggled with him rather than learned from him. Young Lermontov follows in his footsteps the better to challenge him. He picks up Byron discarded by Pushkin en route to do battle on equal ground. He seeks new models for Russian verse in English and German poetry in order to free himself of Pushkin's iambic tetrameter. But Russian verse was fated to go off in a different direction so as to pave the way for a new flowering independent of Pushkin. This alternate track of Russian poetry leads from Tjutchev and Fet to the symbolists. The verse of Nekrasov[4] could stay on the main tract only because he did not do battle with Pushkin, but acted as if Pushkin did not exist. The symbolists began to talk about Pushkin only after becoming victors and masters in their own right, that is, as equals. From the womb of symbolism emerged a new classicism: the poetry of Kuz'min,[5] Akhmatova, and Mandelstam yields a new sense of Pushkin the classicist, an

4. Fëdor Tjutchev (1803–73) and Afanasij Fet (1820–92) were remarkable Russian lyric poets. Around the middle of the century they were overshadowed by the more extroverted and civic-minded poetry of Nikolaj Nekrasov (1821–77).
5. Mikhail A. Kuz'min (1875–1936) was an exquisite lyric poet; his much-quoted call for "beautiful clarity," featured in a 1910 issue of *Apollon*, helped launch the neoclassical secession from symbolism, the so-called Acmeist movement in which Anna Akhmatova and Osip Mandelstam played major parts.

image affirmed by the strikingly paradoxical aphorism of Mandelstam: "The classical poetry is the poetry of revolution."[6]

Against this background of living art we could feel and see Pushkin anew. We saw all the complexity and sophistication of Pushkin's craft that crowned a spectacular period of Russian poetry launched by Lomonosov and Tredjakovskij.[7] We realized that Pushkin's historical mission was to bring the Russian poetic language into equilibrium, to create on the basis of accumulated experience an integrated, vigorous, complete, and stable artistic system. The word in Pushkin became light in the same way in which the most massive material appears weightless and airy in the hands of a skillful architect. The reactionary tendencies of Derzhavin's imitators are overcome, even while all the achievements of old poetry and assimilated and systematized. Pushkin is not at all a revolutionary; he does not quarrel with his mentors; he keeps thanking them. True, Derzhavin is to him "a bad, free translation from some marvelous original";[8] yet he always shows deep respect for his immediate master Zhukovskij: "I agree with Bestuzhev's opinion of Pletnëv's critical essay, but I cannot wholly agree with the severe verdict on Zhukovskij. Why bite our nurse's breast simply because we are teething? . . . Whatever one may say, Zhukovskij did have a decisive influence on the spirit of our letters; besides, his translating style will forever remain a model. Truly, this republic of letters is beyond me. Who will figure out its excommunications, its encomiums? . . . I'm not the result, but merely a disciple who makes his mark by steering clear of the master's path and meandering down a country road."[9]

Pushkin's country road turned out to be the high road of Russian poetry, but for decades after Pushkin's death, it was virtually closed

6. The phrase occurs in one of Mandelstam's most important critical essays, "The Word and Culture" (1921).

7. Mikhail V. Lomonosov (1711–65) and Vasilij K. Tredjakovskij (1703–69) were pioneers of Russian poetry and metrics. Lomonosov's role was especially important.

8. Gavrila R. Derzhavin (1743–1816) was a major eighteenth-century Russian poet. Quote is from a letter to a close friend and fellow, A. A. Delvig (8 June 1825).

9. Vasilij A. Zhukovskij (1783–1852) was the leading figure in Russian preromanticism and one of Pushkin's most influential precursors, "the first pioneer and the accepted patriarch of the Golden Age [of Russian literature]" (D. S. Mirsky). Quote is from a letter to another friend, a minor poet and staunch libertarian, K. F. Ryleev (25 January 1825).

to traffic. Zhukovskij's road veered sideways into a winding foot-
path traveled by two lone figures, Tjutchev and Fet. Zhukovskij
was moving away from the eighteenth-century; Pushkin was returning to it. A study of that period is indispensable to the reconstruction of Pushkin's poetics. Only against such a background
can the system of his artistic devices clearly emerge. Pushkin
exhausted all the verbal and rhythmic possibilities of Russian
verse provided by his forerunners. Here is the source of the magic
of his style: an intricate system of epithets, metonymies, and
paraphrases, which appears simple and light because a symmetry
of the component parts has been attained and their relationships
taken account of, because forms have been found. The classicist
"original" that was still unknown to Derzhavin has been discovered. The old elegies, epistles, and odes appeared in a new
light. Pushkin's narrative poetry derives from these descriptive
epistles and odes. It is significant that in "The Captive of the Caucasus" the dominant element should have been [in Pushkin's
words] an hors d'oeuvre—the description of the Caucasus and the
Circassians that harks back to Derzhavin and Zhukovskij. The
romantic theme was neglected. "The Circassian who captured my
Russian could have been the lover of his deliverer; her mother,
father, and brothers could each have had a distinctive role or
character; all this I neglected."[10] The romantic hero turned into
an element of a landscape whose original source is not Byron
but Zhukovskij ("To Voejkov").[11] In the epilogue the still vital
tradition of the ode is clearly felt:

> But lo—the East raises a howl! . . .
> Hang down your snowy head.
> Surrender, Caucasus—Ermolov's here![12]

There is a direct connection from the above to the historical poems
"Poltava" and "The Bronze Horseman."

By 1830 the lyric strain in Pushkin receded. A gradual shift to
prose is clearly discernible. *Eugene Onegin* paved the way for this

---

10. From a rough draft of a letter to the Russian translator of *The Iliad*, E. E.
Gnedich (29 April 1825).

11. Like the opening passage of Pushkin's "The Captive of the Caucasus,"
Zhukovskij's above quoted epistle contains an extended description of the
Circassian way of life.

12. Reference to the punitive raid on the rebellious Circassian moun-
taineers led by the popular Russian general Ermolov.

transition. We find here both an album of lyrics and the emergence of plot constructions that can dispense with verse.

Pushkin's presentiment came true: not only he, but all Russian literature after the 1820s went the way of "stern prose."[13] It was a clean break rather than a gradual transition. Poetry and prose are essentially different arts, "phenomena nearly opposite and incompatible" (Musset). In Pushkin—the highpoint of Russian verse culture—the break is especially evident. Prose had begun to interest him already in the 1820s: "Prose demands ideas and then more ideas; without them, glittering phrases serve no purpose. Poetry is another matter."[14] He agrees that Russian poetry "has attained a high level of sophistication", but "except for those who are involved with verse, the Russian language cannot yet be attractive enough for anyone. We still have neither literature nor books."[15] In "Roslavlev" he repeats: "Our literature, naturally, presents us with some excellent poets, but we cannot ask all readers to have exclusive interest in verse. In prose we have only Karamzin's history."[16] And readers were already clamoring for prose. Marlinskij spoke for them: "The child is attracted by a rattle before he is attracted by the compass: even mediocre poetry is tolerable, as it is flattery to the ear; but a good prose style requires not only familiarity with the grammar of language but also a grammar of ideas, variety in cadence, in rounding off periods, and does not tolerate repetition. That is why we have a vast number of poets and practically no prose writers. . . . It is true that the poets did not stop chirping into every corner, but no one listened to poems when everyone was writing them. Finally scattered rumblings swelled into a general outcry: 'Prose! prose!—Water, plain water!' "[17]

Russian literature answered this cry by turning to prose. In

13. An echo of the much-quoted lines from chapter 6 of *Eugene Onegin*: "The age impels toward stern prose/ The age chases away that imp, rhyme."

14. From an 1822 essay, "On Diction," first published in 1884.

15. The above assertions are found in an 1824 note on "Factors That Have Impeded the Development of Our Letters."

16. "Roslavlev" (1831) is a fragment of a projected historical novel about the "Fatherland War" of 1812. Nikolaj Karamzin (1766–1826) authored a voluminous *History of the Russian State* along with several sentimental novels.

17. Aleksandr Bestuzhev-Marlinskij (1797–1837) was a floridly romantic poet, fiction writer, and critic. The latter part of the above quotation is drawn from Marlinskij's 1833 critical essay occasioned by a contemporary Russian historical novel.

Lermontov's work both elements are somehow balanced, but there is a telling difference between his poetic style and the style of his mature prose. His prose, initially rich in metaphors, in rhythmic-syntactical parallelisms, and in long sentences ("Vadim")—a legacy of verse—later becomes simple and clear. A kinship with verse is still felt in the prose of Gogol and Turgenev, who actually began with poetry. On the other hand, the prose of Tolstoy, Leskov, and Dostoevsky developed without any relation to verse; in fact, their prose is essentially hostile to it. This is not a special case but a general pattern. In French literature a good case in point is the relation between the prose of Chateaubriand and Hugo on the one hand and that of Stendhal and Mérimée on the other. The difference between poetry and prose is not an external matter of layout; it is basic, organic, no less essential, perhaps, than that between abstract and representational painting. There is a permanent, never-ceasing tension between the two modes. Prose can don the plumage shed by poetry and become in this attire musical, stylistically intricate, and rich in alliteration and rhythmic cadence. (Such is the prose of Marlinskij and Andrej Belyj.)[18] The boundary between prose and poetry is thus practically obliterated until, having won the battle, prose casts off those luxuriant robes and appears again in its natural guise.

Let me cite some relevant pronouncements. In 1817 Batjushkov[19] wrote: "In order to write good verse, to write with variety, with a style both forceful and pleasing, with original thoughts, with feeling, one has to write a good deal of prose, not for an audience, but simply to make notes for oneself. I often found that this method worked for me; sooner or later what one writes in prose will come in handy." "Prose nourishes poetry," said Alfieri, if my memory does not fail me. Young Tolstoy noted in his diary: "I read and wrote verse. It was rather smooth going. I think this will be of great use to me in developing a literary style." The same thought appears in Rousseau's "Confessions." "Occasionally I wrote mediocre poems: this is a pretty good exercise, for it helps develop graceful inversions and improve one's prose." Of special interest are Batjushkov's remarks in a letter to Gnedich,

---

18. See Introduction, pp. 9–10 above. Andrej Belyj's novels, e.g. *St. Petersburg* and *The Silver Dove*, are striking examples of rhythmically saturated prose.

19. Konstantin N. Batjushkov (1787–1855), one of Pushkin's immediate predecessors, a sensuous and urbane lyric poet.

1811, on the prose of Chateaubriand, in which he justifiably sensed a threat to poetry: "He . . . spoiled my mind and my style: I was all set to write a poem in prose, a tragedy in prose, madrigals in prose, and epigrams in poetic prose. Don't read Chateaubriand!"

"The age chases away that imp, rhyme" [see note 13]. This is more than a jest. In "Thoughts on the Road" (1833–35) Pushkin said: "I think that with time we will turn to blank verse. The Russian language has all too few rhymes. One rhyme calls forth another. *Plamen'* [fire] inevitably drags *kamen'* [stone] after it. *Isskustvo* [art] is always on the coattails of *chuvstvo* [feeling]. And who is not tired of *ljubov* [love] and *krov'* [blood], *trudnoj* [difficult] and *chudnoj* [wondrous], *vernoj* [faithful] and *litsemer-noj* [false]?[20]

Significantly, in the first issue of *Sovremennik* [The contemporary], 1836,[21] Pushkin published the essay by Baron Rosen, "On Rhyme," in which the poet is urged to abandon that silly toy unworthy of poetry. In the 1830s Pushkin clearly thought that Russian verse was reaching a stalemate. He himself saw a vast difference between his poetic and his prose styles. While the former had attained its pinnacle within the limits of the classicist canon, the latter was still completely disorganized. "I have been publishing for sixteen years now and the critics have noticed five grammatical errors in my poems (and rightly so); I was always sincerely grateful to them and always corrected the errors. My prose writing is much less correct and I speak even worse, almost as sloppily as Gogol writes."

All this points up the fact that Pushkin's prose appeared not as a supplement to his poems but as a new development that increasingly preempted poetic creativity. During the years 1828 to 1830, Pushkin wrote annually some thirty or more poems, among which were "Do not sing, my beauty in my presence . . . ," "Remembrance," "The Upas Tree," "The Mob," "The Snowslide," "The Hills of Georgia," "As Down the Noisy Street I Wander," "Frost and Sunrise, Day of Splendor . . . ." "To the Poet," "Devils," "Autumn," "Invocation." In 1831 he wrote only seven, in 1832 nine, of which two are incomplete and four are album verse,[22] in

---

20. See "Journey from St. Petersburg to Moscow," *Polnoe sobranie sochinenij* [Complete works] (Moscow, 1949), 11:263.

21. A literary journal founded by Pushkin in 1836 and edited by him until his death.

22. Light and usually gallant verse inscribed in a society lady's scrapbook.

1833 eight, of which only one is a lyric ("Don't Let Me Lose My Mind, Oh God"), in 1834 only three. Prose clearly gains the upper hand.

What should one make, then, of Pushkin's prose? It seems to have no antecedents—the Russian short story was practically non-existent at this time. Neither Karamzin, Marlinskij, nor Narezhnyj[23] had anything to offer Pushkin. What are the sources of the short, simple sentence that shuns rhythmic regularity and stylistic adorn-ments, of the compact, action-centered novella, heavily oriented toward the denouement and intricately plotted? In 1825 Push-kin wrote to Marlinskij: "You have written enough quick tales with romantic transitions. This would do for a Byronic poem. A novel must be chatty; do not keep anything to yourself. . . . Tackle a full-fledged novel and write it with the complete freedom of a conversation or a letter."[24] Marlinskij declaims in prose, Pushkin tells a story. Even Belinskij, who understood nothing in "The Tales of Belkin," sensed this emphasis on storytelling (*conter*).

Pushkin erected his prose on the foundation of his own verse. This is why his prose writings are so distant from his verse. His is not the "poetic prose" of Marlinskij or Gogol. A flimsy fable expands into an absorbing plot couched in a casual, conversational style.[25] These are not "quick" tales; on the contrary, using subtle artistic devices, Pushkin slows down the pace of the novella and makes his every move perceptible. His simple fable is mediated through an elaborate plot structure. "The Shot" may be construed as a single storyline—that of Silvio's duel with the Count. But for one thing Pushkin creates a narrator whose presence motivates the division of the novella into two phases with a hiatus between them (the beginning of the second chapter); for another, the story has two narrators beside the author—Silvio himself and the Count.[26] An element of surprise is injected when the impeded

23. Vasilij Narezhnyj (1780–1820), was one of the pioneers of Russian narrative fiction. He is known mainly as author of a picaresque novel, *The Russian Gil Blas* (1814).

24. Eikhenbaum draws here on two letters to Marlinskij, written respectively in summer and fall of 1825.

25. A note on Eikhenbaum's terminology may be in order: in line with his fellow formalists, he means by "fable" (*fabula*) the basic story stuff, the sum total of events to be related in the work of fiction, and by "plot" (*sjuzhet*) the story as actually told, that is, as mediated through narrative devices.

26. Since the story of "Silvio's duel with the Count" emerges gradually from two chronologically discontinuous confessions of which the main narrator is the

narration is suddenly resumed. The character of Silvio plays a secondary role—no wonder the finale handles his ultimate fate in so
offhand a fashion. What matters here is the pace, the gait of the
tale, its orientation toward plot structure. The same is true of "The
Snowstorm." Of particular interest is the weight given to the ending. This device is not motivated—a playing with the plot is laid
bare. Instead of a single storyline there are two parallel lines that
suddenly converge. A segment of the story—the wedding of Marija
Gavrilovna to an unknown officer—is postponed till the end. It is
left to the reader to piece the picture together—a task that cannot
be accomplished until the curtain goes down. Only at the very end
of the story, when Marija Gavrilovna exclaims, "So it was you!"
do all the separate pieces begin to fall into place.[27] "The Under-
taker" features a playing with the fable through the medium of
pseudo-action: the denouement returns us to the point at which
the fable began and thus obliterates it, turning the story into a
parody. In "The Stationmaster" too one can detect, as Gershenzon
pointed out, a parody of a narrative cliché.[28] The denouement
does not coincide with the story of the prodigal son whose picture
hangs in the station's waiting room. Finally, in "Lady Turned
Peasant" Pushkin parodies the standard theme of lovers who belong to feuding families (*Romeo and Juliet*). Significantly enough,
Aleksej reads with Akulina *Natalija, the Boyar's Daughter*, where

---

recipient, he does provide a "structural" reason or motive for dividing the novella
into two sections.

27. To one who has not read "The Snowstorm" the above may sound even
more cryptic than Eikhenbaum's discussion of "The Shot." Thus a brief synopsis
might be in order. "The Snowstorm" consists of two successive movements.
The. first features a romance between an impressionable young gentlewoman,
Marija Gavrilovna, and an equally responsive young squire. Since the young
lady's parents frown upon the relationship, the lovers decide on a secret wedding
in a neighboring village church at which they are supposed to meet. A violent
snowstorm plays havoc with the carefully laid plan: the bridegroom's coachman gets lost, the carriage does not arrive at the scene until much later. The
bride manages to get to the church nearly on time, but she is delirious and utterly
shaken when her beloved fails to appear. As we learn at the end of the story, an
unknown officer who happens to be around whimsically steps into the breach.
As soon as the ceremony is over, the bride faints. The second section of the
story introduces the young officer and a growing infatuation between him and
Marija Gavrilovna. At some point he blurts out his love but feels unable to
propose because of a marriage to an unknown young woman into which he had
drifted unaccountably. As the "separate pieces" fall into place, Marija Gavrilovna
exclaims, "So it was you!" and faints, this time to good effect.

28. Reference to an essay on "The Belkin Tales" by Mikhail Gershenzon (see
Shklovskij, "Pushkin and Sterne," n. 17).

that theme is used. But Pushkin's Liza does not want to be either Juliet or Natalija, and the unexpected reconciliation of the parents turns the conventional plot around and creates a comic situation.[29]

Such were the beginnings of Pushkin's prose. From *Eugene Onegin,* "Count Nulin," and "The Little House in Kolomna"[30] to the "Tales of Belkin." His interest in plot construction led Pushkin to prose, which his vast poetic experience made concise and simple. Pushkin's prose emerged from verse not in order to compete with it, as was the case with Marlinskij, but in order to counterbalance it. That is why, despite the absence of specifically poetic devices, one can readily recognize in Pushkin's prose narratives Pushkin the poet. In 1834 Senkovskij[31] wrote to Pushkin: "C'est le language de vos poésies . . . que vous transportez dans votre prose de conteur; je reconnais ici la même langue et le même goût, le même charme." It is worth noting in this connection that, while Pushkin pioneers the development of Russian prose, he fails to create a tradition. Pushkin had no followers in prose either. The point is, I guess, that subsequent prose developed on the ruins of verse, whereas Pushkin's prose was borne from verse, from the equilibrium among all its elements. I may add that the original impulse of Pushkin's standard meter—his iambic tetrameter—in contradistinction to the "musical" verse of the romantics, was not "singable" but, if one will, conversational.[32] The pathway to prose thus opened was closed to such poets as Tjutchev, Fet, Balmont,[33] or Blok. It would be interesting to investigate the architectonics of Pushkin's poetic phrase and of its prose counterpart and to bring out the kinship between the two. Pushkin's prose has an effect quite unlike that produced by the prose of prose writers. The quasi-mathematical relationships that

29. *Natalija, the Boyar's Daughter* is a sentimental novel by Nikolaj Karamzin. It may not be clear to the uninitiated that Liza and Akulina (a characteristically peasant name) are the same person. The plot of "Lady Turned Peasant" centers around a young gentlewoman's assuming the guise of a peasant girl.

30. The latter two poems are short whimsical narratives with a parodistic flavor.

31. Joseph-Julian Senkovskij (1800–59), Pushkin's resourceful if unsavory contemporary, was a journalist, publisher, and critic.

32. Eikhenbaum's terminology here derives from a typological study in which he was engaged at the time. In his *Melodics of Verse* (1921) he discerns in Russian lyrical poetry three styles—the rhetorical or declamatory, the conversational, and singable (*napevnyj*).

33. Konstantin D. Balmont (1867–1943) was a mellifluous and prolific Russian symbolist poet.

seem to obtain between the different parts of a prose sentence in Pushkin clearly are a legacy of the poetic idiom.

Pushkin finally becomes our genuine, undeniable, if not our only tradition. Until recently he had been too close to us—as the familiar object is often too close—to be seen clearly. The remoteness from Pushkin that we sense today, having emerged from symbolism only to find ourselves along with futurism in the throes of the revolutionary chaos, is precisely the distance that is needed for true perception. Thus, the artist steps back from his own painting to see it better.

No longer is Pushkin that plaster statuette. He has become an imposing monument. His stature demands that we view him from a distance.

On Tolstoy's Crises

BORIS EIKHENBAUM

Tolstoy began as a liquidator of romantic poetics, a destroyer of established canons. He revolutionized the material, the devices, the form. Instead of a richly metaphorical style, instead of emphatic musical syntax—a simple, though laborious and almost clumsy phrase; instead of a diffuse flow of feeling and emotionally colored landscapes—minute detailed description, dissection, and analysis of psychic life; instead of intricate plotting —parallelism of several lines, linked rather than interwoven.

From the very outset, Tolstoy perceived himself against the backdrop of a disintegrating romantic art. Bypassing the fathers, he returns to the grandfathers, to the eighteenth century. His teachers and mentors are Sterne, Rousseau, Bernardin de Saint-Pierre, Franklin, Buffon, Goldsmith. *Childhood* reflects the influence of Töpffer, born in that same eighteenth century; in *The Sebastopol Stories*, Tolstoy follows in the footsteps of Stendhal— "the latest arrival from the eighteenth century."[1] The struggle with romantic clichés accounts for a great deal in Tolstoy. "Realism" is merely a justification for this struggle. It is a slogan that constantly recurs as literary schools shift and that constantly alters its meaning. Tolstoy wants to write in a way different from that of his fathers. Already in his early diaries he pokes fun at romantic landscapes: "It is said that gazing at the beauties of nature brings thoughts of the grandeur of God and the insignificance of Man; lovers see in the water the image of their beloved, others say that it was as if the mountains were saying such and such, and the trees beckoned in such and such direction. How does one come

---

This essay, translated here by Carol A. Palmer, first appeared in Boris Eikhenbaum, *Skov' literaturu* [Across literature], Voprosy poètiki (Leningrad, 1924), pp. 67–72.

1. Rodolphe Töpffer (1799–1846) was a Swiss writer in whose tales description and introspection loomed larger than external action. *Sebastopol Stories* (1855), an early cycle of documentary narratives based on Tolstoy's experiences during the Crimean War, foreshadowed some of the battle scenes in *War and Peace*. Quotation from an essay by a nineteenth-century French writer Barbey d'Aurevilly (see *Les romanciers*, Paris, 1865).

by a thought like this? One has to try hard to get such nonsense into one's head."[2]

Tolstoy consistently fractures romantic clichés. He deglamorizes and parodies the figures of romantic warriors patterned after Marlinskij[3] and Lermontov. The traditional "poetic" Caucasus, too, is deglamorized: "For in Russia they picture the Caucasus as something majestic, with everlasting virgin ice fields, rushing torrents, daggers, felt cloaks, Circassian girls—all this sounds strange and wonderful, but, in fact, there is nothing jolly about it. If they at least knew that we have never been on the virgin ice fields, and that there would be nothing jolly about being there, and that the Caucasus is divided into provinces: Stavropol, Tiflis, and so on" ("A Wood Feeling").[4] Significantly, Tolstoy long remains silent about the most "poetic" of subjects, love; the critics wait impatiently for his first novel with love interest. At last the novel "Family Happiness" appears, but the hero is an elderly man who does not want to declare his love the way it is done in novels: "When I read novels," he avers, "I always imagine how perplexed the face of Lieutenant Strelsky must look when he says 'I love you, Eleanor' and thinks that something unusual will suddenly occur; then nothing happens, either to her or to him. The eyes and nose stay the same, and everything is just as it was."[5] A wedding serves here not as a denouement, which is usually the case in novels, but as a beginning of the story proper. This is an intentional departure from the canon. In his *Memoirs* [Moscow, 1911, p. 7] V. Lazorskij cites Tolstoy's dictum that "those who conclude their novels with a wedding, as if that were so great that there was nothing more to say—they all talk utter nonsense."

Tolstoy jettisons the very genre of the romantic novella with its central hero and love-centered plot. He gravitates toward the large forms. His works written prior to *War and Peace* are merely preliminary studies that elaborate individual states of mind, scenes, or devices. Having exhausted within the large form the devices

2. See the entry for 10 August 1851, *Polnoe sobranie sochinenij* [Complete works] (Moscow–Leningrad, 1934), 56:81.

3. See Eikhenbaum's "Pushkin's Path to Prose," n. 17.

4. "Rubka lesa" (1855), also translated as "The Wood-Cutting Expedition," was one of Tolstoy's early stories.

5. "The Family Happiness" ("Semejnoe schast'e") was a short novel that appeared in 1859. Its main importance lies in anticipating some of the "domestic" themes of *War and Peace*, especially its first epilogue. Quote taken from *Polnoe sobranie sochinenij*, 5:86.

of minute description, Tolstoy turns to a new mode—the folk-tale. These two junctures in his creative evolution are accompanied by violent crises. It is still widely assumed that Tolstoy's career is divided into two periods—before and after "A Confession"[6]—and that in the latter period Tolstoy became a moralist.

That is not so. Tolstoy's entire life is punctuated by crises, and this is by no means an idiosyncratic phenomenon. Art itself was in the throes of a crisis. Romantic poetics had ground to halt. Art had to take a new look at life in order to claim a new legitimacy. Early on, Tolstoy gets into the habit of interrupting his artistic work for the sake of completely extraneous schemes—he clearly needs this kind of diversion. Already in 1855 Tolstoy conceives a "great, colossal" thought, to the implementation of which he is prepared to devote his whole life, a notion of founding "a religion that corresponds to the development of humanity, the religion of Christ, but cleansed of faith and mystery."[7]

At the core of all Tolstoy's crises lies the search for new artistic forms and for their new rationale. That is why "A Confession" was followed by the tract on art, on which Tolstoy worked for fifteen years [see p. 100 below]. The way was prepared for that tract by another crisis—the crisis of the sixties—which critics unjustly neglect when they speak of the seventies as the turning point. This crisis is discernible already at the end of the fifties, when Tolstoy enters the milieu of St. Petersburg literati, stunning everyone by his sharp paradoxes and his intolerance. He spurns all canons, all authorities and traditions. For a while, Druzhinin, who becomes his guide, seeks to prevail upon Tolstoy to curb his predilection for the pronouns "that," "which," and "this." Several years later, Tolstoy makes a fantastic, dizzying leap from literature to pedagogy, from St. Petersburg men of letters to the Fed'kas and Sëmkas.[8] His friends are under the impression that Tolstoy is about to abandon literature. Druzhinin, aggrieved,

---

6. "A Confession," begun in 1880 and published abroad in 1884, a powerful self-accusatory tract, is generally considered the major watershed in Tolstoy's life and literary career, marking the onset of an obtrusive and ostensibly anti-aesthetic moralism.

7. Eikhenbaum is referring to the 4 March 1855 entry in Tolstoy's *Diaries*, *Polnoe sobranie sochinenij* [Moscow, 1937], 57:87.

8. Aleksandr V. Druzhinin (1824–64) was an influential and a mildly conservative St. Petersburg litterateur. Two peasant boys, Fed'ka and Sëmka, were Tolstoy's prized disciples at his Jasnaja Poljana school—a bold, if short-lived pedagogical experiment.

attempts to bring him back to his senses: "Every writer has moments of doubt and dissatisfaction with himself, and yet, no matter how strong or how legitimate this feeling, no writer has ever abandoned literature because of it. Everyone has kept writing to the end."

In fact, Tolstoy's pedagogical activity emerged from a deep-seated artistic quest. Almost unwittingly Tolstoy changes from a teacher into an experimenter. His essay "Who Should Learn from Whom How to Write: Peasant Children from Us, or We from Peasant Children?" (1862) is no less significant an artistic pamphlet than his future tract on art.[9] Tolstoy contrasts the compositions of Sëmka and Fed'ka with all of Russian literature, where he cannot find anything to match them. He is delighted by their vividness and precision. He is moved and stunned by the force of this naïve creativity that owes nothing to literary tradition.

This stance foreshadows Tolstoy's imminent shift to primitivism. Instead of plots, Tolstoy gives his students proverbs that serve as a sort of canvas for the weaving of a pattern, for interlacing details into a simple and lucid design. He already dreams in this period of producing such work himself: "Among my unrealizable dreams are a number of works—neither stories nor yet descriptions based on proverbs." The shift to deliberate primitivism is affirmed once and for all in the tract *What Is Art?* There Tolstoy inveighs chiefly against the "triviality," that preoccupation with detail, for which his critics once took him to task, labeling it a device of imitativeness. "In literary art, the device of imitativeness consists in describing down to the smallest detail the external aspect of a character, the clothes, gestures, voices, and settings of the protagonists, together with all the chance occurrences one finds in life. . . . Take away from the best novels of our time the details. What will remain?" He is drawn to modes of "folk art and children's art that were not considered truly artistic—jests, proverbs, riddles, songs, dances, children's games, and mimicry." Characteristically, he finds that these "primitive" genres present much more of an artistic challenge than does a "verse epic on Cleopatra or a painting about Nero burning Rome, a symphony in the manner of Brahms or Richard Strauss, or an opera like Wagner's." Tolstoy feels keenly the impossibility of using traditionally "poetic" material. "Maidens, warriors, shepherds, hermits,

9. Reference to the tract *What Is Art?* (1897).

angels, devils in all their guises, moonlight, thunderstorms, mountains, seas, precipices, flowers, flowing tresses, lions, a lamb, a
dog, a swallow, a nightingale,"—these are the clichés he lists,
clichés deemed poetic because "previous artists used them frequently in their works." Not surprisingly, he contrasts *Hamlet*
as interpreted by Rossi with a description of a theatrical production among a "savage tribe," the Voguls, where the entire play
consists in the hunter's pursuit of deer.[10]

Tolstoy marks a crisis in Russian artistic prose. In the new flowering of verse that followed in his wake maidens, moonlight, storms,
seas, flowers, and swallows were subjected to a new poeticiza-
tion. Tolstoy is at once a destroyer and a consummator. Is not he
the one to whom we might return in our quest of a new "non-
poetic" art?

10. The quotations in this paragraph are from *Chto takoe isskustvo?* [What
is art?], *Polnoe sobranie sochinenij*, (Moscow, 1913), 19:71, 110, 127, 70,
225–26.

Dostoevsky and Gogol

JURIJ TYNJANOV

I

The Manor of Stepanchikovo appeared in 1859.[1] Dostoevsky worked on this novel for a long time and valued it highly, but the public took little notice of it. In 1859 Dostoevsky wrote to his brother:

> This novel, to be sure, has major flaws, the chief being its long-windedness. But I am deeply convinced that it also has great virtues, and that it is my best work to date. I was working on it for two years. The beginning and the middle are well done, the end was written hastily. But I invested here my soul, my flesh and blood. The book contains two major *typical characters* which I have been outlining for five years now, flawlessly done, I think, thoroughly Russian, and hitherto poorly handled in Russian literature.[2]

The full title of the novel—Dostoevsky himself calls it in some of his letters a "comic novel," in others, a tale—is *The Manor of Stepanchikovo and Its Inhabitants: From the Notes of an Unknown.* As the title indicates, the novel is written in the form of a memoir, whose chief aim is to present two "new characters." These are Foma Opiskin and the narrator's uncle, Rostanev. The former is a parodistic figure. The material for parody was provided

This essay first appeared in *Arkhaisty i novatory* [Archaists and innovators] (Leningrad, 1929), pp. 434–55. It represents a slightly abbreviated second half of Tynjanov's seminal study *Dostoevsky i Gogol.* The first half, which comprises a brilliantly succinct section on Gogol's imagery and an important discussion of parody as a catalyst of literary change, unfortunately has been preempted. Here are the most relevant of Tynjanov's generalizations on parody: "The essence of parody lies in the mechanization of a device" (p. 430). "The effectiveness of parody depends on the availability to the reader of the model that is being parodied" (p. 433).

1. The title of the first English translation of *Selo Stepanchikovo* is *The Friend of the Family.*

2. F. M. Dostoevsky, *Pis'ma* [Letters] (St. Petersburg, 1883), p. 121.—*J.T.*

by Gogol's personality. Foma's speechifying is a parody of Gogol's *Selected Passages from Correspondence with Friends.*[3]

Dostoevsky's attitude toward Gogol, especially Gogol the man, was complex. When in 1846 a premature rumor about Gogol's death reached Dostoevsky, he added to a long letter the following postscript: "I wish all of you luck, my friends. Gogol died in Florence two months ago." As a writer Gogol represents for Dostoevsky something that has to be overcome, transcended. Thus, in a letter to his brother: "You'll like it [*The Double*] even better than *Dead Souls.*" Dostoevsky's later and better known pronouncements on Gogol are a far cry from received opinion. (Compare Gogol's "laughing mask," "a demon of laughter," or a polemic in *The Possessed* with Gogol's famous self-definition, "visible laughter through invisible tears.")[4] They mark him as a forerunner of more recent Gogol criticism, for example, that of Rozanov, Brjusov [see pp. 8–9 above]. We will recall that the reading and dissemination of Belinskij's letter to Gogol was the main charge proferred against Dostoevsky at the trial of the Petrashevskians.[5] Apparently, as far as *Correspondence with Friends* was concerned, Dostoevsky remained under Belinskij's spell even after the break with his circle. (Practically all the quotations from Gogol that are adduced below occur in Belinskij's review of *Correspondence with Friends.*) Dostoevsky never changed his essentially negative view of Gogol's tract. In 1876 he wrote in *A Writer's Diary*: "In his *Correspondence with Friends* Gogol is weak but characteristic."[6] Likewise, toward the end of 1880, in a letter to Ivan Aksakov, "To envelop oneself in clouds of grandeur (for instance, Gogol's tone in *Correspondence with Friends*) bespeaks insincerity, and insincerity is something even an inexperienced reader can sense. That is what gives the show away."[7]

---

3. Gogol's ill-starred moral tract (1847) couched in the form of letters to friends.

4. A much-quoted phrase from p. 1 of *Dead Souls*.

5. A socialist circle led by Petrashevskij (1821–66). Along with other members of the group Dostoevsky was arrested and tried in 1849. He was sentenced to eight years' penal servitude.

6. See *Dnevnik pisatelja* [A writer's diary] (Paris, 1876), p. 150.

7. After his return from exile Dostoevsky reread Gogol. He was working then on *The Manor of Stepanchikovo* and *The Uncle's Dream*. The year 1857 saw the Kulish edition of Gogol's works, which included two volumes of letters. A few of these will be mentioned below. —*J.T.*

At this point let me emphasize that Dostoevsky's hostility toward *Correspondence with Friends* does not account for his decision to parody it, as his alleged attitude toward Gogol was not necessarily the motive for his parodying Gogol's personality. These factors happened to *coincide*, but they did not need to converge. Parody can stem from various sources; it may dispense with psychological premises. Parodies of the Old Testament are widespread among Orthodox Jews. Pushkin's high regard for Karamzin's *History of the Russian State* did not prevent him from parodying it in his "Chronicle of the Village Gorjukhino."[8] Nor was he averse to parodying in flippant hexameters the style of *The Iliad* and of its Russian translation, which he greatly admired. By the same token, numerous parodies of *The Aeneid* go hand in hand with a high estimate of Virgil's epic. The fact of the matter is that parody, with its dual structure, often appeals to writers as a distinctive and valuable literary strategy.

Dostoevsky enjoyed working with historical and topical materials. The parodistic characters in *The Possessed* (Stepan Verkhovenskij and Karmazinov) are modeled after Granovskij and Turgenev.[9] The projected *Life of the Great Sinner* was to contain a scene where Chaadaev, confined in a monastery, plays host to Belinskij, Granovskij, and Pushkin.[10] (In his notebook Dostoevsky offers a qualification: "I do not mean the real Chaadaev, what the novel needs is that *type*.") Incidentally, one cannot be sure that the portrayal of Pushkin—whom Dostoevsky admired —would not have been tinged with parody. It is a matter of record that Dostoevsky was all too willing to provide his characters with a recognizable literary genealogy. In *The Idiot* Ippolit is described by another character in that novel as "Nozdrëv in a tragedy" [see p. 54 above]. It is a matter of record that Dostoevsky him-

---

8. A little-known story of Pushkin's, begun in 1830 and first published in 1837, after Pushkin's death.

9. Timofej Granovskij (1813–55), a lecturer in history at the University of Moscow, played an important role in the intellectual ferment of the 1830s and 1840s that gave birth to Russian liberalism and the Russian intelligentsia.

10. *Life* was a large-scale novel that Dostoevsky never managed to write. Elements of the grand design went into three major novels of his—*The Possessed, Raw Youth*, and *The Brothers Karamazov*. Pëtr J. Chaadaev (1794–1856), author of the famous *Philosophical Letters*, was brilliantly and harshly critical of the Russian tradition and the Russian society. His first "letter," which appeared in 1836, was found so subversive that Chaadaev was officially declared a lunatic. Yet to nonconformist intellectuals he was an important and a seminal figure.

self wholeheartedly agreed with Strakhov's[11] description of the protagonists of *The Possessed* as "Turgenev heroes gone to seed."

In *The Manor of Stepanchikovo* Gogol the author of the ill-fated *Correspondence with Friends* serves as a prototype for the chief protagonist, a writer manqué and a "sponger."[12]

Foma Opiskin is, above all, a litterateur, a preacher, a moralist—this is the source of his influence. "He [my uncle] put implicit faith in Foma's genius and learning. . . . I forgot to mention that my uncle had the most naïve and disinterested reverence for the words 'learning' and 'literature'. . . . Foma suffered, I need hardly say, 'for a good cause.' "[13]. Here was a new phenomenon, noted, indeed experienced by Gogol: "Among us a simple scribbler who is not a writer and not only has no beauty of soul but is even at times a scoundrel, in the depths of Russia will by no means be taken as such. On the contrary, everyone, even those who hardly ever hear about writers, are convinced that a writer is a superior being, that he must be a noble person" ("On the Lyricism of Our Poets").[14]

Foma Opiskin became a household word ("the type has worked out") so much so that a contributor to *Satyricon*[15] chose it as his pen name. But the extant interpretations of the character have been inadequate. Foma is not simply a crook, he is not merely a hypocrite, a bigot, a dissembler; he is also, as one of the characters put it, an "impractical man, a sort of a poet."

Dostoevsky remains faithful to his contrast-ridden mode of characterization.[16] This mountebank has a moral impact upon his enemies; under his influence Nastja "becomes addicted to read-

---

11. Nikolaj N. Strakhov (1828–91), a contemporary Russian critic and publicist.

12. Interestingly enough, another parodistic figure in Dostoevsky, Stepan Trofimovich Verkhovenskij is also a "sponger." In *The Possessed* the shift that occurs on the character level is accompanied by a shift of setting: Russia—Petersburg—a county town. —*J.T.*

13. *The Friend of the Family*, trans. Constance Garnett (New York, 1923), pp. 14, 4; page citations in text refer to this edition.

14. Gogol, see *Vybrannye mesta iz perepiski z druz'jami* [Selected passages from correspondence with friends], *Polnoe sobranie sochinenij* [Complete works] (Moscow, 1952), 8:261.

15. A St. Petersburg satirical weekly that flourished between 1908 and 1914.

16. In an earlier section of this study Tynjanov argues that, in contradistinction to Gogolian "types," the Dostoevsky characters are marked by complexity that often becomes a matter of unresolvable inner conflicts or contradictions.

ing lives of the saints and says ruefully that ordinary good deeds are not enough—one ought to give everything away to beggars and live happily in poverty." Moreover, Foma's vanity is a literary one. "Who knows, maybe this monstrously inflated vanity is only a false, initially distorted sense of personal dignity, first outraged, perhaps, in childhood by oppression, poverty, filth.[17] . . . But I have said that Foma Fomich was an exception to the general rule. He had been a literary man, slighted and unrecognized, and literature is capable of ruining men very different from Foma Fomich, naturally when it is not crowned with success." [p. 10].

Much of the material detail used in describing Foma Opiskin can be traced back to Gogol's biography. Though in 1859 first-hand reports about him were still scarce, some of his characteristics documented in later memoirs were already widely known. Berg recalls: "It is hard to imagine a more spoiled and more demanding writer than Gogol was at the time. His Moscow friends, or, more exactly, people dancing attendance upon him—it seems that Gogol never had a real friend—treated him with extraordinary reverence. During every visit of his in Moscow he would find in one of their homes everything he needed for a quiet and comfortable existence: his favorite dishes, complete privacy, and a maid ready to cater to his slightest whim. Even the host's close acquaintances were expected to know how to behave should they happen to meet him and have a chance to address him."[18] Dostoevsky's novel offers a close counterpart of the above: Foma is being fussed over: "Tea, only plenty of sugar in it, sister! . . . Foma Fomich likes plenty of sugar in his tea after his nap" [p. 77]. Foma's comfort and privacy are jealously guarded: " 'He is writing!' he [the narrator's uncle] would whisper, walking on tiptoe, though he was two rooms away from Foma's study" [p. 14]. A special man is assigned to Foma, and the uncle carefully instructs his nephew as to how he should comport himself "if he meets him." See also the description of Foma's quarters: "The great man was surrounded by perfect comfort" and so on [p. 159]. Foma's bedroom in the Rostanev family is a replica of Gogol's at the Aksakovs.

17. See Gogol: "In my dealings with people there was much that was repellent. . . . This was due in part to petty vanity, found only among those of us who have risen out of filth and feel that they have a right to look down on others" —J.T.

18. The above is drawn from a memoir by N. V. Berg, published in the journal *Russkaja starina* [Russian antiquity] 5 (1872).

Foma's external appearance also seems to be copied from Gogol's. "Gavrila had been right in saying that he was an ugly little man. Foma was short, with light eyebrows and eyelashes[19] and grizzled hair, with a hooked nose and little wrinkles all over his face. . . . To my surprise he made his appearance in a dressing gown, of a foreign cut, it's true but still a dressing gown" [p. 77]. "Foma Fomich was sitting in a comfortable armchair, wearing some sort of long coat that reached to his heels,[20] yet he wore no cravat" [p. 159]. *The Friend of a Family* abounds in more or less explicit hints at Foma Opiskin's prototype: "He had a rather singular nose." (In one of his sermons Foma actually mentions Gogol's name.) The parallel is suggested early in the novel: "I have myself heard Foma saying after he had become the absolute monarch and oracle of the household: 'I am not going to stay here long,' he would say sometimes with mysterious impressiveness. 'This is not a proper place for me. I will look around, I will settle you all, I will direct you, teach you, and then goodbye: to Moscow to edit a review! Thirty thousand people will assemble every month to hear my lectures. My name will be famous—and then—woe to my enemies!' " [p. 10]. Thirty thousand people attending Foma's lectures: this, of course, is Khlestakov's thirty-five-thousand couriers or else an echo of Gogol's unsuccessful academic career.[21]

But while waiting to become famous the genius insisted upon immediate recognition in substantial form. It is always pleasant to receive payment in advance, and in this case it was particularly so. I know that he seriously assured my uncle that some great work lay before him, Foma, in the future—a work for which he was summoned into the. world and to the accomplishment of which he was urged by some sort of person with wings who appeared to him at night or something of that kind. This great work was to write a profound book of an inspirational nature that would cause a general earthquake and shake Russia to its foundations. And when all Russia was staggered he, Foma,

---

19. In a letter to A. S. Danilevskij, Gogol described himself as "stocky and insignificant looking"; "Gogol was blondish," S. Aksakov.—*J.T.*

20. See S. Aksakov on Gogol's attire: "a jacket that looked like a coat." —*J.T.*

21. Reference to Khlestakov's extravagantly boastful soliloquy in act 3 of *The Inspector General*, and to Gogol's one-year stand as a lecturer in world history at the University of St. Petersburg. This pedagogical episode ended in a fiasco.

spurning glory, would retire to a monastery and pray day and
night in the catacombs of Kiev for the happiness of the Fatherland. [Pp. 10–11]

Gogol's extravagant hopes concerning the impact of his *Correspondence with Friends* are a matter of record. "A time is approaching," he wrote [in October 1846] "when everything will
become clear." "Publication of this book is important for me and
for others: in a word, it is necessary for common weal. This is what
my heart and the extraordinary divine grace tell me."[22] By the
same token, "he would retire to a monastery" is an allusion to
Gogol's 1848 voyage to the Holy Land: "Before the tomb of Our
Lord will I pray for all my compatriots, not excepting one among
them" ("Testament").[23] Dostoevsky spoke about this testament
as early as 1846: "He claims that never again will he pick up his
pen, for his task is to pray," and so forth. The reference to "a general earthquake" may be a parody of Gogol's letter about Jazykov's
poem "Earthquake": "You will find the right words, the right expressions; fire, not words, will fly from your lips, as they did from
the prophets of old. . . . You will lead the true Russian into battle against despondency, you will raise him above the terrors
and tremors of the earth as you raised the poet in your 'Earthquake'!" [*Correspondence with Friends*, pp. 280–81].

Foma Fomich is actively concerned with the peasant question.
No wonder among his posthumous works was found "a meaningless disquisition on the significance and characteristics of the
Russian peasant and how he should be handled" [p. 159]. He
also writes of "productive forces of some sort. . . . Let us talk with
peasants about farming, though he himself could not tell oats
from wheat; after sweetly dwelling on the obligations of the peasant toward his master, after touching lightly on electricity and the
division of labor, subjects of which, I need hardly say, he knew
nothing, after explaining to his audience how the earth went round
the sun, and finally, having moved himself to tears by his own eloquence, he started telling about the ministers. I understood [him].

---

22. "Pis'ma" (Letters), *Polnoe sobranie sochinenij*, 13:112.

23. Actually, the quote is drawn not from "Testament," which constitutes
the first chapter of *Correspondence with Friends*, but from an introduction to
that epistolary tract. (*Polnoe sobranie sochinenij*, 8:218.)

... And the peasants always listened to Foma Fomich with cringing respect" [p. 14].

Foma's farewell sermon elaborates the main thesis of Gogol's epistle in *Correspondence with Friends,* "The Russian Landowner." "You are a landowner," orates Opiskin, "you ought to shine like a diamond in your estate. . . . And so remember you are a landowner," Foma went on. "Do not imagine that repose and sensuality are the destined vocation of the landowning clan. Fatal thought! Not repose, but zealous work, zealous toward God, toward your sovereign, and toward your country! Hard work, hard work is the duty of the landowner, he should work as hard as the poorest of his peasants!" [p. 168].

And now for Gogol: "Shoulder the job of the landowner as it ought to be shouldered in the proper, lawful sense. . . . God will make you answer if you should change this rank for another, because everyone must serve God in his place" [p. 322]. "And you, who have not hitherto served zealously in any special career, will deliver such service to the state in your rank of landowner as no other great official has delivered" [p. 328]. "Be a patriarch, the inceptor of everything, the vanguard of all things . . . and you should dine together with them [peasants], and go out to work with them, and in the work you should be the vanguard, inciting everyone to work robustly" [p. 324].

Foma's pronouncements on literature that follow in the wake of his meanderings on the "dances of the Russian people" parody Gogol's letter "Subjects for a Lyric Poet of the Present Time," and in part another epistle, "On the Theater, on the One-sided View Toward the Theater, on One-sidedness in General."

Foma goes on:

> I wonder, Pavel Semënovich, what all our contemporary writers, poets, scholars, and thinkers are about? How is it they pay no attention to what songs are being sung by the Russian people and to what songs they are dancing? What have *the Pushkins, the Lermontovs, the Borozdins*[24] been about all this time? I wonder at them, the people dance the Kamarinsky, the apotheosis of drunkenness, while they sing of forget-me-nots. Why do

---

24. Probably a reference to Ivan Petrovich Borozdin (1803–88), an obscure lyrical poet. Foma Opiskin's mentioning Borozdin alongside Pushkin and Lermontov is a commentary on his sense of literary values.

not they write poems of *a more moral tone* for popular use, why don't they fling aside their forget-me-nots? It's a social question. Let them depict a peasant, but *a peasant made genteel* so to say, a villager rather than a peasant. Let them paint the *village sage in his simplicity,* maybe even in his bark shoes—I don't object to that—but brimming over with virtues that—I make bold to say—some overlauded Alexander of Macedon may envy. I know Russia and Russia knows me, that it why I say this. Let them portray that peasant, weighed down maybe with a family, with gray hair, in a stuffy hut, hungry too, maybe, but contented, not repining but *blessing his poverty* and indifferent to the rich man's gold. Let indeed on this occasion the virtues of the peasant be united with the virtues of his master, perhaps a grand gentleman. The villager and the grand gentleman so widely separated on the social scale are made one at last in virtue—that is an exalted thought! [P. 81]

Foma's "forget-me-nots" are clearly reminiscent of Gogol's expression "poetic playthings" ("On the Theater," etc.). The motif of the poor man versus the magnate is also found in Gogol's tract: "In a triumphal hymn, exalt the unknown toiler who, to the honor of the lofty Russian race, can be found among the boldest bribe-takers. . . . Exalt him and his family, and his noble wife who would rather wear her old-fashioned bonnet and become a butt of mockery than allow her husband to be unjust and base. Portray their *beautiful poverty* so that, it shines like a holy thing, before our eyes, so that *each of us may wish to be poor* himself" ("Subjects for a Lyric Poet of the Present Time").

Foma's sermon about suffering as a path to virtue contains a direct reference to Gogol: "For myself, I will only say that misfortune is, perhaps. the mother of virtue. That, I believe, was said by Gogol, a frivolous writer, but one from whom one may sometimes glean fruitful thoughts. Exile is a misfortune. I shall wander like a pilgrim with my staff over the face of the earth, and who knows?—perchance my troubles will make me more righteous yet? That thought is the only consolation left me" [p. 188].

Similarly in Gogol ("On Helping the Poor"): "Misfortune softens a man; his nature then becomes more sensitive and more accessible to the understanding of subjects beyond the conception of a man in his everyday condition." ". . . the holy and profound purport of misfortune."

II

An important aspect of Foma Opiskin's speechifying is its style. Foma calls attention to it himself. Citing him, the narrator's uncle maintains that "there is positively something musical in [his] language." Yet one of the ingredients of this exalted diction are vernacular expressions such as "pug-dog," "clod," "Dutch-faced fool," and the like.

Clearly, we deal here with a system, a design. "I called him a Dutch-faced fool with intention, Pavel Semënovich," he observed. "And speaking generally, you know, I see no necessity for softening my expressions. The truth should be the truth. And however you cover up filth it will still remain filth. Why trouble to soften it? It's deceiving oneself and others." "You know as much about art—if you will excuse my saying so, Colonel—as a bull about beef! That's harsh and rude, I admit: anyway, it is *straightforward and just*. You won't hear it from your flatterers, Colonel." "Why did you not wring my neck at the very beginning like a cock's, because he, well for instance, simply because he doesn't lay eggs? Yes, that's just it! I stick to that comparison, Colonel, though it is taken from rustic life and recalls the *trivial tone of modern literature*."

Correspondence with Friends is also a mixture of "high" style with expressions like "unwashed mug," "scoundrel," etc. The mingling was a deliberate one. In a letter [15 April 1847] to a friend Gogol justified it thus: "I included almost by design a number of passages whose aggressiveness was likely to provoke."[25]

The high style is maintained throughout. In Foma's farewell sermons—like in Gogol's preaching—instructions regarding management of the estate blend stylistically with moral directives. "Your hay on the Harinsky waste has not been cut yet. Do not be too late with it; mow it and mow it quickly. That is my advice. . . . It is a pity that you have sown the spring corn so late; it's amazing how late you have been in sowing the spring corn." The tone of the above is not unlike that of Gogol's much-quoted letter to his former classmate Danilevskij [7 August 1841]: "But hearken. . . . now you must hearken to my word, for it has a double power over you—woe to one who will refuse to hearken to my word!. . . .

25. *Polnoe sobranie sochinenij*, 13:278.

Submit and busy yourself for a year, just one year, with your estate. . . . And thus carry out this request of mine unquestioningly and obediently."

Dostoevsky parodies here not only the late Gogol's overall rhetorical thrust but also his individual stylistic devices: "What were you like before I came? But now I have dropped into your soul a spark of that heavenly fire that is glowing there now. Did I drop a spark of heavenly fire that is glowing there now? Did I drop a spark of heavenly fire or not? Answer. Did I drop a spark or did I not?" [p. 15].

"Well, don't you feel now," the torturer went on, "that your heart is suddenly lighter, as though as angel had flown into your soul? Do you feel the presence of that angel? Answer!" [p. 106].

Let us shift to Gogol: "Have I gone completely out of my mind? . . . And what led you to the conclusion that the second volume [of *Dead Souls*] is needed now? Have you actually crawled into my head? Have you grasped the essence of the second volume? Which of us is right? He who already has the second volume in his head or he who does not even know what the second volume is about?" ("The Third Letter *Apropos* of *Dead Souls*").

"Who has told you that their illnesses are incurable? Are you really an omniscient doctor? Why did you not request help of some-one else? Did I not ask you to report everything that goes on in your town? . . . Why have you not done this, especially since . . . you yourself attribute to me a rather uncommon understanding of people? . . . Do you really think that I would not be able to help your incurably ill people?" ("What Is a Governor's Wife?").

In the above instances Dostoevsky's parody rests on bringing together disparate Gogolian mannerisms: images like "the spark of heavenly fire," or an "angel [that] had flown into your soul," are akin to the imagery of *Correspondence with Friends* (for example, the "electric spark of poetic fire" in "The Essence and Distinctive Character of Russian Poetry"). But in Gogol these metaphors are not combined with the syntactical pattern of an interrogative crescendo. In Dostoevsky comedy rests on the incongruity of syntax and semantics.

At times Dostoevsky parodies Gogol's crescendo technique by repeating insistently a single word: "You are vain, immensely vain! . . . You are an egoist and indeed a gloomy egoist. . . . You are coarse, you jar so coarsely upon the human heart, you so egoistically insist upon attention" [p. 106].

Now a passage from Gogol's letter "To A Myopic Friend": "And you are proud; even now you do not want to see anything; you think that all the circumstances of Russia have been revealed to you; you think that no one can teach you anything."[26]

Let us note another striking parallel. Here is Foma Fomich's characteristic outburst. Having browbeaten the narrator's uncle, Colonel Rostanev, and publicly humiliated his favorite, a house serfboy Falalej, the terror of Stepanchikovo rages thus:

> I want to love my fellow man, to love him . . . and they won't let me, they forbid me to love him, they take him from me. Give me, give me my fellow man that I may love him! But where is that fellow man? Where is he hidden? Like Diogenes with his lantern, I have been looking for him all my life and cannot find him; and I cannot love anyone until I find that man. Woe to him who has made me a hater of mankind! I say: give me my fellow man that I may love him and they thrust Falalej upon me! Am I to love Falalej? Do I want to love Falalej? Could I love Falalej, even if I wanted to? No. Why not? Because he is Falalej. Why do I not love humanity? Because all on earth are Falalejs or like Falalej! I don't want Falalej, I hate Falalej, I spit on Falalej, I trample Falalej under my feet. And if I had to choose, I would rather have Asmodeus than Falalej! [P. 189]

Let us now listen to Gogol's "Easter Sunday," and "It Is Necessary to Love Russia." "I cannot embrace this man, he is foul, he is base in spirit, he has besmirched himself by a most dishonorable deed; I will not allow this man to come into my presence. I do not even want to breathe the same air as he; I will go out of my way . . . to avoid him. I cannot live with base and contemptible people— how can I embrace such a man as a brother? . . .

"But how can we love our brothers? How can we love man? The soul yearns to love beauty alone, and poor men are so imperfect, there is so little beauty in them! How shall we do it?"

Foma Opiskin's obsessive repetition of the name "Falalej" is a device often employed by Gogol. Thus, in his eulogy of a contemporary Russian painter we are told that "it is necessary, like Ivanov, to die to all the worldly temptations, to learn like Ivanov,

26. *Correspondence with Friends*, p. 348.

. . . like Ivanov to wear a simple pleated jacket, . . . like Ivanov, to endure all" ["The Historical Painter Ivanov," p. 692].

Opiskin's diatribe achieves remarkable accuracy in parodying Gogolian tautology. The name "Falalej," characteristically, is a meaningful verbal mask. ("Falalej" is reminiscent of "rotozej," Russian for "dumbell.") At the same time the question of the "beautiful man"—that ideal mask in Gogol—is raised by implication and answered in the true Dostoevskian fashion: the beautiful man is the imperfect man.

III

In *The Manor of Stepanchikovo* Dostoevsky draws on all the resources of *verbal* parody. The very vocabulary of *Correspondence with Friends* is parodied here: "Oh, do not put up a monument to me," cried Foma, "do not! I do not need monuments. Raise up a monument to me in your hearts, I want nothing more, nothing, nothing more!" [p. 179]. This sounds very much like the second paragraph of Gogol's "Testament" in *Correspondence with Friends.* "I bequeathe that no monument be raised to me, . . . let the one of my friends to whom I have really been dear erect a different monument to me. . . . Whoever after my death achieves a loftier soul than the one he had during his lifetime will show that he truly loved me and was my friend; only thus will he erect a monument to me" [p. 563]. The only significant difference, which is at the heart of the parodistic effect, is that in Gogol the key term is *pamiatnik* (indigenous Russian for "statue, monument") in Dostoevsky the [French] loanword *monument*. Gogol was among the first Russian prose writers to use for comic effect the device of grafting foreign words upon the Russian text, for instance, "a little *incommodité* in the form of a wart on his right foot." Dostoevesky greatly diversifies this technique. At times it occurs in his works without any comic tinge, for example, "an 'infernal' ["infernalnaja"] woman." The bulk of *Winter Notes on Summer Impressions*[27] is couched in a parodistic lingo, with the Russian words appearing in French transliteration, "outchitel"

27. Dostoevsky's harshly critical West European travelogue, written in 1863.

(*uchitel*, teacher"), "la baboulinka," and vice versa. Dostoevsky is especially apt to use this strategy in a parodistic context: Thus in *The Possessed* Turgenev's "Enough!" becomes Karmazinov's "Merci."[28]

Another device is one of severing the epithet from the noun that it modifies and attaching it to some other word. As quoted above, to Foma Fomich Gogol is "a frivolous writer, but one from whom one can sometimes glean fruitful [literally "grained"] thoughts."

Now this is a direct echo of Gogol: "One marvels at the treasures of our language; every sound here is a gift; everything is *grained* and hard is pearls; now and then the name is still more precious than the thing itself" ("Subjects for a Lyric Poet of the Present Time").

"Grained pearls of language"—"grained language"—"grained thought"—this is how the shift occurs. The epithet ("grained"), bound up with the first element of a metaphor ("pearls of language"), is transferred to the second, which in turn yields to a cognate notion ("thought"). Such a progressive cutting loose smacks of mechanization.

This device of mechanization through repetition is rendered more effective when a phrase is echoed by another party: "I say this uttering a wail of lamentation from my heart, and not in triumphing, not exalting myself over you, as you perhaps imagine.

"But, I am uttering a wail of lamentation from my heart, too, Foma, I assure you" [p. 103].

Once again the recurrent phrase originates with Gogol: "Who knows? Maybe these misfortunes and ordeals that befall you, befall you so as to extract . . . a wail of lamentation from your soul, a wail that would not be heard without these ordeals . . . Everything that matters about your poetry lies in that wail of lamentation from your heart and your genuine thrust toward God" (letter to N.M. Jazykov).[29]

Dostoevsky's heroes often parody each other just as Sancho Panza parodies Don Quixote in his conversations with the latter

---

28. This mawkish piece that the aging writer Karmazinov read at the provincial festival that was soon to degenerate into a pandemonium was a vitriolic parody of Turgenev's lyrical fragment "Enough!"

29. Nikolaj M. Jazykov (1893–1946) was a poet of considerable rhetorical gifts. His best poems had a sonority and verbal magnificence that were greatly appreciated by Gogol. Letter is dated 15 February 1844, in *Polnoe sobranie sochinenij*, 12:261, 263.

(V. Shklovskij). But in Dostoevsky expressions first used by his characters are placed between authorial quotes and become portable parodistic clichés. Thus, Foma Fomich's boast "I know Russia and Russia knows me" recurs without that attribution in *Winter Notes on Summer Impressions.* So too a phrase used by an invalid in *Winter Notes* in speaking of Rousseau, "l'homme de la nature et de la verité," pops up without any reference to Rousseau in *Notes from the Underground.*

Sometimes Dostoevsky borrows entire sequences from *Correspondence with Friends.* Foma's scornful reference to euphemisms—"*Only* a silly *worldly numbskull* can feel the need of such senseless conventions" [p. 78]—echoes a phrase from the "Third Letter *Apropos* of *Dead Souls*": "Such a silly idea could only be formed in a *silly worldly numbskull.*"

IV

The fact that the parodistic tenor of *The Manor of Stepanchikovo* has hitherto escaped the critics' attention is curious, but not unique. Parodies of plots often are artfully concealed. I doubt if anyone would have realized that "Count Nulin"[30] is a parody, had Pushkin not testified explicitly to that effect. One wonders how many works intended as parodies have never been recognized as such. Whenever the parodistic intent fails to register, the meaning of the work changes as does ineluctably the import of any literary work viewed outside its original context. The same thing happens to parody that relies heavily on stylistic detail. Perceived apart from the model that it subverts and that has been forgotten, it loses, inevitably, its parodistic effect. This is closely bound with the question of parody as a comic genre. The comic often accompanies parody, but the former is not coextensive with the latter. Thus the parodistic tenor of the work may fade away while its comic thrust endures. The essence of parody lies in a dialectical play with the device. If a parody of tragedy results in a comedy, a comedy parodied may turn out to be a tragedy.

30. See "Pushkin's Path to Prose" above, n. 30.

The Passion of Aleksandr Blok

VIKTOR ZHIRMUNSKIJ

I

Blok's path is one of coming to know life through love. Its outer boundaries are marked by the religious lyrics "Verses about the Beautiful Lady" on the one hand, and by the gypsy motifs of the poet's last years on the other.[1] Vladimir Solov'ëv appears as the poet's first teacher and Apollon Grigor'ev as his literary fellow-traveler and friend late in life.[2] The changes in the symbolic imagery embodying the love object in Blok's poetry correspond to the successive stages of this inner experience.

Blok's early lyrical poetry is full of romantic presentiments of a first, as yet enigmatic, love. The predominant imagery is that of evening twilight, pale blue mists, transparent dawns, wisps of the azure sky glimpsed through spring clouds—and the first, indistinct summons of the infinite and the mysterious, which had penetrated the poet's soul along with the languor of spring and the expectation of the dawn ("Ante Lucem"):[3]

> Twilight, the twilight of spring,
> Gelid the waves at my feet,
> Hopes not of this world in my heart,
> Waves that run up on the sands.
>
> Echoes, a faraway song,
> But I'm unable to make them out.

This essay, translated here by Stephen Rudy, first appeared as a section of a short study *Poezija Aleksandra Bloka* [The poetry of Alexander Blok], 1921, later reprinted in V. Zhirmunskij, *Voprosy teorii literatury* [Problems of literary theory] (Leningrad, 1928).

1. See pp. 125–26 below.
2. Vladimir Solov'ëv (1853–1900), an eminent philosopher, theologian, and poet. His mystical teachings, especially the myth of Sophia the Divine Wisdom, exerted a powerful influence on the young Blok. Apollon Grigor'ev (1822–64) was a prolific mid-nineteenth-century critic and a minor but gifted poet. It is Grigor'ev's verse, "inspired by his intimacy with the gypsy choruses" (D. S. Mirsky) that attracted Blok during his late period.
3. The title of the first collection of poems (1898–1900) in Blok's *First Book*.

> There, on the opposite shore,
> Lonely, a soul breaks into tears . . .[4]

The first vision of romantic love is the image of the unworldly Beloved. The loved one appears to the poet in a celestial, mysterious radiance: she is the "Beautiful Lady," the "Tsarevna-Bride," the "Mysterious Maiden of the Sunset," the "Mistress of the Universe," the "Majestic Eternal Wife." The poet calls her (always with capital letters) "Radiant," "Luminous," "Golden-Haired," "Unattainable," "Holy." He is the knightly troubadour who is bent in submissive expectation before the image of the Madonna, guarding the "covenant of serving the Unattainable One":

> The fickle shades of day quicken away.
> The churchbell's call is sharp and clear.
> The churchsteps are illuminated bright,
> Their stone alive—awaiting your footfall.
>
> You'll pass through here, touch the cold stone
> Attired in the awful sacredness of ages,
> And, perhaps, you'll let fall a single spring flower
> Here, in these shadows, by the icons grave . . .
>
> [Ss, 1: 156]

In his early verses Blok is the disciple of Vladimir Solov'ëv, the poet of the "eternal feminine," of the religious principle of love. The "Verses about the Beautiful Lady" are filled with esoteric expectation of the actual appearance of the eternal feminine, of the descent of divine love. The eschatological yearnings (for example, of Andrej Belyj, Merezhkovskij, and others) that at the turn of the century had spurred the resurgence of the mystical strain in Russian poetry take on here the aspect of some new and intensely personal revelation through love:

> All visions are so fleeting—
> Shall I believe in them?
> But perhaps I am loved,
> Though accidental, poor, mortal,
> By the Mistress of the Universe,
> By Beauty unutterable.
>
> [Ss, 1: 156]

---

4. Blok, *Sobranie sochinenij* [Collected works] (Moscow–Leningrad, 1960), 1:119. Hereafter cited in text as *Ss*.

These mystical presentiments of the manifestation of the divine
in love ("theophany") ally Blok's verse not only with the lyrical
poetry of Vladimir Solov'ëv, but—through Solov'ëv and perhaps
also directly—with "Hymns to the Night" of the German romantic
poet Novalis and with Dante's *La Vita Nuova*. But this faith in
the reality of the vision that has appeared to the poet is accompanied in Blok by a discordant note of doubt and fear. We find
this expression of an all too human weakness, of powerlessness
before a wondrous gift, in the opening poem of the first collection.
The possibility of betraying the exalted Beloved, indeed, the
entire further development of the poet is prefigured thus:

> I have forebodings of Thee. Time is going—
> I fear for all that in Thy face I see.
>
> The sky's aflame, intolerably glowing;
> Silent, I wait in love and agony.
>
> **The sky's aflame, draws near Thy apparition,**
> **But it is strange. Thy look will change on Thee.**
>
> And in me Thou dost wake a bold suspicion—
> Thy face will change from what it used to be.
>
> How I shall fall! how sorrowful and lowly,
> Unmastered all my mortal fantasy!
>
> The sky's aflame, draws near Thy splendor holy,
> But it is strange. Thy look will change on Thee.[5]
>
> > [*Ss*, 1: 94]

"Unexpected Joy," the second collection of poems (which
was later included in Blok's second volume), develops under the
sign of this duality. The poet is at the "crossroads."[6] The image
of the Beloved recedes into the past and becomes shrouded in
fog. The poet leaves the world of mysterious presentiments and
visions and enters life on earth. Characteristically "modern"
motifs begin to appear in his poems: the city at night, flooded
with electric light, the noise of restaurants at night, and the faces
of earthly women. He seeks in this life reflections of the celestial
vision and catches vague glimpses of another, "more real" reality
in it:

5. This translation is drawn from C. M. Bowra, *A Book of Russian Verse*
(London, 1943), p. 97.
6. The title of the third collection of Blok's poems (1902–04).

> In taverns, on corners, winding lanes,
> Trapped in an electrical daydream
> I sought the infinitely beautiful ones,
> Those forever in love with fame . . .
>
> [Ss, 2: 159]

A woman encountered by chance in the city streets at night
is transformed into the mysterious Stranger, in whose features
the poet sees his only Beloved:

> And every evening, at the appointed hour,
> (Or do I only dream this?)
> A girlish figure, swathed in silks,
> Moves in the misty window.
>
> And slowly, passing amongst the drunkards,
> Always unaccompanied, alone,
> Breathing perfume and mists,
> She takes a seat by the window.
>
> And her resilient silks
> And her hat with funereal plumes
> And her narrow hand all covered in rings
> Are redolent of ancient legends . . .
>
> [Ss, 2: 186]

At this stage in the development of the poet's romantic consciousness we encounter for the first time that dualistic perception of life that found its most complete expression in the lyrical
drama "The Stranger." Each of Blok's poems now unfolds on two
different planes: the first is that of everyday, actual "reality";
the second is that of the "super-real," in which the only events
important and of interest to the poet, spiritual events, occur. Thus,
one of Blok's most memorable poems, "In the Restaurant,"[7] tells
of a chance and, on the surface, insignificant encounter. The poet
sees a woman he does not know in a suburban restaurant, sends
her a rose, meets her indignant look with a bold gaze, and so on.
But then, suddenly, this insignificant event acquires a profound
meaning on another plane, when behind the features of the unknown woman there appears to the poet a vision of his one and

7. For more detail see my article, "Two Tendencies of Contemporary Lyric
Poetry" (Dva techenija v sovremennej lirike) [English translation by J. Glad
in *Russian Literature Triquarterly*, no. 4 (Fall 1972): 175–180]. —V.Z.

only Beloved, whom his soul once glimpsed in a dream, the image
of the mysterious Stranger:

> You tore away like a frightened bird,
> You passed—light as my dream . . .
> And perfumes sighed, lashes slumbered,
> Anxiously silks began to whisper . . .
>
> [Ss, 3: 25]

This is why the account of a "meeting in a restaurant" begins
with agitated words that underscore emphatically its exceptional
significance: *"Never shall I forget* / (Whether that evening was
or not) . . . ." It is also why the poet's courtship of the unknown
lady is set off by a grand, dramatic gesture: "I sent you a single
black rose in a goblet / of Aÿ,[8] that was gold as the sky . . ." [Ss,
3: 25].

The romantic hovering between two worlds known to us from
Hoffmann's *Kunstmärchen*,[9] has its own artistic laws. From the
heights of mystic inspiration earthly reality seems illusory, un-
real; romantic irony distorts it into a hideous grotesque. That is
what happens in the description of the summer resort in the en-
virons of St. Petersburg, with which the ballad "The Stranger"
opens, or in the description of the tavern and of the literary salon
in the lyric drama of the same title:

> . . . Far off, above the dust of lanes,
> Above the boredom of cottages,
> The gilded sign of a bakery glimmers faintly,
> And the cry of a child rings out.
> . . . .
> Above the lake, the rowlocks scrape,
> And a woman's screech rings out,
> While in the sky, inured to everything,
> The moon's disc senselessly grimaces.
>
> [Ss, 2: 185]

---

8. Aÿ is a champagne from the Marne region.

9. Literally, the artistic fairy tale. This genre, which looms large in the work
of such German romantics as Ludwig Tieck and E. T. A. Hoffmann, is a vehicle
for a multidimensional view of reality, with the traditional formulas of the
folk/ fairy tale serving as alibis for the intrusion of the marvelous and the fantastic
upon a workaday, familiar world.

On the other hand, from the viewpoint of common, everyday experience, the poet's mystical insight is subject to doubt, and his vision of the Stranger seems only a poetic illusion, a play of the imagination, or perhaps, a dream vision (compare such expressions, characteristic of the poet's precarious sense of reality: "Or do I only *dream* this?" "You passed, light as my *dream*," "whether it was or not, that evening"). The poet himself half begins to regard his visions as having been induced by dreams or drunken delirium:

> Out of the crystal fog,
> Out of the unseen *dream*,
> Someone's image, someone strange . . .
> (*In the restaurant*, in a private room,
> *Over a bottle of wine*) . . .
>
> [Ss, 3: 11]

In the ballad "The Stranger" and in the lyric drama of the same title the miraculous vision of the one and only Beloved is set in the ambience of a drinking house, and it is induced by the intoxication gradually overcoming the poet:

> And every evening my only friend
> Is mirrored in my wine glass
> And, like myself, is subdued and dazed
> By the tart and mysterious liquor . . .
>
> [Ss, 2: 185]

As in the stories of Hoffmann and Edgar Allan Poe, the features of the celestial Beloved are seen through the midst of the poet's growing intoxication, which obliterates the usual boundaries of daily consciousness:

> . . . And the drooping ostrich plumes
> Wave in my brain,
> And blue fathomless eyes
> Flower on a distant shore . . .

But for the romantic poet intoxication has merely raised the curtain of consciousness, has merely set ajar the door leading from the world of illusions into the world of higher reality: "You are right, you drunken monster; / I know: truth lies in wine" [Ss, 2: 186].

Beginning with the period to which the poems about the "Stranger" belong, one can note certain new facts in Blok's poetic development that the poet himself evaluates from some higher point of view, as a religious sin, a defection or betrayal of the adolescent ideal of eternal love. Yet it is at this time that Blok's work gradually outgrows its prayerlike immobility, its contemplative purity, and is enriched by the complex, contradictory, and chaotic content of earthly life with its sufferings and sins. It is the period of Blok's greatest poetic accomplishments. The basic theme of Blok's new verses (the collection "The Earth in Snow," which was included in the second volume) is the poet's entrance into life, his merging with the creative, superabundant element of life through the medium of vivid and passionate love experience:

> O Spring without end, without limit—
> Endless and limitless dream!
> I accept and acknowledge you, Life!
> I salute you with the clang of my shield!
> . . . .
> At the threshold I meet you—
> With wild wind in your serpent-coiled curls
> With the inscrutable name of a god
> On your cold and tightly closed lips . . .
>
> [*Ss*, 2: 272]

The basic aspiration of the poet's soul has remained essentially unchanged: there is the same expectation of a miracle, the same quest of the infinite that we observed in the poems of his youth. Only the object of these romantic yearnings has changed; they are no longer directed toward the pure and chaste love for the celestial Beloved, but rather toward the caresses of an earthly lover—sinful and passionate. The image of the exalted Beloved now vanishes entirely only to yield to the Snow Maiden, Faina, Valentina, Carmen—figures marking the furthest stages in the history of romantic love:

> They were many. But by one
> Feature did I bring them all together,
> By beauty alone, by mad beauty,
> Whose name is passion and my life . . .
>
> [*Ss*, 3: 160]

These figures have only one thing in common: in the glow of amorous passion, in the kisses and embraces of these worldly lovers, the poet seeks momentary ecstasy, self-forgetfulness, rapture. He reaches toward supreme emotional intensity as a way of transcending the boundaries of ordinary experience, of entering the world of inspiration and delirium, of mystical intoxication.

> Such joy to enfold in my arms your
> Cold shoulders, thus sheltered from wind:
> You think it is a tender caress,
> I know it is rebellious rapture!
>
> Like candles at night, your bright eyes
> Glimmer, and greedily I listen—
> A terrible tale begins rustling,
> The sidereal boundary heaves . . .

[Ss, 2: 264]

The entire "landscape of the soul" changes: instead of the transparent spring dawns and the golden-tinged azure that provided the backdrop for the celestial Beloved in Blok's early poems, we find a "ringing" blizzard, a "turbulent wind" that "singes" the face, "the conflagration of the white-winged snowstorm," a troika run amok, carrying the poet and his love away over the dark, open "abysses," into the "snowy night": "And the blue wind strolls above your sable furs."

The boundlessness of love ecstasy lends Blok's lyrics of this period ("The Earth in Snow," "Night Hours") a boldness and irrationality of design never before encountered in Russian poetry. One almost feels the presence of the primeval chaos of creation, of cosmic forces unleashed, descending upon the poet from the "terrible" night world and inundating the circumscribed realm of daytime consciousness.

> In a light heart—passion and insouciance
> As if a signal had been given me from the sea.
> Over the bottomless gulf into eternity,
> Breathless, a charger speeds.
>
> The snowy wind, your breath,
> My drunken lips . . .
> Valentina, star, dream!
> How your nightingales sing! . . .

> Terrible world! Too narrow for the heart!
> Filled with the delirium of your kisses,
> The dark gloom of gypsy songs,
> The hurried flight of comets!

> [*Ss*, 3: 162]

The love lyrics of Blok's last period represent a movement away from Vladimir Solov'ëv to Apollon Grigor'ev and the gypsy romance. Yet it should be clear from the foregoing that what is at work here is not simply a "canonization of the gypsy song," in other words of an inferior literary branch with its own distinctive themes, which had remained hitherto beyond the pale of "high" poetry.[10] Rather, it is a complex mediation of these motifs, through the resources of romanticism and of a mystical vision of life. Blok was drawn to the gypsy song because he sensed in it an elemental sweep of passion, an untrammeled breadth of revelry and daring. But he was even more responsive to those notes of spiritual frenzy that Apollon Grigor'ev had first overheard in the gypsy choruses (see his poems "The Struggle," "Improvisations of a Wandering Romantic")[11] and that had suggested to Dostoevsky the scene of Dmitrij's orgy with Grushen'ka at Mokroe in *The Brothers Karamazov*. The strange lure of dark passion, the mystical gusts and the flights of inspiration blend with a feeling of sin and suffering, of anguish and disarray. But in this very sin and suffering, in the very image of the sinful beloved there is something irresistibly appealing, a promise of yet unknown, impossible delights, of a reaching beyond the mundane, the everyday:

> Unfaithful one, o cunning one,
> Insidious, dance on!
> And be forever poison to
> My dissipated soul!

> I'll lose my mind, my mind I'll lose
> I'll madly rave, in love,

---

10. This is a mild dig at Viktor Shklovskij and his pet concept of the "canonization of the inferior branch," or periodic reinvigoration of literature by drawing upon motifs and devices of subliterary genres (see especially Viktor Shklovskij, *Rozanov* [Petrograd, 1921]).

11. The speaker in both these poems appears to be in a grip of a debilitating, indeed self-destructive passion.

That you're all night, that you're all gloom,
That you're all drunken too . . .

That you have torn from me my soul,
You've poisoned it all through,
That you I sing, I sing of you,
And numberless my songs!

[Ss, 2: 281]

In his last poems, which were included in the second and third (posthumous) editions of the third volume, Blok is a poet of wild, drunken, gypsy love and of an increasingly oppressive hangover. The enraptured flights of his earlier passionate verses give way to the increasingly oppressive consciousness of spiritual disintegration and fall. Fall and sin are revealed to the poet in the fullness of their terrifying religious aspect as "satanic depth":

I will not hide myself from you,
Look closely at me:
I stand among charred ruins,
Scorched by tongues
Of netherworldly flame . . .

[Ss, 3: 84]

The awareness of spiritual abasement, of sin and fall, saturate all Blok's last poems (see especially "Humiliation," "Black Blood"—in general, the sections "The Terrible World" and "Retribution"), but in this very fall there are mystically rapturous flights that lend the poet's intoxication a cosmic thrust:

Your very name sounds despicable to me,
But when you screw up your eyes,
I hear—the foaming current howls,
The storm approaches from the desert . . .

[Ss, 3: 55]

The image of the celestial Beloved recurs in retrospection ("Do you remember first love, and dawns, dawns, dawns?"), but now it chastizes the "apostate" and threatens imminent "retribution" or belated and useless "repentance" ("The Steps of the Commander"):

What price your repellent freedom
Now that you've known fear, Don Juan?

. . . .

> What are the sounds of bliss to a betrayer?
> Life's instances have been numbered . . .
>
> [*Ss*, 3: 80]

From the depths of his fall the poet again raises a wail of lamentation to the childhood vision of pure and chaste love ("O, moments of kisses not for sale! / O, caresses of unbought maidens!"). The poet's penitential, autobiographical verses project the image of the one and only Beloved:

> The days flew by, whirling in a cursed swarm,
> Wine and passion tore my life asunder . . .
> And suddenly I recollected you standing by the altar,
> I called to you, as if calling to my youth.
>
> I called to you, but you refused to turn your head,
> I wept real tears, but you refused to condescend.
> You sadly muffled yourself in a light blue cloak
> And went out from the house into the damp night . . .
>
> [*Ss*, 3: 64]

But these recollections remain too distant to be of any use in the present. The poet speaks more and more frequently about life as "empty," "needlessly lived to the end," "oppressive and insane," "insane and fathomless." "And it's become mercilessly clear— / Life has finished and gone."

Hopeless emptiness and ennui, like a dull hangover, replace the unrestrained raptures and sufferings of past years. The "gray morning" dawns, only to be followed by "Cruel day, day of iron."

> O, how rich I was once upon a time,
> And all of it—not worth a kopeck coin,
> Enmity, love, fame, and gold,
> And above all—mortal anguish . . .
>
> [*Ss*, 3: 194]

Aversion to the past and despair of the future, and in the present the inescapable grief and ennui, the acedia, or spiritual sloth, well known to the ancient religious writers—or, to use more recent if less significant analogies, Weltschmerz or Baudelairean Spleen—gradually take possession of the poet. He suffers from a metaphysical sickness of the soul, "the ailment mysteriously

and steadily consuming me" (see particularly "Dances of Death,"
"The Life of My Friend," in the cycle Terrible World"):

> Night, a street, a lamp, a druggist's shop,
> A meaningless and dullish light.
> Even if you live another quarter century—
> Everything will be like this. There's no way out.
>
> You'll die—and start again from the beginning,
> And everything will be repeated as of old:
> The night, the icy ripples on the channel,
> The druggist's shop, the street, the lamp.

[Ss, 3: 37]

Perhaps the most profound expression of this final phase in the
development of the romantic poet is to be found in the poem
"To the Muse," which significantly opens volume 3 of Blok's
verse. Here the Muse and the Beloved merge in one image, and
the intimate and personal aspects of love experience expand into
a suprapersonal perspective on the meaning of life sought through
love. In the depth and power of his tragic sense of life Blok approaches here the most mature poems of Tjutchev, dedicated
as they are to his tragic "last love":[12]

> In your hidden melodies
> There are fatal tidings of doom.
> There is a curse of sacred covenants,
> A profanation of happiness.
>
> And such an alluring force
> That I am ready to reiterate the rumor
> That you have brought the angels down to earth,
> With the enticements of your beauty.
>
> . . . .
> I do not know why, at daybreak,
> In the hour when no strength was left to me
> I did not perish, but observed your countenance
> And begged for your consolations.
>
> . . . .
> And your terrible caresses

12. The title of a poignant 1854 lyric by Fëdor Tjutchev, a distinguished
nineteenth-century lyric poet. Its final lines are: "Oh! you, last love! /You are
both bliss and hopelessness!"

> Were more treacherous than the northern night
> And more intoxicating than golden Aÿ,
> And briefer than a gypsy's love . . .
>
> And there was a fatal joy
> In trampling on things held sacred,
> And this passion, bitter as wormwood,
> Was a frenzied delight for the heart.

$$[Ss, 3: 7–8]$$

What is the source of the tragic in this poem, of the most profound disillusionment and despair in the very moment of amorous passion? What one hears in these lines is not the simple, ordinary pangs of love, but a spiritual torment, a religious sickness of particular acuity. The "terrible caresses" of the Beloved (let us also recall: the "terrible tale," the "terrible world," "terrible embraces"), the "trampling on things held sacred," beauty not as joy, but as a curse ("the whole curse of your beauty")[13]—all of this reveals to us a particular realm of experience, the nature of which has been most clearly stated in the works of Dostoevsky:

Beauty—this is a terrible and awful thing! Terrible because it is indefinable, and it cannot be defined because God has posed only enigmas. Here all shores meet, here all contradictions live together. I, brother, am very uneducated, but I have thought much about this. There are fearfully many mysteries! Too many enigmas oppress man on earth. Solve them as you will, you will not emerge dry from the water. Beauty! Here I cannot bear the fact that a man, a man even with a lofty heart and with a lofty mind begins with the ideal of the Madonna, yet ends with the ideal of Sodom. What's even more awful is that the person who, though already with the ideal of Sodom in his soul, yet does not deny the ideal of the Madonna, and his heart glows with it, and truly glows as in his youthful, sinless years. No, man is broad, far too broad, I would narrow him. The devil only knows what it is all about! What to the mind is ignominious, is nothing but beauty to the heart. Is there beauty in Sodom? Rest assured that it is to be found in Sodom for the overwhelming majority of people—did you know this secret or not?

---

13. "The Terrible World" (*strashnyj mir*) is the title of one of Blok's later lyrical collections (1909–16). The other two phrases are drawn from the poem "To the Muse" (1912), which opens the collection.

What is awful is that beauty is not only terrible, but also a mysterious thing. Here the devil struggles with God, but the field
of battle is the heart of men.[14]

These words of Dostoevsky's contain the best interpretation
of Alexander Blok's tragic poetry. What was it that led the poet
of the Beautiful Lady down such paths, what brought him from
"the ideal of the Madonna" to the "ideal of Sodom"? A mystical
craving for the infinite, the quest of an unprecedented intensity
of experience, of moments of ecstasy which, even if leading to
sin and suffering, harbor or promise that *goût de l'Infini* without
which everyday life becomes monotonous and vapid in its simple
and modest joys and sufferings. Thus, as was already indicated,
the chaste adolescent poet's yearning for the appearance of the
"Tsarevna-Bride" can be seen to stem from the same aspiration
that was to serve as the impetus for the amorous and sinful passion of his last years. "Is there beauty in Sodom?" In both his
early and late poetry the romantic poet refuses to settle for anything less than infinite happiness.

> What is happiness? The evening cool,
> In the darkening garden, in remote corners of the woods?
> Or the gloomy, wanton delights
> Of wine, passions, the soul's perdition?

> [Ss, 3: 41]

This spiritual maximalism of the romantic individualist arises
from the feeling of the infinity of man's soul, of its inability to be
content with anything finite and limited. The soul, poisoned by
limitless desires, seeks infinite experiences that alone are capable
of satiating its mystical hunger. Limitless demands on life, the
pursuit of the unprecedented and miraculous makes simple,
commonplace actuality insipid. The sense of emptiness and futility, the oppressive hangover inescapably follow the tormenting
flights of passionate feeling.

This unsatiable spiritual hunger, these limitless demands on
life, coupled with the inability to find a satisfactory outlet for an
awakened religious consciousness, had been spawned by early
nineteenth-century romanticism. Romantic "maximalism" had
many variants ranging from the impiety, disillusionment, and

14. *Brat'ja Karamazovy* [The brothers Karamazov], *Sobranie sochinenij* (Moscow, 1958), p. 138.

religious despair of Byron to the religious humility and the morbid renunciation of personal will and happiness of those German romantics who turned for support to the mystical world view of the medieval church. In the love lyrics of Alfred de Musset or, in particular, of Clemens Brentano, who was in many respects closer to Blok than other of his contemporaries,[15] we find the by now familiar forms of the romantic cleavage between the "ideal of the Madonna" and "the ideal of Sodom." It is Dostoevsky who confronts this problem most directly and thus foreshadows Blok's spiritual quest. In Dostoevsky's novels, as in the verses of the modern poet, the Russian folk element found its fullest expression—that total absence of measure in everything, that maximalism of the spirit for which all that is limited and contingent in *life* is only a barrier to the unconditional, anarchic urge toward creative freedom and self-affirmation. "No, man is broad, far too broad, I would narrow him. . . . Here the devil struggles with God, but the field of battle is the heart of men."

II

The cycle of poems Blok dedicated to his "native land" was composed in the years following the 1905 Revolution, at a time when it had become clear to many that the days which would decide the fate of Russia were drawing near. These "Verses about Russia" stand in the tradition of the religious trend in Russian social thought, the tradition of Khomjakov,[16] Tjutchev, Dostoevsky, Solov'ëv. It is not the political fortunes of his native land that concern the poet, but the salvation of its living soul. The poet views his country's calling, its predestined path, and the victories and battles on that path, in the same way that he had regarded his own fate—as a religious tragedy, a struggle for the divine calling of the human personality. But Blok differs from his predecessors in that he approaches the fate of Russia not as a thinker, through an abstract idea, but as a poet, through intimate love. For him Russia is the Beloved, and as the features of the

15. A German romantic, Clemens Brentano (1778–1842) wrote plays, lyric poems, fairy tales, and short stories.
16. Aleksej S. Khomjakov (1804–60), a publicist, theologian, and poet, was one of the leading figures in the "Slavophile" movement.

Beloved change in his poetry—from the image of the Beautiful
Lady to that of the Muse in his last poems—so also his feelings
for his native land finds its expression in the changing symbols of
romantic love. At first, whether a betrothed, a wife, or a mother,
she recalls the luminous features of the celestial Beloved:

> . . . With a tinkling of crystal
> She filled me with hope,
> Surrounded me with a luminous circle.
>
> . . . This is a light, paradisial image,
> This is your beloved . . .

[Ss, 3: 272]

In "On the Field of Kulikovo" (1908) the celestial Beloved
guards the sleeping warriors:

> . . . In the middle of the plain at nightfall,
> by the sombre Don,
> I heard Your voice in my prophet's heart call
> with the cry of the swan . . .
>
> . . . And when, next morning, the horde moved on
> darkening the field,
> made by no human hands Your image shone
> permanent in my shield.[17]

But the Beloved Russia had already taken on different features
in Blok's poetry. He had glimpsed in her that turbulent, chaotic,
ecstatically passionate, intoxicating aspect that he saw simultaneously in the features of Faina or Carmen. This motif appears
as early as "On the Field of Kulikovo":

> . . . Our road lies over the steppe and through infinite
> anguish, your anguish, Russia:
> even the night beyond the frontier limit
> I do not fear . . .
>
> . . . The wild mare of the steppe sweeps on, on, over
> the feather-grass . . .
>
> endlessly! Milestone and precipice flicker . . .
> draw rein! . . .

---

17. This translation is drawn from Alexander Blok, *The Twelve and Other
Poems*, trans. Jon Stallworthy and Peter Grabel (New York, 1970), pp. 78–79.

... There is no rest. The wild mare galloping
knows no sleep.[18]

"New America" represents the poet's conscious renunciation
of his youthful Slavophile dream of Russia as a bride chosen by
God, a devout maiden ("Holy Russia"):

> "New America"
> You'll pretend to be devout,
> You'll pretend to be an old woman,
> The prayerful voice, the churchbell's peal,
> Behind the crosses—more crosses and more . . .
>
> Yet at times your frankincense and benzoin
> Will be telling a different tale:
> No, the face beneath the colored kerchief
> Is neither senile nor pious!
>
> Through the bows to the earth, and the candles,
> Through litany after litany—
> I can hear quiet, whispered words,
> I can glimpse your burning cheeks . . .
>
> [Ss, 3: 268]

A new image of the Beloved Russia now appears to the poet,
that of "drunken Russia" ("they will hear the voice of drunken
Russia / and rest beneath the tavern's roof"), of a "fatal native
land," whose beauty is "robber-like":

> I cannot offer you my pity,
> I carry my cross as I can . . .
> Squander your wild beauty
> on every new magician!
>
> If they seduce you and deceive you,
> you'll not be broken or collapse;
> though suffering may overshadow
> the beauty of your face perhaps . . .[19]

"The Twelve," dedicated to the October Revolution, has its
place in this sequence of images. At the time of this poem's appearance it was all too often treated as a political document that

---

18. Ibid., pp. 75–76.
19. *The Twelve and Other Poems*, p. 85.

supposedly represented a radical shift in the poet's social views. Actually, "The Twelve" brings to their logical conclusion the most significant elements of Blok's work. Like the poet's entire work, it is completely removed from politics, programs, and the like; the problem it poses is not a political, but a religious and moral one, and its message is individual rather than social. However strange it might seem at first glance, the poem's fundamental theme is not that of a social system, but that of the soul's salvation—the souls of the Red Guard Petrushka, so unexpectedly placed at the poem's center,[20] and of his eleven comrades, and more broadly, the collective soul of Russia in turmoil, her "unencompassable expanses," her "robber-like beauty."[21]

Of course, the "old world" and its representatives—the "Comrade priest," the "writer–orator," the "lady in the astrakhan coat," and the "bourgeois, hungry as a dog"—hardly enjoy the author's artistic sympathy. Such sympathy would be incompatible with his spiritual maximalism, with that instinctive rejection of habit and routine in both private and public life, that thirst for the boundless and the absolute that has already been mentioned. Let us recall a poem of 1908 in which the poet directly addresses his readers:

> You're easily satisfied with a wife and a job,
> And with your piddling constitution,
> But the poet's reach is as wide as the world,
> And constitutions mean little to him!
>
> Even if I die by a fence like a dog,
> If life tramples me into the dirt—
> I'll know: it was the Lord who has bathed me in snow,
> 'Twas the blizzard that held me in its arms!
>
> [Ss, 3: 128]

To be sure, the poet had succeeded in overhearing in the Revolution the new rhythms of an as yet unwritten Marseillaise:

---

20. Petrushka is one of the twelve Red militiamen who on a pitch-black winter night in 1918 patrol the streets of besieged, blizzard-swept Petrograd. These guardians of the new order—half zealots, half roughnecks—are not above using their firepower to settle personal accounts. In a fit of jealous rage Petrushka kills his former lover, the prostitute Katja, only to experience anguish and contrition, which his comrades-in-arms deem unworthy of a soldier of the Revolution.

21. See "Russia" (*Rossija*, 1908), *Sobranie sochinenij*, 3:254.

> The wind plays up: snow flutters down.
> Twelve men are marching through the town.
>
> Their rifle butts on black slings sway.
> Lights left, right, left, wink all the way . . .
>
> . . . Keep a Revolutionary Step!
> The Relentless Enemy Will Not Stop![22]

But Blok's affinity for the Revolution was hardly a commitment to a definite system of political and social ideas. On the contrary, it was the element of popular revolt—"with or against God"—in which Blok sensed a stance closely akin to his own spiritual maximalism, his religious rebellion, his "trampling on things held sacred":

> Grip your gun like a man, brother!
> Let's have a crack at Holy Russia,
> Mother
> Russia
> with her big, fat arse!
> Freedom, freedom! Down with the cross![23]

The essential fact about "The Twelve" is that this poem grows organically out of Blok's entire poetic experience, out of the artistic achievements and symbols in which the religious tragedy of his own life had been revealed to him. The poet had heard the sounds of the snowstorm, which acts as a backdrop to "The Twelve," in his earlier poems about the blizzard, the "snow love," and the "Snow Maiden"; it had become the accustomed "landscape of his soul," a setting for the poet's mystical transports and downfalls. The further development of this artistic theme is found in "Verses about Russia": "Where violently the blizzard piles up / snow to the roof of a frail dwelling"; "You stand in the wild blizzard, / my fatal native land." Significantly, these images coincide with the epigraph from Pushkin's "The Devils," which Dostoevsky used as an inscription in his novel of the same title.[24] The story of the Red Guard Petruskha's love for the prostitute

---

22. *The Twelve and Other Poems*, pp. 145, 146.
23. Ibid., p. 146.
24. Reference is to the Dostoevsky novel *Besy* (which has been translated into English as *The Possessed* or *The Devils*). The epigraph from Pushkin's poem of the same title centers on the image of the blizzard that leads the driver of the speaker's coach astray. Apparently "demons have bewitched our horses."

Katja, which suddenly assumes the dimensions of the central event of this "political" poem, had been told previously in Blok's "gypsy" poems. We confront here once again that spiritual maximalism in love that Dostoevsky had epitomized in Dmitrij Karamazov's words about Grushen'ka ("Grushen'ka, the witch, has such a single curve of a body . . . ") and that permeates the love lyrics of Blok's third volume:

> Oh, brother, brother, brother,
> I loved that girl . . .
> such nights we had together,
> me and that girl . . .
> For the wicked come-hither
> her eyes would shoot at me,
> and for the crimson mole
> in the crook of her arm,
> I shot her in my fury—
> like the fool I am . . .[25]

Finally these triumphal motifs of popular rebellion yield to a mood of inconsolable anguish, of life's emptiness and aimlessness, of a dull hangover, of spiritual torpor, already a religious despair, in the wake of an intoxicating religious rebellion:

> My God, what a life!
> I've had enough!
> I'm bored!
>
> I'll scratch my head
> and dream a dream . . .
>
> I'll chew my quod
> to pass the time . . .
>
> I'll swig enough
> to kill my drought . . .
>
> I'll get my knife
> and slit your throat!
>
> Fly away, mister, like a starling,
> before I drink your blue veins dry
> for the sake of my poor darling
> with her dark and roving eye . . .

25. *The Twelve and Other Poems*, p. 152. See n. 43 above.

> Blessed are the dead which die in the Lord . . .
> I'm bored![26]

Having immersed himself in the congenial turmoil of the popular rebellion, Blok overheard its rhythms and caught sight of its images. But in recreating them he did not conceal their tragic contradictions, just as in confronting his own fate he made no secret of alienation, confusion, or anguish. Therein lies his honesty with himself and his contemporaries. Therein lies his achievement as a poet of the Revolution (not a poet-Revolutionary). In this sense "The Scythians"[27] is much farther removed from primary and genuine creative experience and more discursive and tendentious, as would be any abstract commentary that sought to encapsulate in neat, logical concepts the authenticity and intensity of the poet's vision.

26. Ibid., p. 154.
27. In "The Scythians" ("Skify," 1918), Blok urges the West to come to terms with revolutionary Russia or face a savage confrontation. This "powerful piece of eloquence" (D. S. Mirsky) is indeed a much more explicit and rhetorical statement than "The Twelve," where the distinctive voice of the poet is drowned in the cacophonous roar of the revolutionary street.

On a Generation That Squandered Its Poets

ROMAN JAKOBSON

Majakovskij's poetry—his imagery—his lyrical composition—I have written about these things and published some of my remarks. The idea of writing a monograph has never left me. Majakovskij's poetry is qualitatively different from everything in Russian verse before him, however intent one may be on establishing genetic links. This is what makes the subject particularly intriguing. The structure of his poetry is profoundly original and revolutionary. But how is it possible to write about Majakovskij's poetry now, when the paramount subject is not the rhythm, but the death of the poet, when (if I may resort to Majakovskij's own poetic phrase) "sudden grief" is not yet ready to give in to "a clearly realized pain."

During one of our meetings Majakovskij, as was his custom, read me his latest poems. Considering his creative potential I could not help comparing them with what he might have produced. "Very good," I said, "but not as good as Majakovskij." Yet now the creative powers are canceled out, the inimitable stanzas can no longer be compared to anything else, the words "Majakovskij's last poems" have suddenly taken on a tragic meaning. Sheer grief at his absence has overshadowed the absent one. Now it is more painful, but still easier, to write not about the one we have lost but rather about our own loss and those of us who have suffered it.

It is our generation that has suffered the loss. Roughly, those of us who are now between thirty and forty-five years old. Those who, already fully matured, entered into the years of the Revolution not as unmolded clay, but still not hardened, still capable of adapting to experience and change, still capable of taking a dynamic rather than a static view of our lives.

It has been said more than once that the first poetic love of our generation was Aleksandr Blok. Velimir Khlebnikov gave us a new epos, the first genuinely epic creations after many decades

This translation by Edward J. Brown first appeared in his *Major Soviet Writers* (New York: Oxford University Press, 1973).

of drought.[1] Even his briefer verses create the impression of epic fragments, and Khlebnikov easily combined them into narrative poems. Khlebnikov is epic in spite of our anti-epic times, and therein lies one of the reasons he is somewhat alien to the average reader. Other poets brought his poetry closer to the reader; they drew upon Khlebnikov, pouring out this "word ocean" into many lyrical streamlets. In contrast to Khlebnikov, Majakovskij embodied the lyrical urges of this generation. The broad epic canvas is deeply alien to him and unacceptable. Even when he attempts "a bloody Iliad of the Revolution," or "an Odyssey of the famine years," what appears is not an epic but a heroic lyric on a grand scale, offered "at the top of his voice."[2] There was a point when symbolist poetry was in its decline and it was still not clear which of the two new mutually antagonistic trends, acmeism or futurism, would prevail. Khlebnikov and Majakovskij gave to contemporary literary art its leitmotif. The name Gumilëv marks a secondary branch of modern Russian poetry—its characteristic overtone. For Khlebnikov and for Majakovskij "the homeland of creative poetry is the future"; in contrast, Esenin is a lyrical glance backward. His verse expresses the weariness of a generation.[3]

Modern Russian poetry after 1910 is largely defined by these names. The verse of Aseev and Selvinskij is bright indeed, but it is a reflected light.[4] They do not announce but reflect the spirit

1. Velimir Khlebnikov (1885–1922), one of the leading Russian futurists and, more important, one of the most original and seminal twentieth-century Russian poets. The epic dimension of his work is treated with care and acumen in Vladimir Markov's *The Longer Poems of Khlebnikov* (Berkeley, Calif., 1962).

2. A slightly modified title of Majakovskij's last major poem. "At the Top of My Voice," written in January 1930, two and a half months before the author's suicide, appears in retrospect as his poetic testament.

3. Nikolaj Gumilëv, along with Anna Akhmatova and Osip Mandelstam, one of the founders and chief spokesmen of the short-lived Acmeist movement, combined an essentially neoclassical aesthetics with a strong affinity for Kiplingesque exoticism and flamboyance. In 1921 he was arrested on the charge of conspiring against the Soviet government and summarily executed. Sergej Esenin, a wayward and poignant lyricist, the self-avowed "last village poet," enjoyed in the first years of the Revolution considerable popularity, which, due to his proclivity for drunken rowdyism, was at times un succès du scandale. Plagued by a malaise that clearly antedated the October Revolution and a mounting sense of alienation from the new "iron age," Esenin hanged himself in a Leningrad hotel in 1925.

4. Il'ja Lvovich Selvinskij (1899–), the leader of a modernist group of poets known as "constructivists." Nikolaj Aseev (1889–1963) was a poet close to the futurist movement. —*Trans.*

of the times. Their magnitude is a derivative quantity. Pasternak's books and perhaps those of Mandelstam are remarkable, but theirs is a chamber verse:[5] new creation will not be kindled by it. The heart of a generation cannot take fire with such verses because they do not shatter the boundaries of the present.

Gumilëv (1886–1921) was shot; after prolonged mental agony and in great pain, Blok (1880–1921) died; amid cruel privations and under circumstances of inhuman suffering, Khlebnikov (1885–1922) passed away; Esenin (1895–1925) and Majakovskij (1894–1930) killed themselves. And so it happened that during the third decade of this century, those who inspired a generation perished between the ages of thirty and forty, each of them sharing a sense of doom so vivid and sustained that it became unbearable.

This is true not only of those who were killed or killed themselves; Blok and Khlebnikov, when they took to their beds with disease, had already perished. Zamjatin wrote in his reminiscences: "We are all to blame for this. . . . I remember that I could not stand it and I phoned Gorky: Blok is dead. We can't be forgiven for that."[6] Shklovskij wrote in a tribute to Khlebnikov:

Forgive us for yourself and for others whom we will kill. The state is not responsible for the destruction of people. When Christ lived and spoke it [the state] did not understand his Aramaic, and it has never understood simple human speech. The Roman soldiers who pierced Christ's hands are no more to blame than the nails. Nevertheless, it is very painful for those whom they crucify.

Blok the poet fell silent and died long before the man, but his younger contemporaries snatched verses even from death. ("Wherever I die I'll die singing," wrote Majakovskij.) Khlebnikov knew he was dying. His body decomposed while he lived. He asked for flowers in his room so that the stench would not be noticed,

---

5. When we say "chamber" [kamernaja] we certainly do not intend to detract from the value of their work as poetic craftsmanship. The poetry of Evgenij Baratynskij or of Innokentij Annenskij, for instance, might be called thus. —R.J.

6. Evgenij Zamjatin (1884–1937), one of the most resourceful and intransigent modern Russian writers, is best known in the West as author of the anti-utopian satire We, which for obvious reasons has never been published in the Soviet Union. The above passage occurs in Zamjatin's 1921 memoir reprinted in the collection Litsa [Faces], (New York: Inter-Language Literary Associates, 1967), p. 27.

and he kept writing up to the end. A day before his suicide Esenin wrote a masterful poem about his impending death. Majakovskij's farewell letter is full of poetry: we find the professional writer in every line of that document. He wrote it two nights before his death and in the interval there were to be conversations and conferences about the everyday business of literature; but in that letter we read: "Please don't gossip. The deceased hated gossip." We remember that Majakovskij's long-standing demand upon himself was that the poet must "hurry time forward." And here he is, already looking at his suicide note through the eyes of someone reading it the day after tomorrow. The letter, with its several literary motifs and with Majakovskij's own death in it, is so closely interrelated with his poetry that it can be understood only in the context of that poetry.

The poetry of Majakovskij from his first verses to his last lines is one and indivisible. It represents the dialectical development of a single theme. It is an extraordinarily unified symbolic system. A symbol once thrown out only as a kind of hint will later be developed and presented in a totally new perspective. He himself underlines these links in his verse by alluding to earlier works. In the poem "About That" [Pro èto][7] for instance, he recalls certain lines from the poem "Man" [Chelovek], written several years earlier [1916–17], and in the latter poem he refers to lyrics of an even earlier period. An image at first offered humorously may later and in a different context lose its comic effect, or conversely, a motif developed solemnly may be repeated in a parodistic vein. Yet this does not mean that the beliefs of yesterday are necessarily held up to scorn; rather, we have here two levels, the tragic and the comic, of a single symbolic system, as in the medieval theater. A single clear purpose directs the system of symbols. "We shall thunder out a new myth upon the world."

A Mythology of Majakovskij?

His first collection of poems was entitled *I*. Vladimir Majakovskij is not only the hero of his first play, but his name is the title of that tragedy, as well as of his last collection of poems.

---

7. One of Majakovskij's finest poems, "Pro èto" (1927) is the lyrical landmark of his early Soviet period.

The author dedicates his verse "to his beloved self." When Majakovskij was working on the poem "Man" he said, "I want to depict simply man, man in general, not an abstraction, à la Andreev,[8] but a genuine 'Ivan' who waves his arms, eats cabbage soup, and can be directly felt." But Majakovskij could directly feel only himself. This is said very well in Trotsky's article on him (an intelligent article, the poet said): "In order to raise man he elevates him to the level of Majakovskij. The Greeks were anthropomorphists, naïvely likening the forces of nature to themselves; our poet is a Majakomorphist, and he populates the squares, the streets, and the fields of the Revolution only with himself." Even when the hero of Majakovskij's poem appears as the 150,000,000-member collective, realized in one Ivan—a fantastic epic hero—the latter in turn assumes the familiar features of the poet's "ego." This ego asserts itself even more frankly in the rough drafts of the poem.

Empirical reality neither exhausts nor fully takes in the various shapes of the poet's ego. Majakovskij passes before us in one of his "innumerable souls." "The unbending spirit of eternal rebellion" has poured itself into the poet's muscles, the irresponsible spirit without name or patronymic, "from future days, just a man." "And I feel that I am too small for myself. Someone obstinately bursts out of me." Weariness with fixed and narrow confines, the urge to transcend static boundaries—such is Majakovskij's infinitely varied theme. No lair in the world can contain the poet and the unruly horde of his desires. "Driven into the earthly pen I drag a daily yoke." "The accursed world has me chained." The grief of Peter the Great is that of a "prisoner, held in chains in his own city." Hulks of districts wriggle out of the "zones marked off by the governor." The poet's revolutionary call is directed at all of those "for whom life is cramped and unbearable," "who cry out because the nooses of noon are too tight." The ego of the poet is a battering ram, thudding into a forbidden future; it is a mighty will "hurled over the last limit" toward the incarnation of the future, toward an absolute fullness of being: "one must rip joy from the days yet to come."

Opposed to this creative urge toward a transformed future is the stabilizing force of an immutable present, overlaid, as this

8. Leonid Nikolaevich Andreev (1871–1919), a writer of short stories and plays pessimistic in content and symbolic in manner. —*Trans.*

present is, by a stagnating slime, which stifles life in its tight, hard mold. The Russian name for this element is *byt*. It is curious that this word and its derivatives should have such a prominent place in the Russian language (from which it spread even to the Komi),[9] while West European languages have no word that corresponds to it. Perhaps the reason is that in the European collective consciousness there is no concept of such a force as might oppose and break down the established norms of life. The revolt of the individual against the fixed forms of social convention presupposes the existence of such a force. The real antithesis of *byt* is a slippage of social norms that is immediately sensed by those involved in social life. In Russia this sense of an unstable foundation has been present for a very long time, and not just as a historical generalization, but as a direct experience. We recall that in the early nineteenth century, during the time of Chaadaev,[10] there was the sense of a "dead and stagnant life," but at the same time a feeling of instability and uncertainty: "Everything is slipping away, everything is passing," wrote Chaadaev. "In our own homes we are as it were in temporary quarters. In our family life we seem foreigners. In our cities we look like nomads." And as Majakovskij put it:

> . . . laws / concepts / faiths
> The granite blocks of cities
> And even the very sun's reliable glow—
> Everything had become as it were fluid,
> Seemed to be sliding a little—
> A little bit thinned and watered down. [*Mystery-Bouffe*]

Only in the poem "About That" is the poet's desperate struggle with *byt* fully laid bare. There it is not personified as it is elsewhere in his work. On the contrary, the poet hammers his verbal attack directly into that moribund *byt* which he despises. And *byt* reacts by executing the rebel "with all rifles and batteries, from every Mauser and Browning." Elsewhere in Majakovskij this phenomenon is, as we have said, personified—not however as a

---

9. *Byt* is a nearly untranslatable Russian word that suggests "mores," "convention," "the established way of life," "the daily grind," "middle-class values," and so forth. Komi, an aboriginal non-Russian minority who live north and east of the Ural mountains and speak a language belonging to the Finno-Ugrian group. —*Trans.*

10. See "Dostoevsky and Gogol" above, n. 10.

living person, but rather, in the poet's own phrase, "as an ani-
mated tendency in things." In "Man" the poet's enemy is very
broadly generalized as "Ruler of all, my rival, my invincible
enemy." But it is also possible to localize this enemy and give
him a particular shape. One may call him "Wilson," domicile
him in Chicago, and, in the language of fairy-tale hyperbole,
outline his very portrait (as in "150,000,000"). But then the poet
offers a "little footnote": "Those who draw the Wilsons, Lloyd
Georges, and Clemenceaus sometimes show their mugs with
moustaches, sometimes not; but that's beside the point since
they're all one and the same thing." The enemy is a universal
image. The forces of nature, people, metaphysical substances,
are only its incidental aspects and disguises: "The same old bald
fellow directs us unseen, the master of the earthly cancan. Sometimes in the shape of an idea, sometimes a kind of devil, or then
again he glows as God, hidden behind a cloud." If we should try
to translate the Majakovskian mythology into the language of
speculative philosophy, the exact equivalent for this enmity
would be the antinomy "I" versus "not-I." A better designation
for Majakovskij's enemy could hardly be found.

Just as the creative ego of the poet is not coextensive with his
actually existing self, so conversely the latter does not take in all
of the former. In the faceless regiment of his acquaintances, all
tangled in the "apartment-house spider web,"

> One of them / I recognized
> As like as a twin
> Myself / my very own self.

This terrible "double" of the poet is his conventional and commonplace "self," the purchaser and owner whom Khlebnikov
once contrasted with the inventor and discoverer. That self has
an emotional attachment to a securely selfish and stable life, to
"*my* little place, and a household that's *mine*, with *my* little picture on the wall."

The poet is oppressed by the specter of an unchangeable world
order, a universal apartment-house *byt*: "No sound, the universe
is asleep" ["A Cloud in Trousers"].

> Revolutions shake up violently the bodies of kingdoms,
> The human herd changes its herdsmen.
> But you / uncrowned ruler of our hearts
> No rebellion ever touches. ["Man"]

Against this unbearable might of *byt* an uprising as yet unheard of and nameless must be contrived. The terms used in speaking of the class struggle are only conventional figures, only approximate symbols, only one of the levels: the *part for the whole*. Majakovskij, who has witnessed "the sudden reversals of fortune in battles not yet fought," must give new meaning to the habitual terminology. In the rough draft of the poem "150,000,000" we find the following definitions:

> To be a bourgeois does not mean to own capital or squander gold. It means to be the heel of a corpse on the throat of the young. It means a mouth stopped up with fat. To be a proletarian doesn't mean to have a dirty face and work in a factory; it means to be in love with the future that's going to explode the filth of the cellars. . . . Believe me.

The basic fusion of Majakovskij's poetry with the theme of the Revolution has often been pointed out. But another indissoluble combination of motifs in the poet's work has not so far been noticed: revolution and the destruction of the poet. This idea is suggested even as early as the "Tragedy" (1913), and later the fact that the linkage of the two is not accidental becomes "clear to the point of hallucination." No mercy will be shown to the army of heroes, or to the doomed volunteers in the struggle. The poet himself is an expiatory offering in the name of that universal and real resurrection that is to come; that was the theme of the poem "War and the Universe" [Vojna i mir, 1916].[11] And in the poem "A Cloud in Trousers" [Oblako v shtanakh, 1915] the poet promises that when a certain year comes "in the thorny crown" of revolutions, "for you / I will tear out my soul / and trample on it till it spread out, / and I'll give it to you, / a bloody banner." And in the poems written after the Revolution the same idea is there, but in the past tense. The poet, mobilized by the Revolution, has "stamped on the throat of his own song." (This line occurs in the last poem he published, an address to his comrade-descendants" of the future, written in clear awareness of the coming end.) In the poem "About That" the poet is destroyed by *byt*. "The bloodletting is over. . . . Only high above the Kremlin

---

11. The title "Vojna i mir" is a sort of pun. The Russian sound-cluster "mir" can mean either "peace," as in the title of Tolstoy's epic, or "world, universe" as is clearly the case in the Majakovskij poem. (The traditional, pre-1917 spelling distinguished between the two meanings.)

the tatters of the poet shine in the wind—a little red flag." This image is plainly an echo of "A Cloud in Trousers."

The poet's hungry ear captures the music of the future, but he is not destined to enter the Promised Land. A vision of the future is present in all the most essential pages of Majakovskij's work. "And such a day dawned—Andersen's fairy tales crawled about like little pups at his feet"; "You can't tell whether it's air, or a flower, or a bird. It sings, and it's fragrant, and it's brightly colored all at once"; "Call us Cain or call us Abel, it doesn't matter. The future is here." For Majakovskij the future is a dialectical synthesis. The removal of all contradictions finds its expression in the facetious image of Christ playing checkers with Cain, in the myth of the universe permeated by love, and in the proposition "The commune is a place where bureaucrats will disappear and there will be many poems and songs." The present disharmony, the contradiction between poetry and building, "the delicate business of the poet's place in the working ranks," is one of Majakovskij's most acute problems. "Why," he asked, "should literature occupy its own special little corner? Either it should appear in every newspaper, every day, on every page, or else it's totally useless. The kind of literature that's dished out as dessert can go to hell" (from the *Reminiscences of D. Lebedev*).

Majakovskij always regarded ironically talk of the insignificance and early disappearance of poetry (really nonsense, he would say, but useful for the purpose of revolutionizing art). He planned to pose the question of the future of art in the "Fifth International" [Pjatyj internatsional, 1922], a poem that he worked on long and carefully but never finished. According to the outline of the work, the first stage of the Revolution, a worldwide social transformation, has been completed, but humanity is bored. *Byt* still survives. So a new revolutionary act of world-shaking proportions is required: "A revolution of the spirit in the name of a new organization of life, a new art, and a new science." The published introduction to the poem is an order to abolish the beauties of verse and to introduce into poetry the brevity and accuracy of mathematical formulas. He offers an example of a poetic structure built on the model of a logical problem. When I reacted skeptically to this poetic program—the exhortation in verse against verse— Majakovskij smiled: "But didn't you notice that the solution of my logical problem is a trans-sense solution?"[12]

12. "Trans-sense" (*zaumnyj* [jazyk]) was the term coined by the Russian

The remarkable poem "Homeward!" [Domoj!, 1925] is devoted to the contradiction between the rational and the irrational. It is a dream about the fusion of the two elements, a kind of rationalization of the irrational:

I feel / like a Soviet factory
Manufacturing happiness.
I don't want / to be plucked
Like a flower / after the day's work
. . . .
I want / the heart to be paid
Its wage of love / at the specialist's rate
I want / the factory committee
To put a lock on my lips
When the work is done
I want / the pen to be equal to the bayonet
And I want Stalin / to report in the name of the Politburo
About the production of verse
As he does about pig iron and steel.
"Thus, and so it is / we've reached
The topmost level / up from the workers' hovels
In the Union / of Republics
The appreciation of verse / has exceeded the prewar level."

The idea of the acceptance of the irrational appears in Majakovskij's work in various guises, and each of the images he uses for this purpose tends to reappear in his poetry. The stars ("You know, if they light up the stars, / that means, somebody needs them!"). The madness of spring ("Everything is clear concerning bread / and concerning peace. / But the prime question, / the question of spring, / must be / elucidated.") And the heart that changes winters to spring and water to wine ("It's that I'm / going to raise my heart like a flag, / a marvelous twentieth-century miracle."), And that hostile answer of the enemy in the poem "Man": "If the heart is everything / then why, / why have I been gathering you, my dear money! / How do they dare to sing? / Who gave them the right? / Who said the days could blossom into July? / Lock the heavens in wires! / Twist the earth into streets!"

---

futurists to suggest the poetic experimentation with the sound at the expense of logic and of easily definable meaning, a procedure championed and occasionally implemented by the avant-garde manifesto writers.

But Majakovskij's central irrational theme is the theme of love. It is a theme that cruelly punishes those who dare to forget it, whose storms toss us about violently and push everything else out of our ken. And like poetry itself this theme is inseparable from our present life; it is "closely mingled with our jobs, our incomes, and all the rest." And love is crushed by *byt*:

> Omnipresent one
> You thought up a pair of hands
> Fixed it
> So that everyone has a head.
> Why couldn't you fix it
> So that without torment
> We could just kiss and kiss and kiss?

Eliminate the irrational? Majakovskij draws a bitterly satirical picture. On the one hand, the heavy boredom of certain rational revelations: the usefulness of the cooperative, the danger of liquor, political education, and on the other hand, an unashamed hooligan of planetary dimensions (in the poem "A Type" [Tip, 1926]). Here we have a satirical sharpening of the dialectical contradiction. Majakovskij says "yes'" to the rationalization of production, technology, and the planned economy if as a result of all this "the partially opened eye of the future sparkles with real earthly love." But he rejects it all if it means only a selfish clutching at the present. If that's the case then grandiose technology becomes only a "highly perfected apparatus of parochialism and gossip on the worldwide scale" (from an essay "My Discovery of America"). Just such a planetary narrowness and parochialism permeates life in the year 1970, as shown in Majakovskij's play about the future, *The Bedbug* [Klop, 1928], where we see a rational organization without emotion, with no superfluous expenditure of energy, without dreams. A worldwide social revolution has been achieved, but the revolution of the spirit is still in the future. The play is a quiet protest against the spiritual inheritors of those languid judges who, in his early satirical poem "without knowing just why or wherefore, attacked Peru." Some of the characters in *The Bedbug* have a close affinity with the world of Zamjatin's *We* [My, 1920], although Majakovskij bitterly ridicules not only the rational utopian community but the rebellion against it in the name of alcohol, the irrational and unregulated individual happiness. Zamjatin, however, idealizes that rebellion.

Majakovskij has an unshakable faith that, beyond the mountain of suffering, beyond each rising plateau of revolutions, there does exist the "real heaven on earth," the only possible resolution of all contradictions. *Byt* is only a surrogate for the coming synthesis; it doesn't remove contradictions but only conceals them. The poet is unwilling to compromise with the dialectic; he rejects any mechanical softening of the contradictions. The objects of Majakovskij's unsparing sarcasm are the "compromisers" (as in the play *Mystery-Bouffe*). Among the gallery of "bureaucrat-compromisers" portrayed in his agitational pieces, we have in *The Bathhouse* [Banja, 1930] the *Glavnachpups* Pobedonosikov, whose very title is an acronym for "Chief Administrator for the Organizing of Compromises." Obstacles in the road to the future— such is the true nature of these "artificial people." The time machine will surely spew them out.

It seemed to him a criminal illusion to suppose that the essential and vital problem of building a worldwide "wonderful life" could be put aside for the sake of devising some kind of personal happiness. "It's early to rejoice," he wrote. The opening scenes of *The Bedbug* develop the idea that people are tired of a life full of struggle, tired of front-line equality, tired of military metaphors. "This is not 1919. People want to live." They build family nests for themselves: "Roses will bloom and be fragrant at the present juncture of time." "Such is the elegant fulfillment of our comrade's life of struggle." Oleg Bajan, the servant of beauty in *The Bedbug*, formulates this sentiment in the following words: "We have managed to compromise and control class and other contradictions, and in this a person armed with a Marxist eye, so to speak, can't help seeing, as in a single drop of water, the future happiness of mankind, which the common people call socialism." (In an earlier, lyrical context the same idea took this form: "There he is in a soft bed, fruit beside him and wine on the night table.") Majakovskij's sharply chiseled lines express unlimited contempt for all those who seek comfort and rest. All such people receive their answer from the mechanic in *The Bedbug*: "We'll never crawl out of our trenches with a white flag in our hands." And the poem "About That" develops the same theme in the form of an intimate personal experience. In that work Majakovskij begs for the advent of love, his savior: "Confiscate my pain—take it away!" And Majakovskij answers himself:

> Leave off. / Don't / not a word / no requests,
> What's the point / that you / alone / should succeed?
> I'll wait / and together with the whole unloved earth
> With the whole / human mass / we'll win it.
> Seven years I stood / and I'll stand two hundred
> Nailed here / waiting for it.
> On the bridge of years / derided / scorned
> A redeemer of earthly love / I must stand
> Stand for all / for everyone I'll atone
> For everyone I'll weep.

But Majakovskij knows very well that even if his youth should be renewed four times and he should four times grow old again, that would only mean a fourfold increase of his torment, a horror four times multiplied at the senseless daily grind and at pre-mature celebrations of victory. In any case, he will never live to see the revelation all over the world of an absolute fullness of life, and the final count still stands: "I've not lived out my earthly lot; I've not lived through my earthly love." His destiny is to be an expiatory victim who never knew joy:

> A bullet for the rest
> For some a knife.
> But what about me?
> And when?

Majakovskij has now given us the final answer to that question.

The Russian futurists believed in cutting themselves loose from the "classic generals," and yet they are vitally tied to the Russian literary tradition. It is interesting to note that famous line of Majakovskij's, so full of bravado (and at the same time a tactical slogan): "But why don't we attack Pushkin?" It was fol-lowed not long after by those mournful lines addressed to the same Pushkin: "You know I too will soon be dead and mute. / And after my death / we two will be quite close together." Ma-jakovskij's dreams of the future that repeat the utopian visions of Dostoevsky's Versilov in *A Raw Youth*, the poet's frequent hymns to the "man-god," the "thirteenth" apostle's rejection of God—all this is much closer to Russian literature of an earlier day than it is to official and regimented Soviet "godlessness." And Majakovskij's belief in personal immortality has nothing to do with the official catechism of Jaroslavskij's "godless" move-ment. The poet's vision of the coming resurrection of the dead is vitally linked with the materialistic mysticism of the Russian philosopher Fëdorov.[13]

When in the spring of 1920 I returned to Moscow, which was tightly blockaded, I brought with me recent books and information about scientific developments in the West. Majakovskij made me repeat several times my somewhat confused remarks on the general theory of relativity, and about the growing interest in that concept in Western Europe. The idea of the liberation of energy, the problem of the time dimension, and the idea that movement at the speed of light may actually be a reverse movement in time—all these things fascinated Majakovskij. I'd seldom seen him so interested and attentive. "Don't you think," he suddenly asked, "that we'll at last achieve immortality?" I was astonished, and I mumbled a skeptical comment. He thrust his jaw forward with that hypnotic insistence so familiar to anyone who knew Majakovskij well: "I'm absolutely convinced," he said, "that one day there will be no more death. And the dead will be resurrected. I've got to find some scientist who'll give me a precise account of what's in Einstein's books. It's out of the question that I shouldn't understand it. I'll see to it that this scientist receives an academician's ration." At that point I became aware of a Majakovskij that I'd never known before. The demand for victory over death had taken hold of him. He told me later that he was writing a poem called "The Fourth International" (he afterward changed it to "The Fifth International") that would deal with such things. "Einstein will be a member of that International. The poem will be much more important than '150,000,000.'" Majakovskij was at the time obsessed with the idea of sending Einstein a congratulatory telegram "from the art of the future to the science of the future." We never again returned to this matter in our conversations, and he never finished "The Fifth International." But in the epilogue to "About That" we find the lines: "I see it, I see it clearly to the last sharp detail. . . . On the bright eminence of time, impervious to rot or destruction, the workshop of human resurrection."

The epilogue to "About That" carries the following heading: "A request addressed to (Please, comrade chemist, fill in the name

13. Emeljan Jaroslavskij (1878–1943), a Bolshevik activist who for years was in charge of the Party's antireligious propaganda. —*Ed.* Nikolaj F. Fëdorov (1828–1903) was a Russian philosopher who maintained that the resurrection of the dead should become a major project of Christendom. —*Trans.*

yourself)." I haven't the slightest doubt that for Majakovskij this was not just a literary device but a genuine and seriously offered request to some "quiet chemist with a domed forehead" living in the thirtieth century:

> Resurrect me!
> Even if only because I was a poet
> And waited for you,
> And put behind me prosaic nonsense.
> Resurrect me—
> Just for that!
> Do resurrect me—
> I want to live it all out.

The very same "Institute for Human Resurrections" reappears in the play *The Bedbug* but in a comic context. It is the insistent theme of Majakovskij's last writings. Consider the situation in *The Bathhouse*: "A phosphorescent woman out of the future, empowered to select the best people for transfer into the future, appears in the time machine: At the first signal we blast off, and smash through old decrepit time. . . . Winged time will sweep away and cut loose the ballast, heavy with rubbish and ruined by lack of faith." Once again we see that the pledge of resurrection is faith. Moreover, the people of the future must transform not only their own future, but also the past: "The fence of time / our feet will trample. . . . As it has been written by us, / so will the world be / on Wednesday, / in the past / and now / and tomorrow / and forever" (from "150,000,000"). The poem written in memory of Lenin offers the same idea, yet in a disguised form:

> Death will never dare
> To touch him.
> He stands
> In the total sum of what's to be!
> The young attend
> to these verses on his death
> But their hearts know
> That he's deathless.

In Majakovskij's earliest writings personal immortality is achieved in spite of science. "You students," he says, "all the stuff we know and study is rubbish. Physics, astronomy, and chemistry are all nonsense" (from the poem "Man"). At that time

he regarded science as an idle occupation involving only the ex-
traction of square roots or a kind of inhuman collection of fossil-
ized fragments of the summer before last. His satirical *Hymn
to the Scholar* became a genuine and fervent hymn only when he
thought he had found the miraculous instrument of human resurrection in Einstein's "futuristic brain" and in the physics and
chemistry of the future. "Like logs thrown into a boom we are
thrown at birth into the great river of human time; we toss about
as we float downstream. But from now on that great river shall be
submissive to us. I'll make time stand still, move in another direction and at a new rate of speed. People will be able to get out
of the day like passengers getting out of a bus."

Whatever the means of achieving immortality, the vision of it
in Majakovskij's verse is unchangeable: there can be no resurrection of the spirit without the body, without the flesh itself.
Immortality has nothing to do with any other world; it is indis-
solubly tied to this one. "I'm all for the heart," he wrote in "Man,"
"but how can bodiless beings have a heart? / . . . My eyes fixed
earthward. . . . / This herd of the bodiless, / how they / bore me!"
"We want to live here on earth— / no higher and no lower"
(*Mystery-Bouffe*). "With the last measure of my heart / I believe /
in this life, / in this world, / in all of it" ("About That"). Majakovskij's dream is of an everlasting earth, and this earth is placed
in sharp opposition to all superterrestrial, fleshless abstractions.
In his poetry and in Khlebnikov's the theme of earthly life is presented in a coarse, physical incarnation (they even talk about the
"meat" rather than the body). An extreme expression of this is
the cult of tender feeling for the beast with his beastly wisdom.

"They will arise from the mounds of graves / and their buried
bones will grow flesh" ("War and the Universe"), wrote Majakovskij. And those lines are not just a kind of literary verbaliza-
tion. The vision of a future that resurrects people of the present
is not simply a poetic device that motivates the whimsical interweaving of two separate narrative levels. On the contrary—that
vision is Majakovskij's most cherished poetic myth.

This constant infatuation with a wonderful future is linked in
Majakovskij with a pronounced dislike of children, a fact that
would seem at first sight to be hardly consonant with his fanatical
belief in tomorrow. But just we find in Dostoevsky an obtrusive and neurotic "father hatred" linked with great veneration
for ancestors and reverence for tradition, so in Majakovskij's

spiritual world an abstract faith in the coming transformation of the world is joined quite properly with hatred for the evil continuum of specific tomorrows that only prolong today ("the calendar is nothing but the calendar!") and with undying hostility to that "broody-hen" love that serves only to reproduce the present way of life. Majakovskij was indeed capable of giving full due to the creative mission of those "kids of the collective" in their unending quarrel with the old world, but at the same time he bristled whenever an actual "kid" ran into the room. Majakovskij never recognized his own myth of the future in any concrete child; these he regarded simply as new offshoots of the hydra-headed enemy. That is why we find in the marvelous movie scenario *How Are You?* [Kak pozhivaete?] childlike grotesques, which are the legitimate offspring of the Manilov pair Aristide and Themistocles in Gogol's *Dead Souls*. We recall that his youthful poem "A Few Words about Myself" [Neskolko slov obo mne samom, 1912] begins with the line "I love to watch children dying." And in the same poem child-murder is elevated to a cosmic theme: "Sun! / My father! / At least you have pity and torment me not! / That's my blood you shed flowing along this low road." And surrounded by that very aura of sunshine, the same "child complex" appears as both an immemorial and personal motif in the poem "War and the Universe":

> Listen—
> The sun just shed his first rays
> not yet knowing
> where he'll go when he's done his day's work;
> and that's me
> Majakovskij,
> Bringing as sacrifice to the idol's pedestal
> a beheaded infant.

There's no doubt that in Majakovskij the theme of child-murder and suicide are closely linked: these are simply two different ways of depriving the present of its immediate succession, of "tearing through decrepit time."

Majakovskij's conception of the poet's role is clearly bound up with his belief in the possibility of conquering time and breaking its steady, slow step. He did not regard poetry as a mechanical superstructure added to the ready-made base of existence (it is no accident that he was so close to the formalist literary critics).

A genuine poet is not one "who feeds in the calm pastures of everyday life; his mug is not pointed at the ground." "The weak ones simply beat time and wait for something to happen that they can echo; but the powerful rush far enough ahead so as to drag time along behind them!" Majakovskij's recurrent image of the poet is of one who overtakes time, and we may say that this is the actual likeness of Majakovskij himself. Khlebnikov and Majakovskij accurately forecast the Revolution (including the date); that is only a detail, but a rather important one. It would seem that never until our day has the writer's fate been laid bare with such pitiless candor in his own words. Impatient to know life, he recognizes it in his own story. The "God-seeker" Blok and the Marxist Majakovskij both understood clearly that verses are dictated to the poet by some primordial, mysterious force. "We know not whence comes the basic beat of rhythm." We don't even know where this rhythm is located: "outside of me or within me? But most likely within me."[14] The poet himself senses the necessity of his own verse, and his contemporaries feel that the poet's destiny is no accident. Is there any one of us who doesn't share the impression that the poet's volumes are a kind of scenario in which he plays out the story of his life? The poet is the principal character, and subordinate parts are also included; but the performers for these latter roles are recruited as the action develops and to the extent that the plot requires them. The plot has been laid out ahead of time right down to the details of the denouement.

The motif of suicide, so alien to the thematics of the futurist and "Left Front" groups,[15] continually recurs in the work of Majakovskij, from his earliest writings, where madmen hang themselves in an unequal struggle with *byt* (the director, the "man with two kisses" in the *Tragedy* [Tragedija]), to the scenario *How Are You?*, in which a newspaper article about a girl's suicide induces horror in the poet. And when he tells about a young Communist who committed suicide he adds, "How like me that is. Horrors!" He tries on, so to speak, all possible varieties of suicide: "Rejoice now! He'll execute himself. . . . The locomo-

14. Quotation from Majakovskij's essay "How Verses Are Made" (Kak delat' stikhi, 1926), most notable for its detailed reconstruction of the process that gave rise to the much-quoted poem "To Sergej Esenin," 1925 (see below).
15. The "Left Front" (*Lef*) was a short-lived neofuturist group that tried to combine total political commitment with literary experimentation.

tive's wheel will embrace my neck" [Tragedy"]. "I'll run to the canal and there stick my head in the water's grinning mug . . . ["The Flute-Spine," 1915]. "The heart bursts for a bullet, the throat raves for a razor. . . . Beckons to the water, leads to the roof's slope. . . . Druggist, give me the means to send my soul without any pain into the spacious beyond."

A simple résumé of Majakovskij's poetic autobiography would be the following: the poet nurtured in his heart the unparalleled anguish of the present generation. That is why his verse is charged with hatred for the strongholds of the established order, and in his own work he finds "the alphabet of coming ages." Majakovskij's earliest and most characteristic image is one in which he "goes out through the city leaving his soul on the spears of houses, shred by shred." The hopelessness of his lonely struggle with the way things are became clearer to him at every turn. The brand of martyrdom is burned into him. There's no way to win an early victory. The poet is the doomed "outcast of the present."

> Mama!
> Tell my sisters, Ljuda and Olja,
> That there's no way out. ["A Cloud in Trousers"]

Gradually the idea that "there's no way out" (which appeared first in "A Cloud in Trousers") lost its purely literary character. From that poetic passage it found its way into prose, and "there's no way out" turned up as an author's remark in the margin of the manuscript for "About That." And from that prose context the same idea made its way into the poet's life: in his suicide note he said: "Mama, sisters, comrades, forgive me. This is not a good method (I don't recommend it to others), but for me there's no other way out."

The act was long in preparation. Fifteen years earlier in a prologue to a collection of poems, he wrote:

> Often I think
> Hadn't I better just
> Let a bullet mark the period of my sentence.
> Anyway, today
> I'm giving my farewell concert.

As time went on the theme of suicide became more and more pressing. Majakovskij's most intense poems, "Man" (1916) and "About That" (1923), are dedicated to it. Each of these works is an ominous song of the victory of *byt* over the poet; their leit-motif is "Love's boat has smashed against the daily grind" (a line from his suicide note). The first is a detailed depiction of Majakovskij's suicide. In the second there is already a clear sense that the suicide theme transcends literature and is already in the realm of "literature of fact."[16] Once again—but even more disturbingly—the images of the first poem file past, the keenly observed stages of existence: the "half-death" in the vortex of the horrifyingly trivial, then the "final death"—"The lead in my heart! Not even a shudder!" This theme of suicide had become so real that it was out of the question to sketch the scene anymore. It had to be exorcised. Propaganda pieces were necessary in order to slow down the inexorable movement of that theme. "About That" already initiates this long cycle of exorcism. "I won't give them the satisfaction of seeing me dead of a bullet." "I want to live on and on, moving through the years." The lines to Sergej Esenin are the high point of this cycle. According to Majakovskij, the salubrious aim of the lines addressed to Esenin was to neutralize the impact of Esenin's death poem. But when you read them now, they sound even more sepulchral than Esenin's last lines. Esenin's lines equate life and death, but Majakovskij in his poem can only say about life that it's harder than death.[17] This is the same sort of enigmatic propaganda for life found in Majakovskij's earlier lines to the effect that only disquiet about the afterlife is a restraint upon the bullet. Such, too, are the farewell words in his suicide letter: "Be happy here."

In spite of all this the obituary writers vie with one another: "One could expect anything of Majakovskij, but not that he would kill himself" (E. Adamovich). And Lunacharskij: "The idea of suicide is simply incompatible with our image of the poet." And Malkin: "His death cannot be reconciled with his whole life, which was that of a poet completely dedicated to the Revolution." And the newspaper *Pravda*: "His death is just as inconsistent with the life he led, as it is unmotivated by his poetry." And A.

---

16. The realm of straight reporting where literature and "life" meet. "Literatura fak'ta" was a *Lef* slogan that reflected a bias in favor of the documentary, nonfictional genres.

17. "Esenin's lines" alluded to above occur in his suicide note: "In this life," said Esenin, "there's nothing new about dying./ Nor, to be sure, is there anything new about living." In his "To Sergej Esenin" Majakovskij demurred: "In this life there's nothing hard about dying/ To build life is much harder."

Khalatov: "Such a death was hardly proper for the Majakovskij we knew." Or Koltsov: "It is not right for him. Can it be that none of us knew Majakovskij?" And finally, the poet Demjan Bednyj: "Incredible! What could he have lacked?"

Could these men of letters have forgotten or so misunderstood *All That Majakovskij Composed?*[18] Or was there a general conviction that all of it was only "composed," only invented? Sound literary criticism rejects any direct or immediate conclusions about the biography of a poet when these are based merely on the evidence of his works, but it does not at all follow from this that there is no connection whatsoever between the artist's biography and his art. Such an "antibiographical" position would be the equivalent, in reverse, of the simplistic biographical approach. Have we forgotten Majakovskij's admiration for the "genuine heroism and martyrdom" of Khlebnikov, his teacher? "His life," wrote Majakovskij, "matched his brilliant verbal constructs. That life is an example for poets and a reproach to poetizers." And it was Majakovskij who wrote that even a poet's style of dress, even his intimate conversations with his wife should be determined by the whole of his poetic production. He understood very well the close connection between poetry and life.

After Esenin's suicide poem, said Majakovskij, his death became a literary fact. "It was clear at once that those powerful verses, just those verses, would bring to the bullet or the noose many who had been hesitating." And when he approached the writing of his own autobiography, Majakovskij remarked that the facts of a poet's life are interesting "only if they are borne out by his works." Who would dare assert that Majakovskij's suicide is not borne out thus? "Don't gossip about my deed!" Majakovskij adjured us just before his death. Yet those who stubbornly mark out a strict boundary between the "purely personal" fate of the poet and his literary biography create an atmosphere of low-grade, highly personal gossip by means of those significant silences.

It is a historical fact that the people around Majakovskij simply did not believe in his lyrical monologues. "They listened, all smiling, to the eminent clown." They took his various masquerades for the true face of the man: first the pose of the fop ("It's good when the soul is shielded from inspection by a yellow

18. The title of an early collection of poems.—*Trans.*

blouse"); then the performance of an overeager journalist and agitator: "It's good, when you're in the teeth of the gallows, to cry out: 'Drink Van Houten's cocoa' " ("A Cloud in Trousers"). But then when he carried out that slogan in practice in his advertising jingles ("If you want good luck and good fortune buy a government lottery ticket!") his audience saw the rhymed advertisement but missed the teeth of the gallows. As it turns out, it was easier to believe in the benefits of a lottery loan or the excellent quality of the pacifiers sold in the state stores than it was to believe that the poet had reached an extreme of despair, that he was in a state of misery and near-death. "About That" is a long and hopeless cry to the ages, but Moscow doesn't believe in tears.[19] They stamped and whistled at this routine Majakovskian artistic stunt, the latest of his "magnificent absurdities," but when the theatrical cranberry juice of the puppet show became real, genuine, thick blood, they were taken aback: Incredible! Inconsistent![20]

Majakovskij himself often helped to spread illusions about himself. The record of a conversation we had in 1927 demonstrates this. I said, "The total sum of possible experience has been measured out to us. We might have predicted the early decline of our generation. But the symptoms of this are rapidly increasing in number. Take Aseev's line 'What about us, what about us, can it be we've lost our youth?' And consider Shklovskij's memento to himself!" Majakovskij answered, "Utter nonsense. The way I see it everything is ahead of us. If I ever thought that the best of me was in the past that would be the end for me." I reminded him of a recent poem of his in which the following lines occurred:

> I was born / increased in size
> fed from the bottle—
> I lived / worked / grew oldish
> And life will pass
> As the Azores Islands
> Once passed into the distance.

"That's nothing," he said, "just a formal ending. An image

---

19. A popular saying that served as the title of a novel by Il'ja Ehrenburg.
20. Reference is to Aleksandr Blok's sardonic play *A Puppet Show* (Balaganchik, 1906) in which a clown, stabbed by one of the protagonists, dies oozing cranberry juice instead of blood.

only. My poem "Homeward" in the first version ended with the lines:

> I want my country to understand me
> But if not—so what:
> I'll just pass my country by
> Like a slanting rain in summer.

But you know Brik told me to strike those lines out because they didn't go with the tone of the whole poem.[21] So I struck them out."

The simplistic formalist literary credo professed by the Russian futurists inevitably propelled their poetry toward the antithesis of formalism—toward the cultivation of the heart's "raw cry" and uninhibited frankness. Formalist literary theory placed the lyrical monologue in quotes and disguised the "ego" of the lyric poet under a pseudonym. But what unbounded horror results when suddenly you see through the pseudonym, and the phantoms of art invade reality, just as in Majakovskij's scenario *Bound in Film* a girl is kidnapped from a movie set by a mad artist and lands in "real life."

Toward the end of his life the satire and the laudatory ode had completely overshadowed his elegiac verse, which, by the way, he identified with the lyric in general. In the West the existence of this basic core in Majakovskij's poetry was not even suspected. The West knew only the "drummer of the October Revolution." There are many explanations for this fact. In 1923 Majakovskij had reached the end of the road as far as the elegiac mode was concerned. In an artistic sense "About That" was a "repetition of the past," intensified and raised to perfection. His journalistic verse was a search for something new; it was an experiment in the production of new materials and in untested genres. To my skeptical comments about these poems Majakovskij replied: "Later on you'll understand even them." And when *The Bedbug* and *The Bathhouse* appeared it became clear that his most recent poems had been a huge laboratory experiment in language and theme, a labor masterfully exploited in his first efforts in the area of prose drama and offering a rich potential for future growth.

Finally, in connection with its social setting, the journalistic verse of Majakovskij represented a shift from an unrestrained

---

21. Osip Brik, a close friend and associate of Majakovskij, was an important formalist theoretician and an active member of the *Lef*.

frontal attack in the direction of an enervating trench warfare. *Byt*, with its swarm of heartbreaking trivia, is still with him. And it is no longer "rubbish with its own proper face," but "petty, small, vulgar rubbish." You cannot resist the pressure of such rubbish by grandiloquent, pronouncements "in general and in toto," or by theses on communism, or by pure poetic devices. "Now you have to see the enemy and draw a bead upon him." You have to smash the "swarm of trivia" offered by *byt* "in a small way" and not grieve that the battle has been reduced to many minor engagements. The invention of strategies for describing "trifles that may also prove a sure step into the future"—this is how Majakovskij understood the immediate task of the poet.

Just as one must not reduce Majakovskij the propagandist to a single dimension, so, too, one-sided interpretations of the poet's death are shallow and opaque. The newspaper *Pravda* on the morning after Majakovskij's suicide announced that "the preliminary investigation indicates that his act was prompted by motives of a purely personal character." But the poet had already provided an answer to that in the subtitle of "About That": "From personal motives, but about the general way of life."

The late Bela Kun advised us not to "subordinate the great cause to our own petty personal feelings."[22] Majakovskij had entered his objection in good time:

> With this petty / and personal theme
> That's been sung so many times
> I've trod the poetical treadmill
> And I'm going to tread it again.
> This theme / right now
> Is a prayer to Buddha
> And sharpens a black man's knife for his master.
> If there's life on Mars / and on it just one
> Human-hearted creature
> Then he too is writing now
> About that same thing.

The journalist Koltsov hastened to explain: "Majakovskij himself was wholly absorbed in the business affairs of various literary groups and in political matters. Someone else fired that shot, some

22. Bela Kun (1886?–1940?), Hungarian Communist, was head of the short-lived Hungarian Soviet government in 1919. —*Trans.*

outsider who happened to be in control of a revolutionary poet's mind and will. It was the result of the temporary pressure of circumstances." And once again we recall the rebuke Majakovskij delivered long before the fact:

> Dreams are a harm
> And it's useless to fantasize.
> You've got to bear the burden of service.
> But sometimes—
> Life appears to you in a new light
> And through the mess of trifles
> You catch sight of something great and good.

"We condemn this senseless, unforgivable act. It was a stupid and cowardly death. We cannot but protest most vigorously against his departure from life, against his barbarous end." (Such was the pronouncement of the Moscow Soviet and others.) But Majakovskij had already parodied these very funeral speeches in *The Bedbug*: "Zoja Berëzkin's shot herself—Aha! She'll catch it for that at her cell meeting." Says a doctor in the future world commune: "What is suicide? . . . You shot at yourself? . . . Was it an accident?" "No, it was from love." "Nonsense. . . . Love makes you want to build bridges and have children. . . . But you. . . . Yes, yes, yes!"

In general life has been imitating Majakovskij's satirical lines with horrifying regularity. Pobedonosikov, the comic figure in *The Bathhouse*, who has many features that remind us of Lunacharskij,[23] brags that "I have not time for boat rides. . . . Such petty entertainments are for various secretaries: 'Float on, gondola mine!' I have no gondola but a ship of state." And now Lunacharskij himself faithfully echoes his comic double. At a meeting called in memory of the poet the minister hastens to explain that the former's farewell lines about a "love-boat smashed on daily grind" have a pathetic sound: "We know very well that it was not on any love-boat that he sailed our stormy seas. He was the captain of a mighty ship of state." These efforts to forget the "purely personal" tragedy of Majakovskij sometimes take the form of conscious parody. A group of writers in a provincial town

---

23. Anatolij V. Lunacharskij (1873–1933), the first Soviet commissar of education, was a relatively open-minded and prolix Bolshevik critic and publicist. Though not unsympathetic to the futurists, he was wary of their extremism and of their insistence on being the only truly revolutionary poets.

published a resolution in which they assure Soviet society that they will take very seriously the advice of the late poet not to follow his example.

It is very strange that on this occasion such terms as "accidental," "personal" and so forth are used precisely by those who have always preached a strict social determinism. But how can one speak of a private episode in view of the fact that in a few years' time the whole bloom of Russian poetry has been swept away?

In one of Majakovskij's longer poems each of the world's countries brings its best gift to the man of the future; Russia brings him poetry. "The power of their voices is most resoundingly woven into song." Western Europe is enraptured with Russian art: the medieval icon and the modern film, the classical ballet and the latest theatrical experiment, yesterday's novel and the latest music. And yet that art which is probably Russia's greatest achievement, her poetry, has never really been an export item. It is intimately Russian and closely linked to the Russian language and would probably not survive the rigors of translation. Russian poetry has witnessed two periods of high flowering: the beginning of the nineteenth century and the present century. And the earlier period as well as the later had as its epilogue the untimely death of very many great poets. If you can imagine how slight the contributions of Schiller, Hoffmann, Heine, and especially Goethe would have been if they had all disappeared in their thirties, then you will understand the significance of following Russian statistics: Ryleev was executed when he was thirty-one. Batjushkov went mad when he was thirty. Venevitinov died at the age of twenty-two, Delvig at thirty-two. Griboedov was killed when he was thirty-four, Pushkin when he was thirty-seven, Lermontov when he was twenty-six.[24] Their fate has more than once been characterized as a form of suicide. Majakovskij himself compared his duel with *byt* to the fatal duels of Pushkin and Lermontov. There is much in common in the reactions of society in both periods to these untimely losses. Once again, a feeling of sudden and profound emptiness overwhelms one, an oppressive sense of an evil destiny lying heavily on Russian intellectual life. But now as then other notes are louder and more insistent.

The Western mind can hardly comprehend the stupid, unrestrained abuse of the dead poets. A certain Kikin expressed great

24. These are all prominent poets of the first three decades of the nineteenth century. —*Trans.*

disappointment that Martynov, the killer of that "cowardly scoundrel Lermontov," had been arrested. And Czar Nicholas I's final
words on the same poet were: "He was a dog and he died a dog's
death." And in the same spirit the contemporary newspaper *The
Rudder*[25] carried no obituary on the occasion of Majakovskij's
death, but instead a cluster of abusive remarks leading up to the
following conclusion: "Majakovskij's whole life gave off a bad
smell. Is it possible that his tragic end could set all that right?"

Certain questions are particularly intriguing to journalists.
Who was responsible for the war? Who was to blame for the poet's
death? Biographers are amateur private detectives, and they will
certainly take great pains to establish the immediate reason for
the suicide. They will add other names to that variegated assem-
blage of poet-killers, the "sonafabitch D'Antès," who killed Pushkin, the "dashing Major Martynov," who killed Lermontov, and
so forth. People who seek the explanation of various phenomena
will, if they bear Russia a grudge, readily demonstrate, citing
chapter, verse, and historical precedent, that it is dangerous to
practice the trade of poet in Russia. And if their grudge is only
against contemporary Russia it will also be quite easy to defend
such a thesis with weighty arguments. But I am of another mind.
It seems to me that the one nearest the truth was the young
Slovak poet who said: "Do you imagine that such things happen
only there, in Russia? Why that's what our world is like nowadays."
This is in answer to those phrases, which have alas become
truisms, concerning the deadly absence of fresh air, certainly
a fatal condition for poets. There are some countries where men
kiss women's hands, and others where they only say "I kiss your
hand." There are countries where Marxist theory is answered
by Leninist practice, and where the madness of the brave, the
martyr's stake, and the poet's Golgotha are not just figurative
expressions.

In the last analysis what distinguishes Russia is not so much
the fact that her great poets have ceased to be, but rather that
not long ago she had so many of them. Since the time of the first
symbolists Western Europe has had no great poetry.

The real question concerns not causes but consequences, however tempting it may be to protect oneself from a painful realization of what's happened by discussing the reasons for it.

25. *The Rudder* (Rul') was a right-of-center Russian émigré newspaper in
Berlin.

> It's a small thing to build a locomotive:
> Wind up its wheels and off it goes.
> But if a song doesn't fill the railway station—
> Then why do we have alternating current?

Those lines are from Majakovskij's "Order to the Army of Art" [Prikaz po armii iskusstv, 1918]. We are living in what is called the "reconstruction period," and no doubt we will construct a great many locomotives and scientific hypotheses. But to our generation has been allotted the morose feat of building without song. And even if new songs should ring out they will belong to another generation and a different curve of time. Yet it is unlikely that there will be new songs. Russian poetry of our century is copying and it would seem outdoing that of the nineteenth century: "the fateful forties are approaching," the years, in other words, of lethargic inertia among poets.

The relationships between the biographies of a generation and the march of history are curious. Each age has its own inventory of requisitions upon private holdings. Suddenly history finds a use for Beethoven's deafness and Cézanne's astigmatism. The age at which a generation's call to service in history's conscription comes, as well as the length of its service, are different for different periods. History mobilizes the youthful ardor of some generations and the tempered maturity or old wisdom of others. When their role is played out yesterday's rulers of men's minds and hearts depart from the proscenium to the backstage of history to live out their years in private, either on the profits from their intellectual investments, or else as paupers. But sometimes it happens otherwise. Our generation emerged at an extraordinarily young age: "We alone," as Majakovskij put it, "are the face of our time. The trumpet of time blows for us."[26] But up to the present moment there are not any replacements, nor even any partial reinforcements. Meanwhile the voice and the emotion of that generation have been cut short, and its allotted quota of feelings—joy and sadness, sarcasm and rapture—have been used up. And yet, the paroxysm of an irreplaceable generation turned out to be no private fate, but in fact the face of our time, the very breath of history.

26. From the Russian futurist manifesto "A Slap in the Face of Public Taste" (1912), signed by David Burljuk, Velimir Khlebnikov, A. Kruchenykh, and Vladimir Majakovskij.

We strained toward the future too impetuously and avidly to leave any past behind us. The connection of one period with another was broken. We lived too much for the future, thought about it, believed in it; the news of the day—sufficient unto itself— no longer existed for us. We lost a sense of the present. We were the witnesses of and participants in great social, scientific, and other cataclysms. *Byt* fell behind us, just as in the young Majakovskij's splendid hyperbole: "One foot has already reached the next street." We knew that the plans of our fathers were already out of harmony with the facts of their lives. We read harsh lines alleging that our fathers had taken the old and musty way of life on a temporary lease. But our fathers still had left some remnant of faith in the idea that that way of life was both comfortable and compulsory for all. Their children had only a single-minded, naked hatred for the ever more threadbare, ever more alien rubbish offered by the established order of things. And now the "efforts to organize a personal life are like attempts to heat up ice cream."

As for the future, it doesn't belong to us either. In a few decades we shall be cruelly labeled as products of the past millennium. All we had were compelling songs of the future; and suddenly these songs are no longer part of the dynamic of history, but have been transformed into historico-literary facts. When singers have been killed and their song has been dragged into a museum and pinned to the wall of the past, the generation they represent is even more desolate, orphaned, and lost—impoverished in the most real sense of the word.

3
Early Soviet Marxists

Majakovskij and Russian Futurism

LEON TROTSKY

Early Russian futurism was the revolt of Bohemia, that is, of the semipauperized left wing of the intelligentsia, against the hermetic and coterie-like aesthetics of the bourgeois intelligentsia. Under the thin surface of this poetic rebellion one could feel the pressure of deeper social forces that futurism itself did not quite understand. The struggle against the old poetic vocabulary and syntax, in spite of all the Bohemian excesses, was a progressive revolt against a vocabulary that was restricted and artificially selected with a view to avoiding any unnecessary unpleasantness, a revolt against impressionism, which sipped life through a straw, and symbolism, which went through phony motions in its heavenly vacuum, against Zinaida Gippius[1] and her kind, and against all the other puny pundits of the liberal-cum-mystical intelligentsia. If we survey closely this recent period,[2] we cannot help but realize how vital and progressive was the futurists' impact on poetic language. Without exaggerating the scope of this linguistic "revolution," one must admit that futurism has purged poetry of many hackneyed words and phrases, while restoring vitality to other ways of speaking, and in some instances has felicitously coined many new words and phrases that have entered, or are entering, in the vocabulary of poetry and that are apt to enrich the spoken language. This applies not only to the individual words, but also to their arrangement, that is, to syntax. True, in the realm of word combination, as well as of word formation, futurism has gone well beyond anything a live language can absorb. The same thing, however, has happened to the Revolution and is the "sin" of every dynamic movement. To be sure, the Revolution, especially its conscious vanguard, shows more capacity for self-criticism than do the futurists, but the latter have encountered consid-

---

This essay first appeared as "Futurizm" in *Literatura i revolutsija* [Literature and revolution] (Moscow, 1923), pp. 102–14.

1. Zinaida Gippius (1869–1945), an important figure of the Russian Silver Age, was recently described as Russia's foremost religious poet. To Trotsky her oscillation between faith and metaphysical doubt was an epitome of fin de siècle escapism.
2. The first decade of the twentieth century.

169

erable resistance, which, one trusts, is not likely to slacken. The excesses will cease, but the fundamentally purifying and truly revolutionary work in the realm of poetic language will endure.

The efforts of the futurists in the field of rhyme deserve an especially favorable assessment. Those who do not care about these things or tolerate them merely because they are bequeathed to us by our ancestors, may regard all futurist innovations as troublesome simply because they demand a certain amount of attention. Let me raise at this point a question: in general, are rhythm and rhyme at all necessary? Curiously enough, Majakovskij himself sets out to prove in verses with a very complex rhyming pattern that rhyme is unnecessary. Now a strictly logical approach to the question of artistic form is thoroughly inadequate. Poetry is not a rational but an emotional phenomenon, and the human psyche, which encompasses biological rhythms and the rhythms of collective work, seeks to express them in an idealized form in sound and song, and in verbal art. As long as such a need persists, the futurist rhythms and rhymes, which are more flexible, bolder, and more varied than the traditional ones, represent an indubitable and valuable gain whose import reaches well beyond the confines of the futurist movement.

The futurist achievements in the realm of verse orchestration are equally indisputable. One must not forget that the sound of a word is an acoustic accompaniment to its meaning. If the futurists have been guilty of a monstrous bias in favor of sound as against sense, this overenthusiasm is merely an "infantile disease of leftism"[3]—which, to be sure, must be held in check—a vociferous challenge to sleek verbal routine on the part of a new poetic school that listens with a fresh ear. Of course the overwhelming majority of the working class are not yet interested in these questions. The bulk of the working-class vanguard cannot get excited about them—it has other, more urgent tasks. But there is also tomorrow. That tomorrow will demand a much more attentive and precise, a more craftsman-like and artistic attitude toward language as the fundamental instrument of culture not only where verse, but also, indeed especially, where prose is concerned. Thought can be rendered more precise only by a careful selection of words, a careful weighing of their manifold

3.   The title of a well-known pamphlet by Lenin.

—and this means in part acoustic—possibilities. Here haphazard procedures will not do; what is called for are micrometric instruments. Routine, tradition, habit, and carelessness must yield here as elsewhere to intelligent, systematic work. At its best futurism is a protest against the slovenly, that most entrenched literary school that has very influential representatives in every field.

In Comrade Gorlov's unpublished work, which, in my opinion, traces incorrectly the international origins of futurism and which distorts the historic perspective by identifying futurism with proletarian poetry, the formal-artistic achievements of futurism are, nonetheless, summed up very thoughtfully and succinctly. Gorlov points out correctly that the futurist "revolution" in form, which grew out of the revolt against the old aesthetics, reflects indirectly the revolt against the stagnant and stifling way of life which produced that aesthetics. No wonder in Majakovskij, who is the greatest poet of the school, and in the works of his closest friends this revolution culminates in a challenge to the social order which produced both that repudiated way of life and the repudiated aesthetics. That is why these poets are organically bound up with the October Revolution. Gorlov's analysis is correct, but it must be rendered more precise and more specific. The new words and new word combinations, new rhythms and new rhymes were necessary because the futurist world view has rearranged events and facts and established, that is, discovered, new relationships between them.

Futurism is opposed to mysticism, passive deification of nature, aristocratic and every other kind of laziness, dreaminess, and whining; it is in favor of technology, scientific organization, the machine, planning, will power, courage, speed, precision, and the new man, who is armed with all these things. The connection between the aesthetic "revolt" and the moral and social revolt is direct; both enter fully into the life experience of the active, young, and yet untamed section of the intelligentsia— the left-wing, creative Bohemia. Revulsion toward the constricted and philistine existence—and a new artistic style as both an outlet for this revulsion and a way of siphoning it off. In different configurations and in different historic settings this intelligentsia malaise gave rise to many a new style. But that was always the end of it. This time the proletarian Revolution overtook futurism at a certain stage of its development and

pushed it forward. Futurists became Communists. By virtue of
this act they entered the sphere of more profound questions and
relationships that transcended the limits of their own little
world and that they were not ready to tackle. That is why futurists, including Majakovskij, are weakest artistically in those of
their works that are most consistently Communist. This has more
to do with their spiritual past than their social origins. The futurist poets have not mastered the elements of the Communist
world view sufficiently to find an organic expression for them in
words; these concepts have not entered, so to speak, into their
blood. Hence the frequent artistic, or to be exact, psychological
failures, the stilted rhetoric and noisy posturing. In its most
strenuously revolutionary works futurism becomes stylization.
Conversely, in the poetry of the young Bezymenskij, who owes
so much to Majakovskij, the artistic expression of the Communist
world view is more organic; Bezymenskij was not a mature poet
when he espoused Communism.[4] He was spiritually born into
Communism.

It could be and has been argued, that the proletarian doctrine
and program were also elaborated by members of the bourgeois-
democratic intelligentsia. But this is quite a different matter.
The economic and historical/philosophical doctrine of the proletariat rests on objective knowledge. If that turner Bebel,[5] who
was ascetically economical in life and thought and who had a
razor-sharp mind, had created the theory of surplus value rather
than the erudite doctor of philosophy Karl Marx, he would have
stated it in a much more accessible, simple and one-sided way.
The wealth and variety of ideas, images, and quotations in
Capital undoubtedly reveal the "intellectualist" background of
this great book. But since its content is a matter of objective
knowledge, the essence of Capital became Bebel's property as
it became the property of millions and thousands of other pro-
letarians. In poetry we deal with a perception of the world
through images, and not with scientific cognition of reality. Daily
routine, immediate setting, the range of one's personal experience, all these help shape artistic creation. To overhaul the
world of feelings that one has absorbed in one's childhood in line

4. Aleksandr Bezymenskij (1898–) was one of the leading "proletarian" poets
in the 1920s.
5. Turner by trade, August Bebel (1840–1913) was one of the pioneers of
German Marxism and for many years an influential leader of the German Social
Democratic Party.

with a scientific–ideological orientation is a most difficult inner travail. Not everyone is capable of it. That is why there are so many people in this world who think as revolutionaries and react as philistines. And that is why even when futurist poetry dedicates itself totally to the Revolution, we sense a revolutionary stance that is more Bohemian than proletarian.

Majakovskij is a big, or as Blok put it, an enormous talent. He has the capacity to turn familiar things around in such a way that they seem new. He handles words like a bold master who works according to his own laws, regardless of whether his craftsmanship pleases us or not. Many of his images, phrases, and expressions have entered literature and will remain in it for a long time, if not forever. He has his own way of constructing a poem, his own imagery, his own rhythm, and his own rhyme.

Majakovskij's artistic design is almost always significant and sometimes grandiose. The poet draws into his compass war and revolution, heaven and hell. Majakovskij is hostile to mysticism, to every kind of hypocrisy, to the exploitation of man by man; his sympathies are entirely on the side of the struggling proletariat. Priesthood of art, especially programmatic priesthood, is alien to him; on the contrary, he is entirely ready to place his art at the service of the Revolution.

But even in this big talent, or, to be more correct, in the entire creative personality of Majakovskij, there is no essential correlation between its component parts, there is no equilibrium, not even a dynamic one. Majakovskij is at his weakest whenever a sense of proportion and capacity for self-criticism are needed.

It was more natural for Majakovskij to accept the Revolution than for any other Russian poet; this act was an outgrowth of his entire development. Many roads lead the intelligentsia toward the Revolution (not all of them reach the goal); therefore it is important to define and assess Majakovskij's path more accurately. There is the road of the rustic school of the intelligentsia and of the capricious "fellow travelers"; there is the road of the mystics, who seek higher "music" (Aleksandr Blok); there is the road of the "Changing the Landmarks" group, and of those who have merely reconciled themselves (Shkapskaja, Shaginjan); there is the road of the rationalists and of the eclectics (Brjusov, Gorodetskij, and Shaginjan again).[6] There are many other roads; they

6. The term "fellow travelers," which came to designate, in early Soviet parlance, writers sympathetic with the Revolution but not ready to commit

cannot all be named. Majakovskij came by the shortest route, that of the rebellious, persecuted Bohemia. For Majakovskij, the Revolution was a true and profound experience, because it descended with thunder and lightning upon the very things that Majakovskij hated in his own way, things with which he refused to make his peace. Herein lies his strength. Majakovskij's revolutionary individualism wholeheartedly embraced the proletarian Revolution, but did not blend with it. His instinctive reaction to the city, to nature, to the world is not that of a worker, but of a Bohemian. "The bald-headed streetlamp that pulls the stocking off from the street"[7]—this striking image alone, which is extremely characteristic of Majakovskij, throws more light upon the poet's Bohemian urbanism than any abstract discussion ever could. The impudent and cynical tone of many images, especially of those of the first half of his poetic career, bears an unmistakable stamp of the artistic cabaret, cigar smoke, and all the rest.

Majakovskij is more attuned to the dynamic quality of the Revolution and to its stern courage than to the mass character of its heroism, its deeds and trials. Just as the ancient Greeks were anthropomorphists and naïvely thought of the forces of nature as resembling themselves, so our poet is a Majakomorphist and populates the squares, the streets, and fields of the Revolution only with himself. True, extremes meet. The universalization of one's ego breaks down to some extent the barriers of one's individuality and thus brings one nearer to the collective. But this is true only to an extent. The individualistic, Bohemian arrogance—in contrast not to humility, which no one needs, but to a necessary sense of perspective—runs through everything written by Majakovskij. His rhetoric often rises to a high intensity, but there is not always strength behind it. The poet is too much in

themselves to Communism, was coined by Trotsky. It occurs for the first time in chapter 2 of *Literatura i revolutsija*. "Changing the Landmarks" was a group of Russian émigré intellectuals in the early 1920s who switched from an intransigently anti-Soviet position to an acceptance of the Bolshevik regime on national grounds. The most characteristic and prominent member of this movement was Aleksej N. Tolstoj. Both Marija Shkapskaja (1892–) and Marietta Shaginjan (1888–), who later became an orthodox Soviet novelist, were in the 1920s essentially "private" writers with mildly metaphysical leanings. Sergej Gorodetskij, (1884–) was a minor symbolist, who after a brief association with acmeism, turned into an all-round "eclectic" or, bluntly, opportunist.

7. A line from an early Majakovskij lyric, "From Street to Street" [Iz ulicy v ulicu, 1913].

evidence. He allows too little autonomy to events and facts; it is not the Revolution that is struggling with obstacles, but Majakovskij, who does athletic stunts in the verbal arena. Sometimes he performs genuine miracles, but every now and then he makes a heroic effort—and lifts a hollow weight.

Majakovskij always speaks about himself, be it in the first or the third person, now flaunting his individuality, now dissolving himself in mankind. When he wants to elevate man, he raises him to the level of Majakovskij. He assumes a breezy tone in speaking of the greatest historic events. This is the most intolerable, as well as the most dangerous aspect of his works. It is not the danger of walking on stilts; such props would be too flimsy. Majakovskij has one foot on Mont Blanc and the other on Elbrus. His voice drowns thunder; small wonder that he treats history familiarly and hobnobs with the Revolution! But this is most perilous, for what with such gigantic scale everywhere and in everything, such thunderous shouting (the poet's favorite word), such an elevated vantage point—normal proportions go awry, and it becomes impossible to establish the difference between the big and the small. That is why Majakovskij speaks of the most intimate thing, notably love, as if he were speaking about the migration of peoples and uses the same vocabulary in dealing with the Revolution. He constantly runs the risk of overshooting his target.

That this addiction to hyperbole mirrors, in some sense, the frenzy of our times is undeniable. But to say this is not necessarily to legitimize this style. It is impossible to shout louder than the war or the Revolution; to break down in trying to do so is quite easy. A sense of measure in art is no less essential than a sense of reality in politics. The principal flaw of futurist poetry, even in its best achievements, lies in this absence of a sense of measure; it has lost the measure of the drawing room, and it has not yet found the measure of the street. But to find such a gauge is imperative. The inevitable consequences of straining one's voice at a street rally are hoarseness and shrieking, which destroy the effect intended. It is better to speak in the voice given one by nature than to use a voice louder than one's own. Majakovskij shouts too often when he should merely speak; that is why at moments when he ought to shout, his shouting seems insufficient. The poet's rhetorical thrust is undercut by the audible strain and hoarseness.

Majakovskij's elaborate images, though frequently splendid

per se, quite often clutter up the whole and paralyze the action. The poet evidently feels this himself; that is why he is yearning for the other extreme, for the language of "mathematical formulae," a language unnatural to poetry. Incidentally, the self-generating imagery that imagism shares with futurism—and that seems more at home in peasant-oriented imagism![8]—has its roots in the rural substratum of our culture. It is more akin to the Church of Vasilij the Blessed than to a steel bridge. But whatever the cultural–historical sources of this, the fact remains that what is most conspicuously absent from Majakovskij's works is action. This may sound like a paradox, for futurism appears to be oriented toward action. But here enters unimpeachable dialectics: an excess of violent imagery results in quiescence. Action must correspond to the mechanics of our perception and to the rhythm of our feelings if it is to be perceived physically, let alone artistically. A work of art must trace the gradual development of an image, a mood, or a plot up to its climax and must not fling the reader about from one end to another, no matter how deft the boxing blows of imagery. Each phrase, each expression, each image of Majakovskij's works tries to be the climax, the peak, the limit. That is why the work as a whole has no climax. The spectator has the feeling of being constantly urged to overrespond to the *parts* of the poem. Consequently the whole eludes him. To climb a mountain is difficult but worthwhile. A walk across plowed terrain is no less wearying and gives much less joy. Majakovskij's works have no peak; they lack internal discipline. The parts refuse to obey the whole. Each part wants to be on its own. Each generates its own dynamics, with little regard for the will of the whole. That is why the sense of the whole and of its dynamics is lacking. The futurist experiments with words and images have not yet produced a creative synthesis.

Majakovskij's "150,000,000" [written in 1919] was supposed to be the poem of the Revolution. But it is not. In this broadly conceived work the weaknesses and lapses of futurism are so blatant as to be overpowering. The author wanted to write an epic of mass suffering, of mass heroism, of the impersonal revolu-

---

8. "Imagism" or "imaginism" was a short-lived school in modern Russian poetry. Its chief spokesmen were Vadim Shershenevich and Anatolij Mariengof. The most prominent figure to be associated with the movement was Sergej Esenin, a fact that may account in part for the above description of imagism as "peasant-oriented."

tion of Ivan, who represents 150 million. And the author did not sign it. "No one is the author of this poem of mine." But this state of impersonal ownership does not change the situation. The poem is profoundly personal, that is, individualistic, more often than not in the bad sense of the term. It contains too much that is unmotivated and artistically arbitrary. Here are some of the poem's images: "Wilson swimming in fat," "In Chicago every inhabitant has the title of a general, at least," "Wilson gobbles, grows fat, his bellies grow story on story,"—and so on. These images are on the crude and gross side, not the kind of imagery that makes sense to the present-day masses. The worker, at least the worker who will read Majakovskij's poem, has seen Wilson's picture and knows that Wilson is thin, though admittedly he consumes a sufficient quantity of proteins and fats. The worker has also read Upton Sinclair and knows that Chicago has stock-yard workers in addition to "generals." One senses in these arbitrary and crude images, in spite of their blatantly hyperbolic thrust, a certain proclivity for baby talk. The simple-minded-ness that marks these images smacks not of the robustness of folk imagination, but of Bohemian histrionics. Wilson has a staircase —"If you go on foot, start walking young, and you will hardly get there by the time you are old!" Ivan marches upon Wilson, "the championship [!] of the world's class struggle" takes place, and Wilson has "pistols with four triggers, and a saber bent into seventy sharp blades," but Ivan has "a hand and another hand, [and] that is stuck in his belt." The unarmed Ivan with his hand in his belt facing the infidel armed with pistols—is not this an old Russian motif? Is it not Il'ja Muromets before us? Or is it rather Ivan the Fool who, barefoot, challenges fancy German mechanics?[9] Wilson strikes Ivan with his sword: "He cut him four versts. . . . But a man crawled forth suddenly from the wound." And so on, in the same vein. How out of place, and, more important, how frivolous is this *bylina* [see note 9] or fairy tale–like primitive hastily adapted to Chicago technology and to the class struggle! All this was meant to be titanic, but in fact is at its best only athletic. Nor can this athleticism be taken seriously; it is a sort of tomfoolery with inflated balloons. "The

9. Il'ja Muromets or Il'ja from Murom, a folksy Russian *bogatyr'* (legendary warrior), looms large in a body of Russian oral epic tradition known as *byliny*. Ivan the Fool, the seemingly simple younger brother who somehow manages to outwit all his elders, is a familiar figure in the Russian folktale.

championship of the world's class struggle"! Champ-i-on-ship!
Self-criticism, where art thou? Championship is a holiday
spectacle, quite often combined with hucksterism. Neither the
image nor the word are appropriate here. Instead of a really
titanic struggle of 150 million—a travesty of a half-acrobatic,
half-"heroic" championship. The travesty is unintentional, but
this does not make things any better.

The arbitrary images, lacking inner logic, swallow up the idea
and discredit it artistically as well as politically. Why does Ivan
hold one hand in his belt as he faces swords and pistols? Why
such contempt for technology? It is true that Ivan is not as heavily
armed as Wilson. But that is just why he needs to use both hands.
And if he does not go down, it is because there are workers in
Chicago as well as generals, and because a considerable number
of these workers are against Wilson and for Ivan. But the poem
does not show this. In straining toward false monumentality of
the image, the author amputates the core of his message.

Hastily, nonchalantly, and once again arbitrarily, the author
cleaves the universe into two classes: on th the one hand, there
is Wilson, floating in fat, ermines, beavers, and large heavenly
stars, and on the other there is Ivan, flanked by "work shirts"
and myriad constellations of the Milky Way. "For the beavers /
—the tiny lines of the decadents of the world, / for work shirts /
the iron lines of the futurists." But even though the poem has
quite a few strong and apt lines, brilliant images, and, generally,
much verbal richness, it contains in fact no "iron lines for
blouses." Has Majakovskij's talent faltered? No, what is lacking
here is an image of the Revolution mastered by the nerves and
the brain, an image that could control the devices of verbal craftsmanship. The author is flexing his muscles, catching and throwing about now one image, now another. "We shall finish you, the
world romantic!" Majakovskij threatens. That is right. Romanticism of Oblomov and of Karataev must be given a *coup de grâce*.
But how? "Kill the old and make an ashtray of their skulls!"

But this is romanticism par excellence, only with a minus sign!
Ashtrays made of skulls are inconvenient and unhygienic. And
the savagery of it is, frankly, a bit contrived. By making such an
unnatural use of the skull bones, the poet himself succumbs to
romanticism; at any rate, he has not thought through his images;
he has not integrated them. "Pocket the wealth of all the world!"
In this breezy tone Majakovskij speaks of socialism. But to pocket

something means to put it into one's pocket like a thief. Is this word suitable when at issue is the collective ownership of the land and of the factories? It is totally unsuitable. The author uses such vulgarisms so as to be able to hobnob with socialism and with the Revolution. But when he pokes Ivan, the personification of 150 million, familiarly "under the ribs," instead of the poet's growing to titanic dimensions, Ivan is reduced to one-eighth of his size. Familiarity is not at all a sign of a genuine affinity; frequently it is merely a symptom of political or moral slovenliness. A truly intimate bond with the Revolution would exclude a familiar tone and would bring forth what the Germans call *der Pathos der Distanz*.

The poem has striking lines, bold images, and very apt phrases. The final "triumphal requiem of peace" is perhaps its most effective section. But the work is profoundly flawed because it fails to feature development, to present a gradual intensification of contradictions and their subsequent resolution. Here is a poem about the Revolution that lacks movement! The images live their separate lives, they collide and bounce off one another. The tension between them does not grow out of the historical matrix but is the result of an internal disharmony within the author's revolutionary world view. And yet, when one finishes the poem, not without difficulty, one says to oneself: what a staggering work could have been created from these elements, given a sense of proportion and self-criticism! Perhaps these fundamental defects are due not to Majakovskij's personal characteristics, but to the fact that he operates within a circumscribed environment; nothing is so adverse to self-criticism and a sense of measure as the coterie way of life.

Majakovskij's satiric verses also lack profound penetration into the essence of things and relationships. His satire is hasty and superficial. It takes more than the mastery of a pencil for a cartoonist to be significant. He must see through and know inside-out the world he exposes. Saltykov knew thoroughly his bureaucrats and his squires![10] An approximate caricature—and 99 percent of our Soviet caricature falls, alas, into this category—is like a bullet that misses the bull's-eye by the width of a finger, or even by a hair; it has almost hit the mark, but still it has missed. Majakovskij's satire is approximate; his fugitive, surface observa-

10. See "The Aesthetics of Gogol's *Dead Souls* and Its Legacy" above, n. 28.

tions miss the mark, sometimes by the width of a finger, and sometimes by the span of the whole palm. Majakovskij seriously thinks that the "comic" can be abstracted from its matrix and reduced to form. In the preface to his volume of satires, he even presents "a diagram of laughter." If there is anything about this exercise that can make one smile uneasily, it is the fact that the "diagram" is totally unfunny. But even if someone could draw a more felicitous "outline" than Majakovskij has succeeded in doing, the difference between laughter evoked by a satire that hits the mark and a giggle caused by verbal tickling would remain.

Majakovskij rose above the Bohemia that had nurtured him to scale extraordinarily significant creative heights. But the force that propelled him upward was individualism. The poet is rebelling against the daily grind, against the material and moral dependence in which his life, and above all, his love, is trapped; chafing at the bit and inveighing against the masters of life who have deprived him of a beloved woman, he rises to a call for a revolution and a prophecy that it shall descend upon the society that offers no room for Majakovskij's individuality. After all, his poem, "A Cloud in Trousers," [see pp. 145, 156 above] a poem of unconsummated love, is artistically his most significant, his boldest, and most promising work. In fact, it is difficult to believe that a work of such emotional power and formal originality was written by a youth of twenty-two or twenty-three years. His "War and the Universe," *Mystery-Bouffe*,[11] and "150,000,000," are much weaker, precisely because here Majakovskij leaves his individualistic orbit and tries to enter the orbit of the Revolution. One can only welcome the poet's efforts, for basically no other road is open to him. "About That" [see pp. 150–53 above] is a return to the theme of personal love, but it is several steps behind "A Cloud" rather than ahead of it. Only a wider range and a deeper insight can enable an artist to maintain his creative equilibrium while growing in stature. But it is obvious that a conscious shift to an essentially new social and artistic path is a very difficult matter. In recent years Majakovskij's technique has

11. A flamboyant revolutionary verse drama, written in 1918 and presented on the first anniversary of the October Revolution under the direction of Vsevolod Meyerhold. The advertisement described the play as a "heroic, epic, and satiric portrayal of our era."

undoubtedly become more finely honed, but it has also become more stereotyped. The *Mystery-Bouffe* and the "150,000,000" have splendid passages side by side with dismal lapses into rhetoric and verbal acrobatics. The unmistakable authenticity of "A Cloud"—that poignant howl—is no longer. Some conclude that "Majakovskij is repeating himself"; others add, "Majakovskij has written himself out." "Majakovskij has become official," still others gloat. But is that actually the case? We are in no hurry to make pessimistic predictions. Majakovskij is not a youth, but he is still young. However, let us not close our eyes to the difficulties that lie ahead. That creative spontaneity that throbs in "A Cloud" cannot be regained. But this need not be cause for regret. The youthful talent that spurts like a fountain is supplanted in later years by a self-confident mastery, not only a mastery of the word, but also a firm grasp of historical experience, an insight into the mechanism of life's forces, collective and personal, of ideas, temperaments, and passions. Such mature craftsmanship is incompatible with social dilettantism, with shouting, with a lack of self-respect and a tiresome boastfulness, with nonchalant playing the genius, and with other mannerisms that smack of the intelligentsia cafe. If the poet's crisis—and there is no question but that such a crisis is at hand—is resolved in favor of a mature vision that encompasses the particular along with the general, the historian of literature will be able to say that the *Mystery-Bouffe* and the "150,000,000" marked merely the inevitable and temporary slope at the turn of the road toward a creative peak. We sincerely hope that Majakovskij will grant the future historian the right to make such an assessment.

Isaac Babel

ALEKSANDR VORONSKIJ

I

There is still no collected works of Babel, but the 100 to 200 pages he has published thus far mark him as a writer of unmistakable maturity. This is not to say that his job is done, that he has fully expressed himself. On the contrary, there is still much to come including his most important work. Babel has not yet realized his full creative potential. Not all his works are at the same artistic level, but his prose already shows firmness, maturity, self-assurance and craftsmanship—testimony to sustained, assiduous effort. Babel has his own voice, his own style, but he takes hold not only because he speaks from "the gut," but also because of his intelligence and his capacity for hard work. This is apparent in almost all his miniatures [vignettes]. Clearly he has been to a workshop. He has culture, and this is his crucial advantage over the bulk of Soviet fiction writers who are trying to make it on their "guts" and on the sheer wealth of their observations and who consider study and hard work a tedious bourgeois prejudice. That is why it so often happens in our country that after a debut, an artist begins to peter out and go downhill: his first or second appearance has made an impact because he expressed himself so fully and directly that formal lapses either were not noticed by the reader or were forgiven as a warrant of the author's sincerity. To make predictions about writers is an idle pastime, but it is proper to take note of Babel's culture, his intelligence, and the firmness of his talent. These qualities give one the right to hope that Babel will not deteriorate and will not go the way of several of his young confreres.

Babel is miles away from naturalism or flatly descriptive realism, but he is also a far cry from Andrej Belyj. He has something in common with Maupassant, with Chekhov and with Gorky, yet he cannot be bracketed with them either. Maupassant is a

This essay, translated here by James Karambelas, first appeared in Aleksandr Voronskij's *Literaturnye tipy* [Literary types] (Moscow, 1925), pp. 99-118.

skeptic, Chekhov is sad, Gorky is a romantic, and all this is reflected in each one's style. Babel's manner is epic, at times biblically epic. Here is a fair sample:

> Then Senka dashed water over his Dad's beard and asked him: "You are all right, Dad, in my hands?"
>
> "No," said Dad, "not all right."
>
> Then Senka said: "And Fedka, was he all right in your hands when you killed him?"
>
> "No," said Dad, "things went badly for Fedka."
>
> Then Senka asked: "And did you think, Dad, that things would go badly for you?"
>
> "No," said Dad, "I didn't think that things would go badly for me."
>
> Then Senka turned to the people and said: "And what I think is that if I fell into your hands, there wouldn't be no quarter for me. And now, Dad, we are going to finish you off."[1]

Thus a son relates in a letter to his mother how his brother Senka "finished off" his father—a member of the White Guard. The father, in his turn, has "finished off" his son Fedja. The everyday simplicity of the narration is combined here with unruffled calm. In his miniatures Babel is impassive, calm, slow. He does not hurry, nor does he hurry the reader. He draws out deliberately his spare, weighty, carefully chosen words. He is epic, even in those instances when he becomes lyrical. But Babel's epic is not the kind that is indifferent to good and evil on the assumption that the past has long become ancient history, the topical has evaporated, and all the passions have died out. Babel tries to be epic in his tales about Budënnyj's Red Cavalry [see n.1]. He writes about the stuff of yesterday, follows in the fresh tracks of recent experience; in essence he is writing about the present. His epic is like a campfire that has just gone out: beneath the ashes hot coals are still glowing. Babel's epic quality is *sui generis;* it is an artistic device, calculated and deliberate. The contemporary Soviet fiction writer deals with

1. This quotation is drawn from a tale "Pis'mo" [A letter], which appears in *Konarmija* [Red cavalry, 1926], a collection of stories based on the author's personal participation in the Polish Campaign of 1920. Babel served as a political commissar in the First Cavalry Army—a Cossack unit led by the colorful Semën M. Budënnyj.

extraordinary events and an extraordinary reader. One cannot impress the contemporary reader by an intricate plot, less still by shouting or rhetoric. The most shocking artistic invention will pale before a plot that any one of us could weave from real life. We have grown accustomed to a great deal since the war of 1914 and the Revolution. Were a new Leonid Andreev to appear today with his *Red Laughter, Darkness* or *Abyss*, his devices simply would be out of place, and he would not only fail to "frighten" the reader but would not make one-tenth of the impression Andreev made in some quarters in his day.[2] Today the epic manner seems a more reliable approach to the reader. Our era is essentially epic. Furthermore, the law of contrast is at work here: a narration about what has just been endured in suffering and blood, a tale of extraordinary events, couched in a calm, unruffled, businesslike vein will affect the contemporary reader much more powerfully than shrieking or frenzy ever could.

Actually Babel is not at all impassive, indifferent to good and evil, or calm. He has his own point of view; he has a definite attitude toward the epoch, the people, the events, but he has got a grip on himself as an artist. He speaks simply, without unnecessary verbiage, just as we have become accustomed to living simply and without unnecessary verbiage in the midst of the unusual and unprecedented. More important, he understands that the true artist's task does not lie in hitting the nerves harder, but in touching up the canvas "just a bit," as Lev Tolstoy put it[3] —in singling out unerringly whatever reveals the essence of an object, a person, an episode. "Right in front of my window several Cossacks were shooting an old bearded Jew for spying. The old man was screaming and trying to break loose. Then Kudrja from the machine gun platoon grabbed his head and buried it under his arm. The Jew calmed down and stood with his legs apart. With his left hand Kudrja took out his dagger, carefully slit the old man's throat without spilling any blood on

2. Voronskij is referring to a "put-down" of Leonid Andreev, a popular turn-of-the-century short-story writer and playwright, attributed to Tolstoy: "He is trying to frighten me, but I am not afraid."

3. In *What Is Art?* Tolstoy tells the following anecdote about the nineteenth-century Russian painter Brjulov: "Correcting a pupil's sketch, Brjulov touched it up here and there, and a poor, lifeless sketch suddenly came to life. 'You've touched it up just a bit and everything has changed,' said one of the pupils. 'Art begins precisely where "just a bit is," ' said Brjulov" (*Chto takoe iskusstvo?* chap. 12).

himself" ("Berestechko"). This is a far cry from Andreev or Dostoevsky. Everything is told with a nearly chronicle-like calm, yet every detail is artistically selected, especially "without spilling any blood on himself," so that the picture sticks in one's memory. The ability to strike just the right note marks Babel's best works.

Babel has a way of coupling adjectives with nouns that is startling and apt. "Flaming cloaks," "passionate rags," "a dusty wire of curls," "the thick expanses of the night," "a raspberry-colored wart," "powerful evenings," "the deathly aroma of brocade," "the smoke of a secret murder," "the cool depth of the night," "the orange battles of sunset," "the stuffy air turned sour," "the sparkling sky, inexpressibly empty as always during hours of danger," and so on. Perhaps it is this proclivity for epithets that contributes in part to the slowness, the leisureliness, the expressive, flowing quality of his narration.

Babel is also a lyricist. His lyricism is somewhat dreamy, indolent, cool; it does not hold the reader back, nor does it disturb the rhythm of the narrative. The presence of lyricism, incidentally, exposes the precariousness of his epic manner. Babel plays sly games with the reader; he is not a chronicler, but our passionate contemporary.

Babel is cementing the bond between literature and the Republic of the Soviets and the Communist Party. He is close to us and has a firm sense of what our life and our era are about. One can say without exaggeration that Babel is a new landmark on contemporary literature's tortuous, complex road toward Communism. Though some people fail to see this, the content of Babel's works is absolutely unequivocal.

II

Babel is a miniaturist. Up to now, he has published about thirty miniatures, most from the book *Red Cavalry* and a few separate pieces including some Odessa stories. The book *Red Cavalry* is still not finished nor is *The Tales of Odessa*. The *Red Cavalry* miniatures are the best, the most characteristic, and the most significant, but in order to define the artistic core of the writer, it might be expedient to begin with some of the other stories. They are artistically weaker than *Red Cavalry*, but they give a good idea of Babel's basic thrust.

A true child of his era, Babel is a physiological writer. So are
Boris Pilnjak, Vsevolod Ivanov, Lidja Sejfullina, Nikolaj Nikitin.[4] Each of them has his or her own "physiology," but all are
beholden to their era. Moreover, they share a great forefather in
Lev Tolstoy. It is he rather than Dostoevsky who serves as a
model for contemporary Soviet prose, but that is quite another
subject.

For Babel the given is sacred. He celebrates reality, life, the
elementary human urges, passions, and lusts—everything that is
often labeled "coarse animal instincts." The given is sacred, but
not because "everything that exists is rational."[5] Babel the artist
is a heathen, a materialist, and an atheist. He is inimical to the
Christian, idealistic world view that considers flesh and matter
base and sinful, and the "spiritual" the only positive force. Babel
the artist has little use for mythmaking, for abstract spirituality
and daydreaming, for self-contained fantasies, heavenly utopias,
and a disembodied paradise. He loves flesh, meat, blood,
muscles, flushed cheeks, everything that grows wildly, that
breathes, smells, and is firmly rooted in this earth.

Poets and prose writers who dominated the Russian literary
scene after the abortive revolution of 1905 had spurned life as a
coarse and drunken slattern and sought escape in the enchantment of lovely dreams, in weaving gentle legends. Babel is
ready to tackle this coarse, drunken slattern-life. He knows that
she has a "horribly large belly," a "paunch swollen and com-
bustible," "legs . . . which are fat, bricklike, inflated," and "large
breasts." Every now and then, Babel contrasts this earthy creature with the lovers and devotees of spirituality, with the pure
heaven-dwellers and cherubs who have "neither paunch nor
shoulders, but only incorporeity and [whose] tender snow-white
little wings flutter." The slatterns behave rather disrespectfully
toward heaven-dwellers, even quite coarsely, and the author is
on their side. To one such slattern, Arina, Jesus gave Alfred, an

---

4. Pilnjak, Ivanov, Sejfullina, Nikitin were early Soviet fiction writers.
5. A truncated and inaccurate version of Hegel's famous dictum found in
the preface to his *Philosophy of Right* ([Oxford, 1942], p. 10), "What is rational
is actual, what is *actual is rational*." This mistranslation gained wide currency
in Russia through the good offices of Vissarion Belinskij who, during a brief
period of a conservative "reconciliation with reality" (i.e., acceptance of the
status quo) interpreted Hegel's "what is actual" (*was wirklich ist*) as "all that
exists" (see D. Cizevsky, *Gegel' v. Rossii* [Hegel in Russia] [Paris, 1939], pp.
134–38).

angel. Everything about him was good, but "You can't bear a duckling from him, let alone a baby, for there's a lot of fun in him but no seriousness." The woman was at first unspeakably happy, but then during the night she laid her "paunch" on him and accidentally smothered him, and what is more, she refused to forgive Jesus for palming off someone like that on her.[6] In another tale Ksenija wants a husband. An old woman, Morozikha, brings into her kitchen a "plain" but "playful" Valentine. He gets drunk on his wedding night; instead of doing what is expected of him, he begins to cry and to tell how he was taken advantage of and what unusual dreams he was having. As a result, he is kicked into the yard. Ksenija cries. "It was a booboo," Morozikha admits. "I should have brought a simpler one." In the story "Line and Color," the notorious A. F. Kerenskij refuses to buy a pair of glasses for fifty kopecks in spite of his nearsightedness.[7] He does not want to see lines; colors are enough for him. He cherishes his nearsightedness: "I don't need your lines, vulgar as the truth is vulgar. You live your life as though you were a trigonometry teacher, while I live in a world of miracles, even when I am in Kljaz'ma. . . . To me the whole universe is a huge theater, in which I am the only member of the audience who does not wear opera glasses." This "member of the audience" meets a sad end. The next time the author meets Kerenskij is June 1917 in Petersburg [the first meeting occurred on the eve of the Revolution in December 1916]. "A rally was held in the People's House. Aleksandr Fëdorovich [Kerenskij] made a speech about Russia—mother and spouse. The crowd smothered him with the sheepskins of their passion. He was followed on the rostrum by Trotsky, who in an implacable voice began: . . . 'Comrades and brothers!' " Trotsky stands here for the line, the reckoning, the inexorable.[8]

In acknowledging the supreme rights of the "slattern," Babel is not as straightforward as it may appear. He too is a dreamer. The Alfred strain is not at all alien to him. In the same story about

---

6. The above is a synopsis of a remarkable story "The Sin of Jesus" (1922).

7. Aleksandr F. Kerenskij (1881–1970), one of the major figures in the February Revolution of 1917, became in July the head of the so-called provisional government that was brought down by the Bolsheviks in October.

8. Predictably, the final passage of the story, with its mention of Trotsky, is missing from the 1963 version of the Voronskij essay (*Literaturno-kriticheskie stat'i* [Literary-critical essays] [Moscow, 1963], pp. 276–95).

Kerenskij the writer exclaims: "Oh Helsingfors, refuge of my dreams!" In *Red Cavalry,* his proclivity for dreaming surfaces time and again: "The soul filled with the heady potion of dreams smiled vaguely," "and I awaited with an anxious heart Romeo's coming out of the clouds," "driven out of my mind by the recollections of my dreams," "the dense solemn recollection wearies me," and so on. Clearly the lure of dreaming is well known to Babel. It is here that one should look for the sources of Babel's lyricism, of his aestheticism, which had brought upon him the charge of semidecadence. But Babel is *not* a decadent. It is rather that the dreamer in him clashes head-on with the realist who senses the profound truth of actuality, coarse perhaps, but full blooded and robust. Much of Babel's work is propelled by this conflict, with the realist invariably gaining the upper hand. In the story "Pan Apolek"[9] the author admits: "I then made a vow to follow Pan Apolek's majestic example . . . and the sweetness of rancor, the bitter scorn I felt for the curse and swine of mankind, the fire of silent and intoxicating vengeance—all these I sacrificed to a new god." Apolek's "majestic example" lay in that he, a Polish village icon painter, turned away from traditional church imagery and began to paint "sacrilegious" icons, where the male and female models are local peasants, paupers, beggars, and prostitutes. He rewarded them with family icons; in his Jesuses and Marys they recognized and worshiped their own selves. For the right to paint icons in this way Apolek waged a courageous war against the Jesuits and the Catholic church. He told the author an apocryphal legend about Jesus' sleeping with the newlywed Deborah, lying in her vomit, because she could not abide her wedding night with her bridegroom. Shame fell upon her and her parents, and Jesus, full of compassion, lay with her and saved her from shame.

Thus far, Babel has fulfilled faithfully the promise to follow Apolek's example. Like Apolek, he raises man to a pearl of creation. He writes about the truth of the Arinas and Ksenijas, about the truth of Afon'ka Bida,[10] about the triumph of life, even in moments of deadly battle, for he knows that the Arinas and Ksenijas are the creators of life, while in the Alfreds there is "a

9. One of the *Red Cavalry* "miniatures."
10. See section III below.

lot of fun . . . but no seriousness," that one should take pride in one's essential humanity and leave the scorn for the coarse, slattern-life to feeble Alfreds and self-isolated spectators without opera glasses.

III

Let us turn to *Red Cavalry*. As editor of *Red Virgin Soil*,[11] where Babel has published some of his work, this writer has had to listen to harsh reproaches from some of the most eminent Red Army figures. There were also those who claimed that Babel's miniatures portrayed not the First Cavalry Army, but a bunch of anarchist guerillas. Some of them, it was said, are a lampoon and slander on the Red Cavalry. Only a White Guard, an inveterate counterrevolutionary, could write this way about our army, and so on and so forth.

Strictures such as these are based on a number of misconceptions. Babel's *Red Cavalry* does not set itself immediate propaganda objectives. Until recently, it was customary to write about our army exclusively in propagandistic terms. This was the only appropriate tone under the conditions in which the Republic of Soviets had found itself. Even now discretion must be exercised. Nonetheless, the present, relatively peaceful period allows for a different approach. Today one can demand from an artist not only love for, and burning devotion to, the Red Army, but also an artistically true depiction of it. The propaganda approach was basically accurate, but it lacked depth. It did not offer an artistic portrayal of our army. In Babel's *Red Cavalry*, there is everyday detail that so far has received little attention: the destruction of the shrine of Saint Valentine; Kudrja, who slits the throat of an old Jew; the squadron camp follower Sasha; the vindictive Prishchëpa; the Cossacks making merry at the expense of the foot soldiers in the trenches, and so on. To conclude from this that Babel's stories are politically harmful without relating these episodes to the author's overall artistic world view is to miss the forest for the trees.

11. *Red Virgin Soil (Krasnaja nov')*, founded in 1921, was an influential early Soviet literary journal. Owing to Voronskij's relatively broad-minded editorial policy, *Red Virgin Soil* proved hospitable to a number of talented non-Party writers.

Furthermore, Babel's *Red Cavalry* is not Budënnyj's First Cavalry Army. The writer did not set out to produce a comprehensive epic panorama of the actual Red Cavalry, to capture its essential spirit and character, as Lev Tolstoy did in *War and Peace* with respect to the Russian society and Russian army of the Napoleonic era. Babel's *Red Cavalry* is never shown in action. The writer mentions attacks, but he does not portray them. "And at the Divisional Commander's signal, we moved on to the attack." Period. By the same token, we never see the Red Cavalry as thousands of armed men moving forward relentlessly, a community on the march with a psychology, an ethos of its own. In Tolstoy there is Kutuzov, Pierre, Andrej Bolkonskij, but there is also the army in combat, at rest, on the attack, in retreat. In Babel the Red Cavalry is atomized and dissected. In Tolstoy Kutuzov and Napoleon, Denisov and Andrej are part and parcel of the army, of its way of life, its "style" or spirit. Babel's heroes are alone; they are in the Red Army, but they are not organically bound up with it. Therefore, it is singularly fitting that Babel should have chosen the form of individual vignettes, of autonomous fragments, and that Tolstoy should have embodied his vision of the 1812 war in a four-volume epic: the two writers set for themselves different artistic tasks. Tolstoy offers a synthetic, comprehensive picture of Russian society and the Russian army of 1812 from top to bottom. Babel confines himself to selecting from the Red Cavalry saga a few salient types, personalities, and events to embody imaginatively his own artistic conception of the world. Moreover, these personalities and events are not shown in the round, but from one particular angle. Therefore, to insist that in Babel's *Red Cavalry* there are no real Communists who instill in the army proletarian discipline, that not all women in the Red Army were camp followers, that in Babel the army is not shown in battle, and so forth—all strictures such as these are correct, but beside the point. People who are looking in Babel for a Tolstoyan perspective are presenting the writer with a promissory note that he did not sign and did not issue; they are requesting of him something that was not part of his artistic design.

What is the nature of this design? Clearly the Red Cavalry was for Babel a harsh and wholesome school. He was taught to value truth, authenticity, justice, sturdiness, and the intrinsic worth of that slattern-life and to discard the dreamy abstractions. He realized that the truth of Afon′ka, Balmashev, and Sasha is immeasurably higher than the truth of "spectators without opera glasses" or the pocket-sized Alfreds. Most of all, the Red Cavalry helped resolve the conflict between Babel the dreamer and idealist and Babel the heathen. It was not the "wise and beautiful life of Pan Apolek" that made the writer vow to follow his example and celebrate the essence of man, but the unsophisticated and simple life of the ordinary soldier—Mel′nikov, Timoshenko, Lëvka, Afon′ka.

The types depicted by Babel in *Red Cavalry* are highly varied, distinct, and colorful. Babel does not echo clichés, he does not refurbish old verities. He has inventiveness and originality. He draws amply on the evidence of his senses. To be sure, Babel's vignettes are impressionistic. In each type, each image or picture, he brings out one or two basic characteristics, leaving the rest unilluminated, but what he highlights stands out clearly. His Dolgushovs and Balmashevs are memorable. However, in spite of their differentiation and uniqueness, all his protagonists have something in common. They did not stumble accidentally onto the pages of *Red Cavalry*. How singularly and strangely at the first glance do they conduct themselves on one of the toughest fronts of the civil war! What makes them tick? What are they thinking about? What motive forces drive them, make them fight heroically? Afon′ka Bida seeks revenge on the Poles because they killed his horse; he knows no peace until he secures another good horse for himself, leaving behind a bloody trail across the Polish villages. Mel′nikov, the commander of the squadron, is ready to leave the ranks of the Communist Party because of a horse taken from him by Timoshenko; he finally stays in the Party but quits the Red Cavalry. The political commissar Konkin hunts for the Polish headquarters and engages eight Poles in combat in order to get hold of some junk "for the boys," and in the midst of it cracks a joke: "We'll die for pickled cucumbers and for the world revolution." Shevelëv dies before the eyes of Lëvka, the divisional commander's driver. The latter rapes Shevelëv's mistress, almost within the dying man's sight, yet he goes out of his way to deliver to Shevelëv's mother, who lives beyond the river, her son's underclothes, and a medal for selfless heroism. Prishchëpa lays waste with fire and sword to his native Cossack village because the villagers plundered his property while the Whites were there. During a battle the squad-

ron woman, Sashka is busy mating her horse with a stallion.
Sen'ka Kudrjukov takes revenge for his brother on their "dad"
and "finishes him off." The squadrons attack the Poles and a
"great hush of chopping" is heard about the fields while side by
side flows the quotidian, triumphant, inextinguishable, primordial life, with stallions, women, love, harnesses, cattle mar-
kets, and the plundering of Polish Catholic churches.

What of the social revolution, Communism, the Third International, the Republic of the Soviets? Is this a new revolutionary army or an old one that has always lived by stallions,
mares, camp followers, and canteens? Curiously enough, Babel
seems to be intent on making his heroes intermingle stallions
with Communism and the world revolution. Mel'nikov's letter
about his leaving the Party begins with high-flown words about
the task of the Communist Party. Then he writes: "Now I shall
touch upon the matter of the white stallion, which I recaptured
from peasants who were incredible in their counterrevolutionary
ways." In another letter to Timoshenko, he sends "together with
the working masses of the Vitebsk region a proletarian call:
long live the world revolution!" and expresses his wish that "the
white stallion may ride beneath you long years." Kudrjukov, in
his letter to mother, speaks in the same breath about the Moscow *Pravda,* his "merciless" local newspaper, *The Red Trooper,*
and his horse Stepka. Balmashev shoots a woman for the good of
the social revolution. Afon'ka Bida viciously mocks the deacon
deserter as a traitor to the Republic of Soviets. It may seem that
the author is being ironic in juxtaposing world revolution with
horses, but that is not so. In Mel'nikov's letter to Timoshenko,
in the stories of Konkin and Balmashev, and in the action of
Afon'ka, one senses a genuine revolutionary commitment; not
in vain do they "mercilessly fight the foul Polish gentry." Both
the stallions and the world revolution are very serious matters.
The Afon'kas are far removed from Communism, but their life
spent in harness, the gentry oppression, war, and revolution have
taught them to seek their own truth, their own justice. Oh, they
are not at all the "gray brutes" of old who cared only about
horses! Their life, their struggle, their death testify to a thirst for
truth and justice on earth. Their understanding of this truth is
dim, foggy, incorrect, but it has taken strong hold. Almost all of
them are truth-seekers: Sasha, Balmashev, Lëvka, Mel'nikov,
Sashka the squadron woman, Afon'ka, even Kudrjukov, even

Konkin, who has been "offended" by Makhno's men.[12] "The raw blood of a soldier"—things which the aesthetes and the esoteric dreamers shun scornfully and disdainfully are for them an essential, genuine, ineradicable reality. The white stallions and the underclothes are an inalienable part of man's life, and each infringement of the law of life is perceived here as an untruth. Hence the white stallion alongside the Communist Party, hence Konkin's crack about the world revolution and pickled cucumbers. The truth-seeking of the Babel heroes is abstract not because it lacks concreteness, but only because it is inchoate, instinctive.

Babel does not retouch his heroes. He tells of the desecration of a Polish Catholic church, of reprisals and murders, of everything that in certain quarters is customarily called atrocity, brutality, mindlessness. But underneath the cruelty, the seeming senselessness and savagery, the writer sees a hidden meaning, a yearning for truth. And the incident or the character appears in a new light. There is no room here for facile irony, for philistine sniggering or high-minded fastidiousness. In his letter to the editors, Nikita Balmashev recounts how he at first took a woman with a child into the railroad car and protected her as a mother would from abuse on the part of his comrades; yet when he discovered that she was carrying a bag of salt instead of a child, he threw her out of the train and shot her dead:

> And seeing this unharmed woman, and an unspeakable Russia around her, the peasant fields without an ear of corn, and the desecrated young girls, and the comrades, many of whom go to the front but few of whom return, I wanted to jump off the train and do away with either myself or her. But the Cossacks took pity on me and said: "Give it to her with your rifle."
>
> And taking my trusty rifle off the wall, I wiped the disgrace off the worker's land and the republic. ["Salt"]

Prishchëpa devastated his native Cossack village over the murder of his parents and the plunder of his property. He painstakingly gathered what had been plundered, "arranged the

---

12. Makhno was a leader of anarchical peasant bands that operated in southern Russia during the civil war.

furniture he had taken back in the places he remembered from childhood," and then burned everything, shot the cow, and vanished into the Red Cavalry, because he was seeking not furniture, but his own truth. Afon'ka Bida tries to quench his thirst for truth in cruel reprisals. In his own way, Lëvka the driver, too, is trying to do the right thing, as he worries about Shevelëv's underclothes. Mel'nikov stands up for justice, which in his opinion has been defiled. "The Communist Party," he writes, "was founded, I suppose, for the purpose of joy and solid truth without limit, and likewise it must look after the little people." And here is a description of the death of the telephone operator Dolgushov, a masterful portrayal of a clash of two mentalities and one of the finest passages in *Red Cavalry*:

> The man sitting by the side of the road was Dolgushov, a telephone operator. He sat staring at us, his legs straddled.
>
> "Look here," he said, when we had driven up to him, "I'm going to die. Get it?"
>
> "Yes," answered Grishchuk, pulling up the horses.
>
> "You've got to waste a cartridge on me," said Dolgushov sternly. He was sitting propped against a tree, his boots thrust out and apart. Without taking his eyes off me, he carefully hoisted up his shirt. His belly had been ripped open, the entrails crept down his knees, and the heartbeats were visible.
>
> "Polish gentry will turn up and play their dirty tricks. Here are my papers. Write my mother how things were . . ."
>
> "No," I answered inaudibly and spurred my horse.
>
> Dolgushov laid his dark blue palms upon the ground and looked them over with disbelief.
>
> "Sneaking off, eh?" he muttered, sliding down. "Well, sneak off, then, you bastard."
>
> Sweat broke out all over my body. The machine guns were chattering faster and faster, with a hysterical insistence. Framed in the nimbus of the sunset, Afon'ka Bida galloped up to us.
>
> "We are mopping up what's left," he cried out gaily. "What kind of a show you got here?"
>
> I pointed Dolgushov out to him and rode away.
>
> They had a short conversation. I didn't hear the words. Dolgushov held his papers out to the platoon commander. Afon'ka stuck them in his boot and shot Dolgushov in the mouth.

"Afon'ka," I said with a sad smile, and rode up to the Cossack, "I just couldn't."

"Get out of my sight," he said, growing pale, "or I'll kill you. You guys in specs have about as much pity on chaps like us as a cat has for a mouse."

And he cocked the trigger.

I rode away slowly without turning around, feeling chill and death down my spine.

"Hey, you!" Grishchuk cried out from behind. "Stop fooling around!" And he grabbed Afon'ka by the arm. ["The Death of Dolgushov"]

Here every detail has deep significance: the stern last demand of Dolgushov, who did not want the Polish gentry "to play their dirty tricks," the harsh, merciless pity of Afon'ka, who was not for a minute in doubt as to what had to be done; the intellectual's pathetic "I can't," the bewilderment, the sweat all over the body, and that cocked trigger, which Afon'ka was ready to pull at "guys in specs," and his scorn and fury. A new light is cast on Afon'ka and "traces of his savage and rapacious plundering," his sense of justice and his pity.

Babel looked deep into the human thicket of the Afon'kas and saw under the cloak of atrocities the truth of their life, ineluctable as the dew, the air, the sun, the sea, and the mountains. To accuse an artist of affinity for the counterrevolution on the ground that he failed to create real Communists is to miss the point of his creative achievement. Babel is closer to us than many of those who dutifully stamp upon their productions the official label of Communism and proletarian art.

Babel does not justify the deeds of the Prishchëpas and the Afon'kas; he explains them with the artistic means at his disposal. He heeds Spinoza's wise advice: "Do not cry, do not laugh; understand."

Though Babel concentrated his attention on the Balmashevs and Afon'kas, he also has presented the real leaders of the Red Cavalry, those who kept the Afon'kas in check and disciplined them. Such a man was Timoshenko, who writes to Mel'nikov: "Our Communist Party is an iron line of fighters who gives their blood in the front ranks. And when blood flows from iron, this, Comrade, is no joke, but victory or death." Such, in part, is Mel'nikov or Elijah the rabbi's son, the only one in a retreating peasant crowd to reach toward a leaflet of Trotsky's. Such is the

Jewish lad in glasses who commands an infantry unit made up of local peasants. Budënnyj and Voroshilov[13] are shown briefly. One would hope that in his next cycle of miniatures the Timoshenkos will loom larger. They work out in Babel's tales as well as do his Afon'kas.

The old and the obsolete in its confrontation with the new is portrayed in the stories "Berestechko," "The Rabbi," and "Gedali." The figure of Gedali, the Talmudist who dreams of the "sweet revolution" and the Fourth International is superb: "And I want an International of good men, I want every soul to be listed and given first-category rations."

Babel's fighting men are shown during the Polish campaign of 1920. They are pitted against the small-town mores of the Western borderland, with its Catholic churches, aristocratic castles, and back-breaking peasant toil, its stagnant, backward, Jewish petty bourgeoisie, traditional heders and Sabbaths, smuggling, dirt, and poverty. This milieu forms the essential backdrop for *Red Cavalry*.

Babel is adept at portraying Jewish petty bourgeoisie. He proved this in his *Tales of Odessa*, a cycle, incidentally, which is still unfinished. The hero óf these stories is Benja Krik, the "king" whose prototype is the well-remembered bandit Mishka Japonchik. Outside of robberies he used to take active part in local self-defense units that shielded the Odessa Jews from the czarist pogroms; later he fought the Whites and was shot by them. The *Tales of Odessa* breathe the heady air of Moldavanka[14]—a strange and old mixture of gangsterism and small-town petty bourgeois mores: the marketwomen "Aunt Pesjas," the "aristocrats" and moneybags, Tartakovskijs and Eichbaums, the rabbis and shopkeepers form along with the bandits a unique world with a way of life and a moral code all its own. The "king" himself is a bizarre combination of bourgeois respectability, bandit daring, amazing resourcefulness, and cleverness. Even here Babel remains true to himself. In the bandit Benja he uncovers a truth-seeker, indeed one who bleeds "for the working class." Beneath the bandit's histrionic mask, the misdeeds and robberies as well as the thoroughgoing philistinism, he discerned the truly

13. Another prospective Soviet marshal who distinguished himself during the civil war.
14. The predominantly Jewish section of Odessa.

human traits of a fighter and a rebel, warped but groping toward his own truth. Thus, the basic motifs of Babel's work enter the world of the *Tales of Odessa.*

Babel is a very great hope of contemporary Soviet Russian literature and already its major accomplishment. His talent is extraordinary. Let us hope that he will not lower his sights and will not be spoiled by his early success. There is a good reason for confidence here: Babel is not merely gifted. He is also cultured and intelligent.

4
Emigré Critics

The Enigma of Tolstoy

MARK ALDANOV

The phenomenon confronting us is indeed an enigma.

Nature endowed Tolstoy with an acuity of vision unmatched before or since. This fortune's favorite could see everything—and yet he strained his powers to limit the scope of his vision. No other thinker has been as profoundly convinced as Tolstoy that in the enormous mansion of life only one small room is allotted to thought; that life cannot be contained in any logical or moral dogma; that it is replete with phenomena that are denied to the comprehension of men and consequently lack any sense at all if we repudiate the banal and meaningless phrases of the old, theologically based metaphysics.[1] Yet, at the same time no one else in modern philosophy has devoted so much effort to subordinating life to logic, to screening out the irrational in himself and others; to forcing the whole of man's existence into the confines of the simplest copybook principles. Indeed, Tolstoyanism is the ultimate in narrow rationalism. As we read Tolstoy's dogmatic writings we experience the illusion of unexampled clarity and simplicity. How neatly he delineates the various "shifts"[2] having to do with social intercourse, with physical or intellectual labor; with what mathematical exactitude he lays down the do's and the don'ts. Point one . . . point two . . . point three . . . Never before was the Christian doctrine set forth in a form so closely approaching the bureaucratic. *What I Believe* is, in its own way, a legal code[3] turned inside-out and promulgated by an anarchist.

This essay encompasses two sections of Mark Aldanov's *Zagadka Tolstogo* [The enigma of Tolstoy] (Berlin, 1923).

1. The fact of the matter is that Tolstoy never went as far as to say this. Indeed, without any sense of contradicting himself, he could maintain that "the life of this world is governed by someone's will—through the life of the whole world, and, through our lives, someone achieves some purpose of his own. In order to hope to understand the meaning of this will, it is necessary first of all to carry it out, to do what is expected of us" (*A Confession*). First, carry it out; you will understand it later, if at all. —M.A.

2. "Uprjazhka," the word used in the original means literally a team (of horses, oxen, etc.). In his major tract, *What Are We to Do?* written shortly after his famous *Confession*, Tolstoy borrows this expression from Russian peasant parlance to designate activities in which one would engage successively in the course of a busy, well-spent day.

3. It occurs to one that the well-known dictum of Vauvenargues, "ceux qui

Should we not seek in this fundamental dualism the reasons for
Tolstoy's antipathy to science? The real sin of science is not that
it is "scientific" rather than "true." Tolstoy detests it not simply
because it deals with leukocytes and the Milky Way instead of
tubs and ax handles. He detests it with an almost mystical hatred.
Science for Tolstoy is a cast of thought struck by incurable blindness. For it completely ignores the irrational, or simply fails to
recognize it. And yet it tries to pass off its unwitting blindness as
superior incisiveness; it actually dares to foist itself on people
who have constantly before them something the existence of
which it does not even suspect. All Tolstoy's works, both dogmatic
and fictional, especially the latter, contain a veiled challenge to
science. How will it answer "The Death of Ivan Ilyich"? How
will it get around Khadzhi-Murat's warlike song? How will it
crush Pozdnyshev?[4] Science has no answer to give. Faithful to
the precept of its great prophet, science seeks the "small truth"
and ignores the "big lie."[5] For the majority of scientists the extra-
logical is illogical (in other words, a lie), although, out of courtesy,
they don the comfortable and decorous vestments of positivism.
Wilhelm Ostwald tells us that his first reading of *The Kreutzer
Sonata* caused him a certain amount of anxiety; but then, having
pondered the theses of the book, illustrious scientist was soon
put at ease.[6] This is a highly typical response. *The Kreutzer
Sonata* aroused in Ostwald the same feelings it arouses in us all:
an obscure and unaccountable anxiety before the ominous specter
of the irrational. But the ideas contained in the Afterword could
not even for a moment, of course, embarrass such a logician as
Ostwald. He read the Afterword, checked its arguments against
his own, and happily concluded that he could answer Tolstoy point
by point. And not only that—he could do so without unduly tax-
ing his brain. Scores of ministers before Tolstoy had preached
premarital chastity; and scores of physicians and sociologists

---

craignent les hommes aiment les lois" is applicable not only to written, but
also to moral law. —*M.A.*

4. Khadzhi-Murat, a valiant Circassian mountaineer chief, is a hero of a
remarkable short novel under the same title, which Tolstoy completed six years
before his death. Pozdnyshev is the chief protagonist and narrator of *The Kreutzer
Sonata* (1887–89).

5. "E meglio la piccola certezza che la grande bugie" [Better a small certainty than a big falsehood] (Leonardo da Vinci, *Frammenti e Pensieri*). —*M.A.*

6. A Nobel Prize winning German chemist (1853–1921). It is not clear which
statement of Ostwald's is at issue here.

had answered: "On the one hand . . . , but on the other hand . . . ."
Ostensibly, the answer to Tolstoy lay ready at hand. The trouble is,
though, that the Afterword[7] states only a fraction of what is contained in *The Kreutzer Sonata*. In fact, it says something quite
different. "Maxwell's equations are more profound than Maxwell."[8] It may be easy to counter the Afterword, but there is no
answer to Pozdnyshev.

In this sense Tolstoy remains the victor in his struggle with
science, despite all the complacent pronouncements of men such
as Petzholdt about "eine gewisse Verkümmerung des logischen
Bestandes"[9] in the author of *The Kreutzer Sonata*. But Tolstoy's
triumph was a Pyrrhic victory. In defeating science he defeated
himself. Science has no answer to Anna Karenina, Pozdnyshev, or
Ivan Ilyich. But neither does Tolstoy. To the irrational he gives ra-
tionalistic answers, worth no more than the magnificent silence
of science. Moreover, all these answers flagrantly contradict one
another. *Anna Karenina* offers an apotheosis of marriage; in
Kreutzer Sonata marriage is dragged into the mud.[10] In *The
Death of Ivan Ilyich* people are implored to live godly lives so
that they may die at peace. But *Khadzhi-Murat* shows that life can
be beautiful, even if not lived according to God's law; and Khadzhi-
Murat's death, in any case, is easier and more beautiful than that
of the repentant Ivan Ilyich. These contradictions are inevitable
because they are the contradictions of life itself. They cannot be
smoothed over, of course, though they can be concealed under
the label of "Tolstoy's skeptical world view." But Tolstoy sensed

---

7. A discursive postscriptum to the raving and ranting of Pozdnyshev, "The
Afterword" offers a schematic, point-by-point indictment of sexuality, whether
or not legitimized by marriage.

8. Reference apparently to the eminent Scottish physicist James Clark Maxwell, known especially for his work in electricity and magnetism.

9. "A certain blurring of logical powers." I assume that Aldanov is referring
here to the turn-of-the-century positivistic philosopher J. Petzholdt, author of
Introduction to the Philosophy of Pure Experience. Again I have not been able
to trace the "pronouncement" in question.

10. How acute was Tolstoy's inner conflict in this realm is obvious from an
unmailed letter of his to N. N. Strakhov, written 19 March 1870. Defending
marriage against the "loudmouths," Lev Nikolaevich went as far as offering an
apologia for prostitution: "These unhappy [Mary Magdalenes] have always been
with us and, in my opinion, it would be godless and thoughtless to assume that
God erred having arranged things in this way. . . . The best proof that this kind of
woman is necessary is that we have brought them here from Europe" (*The Tolstoy
Museum*, 2:10). —M.A.

only too clearly that skepticism shattered against the reality of life just as easily as any positive dogma.

In the reminiscences of Count I. L. Tolstoy[11] there is a story about a literary game played at one time at Jasnaja Poljana. Each participant had to state his ideal in writing. When it was Lev Nikolaevich's turn, he answered: "To destroy all one has worshiped, to worship all one has destroyed." How strange! People as a rule fear crises; they brand a man who has changed his convictions with the unsavory sobriquet, renegade. Oh, there are nuances here, of course: to reactionaries, Belinskij is a renegade, while Katkov[12] is a man who had undergone a healthy evolution. To liberals, just the reverse is true. But for all of them a shift in convictions constitutes a black page in man's life. In autobiographies such a shift is usually glossed over; in biographies it is usually attended by remission of sins. Yet here is Lev Nikolaevich openly proclaiming a change of convictions, an achievement, indeed, confidently lifting it to the unattainable realm of the ideal.

What a magnificent spectacle, this auto-da-fé Tolstoy staged at the time of his crisis! The mighty intellect casts off, one after the other, chains forged by centuries, chains that shackle him as they do all living men, great and small. Everything that gave meaning to decades of his life, all the responsibility imposed on him by the graves of his ancestors and the living presence of those dear to him—all this is sacrificed to the God of truth, all is subjected to dispassionate, ruthless analysis. The impetuous torrent of thought burst the dam of prejudice and blind belief. Never before has the Cartesian principle of doubt been implemented in life with such relentless consistency.[13]

We locate Tolstoy's crisis at the end of the 1870s or at the beginning of the 1880s, even though critics have long shown that it began, in fact, much earlier. As a volcanic upheaval is preceded by slow-working processes in the bowels of the earth, so are the crises of great men preceded by years of intensive, though hardly apparent, inner activity. Tolstoy, moreover, is distinguished

11. [In a liberal newspaper] *Russkoe Slovo* [Russian word] (1913). —M.A.

12. An influential nineteenth-century Russian publicist and editor (1818–87) who in the course of his career evolved from a liberal position to an ultraconservative one.

13. I am speaking here about Tolstoy the dogmatic thinker and sociologist. —M.A.

by the singular slowness of those preliminary processes. In order, for instance, to liberate himself from his childhood faith, he first of all deemed it necessary to fulfill its pettiest precepts for a period of three years. Any other high-school boy would have arrived at the same result in a single day, after having read a brochure by Pisarev or Büchner.[14] Therefore it would not be inaccurate to say —and it has already been said—that the crisis is foreshadowed in Tolstoy's first works. The question now becomes, when did it end? Actually the great writer's entire life was a continuing crisis, which at the beginning of the 1880s simply assumed a more acute form. In these years Tolstoy altered his views on society, and these are always more conspicuous than any other views. Besides, in this realm the reversal was extremely abrupt: a Russian landowner, politically disengaged, with a certain bias toward conservatism, becomes more "leftist" than the most left-wing subversive.[15] Yet it is hard to believe that the spiritual growth of the author of *The Kreutzer Sonata* achieved its definitive, immutable form a quarter of a century before his death. Knowing as we do the interminable inner strife, the incessant questioning, the turmoil and discontent of Tolstoy's earlier years, it is difficult to assume that the last twenty-five years of his life constituted a period of peace, certainty, and calm. It seems much more plausible to conclude that Lev Tolstoy could not find peace in any philosophical system.[16]

And yet he said more than once that the doctrine bearing his name brought him full inner well-being. In behalf of this doctrine he inveighed against the secular heresy with all the self-assurance of a man who is certain of the ultimate truth. The Tolstoyans are justified in pointing to this self-assurance in their mentor. How-

14. For Dmitrij Pisarev see pp. 5, 6 above. Friedrich-Karl-Christian Büchner (1824–99) was a German physiologist and pathologist whose book *Kraft u. Stoff*, an exposition of a thoroughly materialist world view, was treated by Pisarev and his followers as the last word of science.

15. So maintains, at any rate, the most eminent representative of contemporary socialism: "Tolstoy, says Jaurès, was an innovator of boldness that makes revolutionary socialism seem tame and routine" (Jean Jaurès, "Tolstoi," *Les droits de l'homme*, 12 March 1911). —*M.A.*

16. "You are in grip of satanic pride when you say you know the truth," said Tolstoy to a man whose profession made it incumbent upon him to know the truth. [The entry in the diary of N. N. Gusev, Tolstoy's erstwhile secretary and biographer, identifies the man as a priest from Tula.] "Here I am, 80 years old, and all this time I have only sought the truth." (Gusev, *Dva goda s Tolstym* [Two years with Tolstoy] [Moscow, 1912], p. 62). —*M.A.*

ever, one could ask them: did Tolstoy *ever* doubt himself or the justness of his views? At a time when he believed not in Christianity, nonresistance, or in being "good," but rather in *comme il faut*, manicured nails, and fashionable bootstraps, he denounced and excommunicated in the name of these convictions, exactly as he did later in the name of Tolstoyanism. Self-assurance is a gift from God; it does not depend on specific beliefs or doctrine. In men like Tolstoy or Schopenhauer it is just as natural and unaffected as the aplomb of a fool is absurd and ridiculous.

Among the characters in Tolstoy's fiction there is one figure whose life is a remarkably close approximation of Tolstoy's own development. He is the Russian Faust, one of the most successfully realized figures in world literature—Prince Andrej Bolkonskij. To be sure, I have in mind here not biographical parallels—though these do exist—but spiritual affinity. Prince Andrej dies at the age of thirty-three; we actually see only seven years of his life. Yet in this brief time span he changes several times and gets involved with several world views. No wonder he has been attacked by men of firm convictions; a considerable number of critics have reacted unfavorably to the hero of *War and Peace*. A certain Navalikhin, a liberal writer well known in his time, who could have been the product of a union of Stepan Trofimovich Verkhovenskij and Marija Vasil'evna Vojnitskaja (Uncle Vanja's worthy mother)[17] called Bolkonskij an obtuse, witless fellow with a filthy view of life. For D. S. Merezhkovskij Prince Andrej is a "noble but not very intelligent failure." To another of Tolstoy's critics, General Dragomirov, Prince Andrej is also a "failure." This military writer says of Bolkonskij: "One feels sorry for him; he is an honest man, to a certain extent perhaps even a man of talent and character, but ineffectual in practical matters; capable of anything, but failing at everything." In a word, Prince Andrej was to no one's liking; he displeased the liberal Navalikhin because he was an officer and a prince; Merezhkovskij because he did not adhere to Merezhkovskij's philosophical teachings; he displeases General Dragomirov, finally, because he failed to attain the rank of general. Koz'ma Prutkov's old dictum, "If you want to be handsome, join the Hussars," has not lost its fascination for critics. But then what else could Prince Andrej be? Where men like the Drubetskojs and the Bergs are successful, the Bolkonskijs can only be "failures."[18] And if fate had not thrust Prince

---

17. S. T. Verkhovenskij, a character in Dostoevsky's novel *The Possessed*, is a fatuous aging liberal; M. V. Vojnitskaja, who appears, to be sure, in Chekhov's *Uncle Vanya*, is strongly addicted to "progressive" clichés.

18. "Koz'ma Prutkov" was a pen name used jointly by the nineteenth-century

Andrej in the way of shrapnel from a French grenade, he might possibly have ended his days even more "unsuccessfully"—on the ramparts of the Peter and Paul fortress, on the thirteenth of July 1826.[19]

Prince Andrej successively goes through the same stages of development as did Tolstoy. In the novel's first scenes he appears as a high-society dandy, "with a tired, bored mien" and a strong sense of personal and class pride. He constantly squints and winces. He uses French expressions like "le général Koutouzoff" stressing the final syllable; his Russian has a dry and disagreeable sound: "if you please, my deah suh." And now this is the way Turgenev described (to Mme Golovachevaja-Panaeva) Tolstoy himself at the time when the latter was twenty-seven years old, exactly the same age as Prince Andrej in the first scenes of *War and Peace.* "There is not one word, one gesture of his that is un-affected. He constantly shows off before us, and I'm hard put to account in an intelligent man for this silly flaunting of his shabby countship."[20] A little further on Mme. Panaeva adds: "And Tur-genev began to criticize Tolstoy's every sentence, the very tone of his voice, his every facial expression." It is superfluous to add that Turgenev was as much mistaken about Tolstoy as St. Peters-burg society was mistaken about Prince Andrej; but the outward appearance of each was the same. Then later on, in wartime, the cadet Tolstoy dreamed of receiving the St. George Cross; the aide-de-camp Bolkonskij dreams of the highest military post. Each, in essence, wants the same thing. Both go through a period of total negation of life, Prince Andrej in 1807, Tolstoy in 1862. "The only possible happiness is animal happiness," says Prince Andrej. And here is Tolstoy in his *Confession*: "I abandoned everything and went into the steppe to the Bashkirs, to breathe fresh air, drink *kumys*,[21] and live an animal life." Both go through a brief period of active involvement with public affairs. Prince Andrej, in collaboration with Speranskij,[22] writes

---

poet and novelist A. K. Tolstoy and his otherwise undistinguished confreres, the three Zhemchuzhnikov brothers. This team produced a considerable body of highly quotable humorous verse. Drubetskoj and Berg are minor characters in *War and Peace,* run-of-the-mill careerists.

19. Reference to the execution of the leaders of the "Decembrist" insurrec-tion. See "Pushkin and Sterne" above, n. 27.

20. [P.I.] Birjukov, *L. N. Tolstoy,* (Moscow, 1906), 1:78–79. —M.A.

21. A fermented liquor prepared from mare's milk, used as a beverage by the Tartars.

22. One of the most enlightened public figures of Alexander I's reign, Speranskij was known mostly for his abortive attempt at constitutional reform. In *War and Peace* he is portrayed as a self-important careerist, overly impressed with legalistic detail.

"enormous tomes" of law, as the old Prince ironically puts it.
Tolstoy serves as a land arbitrator after the freeing of the serfs
and teaches reading and writing to little children. Both dabble
in philanthropy. Prince Andrej makes free farmers of the serfs
on his small estate, which, in his words, "brought in hardly any
income." Tolstoy signs a memorandum dealing with the necessity of liberating the serfs and providing them with land on condition of a "full and honest monetary compensation" to the landowners.[23] Both are soon disillusioned with public affairs and
philanthropy. The death of a person near to them has an overpowering impact on both. Both experience unhappy love affairs:
Prince Andrej with Natasha Rostova, Tolstoy with Valerija
Arsen'eva.[24] At this point they go their separate ways, only to
converge again in the world view each holds in his last days.

"The more he dwelt on a new principle of love everlasting, revealed to him, the more, without actually realizing it, he re-
nounced earthly life. To love everything and everybody, always
to sacrifice oneself for love, meant not to love anyone, meant not
to live this earthly life." In his last years Tolstoy loved everybody and everything, right down to Azef,[25] right down to the rats.
Was he living "this earthly life?"

"In his [Prince Andrej's] words, in his tone, above all in his gaze
—that cold, nearly hostile gaze of his—one could feel an alienation from all things worldly, terrifying in a living man. All living
things he obviously understood now only with difficulty." And
Tolstoy himself? Although loving men with a transcendent love,
he was at the same time never very far from thinking that they
were all insane. He even spoke to us like a psychiatrist to his
patients: gently, cautiously, striving to accommodate himself
to our way of thinking; trying not to upset us, diverting our thoughts
from heavy or sharp objects that could injure ourselves or others.
"If Evgenij Irtenev was out of his mind when he committed his
crime," remarks Tolstoy in the last sentence of *The Devil*,[26] "then

23. Birjukov, *L. N. Tolstoy,* 1:341. —M.A.
24. Ibid., pp. 300–11. —M.A.
25. A repellent but fascinating figure. Azef (1869–1918) was one of the most
famous or notorious *agents provocateurs* of the pre-1917 era. For years he managed to live a double life as one of the leaders of a revolutionary terrorist organization and a Czarist secret police agent. He was unmasked in 1918.
26. *The Devil,* written in 1889 and published posthumously, is one of
Tolstoy's darkest and most powerful narratives. Its hero Evgenij Irtenev, a model
husband and father, obsessed by a passion for an attractive peasant woman, is
finally driven to murdering her. (In an alternate version Irtenev commits suicide.)

everybody is out of his mind. The sickest of all are the very ones who see symptoms of insanity in others, which they fail to recognize in themselves."

Schopenhauer has said that to be the only sane person among teeming thousands of crazy people was like possessing the only clock with the correct time in a city where all other clocks were unwound. A similar fate befell Tolstoy. Perhaps his clock tells the correct time, and ours are slow by a hundred or even a thousand years. Yet we have no other clocks, nor could we live by them if we had. Man is capable of accomplishing his tasks by the dim light of a penny candle, but he has yet to learn how to work by the blinding flash of a lightning bolt. And Tolstoyan meekness is just that—a lightning, instantaneous, brilliant, leaving no trace. On the field of Austerlitz Prince Andrej came to believe in the "lofty, good, impartial sky"; compared to it the puny Napoleon, with all his petty vanity, his joy in victory, seemed pitiful. But when "the weakening of his condition from loss of blood" passes, and the expectation of imminent death leaves him, Prince Andrej returns to the everyday life of men. The place formerly held in his thinking by Napoleon is taken over, at first by Speranskij, who, compared to the sky is even punier and more insignificant, and later by Natasha Rostova and her momentary appendage, Anatol' Kuragin. It could not have been otherwise. A man must live, and perhaps what may be true for a dying man is wrong for one who is alive. "How is it that I never before saw this soaring sky?" the severely wounded Prince Andrej asks himself. "And how happy I am, now that I've come to know it at last. Yes, everything is empty, all is deception, save for these infinite heavens. There is nothing, nothing, save them alone." The dying prince is right; alive he is in error: not *everything* is empty, not *everything* is hollow. But even were it so, a living man should not pull himself up to a height from which Napoleon seems less than a midge.

"It would be a good thing," thinks Prince Andrej, "if everything were as clear and simple as it appears to Princess Mary. How nice it would be if we knew where to seek solace in this life, and what to expect from it, there beyond the grave. How happy and content I'd be now, if I had merely to say, 'Oh, Lord, have mercy!' But to whom would I address such a prayer? Either this power —vague and inscrutable, one to which I cannot turn, one which I cannot even express in words—is a great everything or nothing," Prince Andrej was saying to himself, "Or else it is God sown into

Princess Mary's amulet? Nothing, nothing is certain, except for
the insignificance of all I'm able to understand, and the majesty
of something unintelligible, but most important of all."

"How nice it would be," thinks Prince Andrej. Yes, very nice
indeed. But are the uncertainties of the hero of *War and Peace*
ultimately resolved by Tolstoy? "Where is one to seek solace in
this life?" asks Bolkonskij. "I do not care for the Gospels anymore," said Lev Nikolaevich, four months before his death.[27]
"What can one expect after life, there beyond the grave?" asks
Prince Andrej. "A return to Love," answers Tolstoy. One of
Goya's most terrifying pieces of fantasy shows a convulsively
twisted hand reaching out from beneath the stone of a deserted
grave, desperately clutching at something—the void. The caption
consists of only the one word, *nada* (nothing). A man weary of
life, has found nothingness even there in the depths of his own
gloomy pit. Is Tolstoy's caption "a return to Love" (for all its
being spelled with a capital letter) much better, after all, than
nada?

Human thought is bounded by the same limits that confine life
itself. One of a man's philosophical options is bound to be his
last. But can there really be a genuinely final position for one
whose pride and dream it was "to destroy all one has worshiped,
to worship all one has destroyed?" When a man's past appears
as an extended sequence of speculations, one replacing the other
in a ceaseless striving of the spirit, the natural inference is that
there is no end, there can be no end, to such strivings. The end is
a new beginning. If one is to believe biology, a single individual
in his development repeats the history of his whole species. It is
possible that Haeckel's law also pertains to the nonmaterial
sphere of existence. Perhaps in the history of Tolstoy's life we
should seek a hidden, dark hint at the path man is destined to
travel. Perhaps after "200 or 300 years" Tolstoyanism will have

27. V. F. Bulgakov, *With L. N. Tolstoy* (Moscow, 1911), p. 230—I predict that
this sentence will become as much of a stumbling block for Tolstoy scholars
as "cela vous abêtira" has been for persons known in France as "les pascali-
sants." —M.A. [The full sentence quoted by Aldanov reads: "Naturellement
même cela vous fera craire et vous abêtira." ("This will quite naturally bring you
to believe . . . and will stupefy you"; B. Pascal, *Pensées* [London, 1950], p. 121.)
The import of this puzzling phrase seems to be that "this," i.e. religious practice,
has a momentum of its own: going through ritual motions, behaving as if one
believed, may develop a habit of belief as unquestioning compliance.]

its day. And beyond that? Even Vershinin[28] dared not conjecture beyond this. The process of ontogenesis halted; death occurred, and the tale was broken off—that tale under which one can dimly discern the words "to be continued."

Yet the tale is sufficiently mysterious as it is: we stand perplexed before the insoluble problem of Tolstoy. A Hellene who converted to Judaism, or a Hebrew who lived long years as a Hellene; a misanthrope in love with life; a rationalist who devoted enormous effort to the critique of impure intellect—a genius born to be harsh who yet became inhumanly good, Lev Tolstoy stands before us as a haunting enigma. Who was he really, this man who passed his whole life in a glass house, so close and dear to our contemporaries? When the light from Tolstoy's everlasting sun filters through the paltry prism of analysis, it breaks down into a thousand hues of the rainbow. We study individual bands of light. But who can encompass the iridescent play of this magic spectrum? Who has fathomed the secret unity of the primary thrust? Who can say that he has understood Lev Tolstoy?

---

28. A high-minded and voluble officer in Chekhov's *Three Sisters*, given to speculating about "a new and happy life" that will prevail in "two or three hundred years."

From Chekhonte to Chekhov

PËTR BITSILLI

There is something singularly appropriate about the
fact that Chekhov began his career with the writing of comic
feuilletons for *The Splinters* (*Oskolki*) and *The Dragonfly* (*Stre-
koza*).[1] Each of these pieces was built around an anecdote. Their
themes were borrowed from current jokes. "Marija Vladimirovna
[Kiseleva, his good friend] is well," he wrote to his brother
Mikhail Pavlovich in 1885. "She presented Mother with a jar
of jam and in general is awfully kind. She supplies me with [old]
jokes from French magazines."

The years during which he busied himself turning anecdotes
into short stories were for Chekhov true *Lehrjahre*. The chores
that he often thought burdensome bore fruit: in this process
Chekhov found himself. Traditionally the central motif of the
anecdote is a misunderstanding, an error; the theme of wasted
energy is resolved into a "zero" ending. This theme is at the
core of the stories by Antosha Chekhonte, and more broadly,
of nearly all "comic" tales, novellas, and plays since the beginning
of literature. The comic effect lies essentially in the discrepancy
between what is expected to happen and what actually happens,
provided that the latter is neither terrifying nor depressing. The
simplest and easiest way of achieving this effect lies in having
the plot and its "complications" usher in a "zero" denouement.
The difference between the anecdote on the one hand and the
short story or drama on the other is that, while in the anecdote
the event is presented as an autonomous entity, something that
begins with the entanglement and ends with the denouement,
in the short story or drama it is treated as a phase of an unfolding
process, a "present" that presupposes a "past" and a "future."
That is why the short story tends to require what literary scholars
call *Vorgeschichte* and *Nachgeschichte*.[2] Turgenev, for example,

This essay, translated here by Carol A. Palmer, first appeared as a section of
Bitsilli's *Tvorchestvo Chekhova: Opyt stilisticheskogo analiza* [Chekhov's art:
Attempt at stylistic analysis] (Sofia, 1942), pp. 78–82.
1. Humorous journals to which Chekhov was contributing in 1880–84 under
the pseudonym Antosha Chekhonte.
2. See M. A. Petrovskij, *Morphology of the Short Story* [*Morfologija novelly*],
Ars Poetica, p. 73. —*P.B.*

never fails to introduce the characters of his story to the reader, providing them with brief but comprehensive vitae, and usually lets one know how the events of the tale affected the characters' further destinies.

In this respect, Anton Chekhov remained true to Antosha Chekhonte, from whom he inherited the tendency to tamper with literary clichés. It is fair to assume that Maupassant's influence may have been operative here; the Maupassant short story is typically nothing but an anecdote, elaborated and transferred from the simply comic to the "humoristic," if not tragic, plane. Nonetheless, it is undeniable that Chekhov's literary apprenticeship proved a decisive factor. The Chekhonte legacy is visible not only in Chekhov the artist, but also in Chekhov the literary critic. "Beginning writers," he once said to Shchukin,[3] "often would do well to divide their manuscripts in two and throw out the first half." "It is not necessary," he continued, "to 'introduce' the story. One ought to write so that without the benefit of the author's explanations the reader is able to glean what is going on from the course of the story and from the characters' conversations or actions." Even more significant is another injunction: having written the story, one should cross out the beginning and the end; these sections are the most difficult ones to write, therefore they are liable to prove the weakest: "Here we fiction writers do more lying than anywhere else."[4] Why are these passages the most difficult ones? Because whatever pertains to *Vorgeschichte* or *Nachgeschichte* can and must be conveyed through the medium of allusions, of fleeting hints. This, at least, is how Chekhov always does it. Yet, one may inquire, why is he so convinced that this is the *right* way to do it? As long as we speak about the short story, that is, a narrative genre that derives directly from the anecdote, the answer is relatively simple: a detailed account of proceedings that antedate or follow the central event violates the principle of artistic unity, as rendering is supplanted by reporting.

This, however, does not exhaust the import of Chekhov's pronouncements. It is a significant commentary on his creative evolution that even in his mature period Chekhov wrote a number of

3. From reminiscences about Chekhov, *Russkaja mysl'* [*Russian thought*] (Moscow, 1911), 10:44. —*P.B.*
4. I. Bunin, "Pamiati Chekhova" [Chekhov in memoriam] in a collection under the same title, p. 61. —*P.B.*

short stories that, though not at all "funny," exhibit the formal characteristics of an anecdote in that they lack both a prologue and an epilogue and are built around the motif of a misunderstanding. Thus, for example, in the story "At the Country Estate" (*V usad'be*, 1894), the landowner Rashevich, conversing with a guest, inveighs against the "petit bourgeois" who allegedly are now "setting the tone" and does not learn until the end that he has committed *une gaffe* as his guest turns out to be a petit bourgeois. The same mechanism is at work in "The Grasshopper" (*Poprygun'ja*, 1892), where the heroine deceives her husband as she chases celebrities and "men of genius," only to realize after his death that he was an outstanding scholar, slated to become famous. A wonderful example of a situation where energy is wasted not through a misperception but as a result of a psychic movement is the touching story, "The Letter" (1887). A deacon, having prevailed upon his superior to furnish him with a stern letter to his, the deacon's, wayward son, attaches the following postscript: "They sent us a new inspector. He is smarter than his predecessor, a dancer and a conversationalist; he is good at everything, and the Govorov girls are crazy about him. They say that the military commander Kostyrev will retire soon. Good riddance!" Amusingly enough, he fails to understand that "by adding this postscript, he utterly spoiled the stern letter."

No less telling are the instances where the anecdotal core is, so to speak, turned upside-down: a person decides upon something that seems trivial to him only to realize later that his entire future has been changed by that decision. This is what happens to the relationship between the hero and the heroine in "The Lady with a Dog [1898]." When their liaison begins, the hero does not know that he loves her ardently. It seems to him that this is no more than one of his numerous and inconsequential brief encounters. "The Neighbors" offers another variation on the theme of misunderstanding. Ivashin is on his way to Vlasich's, to whom his sister has run away, with the intention of chastising the seducer: "I will strike him with a whip in her presence and will shower him with insults." Yet what actually transpires is that his friendly relationship with Vlasich is further enhanced. There was no opportunity to expend accumulated energy. The misunderstanding here was an inward one. Essentially, Ivashin himself did not know how he should act. More important, he did not know whether he was truly outraged by his sister's and Vlasich's behavior.

These latter instances contain the germ of still another, more complex transformation of the anecdotal nucleus whereby the zero ending of the story becomes a vehicle for what one might describe as a withering away, an erosion or attenuation of inter-personal relationships. From the viewpoint of "outer form," such works as "Ariadne," "Three Years," "My Life" [1895] have nothing in common with the anecdote, yet these stories too feature the motif of misunderstanding, invested with a new meaning and a new psychological depth. In the above examples, the mis-understanding lies not in having misjudged oneself or the loved one, but in having treated both oneself and the loved one as con-stants. The fact is, however, that just as the river of life never is what it was at an earlier moment, so the one who has stepped into it is no longer the same person he was when he first entered the stream. This is conveyed with special finesse in Chekhov's last short story "The Bride" (1903). Under the influence of Sasha, a friend of the family, Nadja suddenly leaves home and goes off to St. Petersburg to study. Eventually her mother and grand-mother forgive her, and she returns home for a spring vacation. En route, she stops in Moscow to see Sasha.

> He was exactly the same as last summer: bearded, with tousled hair, always in the same jacket, with the same big, beautiful eyes: yet he looked sickly and troubled. He seemed to have grown older and thinner, and he was always coughing, and for some reason, he seemed to Nadja dull, provincial. . . . They sat and talked for a while and now, after spending the winter in Petersburg, she found Sasha, his words, his smile, and every-thing about him somehow out of date, old-fashioned, done with long ago and perhaps already dead and buried.

The point, of course, is not just that Sasha has actually grown older and thinner, that he is already at the edge of the grave. More important, it is Nadja herself who has changed. Sasha had given her all he could give, he had furthered her development. Now—or so at least it appears to her—she has outgrown him. Sasha is the stage of her development she has left behind. Thus, when she re-ceives a letter from him in which he writes of his illness,

> she understood what it meant, and a foreboding verging on a conviction [that he was dying] seized her. It disturbed her that the premonition and the thoughts about Sasha did not upset her as much as they used to. She wanted passionately to go on

living, to be in Petersburg, and her friendship with Sasha appeared to her now as sweet, but far, far away.

It is the ceaselessness of the psychic processes that renders us unable to understand ourselves, to gauge properly what is happening inside us.

It seemed to Nadja that she was quite upset, her heart was heavier than ever, that from now until her departure she would suffer and mentally agonize; but scarcely had she gone upstairs to her room and lain down on her bed than she promptly fell asleep.

The clear implication of the above is that if it *seemed* to Nadja that she was very upset, this *at the moment* was indeed the case. Her error lay in mistaking a moment for an enduring present.

In his dynamic perception of man and life, Chekhov is akin to Tolstoy. The difference between them is that in his insistence on man's fluidity Chekhov is more one-sided than Tolstoy and thus more consistent. True, Tolstoy refused to paint full-fledged portraits of his protagonists on the theory that a human being is too complex to be presented; it is impossible to say of anyone that he is beautiful or ugly, smart or dumb, because everyone is beautiful or ugly, smart or dumb in his own fashion. Moreover, everyone is smart in some cases and stupid in others, good in some and bad in others. And yet—and therein lies Tolstoy's incomparable mastery—even when he sketches his characters impressionistically, with but a few touches, he does it so compellingly that we can see them, sense them, feel close to them. Each has his *character indelebilis*, though one whose essence does not lend itself to paraphrase, and thus his own destiny. Therefore, for all its dynamism, Tolstoy's *roman-fleuve* still retains some affinity with the more static classical tragedy. A Tolstoyan plot does have a denouement, be it a tragic disaster or a happy end.

In Chekhov, one finds two fundamentally different groups of protagonists. First there are comic types—such as one encounters in Gogol—whose *character indelebilis* rests on being in the grip of some fixation, like "the man in a case" or the "hereditary nobleman Chimsha-Gimalajskij," who dreams of his own estate with gooseberries.[5] Then there are sweet, decent, good-hearted people

5. The hero of the "Man in a Case" (Chelovek v futljare, 1898), the school principal Belikov, is a pathologically rigid bureaucrat whose "constant impulse

who resemble one another and whose "indelible stamp" has less to do with their personalities than with their social environment, for example, Laptev and his inferiority complex in "Three Years." They are "typical" in their capacity as gentry, commoners [*raznochintsy*], clergy, peasants, merchants. As personalities, they differ from one another mainly by being more or less likable, good-hearted, responsive to another's joy or woe, by a greater or lesser zest for life. A Chekhov character is least of all a "monad," in the sense of embodying some kind of idea. He is, rather, if one may put it this way, a geometric point of intersection of all possible sensations, an object of external influence rather than a subject, and his residual humanity consists in responding to the outside pressures with his mind and heart. This is attested to by Chekhov's language. Significantly enough, one often encounters in his works, passive, third-person constructions such as "it appeared to him," "it occurred to him," and the like, instead of sentences in which a human being plays an active role, in which he or she thinks, recalls, desires, and so on. These phrases express a condition akin to the one conveyed by Chekhov's favorite verb "to seem" or by passive constructions like "something reminded [him, her, me] of."

Thus in the story "Big Volodja and Little Volodja [1893]": "The peal of the monastery bell was rich, and, as it seemed to Sofija L'vovna, there was something about it that brought to mind Olja and her life. . . . For some reason, she was reminded of that same aunt. . . . Sofija L'vovna recalled Olja and she was overcome by uneasiness" (literally, "it became uncanny to her").

And now a few passages from "The Lady with a Dog": "Tales of easy conquest came to his mind, and a tempting thought of a quick, fleeting liaison suddenly got hold of him" (Here the thought is the subject, he the object toward which the action is directed.) "When the first snow falls . . . it is pleasant to see the white earth, the white roofs; one breathes easily, freely, and years of one's youth are brought to mind." "But now he was in no mood for reflection, he *felt* a profound compassion and was *seized by desire* to be sincere and tender" (literally, "it felt like being sincere and

---

is . . . to make himself a case that would isolate him from external influences." Chimsha-Gimalajskij, a timid clerk turned overbearing landowner, and his fixation on gooseberries are featured in another famous Chekhov story, "Gooseberries" (Kryzhovnik).

tender"). Here "I" for a moment becomes the subject, only to surrender that status promptly.[6]

Many more examples could be adduced; such constructions are quite common in Chekhov.

6. According to philosophers of language, the function of the passive voice is to convey the specifically *human* quality, notably, the ability to *suffer*, to respond *with feeling* to external stimuli. K. Vossler aptly describes the passive voice as "die Leidensform der Verbe" [the suffering form of the verb]. "Ein Leiden," he says, "gibt es, objectiv genommen, nur im eigenen Gefühl. Ja, alles Leiden ist Gefühl und weiter nichts. Wenn wir sagen, die Erde werde von der Sonne bestrahlt, und wenn wir das so ausdrücken, dass die Erde als Trögerin einer Leidensform des Bestrahlens erscheint, so schreiben wir ihr etwas Menschliches zu" [Objectively speaking, suffering is always a matter of feeling. Yes, all suffering is feeling and nothing else. When we say that the earth is illuminated by the sun and thus represent the earth as a bearer of the suffering form of illumination, we ascribe to it a human quality] (*Geist und Kultur in der Sprache* [1925], p. 61). —*P.B.*

Vladimir Nabokov

GEORGIJ ADAMOVICH

Whatever can be said about Vladimir Nabokov, one thing is certain: he is an exceptionally talented writer.

We will take this assertion for granted. Our further discussion will be bound up with and largely predicated upon it. Nabokov is, without any doubt, an extraordinary phenomenon: if I find it impossible to proceed without using the telling little word "but," it is not because his works are not to my liking. Critics would be well advised to remember that their personal affinities or aversions, their likes or dislikes, not to mention their grievances or grudges, matter only where larger considerations are involved. People, particularly critics, usually find art most appealing when it more or less resembles or suits them, and most annoying when it runs counter to their mental habits. But are we justified in demanding this resemblance, this congruence? Is it right to lament its absence? Of course not. In the world there is the tiger and there is the bird of paradise, there is the oak and there is the burdock, all living, all in their own way perfect or in their own way wanting, and one should "criticize" the tiger only for being a bad, unsuccessful tiger, not for being carnivorous or unable to fly. . . . My intention is not to criticize Nabokov. I would simply like to understand him, to make him clearer to myself. As one reads him, one is moved to admiration: how clever, how brilliant! At the same time one wonders: why all this brilliance? Is brilliance essential to genuine literature? What is behind it? Why this constant, obtrusive urge to dazzle? What is the source of this arid and lifeless sorrow that permeates all Nabokov's writings? Something about this uncommon talent is disconcerting. What is it?

Of course, to find a place for Nabokov in our literature and to pin a label on his work would not be difficult. A child of emigration, a bard of rootlessness, or a poet of still something else, why not get hold of one of these formulas, why not conclude that the matter is settled and all that remains is to elaborate on the basic

This essay, translated here by Irene Etkin Goldman, first appeared in *Loneliness and Freedom* [*Odinochestvo i svoboda*] (New York, 1955), a collection of Adamovich's essays.

propositions? However, after yet another bout with the formulas, one has only to open any of Nabokov's books—for example, *Despair*, his best novel in my opinion—to see clearly that the scheme, which hitherto appeared adequate and valid, has little in common with the doubts and uncertainties of Herman or Cincinnatus.[1] The above interpretation seems both logical and reasonable, but Nabokov is so bizarre a writer that the question of logic does not pose itself. To be sure, there is some connection between Nabokov and the notion of emigration, that is, the notion of separation, of discontinuity, but this connection is operative at the level of circumstance, and not at the level of theme. What matters in art, however, is precisely the theme, that is, mastery over the circumstance, the triumph over the demeaning Marxist formula about being and consciousness,[2] which fits everything but creativity.

What distinguishes a literary work of art is chiefly its patterning, in other words, its tone, sound, color, a quality that expresses the very essence of its design, and that the author can neither contrive nor counterfeit. After all, one may contrive any sort of plot just as one may proliferate lofty thoughts or notions without being able to turn verse into poetry. In order to earn the right to judge, to achieve understanding, one must listen intently to the work, rather than rely on unsubstantiated claims! The use of sound in Nabokov's prose is reminiscent of the whistling of the wind, which seems to carry with it "an extraordinary lightness of thought."[3] The reference to Gogol's hero is not entirely accidental: the key to Nabokov is likely to be found in Gogol, and, if—who can tell?—the fate has some creative disasters or transformations in store for him, these might well be impelled, as was the case with Gogol, by a hunger for warmth, light, and life.

Yes, life. . . Gogol's *Dead Souls* begins with the famous, unforgettable conversation about a wheel, one of the most remarkable passages in Russian literature: "What do you think, would that

---

1. *Despair* (*Otchajan'e*, 1934) was Nabokov's first major novel. Herman and Cincinnatus are protagonists in *Invitation to a Beheading* (*Priglashen'e na kazn'*, 1935).

2. Adamovich is referring here to Marx's celebrated thesis found in his introduction to *The Critique of Political Economy*: "It is not the consciousness of men that determines their being, but on the contrary, their social being that determines their consciousness."

3. This priceless self-definition belongs to Khlestakov, the frivolous and mindless hero of Gogol's "The Inspector General."

wheel make it to Moscow, if need be, or wouldn't it?"—"It would." "But it wouldn't make it to Kazan, I'm thinking, or would it?"— Not to Kazan, it wouldn't."[4] It seems that nothing could be more alive than this auspicious prelude. After all, this is only a vignette on a dustcover, deliberately two-dimensional and lopsided. The author's full resources are yet to come into play. It is as though all that the author needed to do to bring off wonders of vividness was to press the pedal "just a bit."[5] Yet later the author presses not just a bit but all the way; extravagantly he deploys an incredible profusion of devices—and for all that, life keeps eluding him, as the tortoise eluded Achilles, and the ever-so-slight distance remains. At times one has the feeling that the writer has overdrawn the picture, that he has overexerted himself. Otherwise, it is impossible to understand why Sobakevich or Nozdrëv,[6] illuminated as they are by the rays of thousands, no, tens of thousands of candles, somehow appear bloodless, so unlike the most insignificant, the most casually outlined character in Tolstoy. All Gogol's protagonists without any exception are like this, even Akakij Akakievich, even the old-fashioned landowners.[7] Their creator fails to bring out the difference between an organism and a thing, his images seem to lack the life-giving substance.

Nabokov leaves us with nearly the same impression. Now Gogol's example shows clearly that such congenital aridity is not incompatible with true genius. Leaving aside *Despair,* a novel whose basic design makes everything bifurcate and throw off fantastic and sinister shadows, let us recall that some of Nabokov's stories address themselves to ordinary emotions. Yet even here his heroes do not evoke sympathy so much as curiosity. . . . The people about whom Nabokov writes are described with meticulous precision, but, as with Gogol, something is missing here, something elusive and yet crucial; they lack the final breath of life—to put it more simply, they lack soul. In fact, the picture may well be so starkly clear just because it is taken from

4. Quoted from *Dead Souls,* trans. B. G. Guerney, (New York, 1948), p. 1. The above, we will recall, is an exchange between two "native peasants" assessing the range of Chichikov's "light traveling carriage."

5. An echo from Tolstoy's *What Is Art?* See "Isaac Babel" above, n. 3.

6. Characters in *Dead Souls* (see "The Aesthetics of Gogol's *Dead Souls* and Its Legacy" above, nn. 12, 13).

7. Akakij Akakievich is the unheroic hero of Gogol's "The Overcoat"; "the old-fashioned landowners" are featured in the seedily idyllic story under the same title.

a dead, stagnant universe, from brilliantly painted and ingeniously arranged puppets displayed in some super-shop window, rather than from a living world where this mechanical glitter, this incessant play with plots and denouements could not abide.

Gogol was a writer with a tragic bent. And even if *Selected Passages from Correspondence with Friends* did not exist,[8] we could tell from *Dead Souls* how heavily his perception of reality weighed upon him. Far be it from me to wish tragedy upon Nabokov. . . . Yet I cannot help but note with surprise that in Nabokov this burden is turned into a bit of fluff, that he composes novel after novel, one more frightening and "despairing" than the other, with apparent pleasure and without any inner compunctions. His uncommon productivity in and of itself is legitimate and natural, but it is also suspect and telling, for it suggests that there is something mechanical about Nabokov's craft that seems to dwell in a kind of vacuum. To label Nabokov, as some do, simply a "virtuoso," a technician, a man who writes for the sake of writing, would be grossly unfair: no, he does have a theme, he is obsessed with it, perhaps without fully realizing this. At first glance it should become clear that the creative vision of Nabokov is bound up with a dread of the allegedly inescapable downward slide of humanity toward leveling social patterns, toward an enforced collectivism. It seems that Nabokov is actually in the grip of this dread. Yet, as with Franz Kafka—with whom the author of *Despair* has very little in common, a widespread opinion notwithstanding—this is not what his writings are essentially about.

A lifeless life, a world peopled with robots, a general tailoring of the individual to a pattern of mediocrity, an absence of adversities and joys, a well-functioning "anthill," in short, an image of the future that today is rather widespread. No doubt this theme is fairly close to Nabokov's heart. One of his novels, *Invitation to a Beheading*, is dominated by it. Yet I cannot think of another writer whose plots would be so thoroughly divorced from his themes, instead of encompassing them or coinciding with them. *Invitation to a Beheading* is an example of this duality. The plot of the novel is not exactly distinctive or original in concept. It smacks of the stereotype that is all too familiar, indeed almost

8. See "Dostoevsky and Gogol" above, n. 3. Adamovich must be referring specifically to "Four Letters on the Subject of *Dead Souls*," where Gogol confesses to having been haunted by moral monsters in the process of writing the novel.

cheaply topical. The plot is worthy of the countless utopian novels published in popular journals, and, if in the days when Dostoevsky wrote about "Shigalëvism"[9] it called for incisiveness and perspicacity, today, diluted and vulgarized, it can easily dispense with such qualities. These resolutely "nightmarish" visions of the future, where people have numbers instead of names, where feelings are pigeonholed and passions are regimented, all this has become a literary commodity.[10] The main thing is, though, that no matter how engrossing all this may be as a horror story or a screenplay, the prophetic value of such visions is highly dubious. Is the leveling urge so irresistibly strong as to obliterate the centuries-old, powerful, every-resurging diversity of our world without a trace? Can our personal fears born from an experience of several decades be extended with impunity into the future of the whole mankind? It is hard to give credence to this notion—"they are out to scare us, but we are not afraid."[11] In fact, I find it is rather hard to believe that Nabokov would not transcend this theme, whether instinctively or consciously.

What, then, is he writing about? I am afraid that the matter is much more serious than would be the establishment of an ultra-Communist system in the thirty-sixth or seventy-second century. Without actually naming it, Nabokov moves closer and closer to that eternal and eternally enigmatic subject, death. . . . He approaches it without the rage and the anguish of Tolstoy, without the prettily gentle, hopeless musings of Turgenev in "Clara Milich,"[12] but with an odd and uncanny feeling of perfect naturalness. The theme of death was the theme of many great and supreme poets, but these poets were great only because they endeavored to overcome it, or at least beat their heads against a wall in search of liberation and escape. In Nabokov, we confront a dead world too deeply permeated by chill and indifference to be brought back to life. It is like a lunar landscape where,

---

9. A minor character in Dostoevsky's *The Possessed*. A mad radical theorist, Shigalëv evolves a scheme of a perfect society that, in his own words, starts from total freedom only to usher in total slavery. This aspect of the novel has been termed prophetic.
10. Clearly, a dig at the twentieth-century anti-utopian novels, e.g. Zamjatin's *We* or Huxley's *Brave New World*.
11. See "Isaac Babel" above, n. 2.
12. The last story by Turgenev (1883) and one of his few tales featuring the fantastic and the mysterious; "it has all the inevitable flatness of Victorian spiritualism" (D. S. Mirsky).

in the absence of the earth's atmosphere, one would not even
have the strength to scream. And the one who invites us there
not only remains completely calm, but deploys all the sorcery of
his art in order to render the transition painless. To be sure,
"transition" has to be understood figuratively, only as an exposure
to a state of mind, compared to which even the past dreams of
Fëdor Sologub may seem a manifestation of a healthy, ebullient,
youthful enthusiasm.[13]

By the same token, if Eros—in the highest, purest sense of the
word—is the basis, essence, and justification of all creativity,
Nabokov's anti-eroticism, the entrapment in himself, the spiritual hopelessness of his writings, are disturbing symptoms. He
does not seem to care about anything. He lives off himself, he
is turned into himself. He raves rather than thinks, he stares
at the phantoms of his own devising rather than at what actually
surrounds him. . . . It would be simple to assume one of the familiar, didactic critical postures and, in the manner of a new
Dobroljubov [see pp. 5–6 above], offer some hackneyed advice,
for instance, what the author needs is more faith in man and a
stronger desire to improve himself. But advice rarely reaches
those for whom it is intended and, in any case, it would not reach
such an addressee as Nabokov. Besides, who has the right to ad-
vise him? And yet one cannot live by despair alone, and even
the most intricate verbal designs will not shield one from it.

However, Nabokov keeps returning to the imminent "anthill."
Apparently this notion continues to interest or bother him (I was
about to say "trouble," but this is hardly the right word to use
in speaking of Nabokov). Thus his story "The Annihilation of
Tyrants" (1936) could easily be inserted into *Invitation to a Beheading*. It is a variation on the same theme, with the same apparent breakthroughs into a more terrifying, darker world.

A brilliant and bizarre tale! One could hardly feel the slightest sympathy toward the tyrant as described by Nabokov. And
yet that defiantly individualistic, ostentatiously aristocratic stance,
that air of unruffled snootiness which permeates the tale, is disturbing. If this is all that one can pit against tyranny, is it worth
the battle? How much better is this than what Nabokov so clever-
ly mocks? If a battle is indeed impending, if it is already being

13. See "Gogol" above, n. 18. A typical Sologub lyric is exquisitely morbid.

fought in this world, will not the contest be lost because it lacks sense, because the alternative offered by the presumably just and righteous camp cannot generate enthusiasm? The question remains unanswered.

Nabokov's tyrant is a most ordinary, mediocre man; his story is told by another ordinary man, who in his youth was the tyrant's friend and companion. The narrator recalls his actions, his words, and shudders in helpless contempt. He comes close to hallucinating. He is contemplating an attempt on the tyrant's life and vividly anticipates the "scrap" that is to come; he sees a "human whirlwind, grabbing me, the Punch-like abruptness of my movements among greedy hands, the sound of torn clothing, the blinding flush from the blows and then (if I get out of this whirlwind alive) the steely grip of the guards, the prison, a quick trial, the torture chamber, the block, and all this to the thunderous rumble of mighty happiness." Anger drives him to near-insanity. It seems to him that suicide is the surest method of ridding himself of the tyrant, "for he is within me, nourished by the strength of my hatred." But he is saved—by laughter. The tyrant is not frightening, the tyrant is ludicrous, and he has no power over those who understand this.

The moral of the story, then, comes down to the fact that everything can be rendered harmless through laughter. If this were only true! We would burst out laughing at the right moment and all threats and fears would disappear. But I am not sure Nabokov is really convinced of this. In his story there is something of *Notes from the Underground*, something of *Envy* by Jurij Olësha, yet in essence it is rather the current variant of the diary of the contemporary "superfluous man" protesting in helpless despair against the stultification and brutalization of the world.[14] The composite "tyrant" modeled partly after Stalin, partly after Hitler, but clearly more stupid than either historical "tyrant," is a caricature rather than a portrait. The caricature is vivid and apt. How masterful, for instance, is the scene of the official reception

---

14. *Envy* (1922), one of the most sophisticated early Soviet novels, features a gifted and embittered misfit. "The Diary of a Superfluous Man" (1850) is a short story by Turgenev. In a diary begun on the eve of his death, the hero diagnoses himself as an odd man out. "The superfluous man" was soon to become a critical and journalistic cliché, suggesting alienation, maladjustment and the like and applied to literary characters as disparate as Pushkin's Eugene Onegin, Lermontov's Pechorin, and Turgenev's Rudin.

for an old woman who grew a two-pound turnip. " 'Now this is poetry,' he [the tyrant] gruffly told the people around him. 'Here is the person from whom the poets should learn'—and angrily ordering them to cast the mold in bronze, he stalked out."

Yes, the tyrant is contemptible and revolting. He is a sinister figure. Nabokov is justified in recoiling from him. But once again: What alternative does he offer? Freedom? Freedom for what? I ask this question without the slightest irony, without any suggestion that if one has nothing positive to offer, one should not denounce. No, it is essential to denounce. It is necessary to repudiate. It is necessary to seek acceptable solutions to all the disorders and crises. But what does Nabokov think about the chances of finding such solutions? Does he think at all? Does he deign to think? Having created another gallery of "pig snouts" no less awful than the Sobakeviches and Pljushkins, though often draped in quasi-poetic mantles, will he settle for the position of a highly successful litterateur, or at long last uneasily confront the travail that ultimately lent the Sobakeviches and the Pljushkins their depth and meaning: the night, the hearth, the smoldering pages of a manuscript about "souls," this time far from "dead."[15] . . . Nabokov is a major Russian writer. Is not there, after all, a special kind of authority in our literature that exacts from a major Russian writer respect for its fundamental laws?

"A child of emigration" . . . In the very beginning of this essay these words were used ironically and lightly. Not only in a novel or poem, but also in a most ordinary article, it is difficult to foresee where an argument might lead. In concluding the above observations about Nabokov I am now ready to ask myself a question: is he not, in fact, a child of emigration?

Emigration is a complex phenomenon with numerous ramifications in the realms of politics, mores, national existence; it can be approached from different vantage points. What is undeniable, though, is that emigration always entails some slackening of activity, some impairment of the conviction that every person has a function and place in this world. Clearly, emigration is by its very nature a "flawed" condition: an artist affected by it— especially a truly sensitive one—may feel thrown not merely out of balance, but out of life itself. Thrown out whither? If we

15. For Sobakevich, Pljushkin, and Gogol's somber auto-da-fé, see "The Aesthetics of Gogol's *Dead Souls* and Its Legacy" above.

only knew that, there would be no need to worry about the "flaw" that, incidentally, is blithely ignored by people, who are engrossed by questions of a pragmatic or topical nature: today one meeting, tomorrow another, today a lecture, tomorrow a counter-lecture, and so forth. . . . For the artist, especially an artist of Nabokov's bent, the answer is different: thrown out into nowhere. To be sure, he does not say this in so many words. But he writes within an ambience where nothing comes from anywhere or is going anywhere. In his world all ties are severed. He plays with life and does not live in what he writes. He does not listen for the ring of truth in his writings, because for him such a quality does not exist—all that was said along these lines is nonsense, sham, it was all dreamed up by obtuse hacks like Chernyshevskij, whom he attacked with such self-indulgent flippancy in *The Gift*![16] There is, incidentally, something strikingly and profoundly un-Russian about Nabokov's cavalier attitude toward "simplicity and truth" in the Tolstoyan or any other sense of the word, about that dandyism, that noiselessly surging prose, about the studiously cold, boyishly impudent air, the self-assured and unruffled tone of his writings.

But if he is a "child of emigration," is not this, in fact, a stance that the son of emigration is doomed to take? The assumption is more plausible than it would appear at first glance. Given this assumption, it suddenly becomes clear how it could happen that a major Russian writer found himself out of step with Russian literature. If we accept this hypothesis, could it have been otherwise? Has Russian literature ever before been forced to live in a vacuum? How could this loneliness fail to instill in someone indifference or even bitterness, how could it fail to be embodied in a vision, a creative thrust hitherto unknown to us? There is nothing impossible in the assumption that, precisely because of his spiritual dependency upon the fact of emigration, and as a consequence of this fact, Nabokov will be assigned someday a significant position in Russian literature.

A few words about Nabokov's poetry.

He is, without a doubt, the only authentic émigré poet who

16. *Dar* (Paris, 1938), one of the landmarks of Nabokov's Russian period, is in part a brilliant and cruel spoof on Nikolaj Chernyshevskij (see p. 5 above) whose naïvely realistic aesthetics proclaimed the superiority of "reality" to art. For the English translation, see *The Gift* (New York, 1963).

has studied Pasternak and learned something from him. We constantly hear about Pasternak's influence, though more often than
not the references are mechanically unselective: if a poem is
not completely understandable, the author must have been following in Pasternak's footsteps. Opinions such as these occur
not only in conversation, but also in print. . . .

There is nothing enigmatic about Pasternak's poetic devices.
Doubtless his poems, in contradistinction, say, to Blok, arise
out of verbal combinations that at the moment of their emergence
were not associated with any emotions or feelings. In Pasternak
words give rise to emotions, and not the other way around. Blok
once described his own poems as "only slightly verbal." The
poems of Pasternak are heavily verbal, time and again they become a sheer riot of words, images, sounds, and metaphors that
seem to be crowding and urging each other on. In this turbulence
the poet has no time to look closely at his images. As a result,
if one were to tamper with the rhythm of some of his poems and
try to read them like prose, an utter muddle would ensue. In a
poem dedicated to Anna Akhmatova, for example, we are told
that she "had nailed to the rhyme the fear of looking back with
a pillar of salt."[17] I chose this appalling quotation at random,
for one could have cited a thousand lines. There is no deliberate
break with logic here, as in many Western poets. Logic as a matter of linking concepts is technically preserved here, but what
ordeals it has to undergo, poor thing! Pasternak is merciless and
indifferent to it. He rushes, he spins, and along with him his
lines rush, spin, and whirl, as though racing toward a distant
objective. It is impossible not to recognize that at times their
élan is irresistible. Pasternak is one of the few contemporary
poets to whom one can apply the word "inspiration" without a
smile. The sounds? The sounds are quite barbaric; a clash of
five or six consonants does not disturb Pasternak in the least (for
example, "kak kost' vzblesnet kostel . . . "). His sounds are more
like Derzhavin's,[18] not so much in the intonational pattern as in
the pervasive urge to bend and twist the line so that, for better
or worse, all the requisite words can be squeezed into it.

At one time Pushkin was carried away by a line by Batjushkov

17. See "To Anna Akhmatova" (1928) in Boris Pasternak, *Stikhi i poemy
1912–1932* (University of Michigan Press), p. 224.
18. See "Pushkin's Path to Prose" above, n. 8.

—"ljubvi i ochi i lanity"[19]—and noted its magical Italian light-ness. From then on, in the course of over a hundred years, this Italianate mellifluousness has faded and petered out. As often happens in art, a reaction was bound to set in. Pasternak began to yearn for Derzhavin's sonorous jumble that Pushkin had found hopelessly outmoded. Just as Derzhavin does not hesitate to break the structure of a phrase, to reshuffle words at random, just as Derzhavin rages in his verse in Asiatic frenzy, so Paster-nak mangles, squeezes, cripples, piles up absurdities and pro-liferates wild comparisons. Another example, taken at random: "youth floats along in bliss, like a pillowcase in a child's snore." How false it is, how outrageously arbitrary, what sloppy work! —one might protest, if only one did not detect in this torrent of absurdities a tragic challenge to reason, a challenge to clarity and harmony, to Pushkin's marvelous but increasingly arid poetic soil. If one were not aware of a passionate, headlong urge to plough up that soil anew. If one did not sense here a true poetic intoxication, or did not hear the hollow underground rumble of a lofty, though still indistinct music. Sometimes, incidentally, all that usually appears vague suddenly becomes clear. Some-times Pasternak's mumbling reaches an eloquence in which the ore of his poetry melts and begins to glisten—as in the remark-able, majestic closing lines of the otherwise murky poem "Sum-mer" (1930), where themes drawn from Pushkin and from Plato are oddly interwined.[20] Or as in the poem "There will be no one in the house . . . " (from "The Second Birth")[21]—a poem decep-tively plain, full of meaning, feeling, and beauty, one of those poems that should remain forever in the treasure house of Russian poetry.

Some of Nabokov's comparatively early poems sound so much like Pasternak that the illusion is total:

19. Ibid., n. 19. This line drawn from Batjushkov's epistle "To a Friend" means roughly "the gaze and blush of love." Pushkin praised it in his "Notes on the Margin of K. N. Batjushkov's Verse and Prose" *(Pushkin o literature* [Moscow: Academia, 1934], p. 128).

20. This interweaving occurs in the last three quatrains of "Summer," where motifs drawn from Plato's "Symposium" (the banquet, Priestess Diotima) mingle with the themes of Pushkin's dramatic fragment "The Feast During a Plague." The poem's last line, "Perhaps, the last warrant of immortality" *(Bessmert'ja, byt' mozhet, poslednij zalog)* is drawn from "The Feast," more specifically from the much quoted set-piece, "The Chairman's Song."

21. A collection of poems written in 1930 and 1931.

> Kind of green, Kind of gray, i.e.
> Striated all over with rain,
> and the linden fragrance, so heady
> that I can hardly—Let's go!
> Let's go and abandon this garden.[22]

Here everything is borrowed, the images as well as the intona-
tions. These lines appear to have come right out of "The Second
Birth" or "Beyond the Barriers."[23] But they were written twenty
years ago, and since that time Nabokov has liberated himself
from influences and has found himself in poetry.

To my ear there is less romantic music in Nabokov than in
Pasternak. Whatever one's objections or misgivings, the latter's
overall image is remarkably appealing. No matter how one might
wince at some of his verbal tricks, Pasternak is a poet down to the
marrow of his bones; he lives by verses, he breathes poetry. Like
Pasternak, Nabokov shuns neither verbal excesses nor verbal
innovations, and the mirage of an ultimate, unattainable simplicity—which has worn down some contemporary poets—holds no
magnetic attraction for him. His inspiration does not attempt
to rise above the word, but instead luxuriates in it; he tells fortunes, he mumbles, he chants, all the while moving further and
further away from what one might call a poetic miracle, from
the two or three magically shining lines where there is nothing
to add, nothing to explain. From whatever glimpses of Nabokov
the man we find in his writings, concern for the future seems to
be thoroughly alien to him. Any notion that Nabokov would actually want to labor in the vineyard of Russian literature could
be advanced only tongue-in-cheek. Nevertheless, consciously or
unconsciously, he ploughs up the earth for some future Pushkin,
who once more will take it upon himself to put our poetry house
in order. Perhaps the new Pushkin will never appear. But the
anticipation, the yearning for him shall remain—for precious
few will claim that all these cryptic mutterings should be viewed
as achievements, rather than as experiment and quest.

However, Nabokov is a born poet, a fact that is evident even

22. Nabokov's own translation found in his recent miscellany, *Poems and
Problems* (New York, 1970), p. 79. The poem "How I Love You," which begins
with the above five lines, was written in 1934.

23. Poems that comprise this collection were written between 1914 and
1916, yet published considerably later.

in his quest. Some of his poems are beautiful in the full sense of the word, and just one poem like "Poets" or "Will you leave me alone? I implore you! . . . " would be enough to erase any doubts on this score. How fine they are! How amazingly fine are the "phosphoric rhymes" with the "last, barely perceptible glow of Russia" on them![24] Here mastery is inseparable from feeling, the one fusing with the other. The author is clearly a complex figure; the poem "Fame" is a singularly revealing autobiographical document; all that is appealing and all that is disturbing about Nabokov blend here into a bizarre symphony.[25]

This poetry is far removed from the poetic canon established in the emigration, especially, from what has become known as the "Paris note."[26] (Before the year 1939 there was no collective "note"; only individual voices were heard, scattered by history across the world: literary life was concentrated in Paris.) The distance between Nabokov and this "note" is roughly the same as that between Lermontov and the Pushkin Pleiad.[27] Just as Zhukovskij,[28] having taught so much to the Pleiad, shook his head over some of Lermontov's poems—not the best ones, of course—so the present-day purists, the sworn foes of rhetoric, of poses and phrases, profess bewilderment over a collection of Nabokov's poems. In their own terms they are right and so in his own terms—but only in those!—was Zhukovskij. But in literature, as in life, thee is room for contradiction and conflict, and no principle, school, or method, still less a "note," can claim a monopoly. It is not methods or schools that give life to poetry, but inner energy seeking an outlet: one has to be deaf to miss hearing it in Nabokov.

24. See V. Nabokov, *Stikhotvorenija* [Poems] (Paris, 1952), p. 20.
25. "Fame" (1942), which opens as an encounter between the persona and an intrusive, loquacious, and insidiously clever vulgarian (oddly reminiscent of Ivan Karamazov's devil), only to usher in a pithy self-definition, is a poetic credo rather than an "autobiographical document." Yet it is unquestionably revealing and quintessentially Nabokovian: "But my word arches like an aerial bridge /above the world, and I walk across it incognito/ into the fire-lit darkness of my native land" (ibid., p. 24).
26. The phrase "the Paris note" has come to designate in Russian émigré parlance a style that dominated much Russian verse written in Paris on the eve of World War II. The salient characteristics of this manner were lyrical reticence and artful "simplicity."
27. A cluster of Pushkin's contemporaries and associates which includes, in descending order of distinction, such poets as Evgenij Baratynskij, Anton Delvig, and Wilhelm Küchelbecker.
28. See "Pushkin's Path to Prose" above, n. 9.

5
The Recent Scene

On Boris Pasternak

ANDREJ SINJAVSKIJ

Landscape in Pasternak's work often becomes not the object of a representation but the subject of an action, the principal hero and mover of events. All the fullness of life in its varied aspects enters a fragment of nature that, it seems, can perform actions, feel, and think. The assimilation of nature to man, which is characteristic of poetry, goes so far with Pasternak that the landscape takes on the role of preceptor and moral example. "The forest drops its crimson attire" remains the classical formulation in Russian poetry for autumn.[1] With Pasternak we often meet this thought in reverse: "You throw off your dress / just as the copse throws off its leaves"; "You are undesigning like the air," the poet addresses his beloved. Man is defined through nature, by comparison with her he assumes his place in the world. This power, or more properly intercession, of nature does not humiliate man since by submission and assimilation to her he follows the voice of life. Moreover in Pasternak's art nature is so close to man that being dislodged and superseded by nature he comes to life in her anew. Here the degree of the world's humanization is such that wandering through forests and fields we have to do actually not with pictures of these forests and fields but with their character and psychology.

Pasternak's poetry is metaphorical through and through. But often one is less aware of these similitudes as metaphor than as something vividly at work before our eyes. Quite literally "the garden weeps" or "the storm runs"; they are presented in all the immediacy of an uncontrived, genuine act:

> The storm is at the gates! outside!
> Transfigured and dazed

This essay, translated here by Henry Gifford, is reprinted with permission from *Encounter* (London, April 1966), pp. 46-50. It represents excerpts from Sinjavskij's introduction to Boris Pasternak, *Stikhotvorenija i poèmy* [Verses and poems] (Moscow–Leningrad, 1965), pp. 5–62.
   1.   First line of a poem by Pushkin, "October 19" (1825).

> In darkness, in thunder-peals, in silver,
> It runs down the gallery.[2]

Metaphor in Pasternak's poetry has chiefly a linking role. Instantly and dynamically it draws into a single whole the discrete parts of reality and thereby bodies forth the great unity of the world, the interaction and interpenetration of things. Pasternak's starting point is that two objects when juxtaposed have a close interaction, penetrate each other, and so he connects them not by resemblance but by proximity. The world is described "whole," and the job of unifying it falls to metaphor:

> Spring, I am from the street, where
> the poplar is astonished,
> Where the distance is scared, where
> the house fears to fall,
> Where the air is dark blue like
> the bundle of linen
> Of a man discharged from hospital.[3]

The last line shows why "the distance is scared" and "the house fears to fall": they too have just been discharged from the hospital like the man whose bundle made the air blue.

Landscape—broader still, the whole ambient world—gains with Pasternak a heightened sensitivity. It reacts sharply and instantly to the changes that go on in man, not merely in response to his feelings, thoughts, and moods (a thing common enough in literature) but by becoming his full likeness, an extension, his alter ego. The mechanism of these changes is revealed in Pasternak's story *The Last Summer*:

> Of course the whole alley in its utter gloom was fully and entirely Anna. Here Seryozha wasn't alone and he knew this. And indeed this had happened to all sorts of people before him. However the feeling was still more spacious and precise, and here the help of friends and predecessors stopped. He saw how painful it was for Anna to be the morning in town. . . . In silence she looked lovely before him, and did not call for his aid. And faint with longing for the real Arild. . . . He saw how, sur-

2. From "Jul'skaja groza" [Storm in July], in Boris Pasternak, *Sochinenija* [Works] (Ann Arbor, Mich., 1962), 1:208.
3. From "Vesna" [Spring, 1918], ibid., p. 95.

rounded with poplars like frozen towels, she was sucked in by the clouds and slowly tossed backward her gothic brick towers.[4]

Notice: the feeling that seized Seryozha was more spacious and precise than similar things experienced by others. For here Pasternak speaks of himself.

The Invisible Poet

The task that fascinated Pasternak was to re-create within the limits of verse the all-embracing atmosphere of existence, to communicate "the sense of intimacy with the universe" that possessed the poet. In his verse the lyrical narrative does not proceed in order from one thing to the next but leaps "over the barriers,"[5] tending toward an exquisite breadth, a bold depiction of the whole. Things are shifted by metaphor from their long-occupied places and come into violent chaotic movement, the purpose of which is to set down reality in its natural disorder:

> I want to go home, to the vastness
> Of the flat which induces grief.
> I shall enter, take off my overcoat, collect
>   myself
> I shall be illumined by the streetlights.
> The thin sides of partitions
> I shall pass through, pass through like light.
> Pass through as image enters image
> And as object cuts across object.[6]

In this immaterial space intersected by metaphors the poet holds a peculiar position. Except in a few works he does not stand out developed as a fully independent and separate character. He differs from Blok, Tsvetaeva, Majakovskij, Esenin, in that he rarely assigns the lyrical part to the first person. With the others the poet's personality stood at the center, and his art extending into a diary of many years, a tale "about the time and oneself," composed a kind of saga, a dramatic biography enacted before the eyes of its readers and surrounded by an aureole of legend. Pasternak

---

4. See "Povest" (1929), *Sochinenija*, 2:196.
5. The title of Pasternak's second collection of verse (1917).
6. A poem from the cycle *Vtoroe rozhdenie* [Second birth, 1934], *Sochinenija*, 1:320.

departs from this conception, which he designates as "romantic," the "idea of a poet's biography as a spectacle."[7] He has little to say about himself or in his own person and takes trouble to conceal his ego. When reading his poetry you have at times the illusion that the author doesn't enter into it, that he is absent even as narrator and as a witness who has seen all that is depicted there. Nature speaks in its own name:

> In the open windows on their handiwork
> Dovelike the clouds sat down.
> They noticed the water had made thin
> The fences—markedly, the crosses—slightly.[8]

Not the poet but "the clouds . . . noticed."

In one of Pasternak's late poems, "First Frost," we again encounter just such an unusual image in which landscape and spectator seem to have exchanged roles, and the picture itself looks at the man standing in front of it:

> This cold morning the hazy sun
> Stands like a pillar of fire in smoke.
> I too, as in an awful snapshot,
> Simply can't be made out by it.
>
> Until it issues from the mist
> Shining beyond the pond on the meadow
> The trees can't see me properly
> On the distant bank.[9]

If Majakovskij or Tsvetaeva wants to speak for all the world in their own person, Pasternak prefers that the world should speak for him and in his stead. "Not I about spring, but spring about me." "Not I about the garden, but the garden about me."

> By the fence
> Between damp twigs and the pallid air
> A quarrel went on. My heart sank.
> About me!

---

7. This revealing phrase occurs in Pasternak's autobiography "Safe Conduct" (Okhrannaja gramota, 1931), *Sochinenija*, 2:282.

8. From a 1919 poem featured in the cycle "Themes and Variations," ibid., p. 97.

9. From a 1956 poem, ibid., 3:76.

A New Poetic Language

"The inability to find and tell the truth," Pasternak declared, "is a defect that no ability to tell untruth can hide." Realism as he understood it—the heightened receptivity and honesty of the artist when he communicates real being which, like a living human character, is always entire and unique—inheres in all genuine art and shows in the work of Tolstoy and Lermontov, Chopin and Blok, Shakespeare, and Verlaine. On the other hand, for Pasternak, romanticism was a negative idea, for it slips into the fantastic and easily neglects fidelity of expression.

This aspect of his aesthetic views is the more interesting because Pasternak for a long time was associated with a futurist group and later with LEF. They went in extensively for the so-called formal method that treated a work of art as the sum of its technical procedures.

The trends of today (Pasternak wrote early in the 1920s) assume that art is a fountain when really it is a sponge. They have decided that art

> must spurt forth when really it must absorb and become saturated. They have reckoned that it may be broken down into the means of expression, when really it is made up of the organs of sensibility. It always has to stand with the spectators and look on the most purely, sensitively, and accurately of all, but in our days it has come to know powder and the dressing room, and to show itself from the stage. . . .[10]

Art so understood presupposes a renewed vision of the world that is perceived by the artist as if for the first time. "The whole steppe, as before man fell."

In his search for new words that could restore to the world its individual face Pasternak turned to live conversational speech. He took part in that decisive democratization of poetic language that in the 1910s and 1920s affected many poets and ran with most turbulence in the work of Majakovskij. Now Majakovskij enlarged his vocabulary in the main by drawing on the language of the street, which had begun to speak with its full voice, where vulgarisms alternated with the idiom of political speeches; this was

10. See Boris Pasternak, "Several Propositions," *Sovremennik* [Contemporary], no. 1 (Moscow, 1922), p. 6. —A.S.

dictated by his broadening the theme to include the city, the war, the revolution. Pasternak, however, kept for a long time to the circle of traditional themes well worn by poets of the past and present. Yet he spoke of traditional springs and sunsets in a new way; he told of natural beauty not in the language of the accustomed poetic banalities but in the current words of the everyday prose of life. Thereby he restored to it a lost freshness, an aesthetic significance. The trite subject in his rendering became a living event.

He boldly introduces into elevated poetic speech the low language of life, of the city in our time. Pasternak does not shrink from officialese, the license of daily talk, conversational idioms. In their new application these forms, the worn coins of everyday use, sound fresh and unexpected. Thus the set phrase in general currency becomes a weapon against literary cliché. Pasternak is inclined to treat the highest themes with a homely directness. The unquiet grandeur of the Caucasus he will convey with a simplicity in the tone of familiar everyday talk—"it's out of sorts"—or "Caucasus seemed all spread on your palm, / All like a rumpled bed." His singularity is that he poeticizes the world with the help of prosaisms, which infuse into his lines the truth of life.

Pasternak's innovation in language was largely dictated by the search for the greatest possible unfettering and naturalness of poetic expression. That was fully revealed and confirmed in his works of the thirties and particularly of the forties and fifties. Then these tendencies, earlier hidden by Pasternak's irrepressible imagery, became clear and sharply intensified. Originally they were not obvious and acted, as it were, undercover. The author was fully aware of them, but seldom were they accessible to the reader. In this connection the poet wrote at the beginning of the thirties in his lyrical sequence *The Waves*:

> Making sure of kinship with all that is
> and familiar with the future in daily life
> You are bound to fall into that heresy at last—
> A strange simplicity.
>
> But we may expect no mercy
> So long as we do not hide it.
> Men need it most of all
> But are more at home with complexity.[11]

11. *Sochinenija*, 1:327–28.

"Complexity" here means the banal—the poetic stereotype. But simplicity is affirmed as the inner foundation, the spur and ultimate aim of his endeavours that had still to be realized.

The Sense of History

Pasternak called art "the extremity of an age" (and not its resultant), and he related works of art with historical events as kindred phenomena on different planes. Thus he thought Tolstoy kindred to the Revolution. In his own book *My Sister Life* he saw a certain parallel with its revolutionary time and even counted it a book about the Revolution, although it speaks not about social but just ordinary storms and dawns, and to treat it in an allegorical spirit would do violence to the meaning.

Nonetheless history came into Pasternak's work, even when he demonstratively refused to touch it, pretending not to remember "what millennium, my dears, it is outside." Echoes of war and revolution rolled across a number of his landscapes, and history set its stamp on his representations of nature. This penetration of historical actuality into the realm of nature was nothing odd for the poet, since he rendered landscape through the perceptions of a contemporary city-dweller, who drags after him on his walk, along with the everyday quality of life, a chain of social and political references, involving the meadows and woods in the round of events among which his life passes.

In his representation and actual impression of history Pasternak comes close to Blok. This closeness results from their ability to catch the ground-rhythm of an epoch, not only in the obvious course of events lying on one plane but in all the departments of life and from the poets' attempt to seek some common historical equivalent in all that goes on about him, and to show the world in the complete unity of its constituent parts, be they revolution, earthquake, or love. Pasternak in his poems hastens to deduce a common denominator of human actions, sunsets, and city streets. And if, for example in "Lieutenant Schmidt," the setting is the Russo–Japanese war, in fact the eve of revolution, then this troubled state of the world is reiterated by everything, even the Kiev racecourse. History penetrates all the pores of life, converting the smallest details of the environment into her likeness.

Hamlet and Human Destiny

The idea that the individual human being has an exalted historical mission has been developed in Pasternak's poetry. From
"Lieutenant Schmidt," where the moral ideal of man was made
concrete in the character of the poem's protagonist (Schmidt
sacrifices himself, performs a feat of historic renewal, and accepts
a tragic destiny as his due), through the lyric poetry of the thirties
and the war period there run threads to the works of Pasternak
that complete his career as artist. Their philosophical content may
be disclosed from the remarks that Pasternak made about *Hamlet*,
on a translation of which he was working:

> Hamlet renounces himself in order "to do the will of Him that
> sent him." *Hamlet* is not a drama of characterlessness but a
> drama of duty and self-renunciation. When it becomes plain that
> appearance and reality do not meet and are separated by a gulf,
> it is not material that the intimation of the world's delusiveness
> comes in supernatural form and the Ghost demands vengeance
> of Hamlet. It matters far more that by the will of chance Hamlet
> is chosen as judge of his time and servant of what is farther off.
> *Hamlet* is a drama of high destiny, of an enjoined feat and a
> mission entrusted.[12]

The lyric poetry of the later Pasternak discloses to us the poet's
position—with regard to the world and to time—in a rather different perspective from his work of former years. The idea of moral
service here prevails over all else, though Pasternak does not
cease to affirm the receptive power of poetry—its ability to seize a
living picture of the actual (and the moral element in an artist's
perception of the world even earlier was essential for him). If once
in his aesthetic notions the image of "poetry as sponge" held the
central place, now without canceling the first another motif prevails: "the aim of art is self-surrender."[13] Simultaneously, at the
end of the poet's life there is deified in his art and there sounds
with full force the consciousness of having accomplished his historic role. Hence in particular the uncommonly bright tonality of
his late lyrics, despite the tragic note of separate poems, and the
prevailing sense of confidence in the future.

12. Ibid., 2:196–97.
13. The latter image occurs in Pasternak's much quoted 1956 poem "It's
unbecoming to be famous" (Byt' znamenitym nekrasivo), ibid., 3:62.

Both his ideas about morality and history and his understanding
of the problems of art reveal traits, views, habits that approximate
the poet to the present epoch and at the same time challenge
certain of its assumptions and demands. "You are the outskirts
[*prigorod*] and not a refrain [*pripev*]," Pasternak said about
poetry.[14] It seizes the actual and sidles to it like the outskirts of a
town, but—so Pasternak thinks—it does not repeat word for word
the refrain of accepted truths.

The special way he understands the problem of art (in relation
to nature, reality, its original) is so organic for Pasternak's vision
that similar habits and conceptions are to be found in his translation work too.

It is not difficult to see that his ideas on the art of translation are
very close to his ideas on art in general. He tries above all for
"that conscious freedom without which you cannot come near to
great things." Comparing his own work with the performance of
other translators, Pasternak observes:

> We challenge no one with separate lines, but the contest is
> about entire structures, and in carrying them out, along with
> fidelity to the great original, we come to submit more and more
> to our own system of speech.[15]
>
> . . . .
>
> An original should be related to its rendering as . . . the stock to
> a cutting. A translation should come from an author who has felt
> the influence of the original long before this work. It should be
> the fruit of the original and its historical consequence.[16]

His translation of *Hamlet* appeared in a separate edition in 1941
and became the first of a series of translations of Shakespeare's
tragedies. But already in a poem of 1923 we meet the idea that
was developed in his translation work: "Oh, all Shakespeare
perhaps is just in this, / That Hamlet converses freely with the
Ghost." To "converse freely"—in other words, to speak unre-
strainedly and colloquially on the most elevated themes—this we
know was the rule with Pasternak, who had other traits allying
him in his own fashion to the realism of Shakespeare, his freedom,

14. See "Poèzija" (1922), ibid., 1:101.
15. Boris Pasternak, "Novyj perevod 'Otello' Shekspira" [A new translation
of Shakespeare's "Othello"], *Literaturnaja gazeta* (9 December 1944).
16. "Zametki perevodchika" [Translator's notes], *Sochinenija*, 2:183.

vividness, and so on. The "influence of the original" (of course not always direct, but often complicated and refracted in the various manifestations of world culture) here began long before his immediate work on Shakespeare's tragedies and in some measure fell in with his own interests and purposes as an artist. That is why Shakespeare transplanted so well in Pasternak's poetic soil, and his work as translator, which was visibly influenced by the individual tastes, passions, and procedures of Pasternak the poet, had in its turn an influence on his original work.

"Impressionism of the Eternal"

The meaning of existence, the purpose of man, the essential nature of the world—these are the questions that excited Pasternak over many years, particularly at the end of his life.

This concern about essences, about the nature of things, puts the poet in a very interesting and ambiguous position with regard to impressionism, traces of which are to be seen in his work (especially of the early period). Pasternak's images at times recall the canvases of Monet and Renoir, Pissarro, and Vuillard. Like these artists he often tries to set down his momentary impressions of objects and, setting aside his previous knowledge of the world, to represent it as he sees it at that particular moment. Here, for example, is a sketch fully in the spirit of impressionism:

> The barman's dishes resounded.
> The waiter yawned counting the crockery.
> On the river, at the height of a candlestick,
> Swarmed the fireflies.

> They hung in a glittering thread
> From the riverside streets. It struck three.
> The waiter with a napkin tried to scrape off
> Tallow grease that had appeared on the bronze.[17]

Lights on shore, their reflection in the water, the waiter on the steamship—all this is taken in at a single glance that seeks only to absorb the picture suddenly revealed and to fix it in this position seen once "at the height of a candlestick."

But impressionism as a rule has to do with the sensuously perceived surface of an object, not with its essence. Drowning in a

17. From an early poem "Na parakhode" [On board ship, 1915], ibid., 1:216.

sea of colors and scents, impressionism seeks to avoid a priori knowledge, concepts, and ideas that can trouble the purity of apprehension. Impressionism has no interest in eternal values.

Now it is curious that the young Pasternak, clearly going beyond impressionist ideas, should devise for himself such a formula for art as "impressionism of the eternal." It combines the poet's liking for an immediate apprehension of life, for pure color painting, *plein air*, with his passion for the philosophical quest of absolute categories. So in his poetic images he tries to unite sensation and essence and describes "a storm, momentary forever. . . ."[18] The favorite "instant" of the impressionists is given so much significance by Pasternak that it tells no longer of the transient and unique, but of the constant and universal.

Having achieved the simplicity he wanted, Pasternak kept also the most valuable of his former gains—that wholeness in the perception and representation of the world. But in the past the partitions between things, between man and nature, the temporary and the eternal, were overcome chiefly by aid of metaphor, by shifting objects and signs from place to place and introducing at the same time a commotion, a babel of images. But now metaphor, while it continues to play an important connecting role, has ceased to be the sole mediator between things. Their unity is now achieved through that breadth and clarity of poetic vision, that winged inspiration of feeling and thought before which every barrier falls, and life stands forth as a great whole where "nothing can be lost," where man lives and dies in the embrace of the universal, and the wind

> Rocks forest and dacha
> Not each fir by itself,
> But all the trees absolutely
> With all the limitless expanse.[19]

In the work of the later Pasternak not only do the connection of things and the poet's unity with the world take more simple and direct forms than hitherto, but the very "universe is simpler / Than some wily man may suppose," and it is founded on the supremacy of a few simple, elemental truths that everyone may

18. Title of a poem from Pasternak's early collection of verse, *My Sister, Life*.
19. From a Jurij Zhivago poem, "Veter" [The wind], *Doktor Zhivago* (Ann Arbor, 1959), p. 540.

understand—land, love, bread, sky. Sometimes a poem rests wholly on the affirmation of one such cornerstone in human existence. Together with this, ordinary life still more widely enters Pasternak's lyricism.

In half a century of Pasternak's writing, much changed and refashioned itself. But to a series of ideas, principles, and partialities he remained faithful until the end. One of Pasternak's deep convictions was that true art is always greater than itself, for it testifies to the significance of being, the greatness of life, the immeasurable value of human existence. This witness can dispense with declarations, profound symbols, and exalted allegories: the presence of greatness shows in the unaffected liveliness of what is being told, in the heightened awareness and poetic inspiration of the artist, who is possessed and stricken by the miracle of actuality itself and who tells constantly of one thing—of its notable presence, of life as it is, although the subject may be only the snow falling or the forest stirring.

The most sublime, as always with Pasternak, turns out to be the simplest—life that fills and exhausts everything. "Poetry," says Pasternak, "will always remain that celebrated height above all the Alps, which lies around in the grass at your feet, so that you need only bend down to see it and pick it up from the earth. . . ."[20]

---

20. From Pasternak's speech at the International Congress of Writers in Defense of Culture, June 1935, *Mezhdunarodnyj kongress pisatelej v zashchitu kultury v Parizhe* (Moscow, 1936), p. 375.

Mikhail Bulgakov's
The Master and Margarita

VLADIMIR LAKSHIN

> *Where there is no love of art,*
> *there is no criticism either.*
> *"Do you want to be a connois-*
> *seur of the arts?" Winckel-*
> *mann says. "Try to love the*
> *artist, look for beauty in his*
> *creations."*
>
> Pushkin[1]

On a strange, fantastic moonlit night after Satan's Ball when Margarita is united with her beloved by the power of magic charms, the omnipotent Woland asks the Master to show him his novel about Pontius Pilate. The Master is in no position to do this. He has burned his novel in the stove. "This cannot be," retorts Woland. "Manuscripts don't burn." And at that moment the cat, holding in his paws a thick manuscript, offers Messire with a bow a neat copy of the destroyed book.

"Manuscripts don't burn . . ." Mikhail Bulgakov died with this belief in the stubborn, indestructible power of art, at the time when all his major works lay unpublished in his desk drawers only to reach the reader one at a time after a quarter of a century. "Manuscripts don't burn"—these words served the author as an incantation against the destructive work of time, against the dismal fate of his last and, to him, most precious work, the novel *The Master and Margarita.*

And the incantation worked. The prediction came to pass. Time became Bulgakov's ally. Not only did his novel see the light of

This essay, translated here by Carol A. Palmer, first appeared in *Novyj mir* 6 (1968): 284–311.

1. From posthumously published "Notes on Criticism and Polemics" in *Pushkin o literature* [Pushkin on literature] (Moscow: Academia, 1934), p. 208. Johann J. Winckelmann was an eighteenth-century German art historian.

day. Along with his other, more topical books, it has proved to be
an essential, a vital work.

I

> *To immortalize all that is real,*
> *to humanize all that is imper-*
> *sonal.*
>
> A. Blok, "Iambics"[2]

Even as he turns the last page of the book, the reader is not yet
ready to sort out his impressions, to encompass the manifold images, observations, and thoughts stirred by the novel, but the
voices of a vast throng rumble in his ear, faces, colors, sounds
crowd his memory . . .

People in contemporary jackets and ancient tunics, in caps and
in golden helmets with plumes, people with briefcases under
their arms and with lances atilt, people of various epochs and
ages, professions and circumstances: a writer, a bookkeeper, a
house manager, the Procurator of Judea, a high priest, a centurion,
the Variety Theater's barman, a master of ceremonies, a railway
conductor, a literary critic, Roman soldiers, robbers, martyrs, civil
servants, actors, administrators, doctors, waiters, housewives, detectives, cab drivers, ticket takers, policemen, vendors of car-
bonated water, members of the management of a housing cooperative, editors, nurses, firemen—it is hardly possible to name them
all. And yet the main characters have not been mentioned here,
nor those whom one hesitates to call dramatis personae—the
Devil and his retinue, witches, corpses, water nymphs, demons of
all aspects and of every stripe, and finally an enormous talking car
with a cavalry mustache. Oh, yes, there is much here to throw a
literary pedant into confusion![3]

This densely populated and vividly costumed world teems with
unexpected encounters, transformations, closeups—a kaleidoscope
of wonders, performed against the most commonplace, most mun-

---

2. From a 1914 poem which opens the cycle "Iambics" (Jamby, 1907–1914),
Sobranie sochinenij (Leningrad–Moscow, 1960), 3:85.

3. Reference to some unidentified Soviet "professors of literature," alluded
to in an earlier, omitted section of Lakshin's essay.

dane background. The free, playful, light but not facile talent of
the author, overflowing with an excess of creative powers, generates a narrative flow of astounding tempo and variety. A funny
anecdote is cut off by a scene of horror, mystical fantasmagoria
rubs shoulders with farce, and a lyrical page is charged with explosive comic detail. One sequence moves to laughter, another to
rumination, another still leaves one uneasy, troubled. But, as always after an encounter with true art—be the tale it tells merry or
sad—there is a sense of having just returned from a holiday.

The most striking thing about Bulgakov's novel, I believe, is its
form, brilliant, captivating, unusual. But I do not want to rush to
conclusions. I would rather proceed not by the shortest but by the
most attractive and picturesque route, and having read the last
page, yield to the temptation to retrace my steps and begin reading anew, listening to the music of the Bulgakovian phrase: "At
that hour when it seemed already that people hadn't the strength
to breathe, when the sun, having scorched Moscow, tumbled in a
dry haze somewhere behind Sadovyj Circle, no one came to stroll
beneath the linden; no one sat on a bench, empty was the av-
enue."

Out of this arid heat an extremely strange gentleman will
materialize, a beret cocked over one ear, one eyebrow higher than
the other, a cane, eyes of a different color. But along with this
uncanny and disturbing riddle there is genre painting, everyday
life, humor, and accuracy of mundane detail right down to the
physiology of the debilitatingly hot day in the city, Moscow literary men, seeking shade beneath the lindens—and the lukewarm
orange soda on the stand that induces hiccups. And then—the
strange conversation on the bench, and with amazing smoothness,
almost without flaws or obvious transitions, the narrative shifts to
another register: "In the early morning of the 14th day of the
spring month of Nisan, in a white cloak with blood-red lining,
shuffling with his cavalryman's gait, there emerged into the covered colonnade between the two wings of the palace of Herod
the Great, the Procurator of Judea, Pontius Pilate." These lines,
cast, it would seem, from ancient bronze, are lines to remember, to
learn by heart, to recite. It is not enough to read them; they call for
sonorous oral delivery.

Already in the first and, incidentally, the most harmonious, most
polished section of the novel, Bulgakov, without doing violence to
our imagination, brings together the high and the low, the tem-

poral and the eternal: the Procurator of Judea's interrogation of the tramp-philosopher in the blue tunic on the balcony of the palace in ancient Jerusalem—and the laughter of "some citizeness in the boat" gliding across the Patriarch's Ponds; the hideous death of Berlioz, and the cat seating himself at the trolley stop and cleaning his mustache with a dime.

The fact that the author freely blends the unblendable—history and feuilleton, lyricism and myth, everyday life and fantasy —makes it difficult to define the book's genre. Through the good offices of M. M. Bakhtin attempts have already been made to label it Menippean.[4] I shall not object, but with equal success it could probably be called a comic epic, a satirical utopia, or still something else. Does this bring us any closer, however, to understanding the book?

Tolstoy was probably right. He maintained that significant art always created its own forms, defying the usual hierarchy of genres. Bulgakov's book is further proof of this. One might as well label it simply a novel. What matters is that its free, dazzling, and sometimes bizarre form provided ample scope for the author's thoughts, moods, and life experiences during the time he wrote this book. He wrote it over a long period without hope of early publication, warming himself by the very process of writing and seeing in it his last will. All that the author thought about and experienced was expressed in the novel with completeness and sincerity. He constructed it the way a snail builds its house, measuring it against himself and leaving no empty spaces. In *The Master and Margarita* Bulgakov found the form most adequate to his remarkable talent. Thus, many elements that occur separately in his previous works merge here into an artistic whole.

One of Bulgakov's vital assets has always been a rare power of description, that concrete perception of life that was once called "clairvoyance of the flesh,"[5] an ability to re-create even metaphysical phenomena with a limpid clarity of outline, without any diffuseness or schematicism. Bulgakov possessed the power of artis-

4. For Bakhtin, Introduction, p. 15 above. According to Bakhtin, the half-discursive, half-fictional genre, known in classical antiquity as the "Menippean satire" or "Menippeia" (the terms were derived from the name of an ancient Greek philosopher), foreshadows such hybrid or syncretic literary modes as the Dostoevsky novel.

5. The phrase was given wide currency by Merezhkovskij, who used it in his influential study *Tolstoy and Dostoevsky*. (See Introduction, p. 8 above).

tic suggestion and could make the reader feel that along with Berlioz he was clinging in vain to the ill-fated turnstile and irresistibly sliding down the rails to meet his death:[6] so vividly could he depict a cat with a glass of vodka in one paw and a marinated mushroom on a fork in the other that we were ready to bet that we ourselves have seen this miraculous phenomenon of nature and even succeeded in noticing how discontentedly his mustache bristled in embarrassment at being caught in such a relaxed pose.

Legend and faith in miracles feed on convention and allegory. Though Bulgakov introduces the mystical and religious element, he immediately undercuts it by his fidelity to earthy detail. As a result, the overall poetic meaning of the book clearly emerges.

A special concern of the author was with accurate rendition of the flavor of time and place. First, there is Bulgakov's Moscow, the Moscow of the thirties. Moscow for Bulgakov is not merely the locale of his novel, not only a city like a thousand others, but a beloved, familar, thoroughly explored city that has become his home. Having celebrated in *The White Guard*[7] Kiev, the city of his childhood, Bulgakov pays here a poetic tribute to Moscow. His urban topography is usually so reliable that even now we seem to have no difficulty in finding the bench in the square "at the very crossing of the Bronnaja Street," on which the two litterateurs made the acquaintance of the mysterious consultant, and in following Ivan along the entire path of his chase on the trail of the evil gang, from Patriarch's Ponds to Spiridonovka, on to Nikitskij Gate, to Arbat and Kropotkin Street, then through an alley to Ostozhenka Street.

It is not surprising that the author knows his Moscow so well. But how does he manage to describe with such unassailable accuracy ancient Jerusalem, which he never visited, with its suspended bridges, the colonnade of Herod's Palace, the gloomy tower of Antonia, the squares, the temples, the noisy, filthy bazaars, and the narrow winding alleys of the Lower City? Of course he read the works of historians and archeologists and was acquainted with the geography and topography of ancient Judea.

---

6. Reference to the first of the magically produced disasters featured in *The Master and Margarita*.

7. The first full-length novel of Bulgakov's dealing with the Civil War in the Ukraine, written in 1923–24. It served as the basis for a popular and controversial play *The Days of the Turbins* (1926).

But more important, he had the imagination of a truly realistic master. Thus we cannot help but feel that the heavy attar of roses, the clang of armor, the cries of water-bearers scorched by the fiery Jerusalem sun, have been copied from nature and are no less real than the trolley bus, the Moscow department store, a performance at the Variety Theater, the House of Writers, Massolit,[8] and other landmarks of Moscow of the thirties for whose authenticity we can more easily vouch.

The Master's beloved city Moscow and the "barbaric" Jerusalem that Pilate hates seem totally unlike. But there is one detail in Bulgakov's urban landscapes that artistically links episodes so distant in space and time. All major scenes of action, conversations, and pageants are accompanied in the novel by two mute witnesses whose presence is invariably brought to our attention. Moonlight and sunlight that flood the pages of the book provide not merely an effective illumination of a historical stage set but also the dimension of the eternal—a bridge between the swelteringly hot day of the 14th of Nisan in Jerusalem 2000 years ago and the four April days in 1930 in Moscow. Two heavenly luminaries alternately shedding their light on earth for all practical purposes become participants in the events, active forces in the novel.

The hot late-afternoon sun over Patriarch's Ponds and the bright circle at which Pontius Pilate gazed with despair at the moment of announcing the verdict, the broiling sun over the scorched Bald Mountain in Jerusalem, and the moonlight: a full moon that shatters to pieces as Berlioz is sliding down the streetcar rails; the moon over the balcony of the Roman Procuratory, and in the garden where Judas was stabbed; and the moonlit road seen from the window of the hospital where Ivan Nikolaevich languishes; and the endless moonlit ribbon along which, in the finale, Yeshua and Pontius Pilate walk in friendly conversation.

The sun—the customary symbol of life, joy, genuine light —accompanies Yeshua on his way of the cross as the emanation of hot, searing reality. In contrast the moon's is a fantastic world of shadows, mysteries, and eeriness; it is the kingdom of Woland and his guests, feasting in the full moon at the spring ball, but it is also the cooling light of peace and dreams. Finally, the luminaries of day and night are the only two indisputable witnesses of what

8.   An abbreviation that stands for the name of a Moscow literary club.

occurred who-knows-when in Jerusalem and of what happened recently in Moscow. They vouchsafe the unity of human history.

And this is only one of the imagistic correspondences, of the secret mutual echoes and mutual reflections that define the artistic structure of the book.

II

> *There are miracles which at close range turn out to be firmly rooted in reality.*
> Saltykov-Shchedrin[9]

There is something paradoxical about the very nature of Bulgakov's novel. It features irony, not as an element of style or a device but as part of the author's overall world view. Bulgakov dazzles the reader by the novelty and strangeness of his plot, by his treatment of events and characters.

Each of us imperceptibly adopts a number of truisms, ready-made and untested notions, inherited preconceptions. Paradox destroys didacticism and routine—this is why art loves it so. But there are two kinds of paradoxes. Some merely demonstrate the incisiveness and inventiveness of the author's mind. Others seem paradoxical only at first, giving pause, as they do to unventuresome reason and sluggish imagination. As we grow accustomed to these propositions, we begin to treat them as incontestable truths.

Realistic art challenges the reader's preconceptions, showing him the unusualness of the usual, the ordinariness of what seems extraordinary. What can be more miraculous and extraordinary than the story of Jesus Christ canonized by the Church, ensconced as a central religious dogma? Yet Bulgakov tells the story as though he were reconstructing an actual historical episode that occurred in Roman Judea in the first century of our era, and later provided material for legendary interpretation and religious canons. The very name of the hero—so jarringly plebeian Bulgakov uses the earth bound and secularized "Yeshua Ha-Notsri" instead of the solemn, rabbinical "Jesus"—vouchsafes the genuineness of

9. See "The Aesthetics of Gogol's *Dead Souls* and Its Legacy" above, n. 28.

Bulgakov's story and its independence from the evangelical tradition. Let us also recall the complaint voiced by Bulgakov's Yeshua about his disciple Matthew the Levite who walks around with a goat parchment writing down Yeshua's every word and always incorrectly. "I said nothing at all of what is written there"—it is as if he were refuting beforehand the prospective text of the Gospels. The fate of the tramp-philosopher who falls victim to the religious fanaticism of his compatriots and the cowardly treachery of the Roman procurator is deprived by Bulgakov of the usual mythical trappings. The religious cover of the miraculous is removed from the old gospel legend: we are faced with a human drama and a drama of ideas. But in contradistinction, say, to Renan, who in his study *The Life of Jesus* sought to portray Christ as a real historical figure,[10] Bulgakov's Yeshua is first of all an artistic creation, and his realistic "authenticity" is merely a vehicle for confronting the reader with vital moral and philosophical questions.

Bulgakov uses motifs from the evangelical legend the way Chekhov employed them in his remarkable tale "The Student," which he called his favorite story. On a cold spring night, returning home through an empty field, the student Ivan Velikopolskij meets two gardener women at the campsite. Warming himself at the campfire he tells them how on just such a spring night the apostle Peter thrice denied Christ and how heavy penitence was visited upon him. Whether due to the chance encounter and the setting or to the student's clear and beautiful narration, the story they must have heard many times in a priest's hasty mumbling suddenly comes to life and acts upon two women with a kind of irresistibility reserved for great art. The old woman Vasilisa and her daughter, the village woman Lukerja, for some reason become upset and cry, and the student understands that Vasilisa is involved with her whole being in Peter's travail. He realizes that the past is linked to the present by an unbroken chain and that "truth and beauty that guided human life there in the garden and in the courtyard of the high priest have endured to this very day and evidently have always been the most important thing in human life."

Thus it is with Bulgakov: the unusual and the legendary yields the humanly comprehensible, actual, and accessible, but no less

---

10. Ernest Renan (1823–92) was a nineteenth-century French philologist and historian. His *Vie de Jesus* (1863) was an eloquent but essentially heterodox tribute to one whom Renan had declared earlier "an incomparable Man."

significant for its accessibility; what is revealed is not faith but truth and beauty. Conversely, the writer's keenly ironic view detects in the ordinary and familiar much that is enigmatic and baffling.

The author of *The Master and Margarita* pokes fun at self-satisfied sobriety that hastens to find the simplest and most commonplace explanations for incomprehensible phenomena. Pontius Pilate, astounded by Yeshua's astuteness in divining his sickness and predicting relief from the attacks of hemicrania, nervously inquires: "Perhaps you are a great physician?" and vainly awaits confirmation of his guess. Likewise, Woland's interlocutors want to see in him no more than an artful hypnotist, while the breezy master of ceremonies Jurij Bengalskij, smiling a "wise smile," tries to assure his audience at the Variety Theater that the maestro simply has an excellent mastery of the techniques of magic. Finding such a tangible and handy explanation, people regain their complacency; the situation becomes viable again. If such an explanation is not found at once, they fall back, like the frightened Varenukha, on the flat and, as the author puts it, "utterly absurd" assertion: "This cannot be!"

Bulgakov's ironical mind challenges this complacency and sobriety without attempting to turn his readers into partisans of superstition or mysticism. It compels us to inquire: and what if one April evening the Devil really visited Moscow? An unlikely event, no doubt, but it is still interesting to find out who would react to this unsolicited appearance and how. This would be the more instructive, since people who seem so irreconcilable to all deviltry and mysticism easily come to terms with much that is wondrous and inexplicable in their daily lives.

Bulgakov detects general miracles and mysticism where few see them, notably, in the daily routine that sometimes plays jokes on one that are stranger than Korov'ëv's tricks. This is the chief technique, the basic lever of Bulgakovian satire, fantastic in its form like the satire of Saltykov-Shchedrin, but no less reality oriented in its import.

Actually, the forces of evil are not capable of original invention. More often than not Korov'ëv's swindles are merely the absurdities of life brought to light and pushed to the limit of the grotesque. When at the instigation of the branch director the bookkeepers, couriers, and secretaries of a reliable establishment, in the middle of a working day, burst into singing "Beautiful Sea, Sacred Baikal" and cannot shake off this popular tune so that in the end truck drivers carry them off singing, as at a mass rally, to the Stravinskij clinic, this is no more than a logical consequence of that mania for organizing clubs that the branch director regularly displays.[11]

Korov'ëv performs what seems to be an authentic miracle when at his behest there sits behind the desk of a branch director only an "executive" suit busily signing papers (a purely Shchedrin-like technique of ridicule, one might add). However, even here Korov'ëv's invention is outstripped by reality. What is truly amazing is not what the evil spirit did to Prokhor Petrovich, but the fact that, having "returned" to his suit, the chief approves all the memoranda that the suit signed in his absence!

Bulgakov's ironic vision uncovers a myriad of everyday miracles and mundane mysteries within the sphere of reality, eminently worthy of satire, that have to do with mistrust, fear, suspiciousness, and other psychological consequences of the violations of legality epitomized by the events of 1937.[12] The distinctive marks of that era are unobtrusively scattered across the pages of Bulgakov's book.

Woland is a master at arranging mysterious disappearances of people. Thus, in order to secure apartment no. 50 for himself, he dispatches Berlioz under a streetcar, while magically transferring Stëpa Likhodeev to Yalta. But Bulgakov drops a hint *en passant* that this "bad apartment" had already enjoyed ill fame: even before Woland's appearance its tenants had been disappearing without a trace. Under the circumstances Stepa Likhodeev's first reaction is quite understandable: having just witnessed the sealing of the dead Berlioz's apartment and still knowing absolutely nothing of the latter's fate, he turns yellow, as usual, and recalls with chagrin that he had recently palmed off on Berlioz an article for publication and had a questionable conversation with him.

Traces of the same atmosphere are easily detected in the nervous suspiciouness of Ivan, who in a conversation with the

11. Baikal is the largest lake in Siberia. The song, sung by an escaped convict, was an "old favorite." In his lively but not always accurate translation, Michael Glenny substitutes blithely "The Song of the Volga Boatmen." Stravinskij is the psychiatric clinic where the Master meets the hapless poet Ivan Bezdomnyj, traumatized by the strange events.

12: A pointed if characteristically euphemistic reference to the mass purges of the late 1930s.

"foreigner" suggests dispatching the philosopher Kant to Solovki[13] and, after landing in a psychiatric clinic, greets the doctor with the words "Hi ya, saboteur!" They are present in the hasty excuse of the chairman of the housing committee Bosoj caught taking bribes, "Enemies have sneaked it in"; in the sinister figures of the slanderers and informers Baron Majgel and Aloysius Mogarych, who went after the master's apartment; in the orgy of suspiciousness caused in the provinces by the rumors about Woland's gang, with a citizen in Armavil delivering to the police a black cat whose four paws he bound with a green neck tie, while in some other city citizens are arrested whose names sound like "Woland." (For good measure—"and quite unaccountably . . . so was the candidate of chemistry Vetchinkevich.")

Life is thus full of oddities and wonders to which people have become accustomed—they are too lazy or timid to notice them. The simplest confirmation of this is the behavior of the conductress of the trolley on which the cat tries to ride. Watching him grasp the handrail with a paw and offer a dime for the ride, the conductress yelled with anger, "No cats allowed!" "Neither the conductress nor the passengers," comments Bulgakov, "were struck by the very essence of the incident: that the cat was climbing on to the streetcar would have been a bit of a problem, but, to top it all, he intended to pay!"

Paradoxes of art are merely a reflection of paradoxes of life. Having rendered tangible phenomena usually assigned to the department of mysticism and miracles, the author was at the same time able to show how much of the strange and eerie lurks beneath familiar commonplaces.

It is hardly surprising that Ivan Nikolaevich, "virginal" in regard to education, fails to recognize on the bench at Patriarch's Ponds the traditional literary Mephistopheles. It is even harder to divine the Devil in his everyday disguise—in the form of Korov'ëv with his tiny moustache and trembling pince-nez, dirty socks, and checkered trousers. Thus he once appeared to Ivan Karamazov and since then has not haunted the reader's imagination.

On the other hand, it is not so difficult to see how peoples' lives are poisoned by malice, cowardice, suspicion, and lies, to grasp, that is, what in popular parlance is known as "the devil's power." "The Devil made me do this." Bulgakov deploys and realizes this metaphor in his novel.

13. An old monastery converted in the early 1920s to a prison camp designed mainly for political offenders.

III

> *Room! Sir Voland is coming!*
> *Rabble, clear the ground!*
> Goethe, *Faust*[14]

The Evil One has innumerable names, nicknames and sobriquets. The popularity of this figure in the oral legends of various peoples is indisputable evidence of how often man has had to deal with evil, destructive, and hostile powers. Unable to understand them and even less to cope with them, he found for these forces a most frightening and uncomplimentary personification.

The name Faland, which means "deceiver" or "cunning one" was already used by medieval German writers to signify the devil. Therefore when the cashier of the Moscow Variety Theater, straining her memory, recalls at the investigation that the mysterious magician who caused the commotion at the theater was called something like Faland, she is not entirely mistaken. And very similar-sounding Woland, "Herr Voland," appears once under this very name in the text of *Faust* as one of the allegorical designations of the devil.[15]

But no matter how different the sobriquets of Satan, his traditional occupation is always the same: he tirelessly sows temptation, destruction, and evil, confusing good people. Thus at first one is inclined to assume that the author had in mind a simple juxtaposition of the two forces eternally at war in the world, the antithesis of good versus evil embodied here in the figures of Yeshua and Woland.

However, upon closer examination one must conclude a bit uneasily that for so hard-and-fast an antithesis of shadow and light, Woland's portrayal is not sufficiently negative. Moreover, the author too readily gives him the floor for the purposes of explanation and self-justification.

There is something indisputably attractive about Bulgakov's Satan; he is even, one hesitates to say, likable. Scarcely having recovered from the first fright of the villainous killing of Berlioz

---

14. These words are spoken by Mephistopheles in Johann Wolfgang von Goethe, *Faust,* trans. Alice Raphael (New York, 1930), p. 224.

15. See the preceding note. In the epigraph above, "Voland" appears to be one of Mephistopheles' assumed names.

and still vexed, along with Ivan, at the unsuccessful chase of the mysterious trio, we note with astonishment that little by little we are beginning to like the members of this gang. Even the impertinent and enterprising Korov'ëv, upon brief acquaintance, no longer seems as repulsive as he did at the first glance. Still greater sympathy is gained by the gloomy and taciturn Azazello in his starched linen and with a gnawed chicken bone in his pocket, clumsily but persistently coaxing Margarita on a bench of the Aleksandrovskij Gardens, not to mention the cat whose appearance on the scene evokes a smile from us every time, insuring him against our hostility. Bulgakov's cat is a full-fledged character; mischievous, vain, boastful, touchy, unmannerly, and finicky. Let us recall how he wishes to appear as a gentleman and to shine at the ball in his tie, how at supper with Satan he peppers and salts a pineapple, arrogantly rejecting all attempts to teach him good manners: "I'm behaving at the table, don't bother me, I'm behaving!" And how with the primus stove in his paws he's sitting at the fireplace and inwardly preparing himself for resistance before the storming of apartment no. 50: "I'm not playing tricks. I haven't touched anyone. I'm fixing the primus," muttered the cat with an unfriendly frown, "and furthermore I consider it my duty to warn you that the cat is a most ancient and untouchable animal."

Woland himself is full of unhurried dignity, calm, and wisdom. Though portrayed by the author as Mephistopheles, he is actually a far cry from the traditional demon, the devil-tempter.

To understand Bulgakov's unorthodox treatment of Woland, it is necessary to examine the literary genealogy of this hero. *The Master and Margarita* teems with echoes of Goethe's *Faust*: the link between Woland and Mephistopheles is obvious. This is not to say that Bulgakov's Woland is only a new name for that same character, a variation on a familiar theme.

Goethe's Mephistopheles is evil, selfish, immoral. With a jesuitical grin he worms his way into one's confidence, operates by treachery, seduces into sin, and gleefully destroys the souls that have fallen into his lair. He reduces Faust to low sensuality, leads him to bear false witness, compels Gretchen to commit crimes—to drown her child and to administer poison to her mother. He murders noble Valentin and gloats nastily as he surveys his handiwork.

But along with Mephistopheles, in a complex relationship of submission to and rivalry with him, rises the figure of Goethe's Faust—the embodiment of thirst for knowledge, dominance over nature, omnipotence of man, determined to discover all the mysteries of the universe and to explore all the meanness and grandeur of life. Faust obtains from Mephistopheles a mighty power, not a power of evil and destruction but a power of knowledge and discovery. The passion for omniscience, for total knowledge was for too long considered the original sin. Goethe rehabilitated it, leaving to the Devil the sphere of active evil but taking from him the privilege of knowledge, which he had given man.

Bulgakov's Woland is capable of doing all the ancient legend ascribes Dr. Faustus. But at closer range one may recognize in Bulgakov's hero certain features of the later Faust of the classical tragedy. It would not be an exaggeration to say that Woland somehow encompasses both the devil Mephistopheles and the Magus Faust with his passion for investigation and knowledge.

In Woland, as he is described by Bulgakov, we see clearly the motif of activism, of protest against routine, stagnation, prejudice. In his Moscow adventures he seems to put into effect the mission with which the Lord entrusts Mephistopheles in the "Prologue in Heaven":

> Too quickly stilled is man's activity,
> to soon he longs for unconditioned rest;
> Hence I bestowed this comrade willingly,
> Who goads, and as a devil, creates best.[16]

However, Goethe's Mephistopheles is not so much an envoy of benign power as a sovereign of shadows, a tempter and destroyer. Not for nothing does Faust fling at him the reproach that "to eternal motion and salutary creative activity" he counterposes his "icy devil's fist." Bulgakov's Woland is something else again. Whatever one's view of him, he exhibits infinitely more good sense and nobility; he is even, quite unexpectedly, something of a moralist.

The Prince of Darkness, the Devil, Satan, Beelzebub, the Demon—from ancient times this power has had two principal roles, two callings: one is to confuse good people, to lead them into temptation, to seduce them, to engage in destructive villainy. The other, more noble, is to serve as executioner of vices, to bring retribution for sins: not for nothing are caldrons of boiling oil in hell serviced by devils. First the Devil ruins the human soul, then he lustfully punishes and executes it.

16. *Faust*, p. 18.

Woland seems to limit his own functions intentionally: he is inclined not so much to seduce as to punish. In fact, what is it that he and his cohorts are engaged in while in Moscow? To what purpose did the author let them cavort and carry on outrageously in the capital for four days?

Of those caught up in the actions of the evil gang too many reeked, as was pointed out in the investigation, of "blatant, obvious deviltry with an admixture of hypnotic tricks and distinctly criminal acts." Some perished, others were scared out of their wits, still others landed in insane asylums. Nonetheless, it is impossible to claim that these punishments fell on the heads of completely innocent victims. On the contrary, more often than not the reader accepts them as well deserved. Even if one is taken aback by the abruptness and ease of these reprisals—burdened by his omnipotence, the Devil does not always seem capable of calculating the force of his blow—one is not inclined to question their essential fitness. After nearly every one of Woland's escapades, the reader is apt to say to himself with a smile: "And serves him right, too!"

Ivan Nikolaevich is punished by insanity for his bad and false verse, Stëpa Likhodeev for sloth and debauchery, the house committee chairman Bosoj for graft, Varanukha for lying, Semplejarov for bigamy, the branch director for bureaucratism, Berlioz's uncle for being so greedy, the barman for swindling, Annushka for selfishness, Baron Majgel for informing. Arguably, Berlioz was an innocent victim of satanical pranks, but, perhaps, there is a measure of justice here, too. A self-satisfied windbag, a stranger to art, he put on too many airs, he was too vainglorious, too boastful about his intelligence and for this he lost his head. Granted this devilish joke is cruel, but Satan needs to have his fun. The fact of the matter is that with Berlioz's death literature did not sustain a major loss. Having grown wise and sober, Ivan Nikolaevich muses: "Big deal—a magazine editor was crushed! So what? Would the magazine be closed down on this account? There will be another editor, for all I know, even more eloquent than the former!"

It turns out that the forces of evil in Bulgakov's novel are not at all interested in their traditional pastime. Only one scene in the novel, that of mass hypnosis at the Variety Theater, features the Devil in his traditional role as tempter. But even here Woland behaves precisely as a corrector of morals, in other words as a satirist. He exposes low desires and passions only to stigmatize them with contempt and laughter. There is not the slightest shade of gloating in his attitude toward the people gathered at the Variety Theater. He awakens the crowd's greed and compels the audience to reach for the shower of banknotes and arouses feminine vanity with the latest Paris fashions, but not in order to ruin sinful souls. On the contrary, he seems to keep aloof fastidiously from the vices acquired by people without any assistance on his part. When he tests the audience's potential for cruelty as Fagot tears off the head of the verbose master of ceremonies and compassionate women demand that it be put in its place, the great magician says in a tone of tired understanding: "Well, now . . . they are people like any others, just thoughtless . . . but compassion does knock at their hearts sometime . . . ordinary people . . ." Then he commands loudly, "Put back his head!" How little does this pensive humanist resemble the merciless demon of the netherworld!

Still more unexpected is Woland's, and his henchmens', readiness to help good people who have fallen into misfortune or been treated badly by fate. It is they who reunite the Master and Margarita and return to the writer his manuscript. Toward the principal characters of the novel they act not as devils but rather as guardian angels. They are not incapable of chivalric conduct. Thus it is not altogether surprising that when the magical black horses carry them away from Moscow, the unpresentable members of Woland's gang acquire the lithe appearance of the heroes of an old German ballad: there gallops off with a quiet dangling of his golden chain a dark violet knight with a gloomy face, and with difficulty we recognize in him the "king of con artists," the self-styled translator Korov'ëv, and beside him, clad in steel armor, Azazello and the former cat Behemoth, "the best jester that ever existed," transformed into a slender youth, a demon-page.

Bulgakov has creatively reinterpreted the image of Woland–Mephistopheles and his cohorts. The juxtaposition of Woland and Yeshua is no simple antithesis of good versus evil. Unmitigated terror to the uninitiated, Woland turns out to be an avenging sword in the hands of justice and almost a champion of good.

Now it is easier for us to understand the meaning of the crucial epigraph to the novel taken by Bulgakov from Goethe's tragedy:

> Which then are you?
> A part of that Power which operates
> Ever in evil, yet good forever creates.[17]

17. Ibid., p. 63.

It is a matter of some significance that in *Faust* these words of Mephistopheles have quite a different import than the one they acquire when reproduced on the title page of the novel *The Master and Margarita*. The words of Goethe's Mephistopheles sound like a dexterous dodge by an experienced debater: the fact of the matter is that "good" when uttered by the Devil is tantamount to "evil." Let us recall the well-known dialogue where Mephistopheles spells everything out. "Tell me what this riddle of yours implies," says Faust, referring specifically to the words cited by Bulgakov in his epigraph, and here is the cynical reply:

> I am the Spirit that ever denies!
> And justly so; for all that's borne
> deserves to be destroyed in scorn.
> Therefore 'twere best if nothing were created!
> Destruction, sin, wickedness, plainly stated.
> All which you as evil have classified.
> That is my element, there I abide.[18]

The Devil, as usual, is a trickster. "Good" which he was just invoking, means for him the destruction of all that lives. But in Bulgakov the words about the "power which operates ever in evil, yet good forever creates" convey quite another meaning, free from dark irony and much more literal. It is as if the author of *The Master and Margarita* refused to understand the diabolical mockery of Mephistopheles and treated the above words as a credo that actually guided Woland's behavior.

Indeed how do the words "which operates ever in evil" apply to Woland? Only in that Woland embodies the element of doubt, negation, skepticism—qualities, needless to say, scarcely alien to Bulgakov the satirist. What is then the significance of the admission that even while wishing evil he "yet good forever creates"? It lies in that, in contrast to the cold and insolent Mephistopheles, evil is for Bulgakov's hero—by now we can call Woland this —not an end but a means, a way of coping with human vices and injustices. Woland shatters daily routine, punishes baseness and meanness, humbles scoundrels, petty cheats, swindlers, informers, profiteers, and thus emerges ultimately, in a most paradoxical and unexpected manner as virtually a servant of good.

18. Ibid., p. 64.

IV

> *By playing a treacherous role*
> *in the execution on Golgotha,*
> *the state dealt itself a very*
> *heavy blow. A legend full of*
> *disrespect for authority pre-*
> *vailed and swept the world.*
> *In this legend the powers-*
> *that-be play a foul role, the*
> *defendant is right, and the*
> *judges and police join forces*
> *against the truth.*
>
> Ernest Renan, *The Life of*
> *Jesus*[19]

The chapters about Jesus and Pontius Pilate that interrupt three times the narration of contemporary events, appear to lead an independent life in the novel. Nor are we inclined to begrudge them this status, so vivid, so truthful, so thought-provoking, and moving are these scenes. However, as one ponders further the place of these inserted chapters in the overall structure of the novel, one begins to see them as an organic part of the whole. A philosophical novel—and we are justified in labeling *The Master and Margarita* thus—is propelled not so much by the dynamics of the plot as by the development of the author's thought, capable of finding support in episodes seemingly distant from one another. Thus as we follow the duel between Pontius Pilate and the tramp-philosopher Yeshua Ha-Notsri and then become witnesses to his terrible execution, we confront the same problem of good and evil, of the weakness and power of the human will that underlie the story of Woland's Moscow adventures. Only here the issues are transferred from the plane of the contemporary and everyday to that of the historical and legendary and are elaborated and complicated by new motifs and nuances of thought.

One who has read Bulgakov's book will recall, no doubt, the large terrace in the garden, the spacious colonnade, the singing of the water in the fountain, the heavy, oppressive odor of attar of roses, the Procurator, tortured by hemicrania in an armchair on the

---

19. *Vie de Jésus* (Paris, 1879), p. 456.

mosaic floor, and off to the side the secretary taking down the interrogation on parchment and from time to time glancing up in astonishment at the audacious prisoner.

Pontius Pilate, who conducts the interrogation in a monotone, suddenly senses in the words of the beggarly philosopher a strange power, the power of calmly uttered truth. This elicits from the Procurator involuntary respect. True, he still tries to silence this feeling by cheap rhetoric as he flings at Yeshua the question famous in the annals of hypocrisy, "What is truth?" He still tries to scoff at the naïveté of Ha-Notsri, who asserts stubbornly and in spite of everything that man is good, and falls back on the traditional conventionality of all morals and relativity of all truth. But deep in his heart he already knows that in some sense the tramp is right.

Though the moral verdict upon Pontius Pilate had already been passed, he is portrayed by Bulgakov from inside as a complicated and a dramatic figure. He is no stranger to contemplation, to human feeling, to active sympathy. He clearly does not wish to destroy wantonly Yeshua's life. The wandering philosopher whose bold speeches sound strange to the Procurator's ears attracts and interests him. It is indeed interesting to observe a man free from internal inhibitions and taboos that always weigh heavily upon us, a man who fiercely and simply speaks the unspeakable. Pilate is ready to hide him in his own place at Caesarea, to save him from the fanaticism of his own countrymen, and to make him something like a court philosopher.

But there is a limit to everything. As long as Yeshua propounds that all men are good, Pilate is inclined to gaze condescendingly at this harmless nonsense, the fruit of childish idealism. He is prepared even to forgive the philosopher for knowing much about him that the Procurator would not dare to admit to himself, notably that he is lonely, friendless, seriously and perhaps hopelessly ill, that he is tired of ruling the Jerusalem he hates, and that he has lost faith in man once and for all.

But then the suspect from Galilee carelessly touches upon the supreme power and rashly declares that there will be a time when Caesars will no longer rule over man. And his fate is sealed.

Pilate is pierced by an acute fear that he has been conversing confidentially with a state criminal. Before his mind's eye appears the bald head of Caesar in his golden crown and a nasal voice draws the words: "The law regarding high treason . . ." Pilate's patience and liberalism are at an end.

The Procurator already knows that he cannot rise above himself, that he is pitiful and weak, that his fear of Caesar is stronger than he and that he will surrender Yeshua to death. But he still tries to make a deal with his conscience, still tries to persuade Yeshua to compromise in order to save his life. By his questions he wants to suggest inconspicuously to the prisoner answers that would ease his fate. He hints, winks, prompts, but Yeshua, as if refusing to understand him, stubbornly scorning the slightest compromise with his conscience, heads straight for certain death. What a pity! If he would only yield a little, keep quiet, use cunning, but the naïve prisoner reiterates: "To tell the truth is easy and pleasant," thus robbing the Procurator of the last hope of saving him.

By now the all-powerful Procurator is entirely in the grip of fear; he loses what remains of his pride, dignity, and calm. "I don't share your thoughts!" he exclaims with ostentatious haste. And fearful lest he be suspected of sympathizing with seditious ideas, he shouts, hastening to reject Yeshua's dangerous prophecy that the kingdom of truth will come: "It will never come!" This terrible cry is supposed to silence the calm, steady, and unconquerable voice of truth. It is not destined solely for long ears. Pilate tries to convince and calm himself to maintain his customary equilibrium. His only defense is not to believe that justice or truth will come in the end, because otherwise he is lost. He is lost because he has long taught himself to think that he has a single duty on earth, to glorify Caesar without peering into the past or thinking about the future. Belief in the imminent triumph of justice would undermine this short-range outlook.

One must conclude that this brave soldier, clever politician, a man possessing an unheard-of power in conquered Jerusalem, is guilty of shameful cowardice. He shudders at the thought of Caesar; he is apprehensive about informers, frets over his career, then, to his own surprise, he grows timid before Yeshua, vacillates, becomes confused, as he desires but does not dare to save him. After Yeshua has already hopelessly compromised himself by his dangerous outburst against the power of Caesar, Pontius Pilate makes the last attempt to help him and, transcending his own weakness, tries to persuade Caiphas to have mercy on the harmless dreamer. But religious fanaticism is more terrible and stubborn than the fanaticism of state power and the Procurator yields before the High Priest. Realizing that he is committing a horrible crime against his conscience, he agrees to execute Yeshua.

His cowardice is also treachery since he inwardly sympathizes with the unfortunate wanderer. That is why, even when everything is ended and the storm has washed off the Bald Mountain the traces of the terrible execution, the author does not release Pilate from the pincers of psychological analysis eternally extending the torment of his conscience.

For it is Bulgakov's Pilate who tries to ease Yeshua's last suffering on the cross, sending via Arthinius a secret order to finish him with a spear. And it is he who with the aid of secret service vengefully murders the betrayer Judas and shames the Sanhedrin by ordering that the thirty accursed pieces of silver be thrown over the fence of the High Priest's palace. Thus, he takes upon himself and accomplishes exactly what Yeshua's disciple Matthew the Levite wished but was unable to do—to save his teacher from the tortures of the cross by stabbing him with a knife and then to avenge him by killing Judas.

But there is and there can be no easy way to redeem betrayal. Pontius Pilate hopes in vain that the vengeance wreaked on Judas will purify him and lighten his guilt. In his soul both of Ha-Notsri's disciples—the faithful Levite and the traitor Judas —seem to dwell and fight each another, but, having killed the one, he does not obtain the confidence of the other. The Procurator tries to persuade the Levite to come to Caesaria, and as previously, with Yeshua himself, offers him protection only to face a decisive refusal: "No . . . you'll be afraid of me. It won't be very easy for you to look me in the face after you've killed him." This is the first punishment of the Procurator and the first confirmation from without that his conscience is forever stained and that he cannot expect forgiveness.

Cowardice is Pontius Pilate's major curse. But can a soldier fearless on the battlefield, a knight of the Golden Spear, actually be a coward? Why does Bulgakov insist so strenuously on this accusation? "Cowardice, without a doubt, is one of the most terrible vices"—these are Yeshua's words which Pontius Pilate hears in a dream. "No, Philosopher, I object: it is *the* most terrible vice," the author of the book interrupts unexpectedly, speaking in his own voice. Why did his usual restraint betray Bulgakov here and compel him, in violation of the conventions of narrative fiction, to express a personal condemnation of his hero?

The Procurator did not wish Yeshua harm; cowardice brought him to cruelty and treachery. Yeshua cannot condemn him—to

him all men are good. But Bulgakov condemns him without mercy
or condescension, condemns because he knows that people who
pursue evil as their goal are not as dangerous—there are in fact not
many such people—as those who are supposedly ready to help
good along but are faint-hearted and cowardly. Cowardice, which
easily subjugates a man to evil, which makes him a spineless tool
in the hands of others, that is, for Bulgakov, the heaviest curse. It
can turn a clever, brave, well-intentioned man into a pitiful
wretch; it can weaken and debase him. The only thing that can
save him is inner staunchness, confidence in his own reason, and
the voice of his own conscience.

In Bulgakov's conception that is of what the prisoner standing
with bound hands before the armchair of the powerful Procurator
was to remind us. The wondering philosopher is strong in his
belief in good, a belief that could not be taken away from him
either by fear of punishment or by the spectacle of howling injus-
tice whose victim he himself becomes. Yeshua is the embodiment
of the pure idea of good, of stubborn and enduring faith that transcends conventional wisdom and runs counter to the obvious les-
sons of life.

The weakness of Yeshua's preaching lies in its idealism. Pontius
Pilate surrenders him into the hands of the executioners, Mark the
Ratfighter whips him, other "good people" hoot at him in the
square when the Procurator announces his sentence. But Yeshua
is stubborn; the absolute integrity of his belief in good is compelling. Huge, cruel, and bestial, his face disfigured by a German
club, Mark the Ratfighter does not seem hopeless to him: he is
merely an unfortunate man made cruel by his misery. "If only one
could talk to him . . . I am certain he would change radically,"
Yeshua says dreamily.

To be sure, this faith in the man's essential goodness and the
ultimate triumph of justice is close to Bulgakov's heart. But he
does not share the utopian hope of achieving such a triumph
solely by inspirational preaching or even at the cost of a great
sacrifice or self-immolation. The author of *The Master and
Margarita* is ill-suited to be an orthodox disciple of Yeshua; his
outlook is more earthy, more realistic, tough. In Yeshua's beautiful
and humane teachings there was no place for the punishment of
evil, for the concept of vengeance. It is hard for Bulgakov to accept this. That is why he was in so much need of Woland, free
from his customary wallowing in destruction and evil and acting

as if entrusted by the forces of good with an avenging sword. Woland seems to feel Yeshua's power and, submitting to it, implements the law of justice in the proximate realm. But prior to that Yeshua's disciple, Matthew the Levite, despite the precepts of his teacher, wants to punish immediately the traitor Judas. If he fails to accomplish this, it is only because the Procurator's secret service has already beaten him to it. Bulgakov does not want to wait until the idea of justice captures men's hearts on its own; he hastens the punishment of betrayal.

Defenseless and weak in earthly life, Yeshua is great and forceful as a harbinger of new human ideals. Bulgakov's version of the Christ legend emphasizes the motif of Christian socialism, of democratic tendencies inherent, as historians have pointed out, in early Christianity and so diversely interpreted later on. In contradistinction to the Gospel Jesus, who evasively proclaimed "Render unto Caesar what is Caesar's and unto God what is God's," Bulgakov's Yeshua will have no truck with the power of Rome. The "kingdom of truth and justice" he dreams about has social rather than religious implications. This is why the very scene of execution, portrayed by Bulgakov with the vividness of an eyewitness, is in many ways independent of Church tradition.

. . . The crowd of the curious has long since dispersed, the soldiers are exhausted from heat and boredom; the sun has begun to set behind Golgotha, and on a post, spread-eagled and scorched by the sun, Yeshua Ha-Notsri, who believed unreasonably in good, is experiencing his last moments. His head in its unwound turban hangs weakly to one side; tortured by horseflies, he is dying not as an omnipotent god who will be resurrected in the morning, but as a mortal, powerless man who has gone to the extreme for his convictions, accepting the torture of crucifixion for them and thus giving them unconquerable power. The import of this image grows, swelling in significance, and behind that disgraceful execution in Jerusalem, we discern through the haze of two millennia, Giordano Bruno in the flames and Joan of Arc executed and the five shadows of those hung from the battlements of the Petropavlovskaja fortress[20]—the long line of sacrifices borne by mankind on its path to justice and truth. These people wanted to remain true to themselves and their ideals that seemed to their

---

20. Reference to the execution at Nicholas I's orders of the leaders of the "Decembrist" insurrection (see "Pushkin and Sterne" above, n. 27).

contemporaries too novel, too audacious, or too dangerous, and they had to pay for it with their lives and win for their cause immortal glory.

This is why Yeshua, for all his helplessness, is so strong and unconquerable: this is why the mere memory of him causes the all-powerful Procurator to shudder and eternally haunts his conscience "beaten black and blue." No, the author sees in him more than a religious preacher and reformer. In Bulgakov the figure of Yeshua becomes a symbol of free spiritual activity.

The poet–prophet scorned, insulted, persecuted, misunderstood, is an old theme in poetry. It resounds in the deathless verse of Pushkin: "Lone sower of freedom / I set out early before the star . . ."[21]

In Yeshua Ha-Notsri Bulgakov sees just such a prophet who "set out before the star," whose preaching anticipates another, better era. Thus there emerges in the perspective of ages the problem of spiritual power pitted against the authority of prejudice and brute force, in essence the same problem that occupied Bulgakov in his biography of Molière and in his play about the last days of Pushkin.[22]

Molière and Louis XIV, Pushkin and Nicholas I, Pushkin and D'Anthès, Yeshua and Pontius Pilate—these names are paired in Bulgakov's universe, where those who have been granted immortality as a deserved reward bestow it upon others as a badge of shame. The king of France would not have been too pleased to find that several centuries later people would recall his name most often on the anniversary of his court comedian. Within one century the object of persecution and ridicule, the chamberlain of Nicholas I, has turned the omnipotent ruler into a minor protagonist in his biography.[23] And Pontius Pilate is ready for any penance to shake off the onerous fame as a destroyer of the Galilean itinerant philosopher, to free himself from the yoke of a shameful immortality.

The stubborn power of art, of truth, of the creative spirit will inexorably prevail, whatever the obstacles, large or small, that lie

21. A quotation from an 1823 Pushkin lyric.
22. Lakshin speaks here of the fictionalized biography, *Life of Monsieur Molière* (1932–33) and the play *The Last Days* (1934–35), which portrayed the events immediately preceding Pushkin's fatal duel.
23. Reference, clearly, to Aleksandr Pushkin.

in its path. Linked at one level to the mysterious presence of Woland, the story of Yeshua and Pontius Pilate points directly, at another level, toward the strange fate of the Master and his beloved.

V

> *But you my poor and bloodied master! You did not want to die anywhere—either at home or away from home!*
>
> Bulgakov[24]

The hero whose name is part of the novel's title appears only toward the middle of the first part of the book. His appearance is sudden and strange: clad in a hospital gown, glancing around fearfully, he slides into Ivan Nikolaevich's ward from the balcony that surrounds the facade of the Stravinskij clinic.

In the description of the hero's outward appearance there is a flash of something remarkably familiar: "clean-shaven, dark-haired, with a sharp nose, an anxious expression and a lock of hair hanging down his forehead, a man of about thirty-eight." This looks like a cagey attempt at a self-portrait, a face that is quite different from the author's and yet recognizable. It is as if the artist had painted over a canvas: it is enough to remove the top layer of paint, to wash the canvas thoroughly in order to see the profile of the author of *The Days of the Turbins* [see note 7 above]. The same may be said of the Master's entire life story and his vicissitudes; behind them one divines much that is poignantly personal, autobiographical.

Such closeness to his hero, though offering certain advantages, must have inhibited the writer, adept at graphic portrayal of characters seen from the outside. In fact, the Master is somewhat conventional, diffuse, as if he were drawn so as not to resemble his creator too much, yet at the same time to embody the author's personal impressions and experiences. In that figure there is less

---

24. *The Life of Monsieur de Moliére*, trans. M. Ginsburg (New York, 1970), p. 5.

living flesh, less vivid detail than we usually find in a Bulgakov protagonist. Surrounded by everyday life, the Master is at the same time elevated high above it. But the somewhat vague and shadowy quality of the hero is redeemed by the poetic significance of two motifs, two themes that pervade the figure: creativity and love. It is appropriate that the title of Bulgakov's teeming and multidimensional novel should have featured the names of the Master and his beloved. What is at issue here is not so much a title as a burden, not just a tribute to the thematic importance of the protagonists, but an act of self-expression.

To outsiders the Master would seem a man "not of this world." He is entirely in the grip of his imagination, capable of summoning from the silence of the millennia the shades of Yeshua and Pontius Pilate. Work and creativity are his all-consuming passions. Days and weeks fly past the windows of the basement of a small house with a garden, the seasons of the year follow each other impetuously. Now snowdrifts pile up at the fence and the snow creaks below the window, then the sun peaks into the basement and the spring torrents flow, threatening to inundate the quiet shelter, and in the yard the lilac bursts into bloom. Never through all this does the Master raise his head from the manuscript.

He is consumed by worry, racing against time, anxious to say it the best way he can. The novel does not promise him early recognition or success; his reward lies elsewhere. He is destined to experience only one extremely brief moment of triumph, when he realizes with pride that he has correctly divined his characters and resurrected the dead past. "Oh, how I guessed it! I guessed it all!" he rejoices hearing Bezdomnyj's tale of Pontius Pilate.

The Master stubbornly declines the honor of calling himself a professional writer. This is not modesty but pride. He does not regard his writing as merely belles lettres, as a matter of earning a living or meeting a demand, but as a sort of a mission, a fulfillment of a voluntary vow. His attitude toward the Writers' Union, toward the professional literary milieu, is apprehensive and almost hostile. Without even knowing the verse of Ivan Nikolaevich, he is convinced beforehand that it is hopelessly bad ("Monstrous," Ivan agrees unexpectedly) and begs him to give up writing. He is almost outraged when his interlocutor recognizes in him a brother of the pen.

"You are a writer?" the poet asked with interest.

The visitor's face darkened and he threatened Ivan with his fist, then said, "I am a Master!"

For Bulgakov, a master is more than a writer. The word is capacious; it has a wide semantic resonance. It suggests respect for consummate skill, for perfect mastery of a craft. It also conveys a sense of dedication, of service to some lofty spiritual mission, utterly foreign to that empty life *around* art led by the litterateurs at the little table of the Griboedov Restaurant or in the corridors of Massolit. In a certain sense Yeshua, too, could be called a master.

In fact, the Master shares several traits of Yeshua's: fidelity to his convictions, inability to hide the truth, an inward independence that plays havoc with his personal welfare. Like the vagabond from Galilee, the Master has grown sensitive to human suffering and pain. "You know I can't stand noise, disturbance, violence, anything of that nature," he tells Ivan Nikolaevich. I especially hate a human scream, whether it's a scream of suffering, rage, or any other kind of scream."

But we would be rushing to conclusions if we were to consider the Master a blind follower of Yeshua. In one very important aspect they differ crucially. Bulgakov's hero does not share the idea of all-forgiveness; it is difficult for him to believe that every man is good and that people should forgive every insult. That is probably why he who has told us of Yeshua's infinite goodness finds a protector and intercessor in the mighty Devil–Woland.

You recall how strangely the Master reacts to Ivan's doleful tale of Berlioz's horrifying death. His eyes gleam with malice. "I'm only sorry that instead of Berlioz it wasn't the critic Latunskij, or that writer Mstislav Lavrovich!" he exclaims in an attack of uncontrolled fury. But then the Master had good reason to hate that clique. While he sat in basement with pen in hand, his only concern was to bring out his novel, to "divine" his heroes, to breathe life into his book. But novels are written to be read; the day comes when a book must appear, must face the people, and how difficult, at times, is its path to the reader! At the gates to the literary world the Master meets the editorial secretary Lapshennikova with her "eyes crossed to her nose from constant lying." The editor conversing with him is more interested in the irreproachability of the author's biography than in his manuscript and asks the Master the "idiotic" question: who had advised him "to compose a novel on such a strange subject?" Critics closely associated with the magazine read the manuscript, and shortly after Lapshennikova returns his book to the author and explains that its publication is "out of the question," articles appear in the paper stigmatizing the unpublished novel. The critic Ariman castigates the Master's book

as an attempt at an "apologia for Jesus Christ." The writer Lavrovich urges people "to strike and strike hard at Pilatism." And
Latunskij surpasses them all in coarseness by publishing an article
under the venomous title "A Militant Old Believer." (There was
hardly any need for inventiveness here. All Bulgakov had to do
was to draw on an appropriate body of RAPP criticism.[25] The
author of *Days of the Turbins* had collected in a scrapbook 298
hostile and abusive reactions to his work).

No wonder that like Maksudov, in *A Theatrical Novel*,[26] who
has just stumbled into the literary milieu, the author subsequently
recalls it "with horror." Hatred boils in him against Lapshennikova and Ariman, Lavrovich, and Latunskij. Having experienced
the tragedy of nonrecognition and victimization at the hands of his
confrères, the Master cannot easily forgive his foes. He little resembles a righteous man, a Christian, a martyr. Is this not why, in
the symbolic finale of the novel, Yeshua refuses to take him into
his realm of "light" but contrives for him a special fate, rewarding
him with "peace," of which the Master had known so little in his
life?

But a book should outlive its creator, for "manuscripts don't
burn." And though the Master's chief detractor Latunskij is far
lower and pettier than Yeshua's oppressor Pontius Pilate, and the
problem, having been transferred to a more recent era, is resolved
by Bulgakov on another, more mundane plane, we can distinguish
in the tale of the Master's fate the throbbing of a familiar belief:
genuine spiritual power will inevitably prevail and demonstrate
its virtue. Whatever may happen, people will still read the
Master's book and Latunskij will get what he deserves from pos-
terity: his name will be covered with scorn, his malicious slander
will never be forgiven.

But the comfort of his faith in the future cannot undo misfortunes and anxieties of the present. And until the time of justice
comes what can sustain the tired, drained Master? Belief in the
importance of his work. Inner firmness. And the devotion and love
proffered by few, for that matter, by one person only, Margarita

---

25. The abbreviation stands for the Russian Association of Proletarian
Writers. RAPP was a doctrinaire literary faction that in the years 1928–32 exercised a virtual dictatorship over Soviet literature.

26. Another work of Bulgakov's written "for the drawer" and published
recently in the West, *A Theatrical Novel* (1936–37) is a pointedly satirical
account of the author's precarious association with the Moscow Art Theater.

who helps him to believe that he is not living in vain, who comforts and protects him in moments of confusion and perplexity.

The woman who was to become the Master's "secret wife" appeared in his life at just the right time, and not only to make him coffee in the morning and beautifully to set the oval table for breakfast. Like Matthew the Levite, she is ready to cast everything aside along the way, just as the tax collector once threw his money into the dust, and as she herself threw the flowers into the gutter in order to follow the Master and if necessary to perish with him. Her faith in the novel about Pontius Pilate is a genuine feat of loyalty. She is his only reader, his sympathetic critic, his defender and heir, and as long as she is with the Master, let all the Latunskijs of the world choke in powerful rage—he is not crushed, he works, he will write a great book!

The author arouses in us a tender, grateful feeling toward this woman: devotion in love and fortitude in creativity are for Bulgakov essentially phenomena of the same nature. Is this not why the Master and his beloved understand each other so well?

Margarita cannot shield the Master from the adversities that threaten him. But she does everything in her power to try to struggle with the terrible and incomprehensible illness that is poisoning their whole life. What is this disease? Where has it come from? The Master calls it *fear*. "Cold and fear, after becoming my constant companions," he tells Ivan "drove me to exhaustion. . . . Fear rules every cell of my body."

Gloomy forebodings grip the Master. Dark autumn evenings bring melancholy that envelopes him like an octopus. At such a moment he flings the manuscript of his novel into the fire; only Margarita can ease the effect of the ominous illness, only she can sustain in him the will to live and feed the weak flame of hope. She retrieves from the stove the fragments of the charred manuscript so as to rescue the best part of the Master's soul—his novel.

The Master's illness is difficult to cure because it does not fall under the rubric of standard mental ailments. It seems to belong in the same category as the malady hinted at in A. Afinogenov's play *Fear* and in Leonid Leonov's *The Snowstorm*.[27] I am speak-

27. Both plays were written during the thirties. It is curious that Lakshin should mention them here: A. Afinogenov's *Fear* (1931) deals with a politically naïve old scientist who becomes a tool of anti-Soviet elements; L. Leonov's *The Snowstorm* portrays a crafty "enemy of the people." Yet in spite of an

ing about the kind of fear that was aroused by the airborne bacilli of suspicion, distrust, expectancy of a sudden knock on the door in the night, a symptom, that is, which we associate today with the atmosphere of violation of legality at the end of the thirties.

That is why Margarita was able to struggle with the Master's sickness only to a certain point; beyond that even she was powerless. What was in her power was to share to the end the fate prepared for him. But once, having parted from the Master at midnight and promised to come the next morning, she does not find him in the basement. "Yes, like the unhappy Matthew the Levite, I return too late!" Margarita showers herself with reproaches. (The Levite and Margarita—Bulgakov does not draw this parallel accidentally.)

Where did the Master vanish to from his little apartment that November night? Why did he appear again in January beneath the windows of his house, shifting in the cold from foot to foot, in a coat with its buttons torn off? Where did he spend those three long months, and why, hearing the sound of a gramophone coming from his basement, did he promptly leave the yard and walk through the frozen city to the Stravinskij clinic?

Here much remains vague and nebulous. One thing is clear: it is Latunskij's article that dealt with Master the decisive blow. Having read it, the resourceful Aloysius promptly concluded that it did not require much effort to liberate the Master's little apartment for himself. No wonder the vile feeling of fear seized the Master right after he read the articles about his novel.

But perhaps the Master is simply a coward and deserves the same verdict as the one passed on Pontius Pilate. No, cowardice and fear are positively not the same. The Master is no coward. Fear may drive him to distraction, but it cannot push him to a dishonorable act. For cowardice is fear multiplied by baseness, an attempt to preserve peace and well-being at any price, even by compromising one's conscience.

The Master never forgoes his conscience, his honor. All the same fear acts destructively upon the human soul, especially on the soul of an artist. It produces revulsion toward one's work, apathy, and a debilitating sense of being trapped. Though only

---

ostensibly orthodox message, each play does suggest the climate of all-pervasive fear. Incidentally, *The Snowstorm*, though written in 1939, was not published until the sixties.

yesterday he was proud of his novel, the Master grows cold toward his beloved labors and is ready to hate them. He does not want to remember his novel so as not to cause himself pain, and after a three-month absence from home, poisoned by fear, voluntarily sets off for Stravinskij's clinic—the most convenient place for quiet meditation and candid conversation with those who are insane like he is. Terrible is this apathy of the Master, the indifference oppressing his soul, the satisfaction with the four walls of the ward in a man who once dreamed of traveling all over the globe so as to see everything for himself . . .

Margarita resists this numbness of the soul. She refuses to reconcile herself to the death of the Master. She endeavors to dispel the fear that dictates resignation and weakness and to conquer it by courage and fidelity. Loudly she adjures fate: "Why is it happening? But I will save you. I will save you."

And so that this supplication be not in vain, that the promise be fulfilled, the author crosses a certain threshold in his book, alters the scenery as in a fairy-tale spectacle: the bleak reality wanes and Margarita's magical dream begins—her wish and hope transform into a fantastic reality.

For the sake of meeting with the Master, Margarita is prepared to become a witch, and she accomplishes her merry flight along the Arbat on a broom. Flying above electric wires and signs of gas stations, she now feels strong enough to accomplish everything that formerly seemed unrealizable. If she does not poison Latunskij as she promised, she at least creates a marvelous mess in his fashionable apartment. And if she does not succeed in saving the Master, he is returned to her at the spring ball of the full moon, and the manuscript he burned is again resurrected in a miraculous manner. Thus, be it in a fairy-tale-like, fantastic dream, Margarita restores desecrated justice and demonstrates her "genuine, eternal, true love."

VI

> . . . to embody what never was
> A. Blok[28]

Now that the fates of all the principal protagonists have passed before us, it is time to note the links that bind the disparate and

28. A sequel to the lines quoted as an epigraph of section I. (See n. 2 above.)

seemingly autonomous strata of the narrative. In Woland's Moscow adventures, in the spiritual duel of Yeshua with Pontius Pilate, and in the dramatic fate of the Master and Margarita, one
unifying motif resounds incessantly. It is faith in the law of justice,
of righteous judgment, of inexorable retribution.

Bulgakov believes in this law with exemplary fervor. Such un-
swerving faith in justice bespeaks great moral strength, but there
is something touchingly naïve and helpless about it. One has had
to go through a great deal, to have had many a bout with despair in
order to summon Satan's aid and turn Woland and his gang into
Robin Hood–like good robbers. In Bulgakov's novel justice invariably triumphs, but this victory is most frequently secured by inscrutable devices of black magic. I have already mentioned the
threat that Woland and his retinue pose to every kind of petty
swindler and liar. But the real payoff of Woland's punitive raids is
his pursuit of informers and spies. At Satan's Grand Ball, Azazello
ruthlessly kills Baron Majgel, notorious in Moscow for excessive
inquisitiveness "and no less developed loquaciousness," and
Messire drinks with pleasure from a chalice the blood of the guest
who had crashed the party in order to spy and eavesdrop. A little
later Woland summons before his formidable eyes the shadow of a
man wearing nothing but his underwear, with a suitcase in his
hands and nearly delirious. This is our friend Aloysius Mogarych
who brought a complaint against the Master in order to move into
his little apartment. "I put in a bathroom," cried Mogarych, his
teeth chattering and babbling with fright. "I gave it a coat of
whitewash." But the informer's pathetic excuses are of no avail.
Aloysius, frightened out of his wits, is blown away and the little
apartment is restored to the Master and Margarita by their mag-
nanimous patron.

That same law of justice triumphs ineluctably in the ancient
story of Yeshua Ha-Notsri. To Bulgakov it was not enough that the
traitor Judas should punish himself. In defiance of the Gospel he
has him killed by the hired murderers sent by Pilate. To allow the
traitor repentance and suicide, inspired by remorse, would have
been too great an honor. By the same token, the author punishes
Pontius Pilate with eternal torment, making him suffer for two
thousand years insomnia, headache, and the anguish of remember-
ing forever that fatal moment when he delivered Yeshua to the
executioners. Let the cowardly ruler of Judea squirm in his stone

armchair on the joyless flat hilltop, seeing always before his eyes that drying red-black pool—be it wine once spilled by a clumsy slave or a reminder of Yeshua's innocent blood—and yearning hopelessly for an end to his ordeal.

The return to the Master of his charred manuscript and his reunion with Margarita under the roof of their beloved home are also acts of justice wrought by black magic. Having arranged this miracle, Woland smiles the pleasant smile of a benefactor and wishes happiness to the heroes of the novel, as their good spirit, their godfather, and matchmaker. He shows much more solicitude for the Master's literary career than does the magazine's editor and inquires with interest about his further creative plans. "But shouldn't you latch on to something real?" says Woland reproachfully to the master. "If you have exhausted the Procurator, why don't you write about, say, Aloysius?"

True, the law of justice has one aspect that its unorthodox champion is bound to find uncongenial. Woland makes retribution his guiding principle; he is completely deaf to the idea of mercy. Yet to Bulgakov there can be no justice without mercy, just as there can be none without retribution. It falls to Margarita to voice this belief.

Margarita rejects Woland's polite offer to punish Latunskij with instant death and calms down Azazello, who is ready at the queen's first words to empty his revolver into the scoundrel. Her modest feminine revenge, the havoc wreaked in the critic's apartment, is enough for her. Even more annoying for Woland is the deal with hapless Frieda who, deceived by a café owner, suffocated her infant with a handkerchief, this a variant of Goethe's Gretchen. Margarita promises to intercede in her behalf; she cannot disappoint her. She turns to Woland with a request that he reprieve Frieda. This is beyond Woland's power: forgiveness is not his department. It is easier for Margarita to rescue the wretch herself; all Woland can do is to shut his eyes to her whim.

Mercy and all-forgiveness are not the same thing. In contradistinction to Yeshua, who forgives everyone for everything beforehand, Margarita is not inclined to forgive evil. She knows the sweet feeling of revenge, but her heart is compassionate, easily appeased. What can you do if Margarita feels pity for Frieda, who every morning for thirty years has been given the poisoned handkerchief reminding her of her crime? She even pities Pontius Pi-

late, who has been sitting for two thousand years in his stone
armchair. These just punishments, drawn out endlessly, seem to
her cruel and almost excessive.

Human sensitivity is apt to play havoc with the Devil's efforts at
punishing criminals. Yet curiously enough, it is Woland himself,
dissatisfied as he is with Margarita's attempt at intercession for the
man sitting in the stone chair, who formulates *en passant* the
central idea of the novel in words chiseled like a commandment.
"Are you going to repeat the business with Frieda again?" said
Woland. "But you needn't distress yourself, Margarita. All will be
as it should: that is how the world is made."

"All will be as it should; that is how the world is made"—in
these words resounding from the lips of the Devil, the author's
undying faith in the law of justice is again affirmed. But, as we are
now beginning to realize, justice according to Bulgakov cannot be
reduced to punishment, retribution, and reward. Justice is dis-
pensed by two departments whose functions are strictly separated:
the department of retribution and the department of mercy. This
striking metaphor embodies an important concept: even while
calling for vengeance, a truly righteous power is incapable of becoming intoxicated with cruelty, savoring endlessly the vengeful
feeling of triumph. Mercy is the other face of justice.

Pontius Pilate, like Frieda, obtains forgiveness in the end, and
Woland tells the Master that he can now conclude his novel with a
single sentence. "You are free!" cried the Master, cupping his
hands into a megaphone. These words of *forgiveness*, recalling the
voice from heaven "You are saved!" in Goethe's *Faust*, are the last
words in the Master's novel about Pontius Pilate.

But we are not yet finished with Bulgakov's own novel. Its overall impact calls for further comment.

It is a well-known fact that Bulgakov gravitated toward the
broadly conceived humanistic ideal. He never evolved a clearcut
political world outlook. Strictures about his imperfect understanding and acceptance of the new revolutionary order are, for the
most part, well taken. Portrayal of the new social realities was not
his forte. Yet, in line with the old Marxist tradition, we shall judge
the artist not by what he fails to offer but by what he does offer.
"Universalist" art may prove a mode of escape from social issues,
yet it may also be a way of confronting them. At times the
humanism of universal scope, as with Tolstoy and Dostoevsky, can
cast a new light on social reality. Bulgakov leads us into the realm

of moral values, for example, conscience, honor, justice, and his observations and discoveries are of great moment to us and the quality of life in our society.

This is not to say that Bulgakov resolved the enormous problems that confronted him. Far from it—he piled new queries on top of the old ones and provided in the context of the novel a purely conventional, illusory resolution. Yet he deserves credit for daring to approach the major moral–philosophical dilemmas of our time, for refusing to forget or ignore them. Instead he placed these issues at the center of a dazzling and unorthodox novel, hoping to rivet the reader's attention upon them.

The writer shows anguish and pain at the sight of people who pay lip service to the sense of social responsibility but actually are ready to jettison personal morality, and who live mindless lives. "You and I don't have to think. The leaders are doing our thinking for us." That is how Majakovskij epitomized this mentality. This kind of attitude, while respecting social proprieties, was compatible with self-seeking and acquisitiveness.

Nikanor Ivanovich Bosoj, caught at taking a bribe, remonstrates: "I took the money—I admit that—but it was Soviet money. . . . Yes, I would sign tenants up for money. . . . But I never took any foreign currency." Note the fine distinction Nikanor Ivanovich draws between his self-image as a Soviet citizen and as an ordinary crook. He expects leniency for being able to separate his public morality from his personal ethics.

Today, from the vantage point of the sixties, we can see more clearly than ever that communism not only does not spurn morality but is a necessary condition for the victory of new principles in the consciousness of those individuals who comprise our society. Social morality is inseparable from personal morality, for social justice, in the final analysis, is nothing other than a sense of personal justice, of a moral ideal, transposed to the scale of all society.

That is why Bulgakov's book, written in the thirties, proved surprisingly relevant to the literature of the sixties, the period when our writers' basic concern with social problems blended with an especially keen interest in the problem of moral choice, of personal morality. To be sure, Bulgakov's novel bears the distinct imprint of his times and his personal destiny. In the book's artistic philosophy we find a reflection of the author's literary adversities and somber thoughts on the eve of death. Bulgakov believed in the ultimate triumph of justice. He knew that sooner or later real art always won recognition. Sooner or later—but everyone would like this to happen sooner, at any rate within his lifetime. In order to banish the feelings of futility and frustration that were undermining his will to create, Bulgakov urged time forward, hurried justice along to make it triumph immediately, be it in the realm of poetic fantasy.

This possibility of punishment, of immediate restitution of justice, remains in the novel's plot Woland's prerogative, but there is another protagonist who enjoys the same privilege. This is the author–demiurge who shapes the fate of his characters. He knows all about them beforehand and preassigns to each his lot.

He made this kind of choice also for his master. In the last chapter of the book you sense all the bitterness of the approaching departure from life, the final settling of accounts with it. In the foreword to the novel, Konstantin Simonov truthfully wrote that there is in this book "a kind of last-gasp brilliance of an immensely gifted writer who knew deep in his heart how little time he had left."[29]

But for all the infinite sadness of the novel's finale—wherein a heavy black curtain is drawn across the death of the Master and Margarita—the last chapters of the book also contain wise solace gleaned by a warm heart.

The Master and his beloved are not destined to remain in the house with the garden. Neither will they follow Yeshua "into the light," for the Master has not earned the light. Woland seduces them with another "eternal home" where the Master will stroll with Margarita beneath the blossoming cherry trees and in the evening will listen to the music of Schubert, where he will write with a quill by candlelight and, like Faust, will sit over his retort in hopes of fashioning a new homunculus. "This way, Master, this way," Woland urges him on.

The Master is given "peace," but a strange, active peace. Again labor at a writing table, again meditation, and again insight. In this other life the Master is destined to delight in quiet and concentrated effort, in the tenderness of his beloved. Margarita can already see the Venetian window of their home, a grapevine climb-

29. The foreword by Konstantin Simonov (1915–), a popular and versatile Soviet writer, appeared in the November 1966 issue of the journal *Moskva*, which featured the first installment of *The Master and Margarita*.

ing up the roof, the quiet strolls along the stream, and at night the calm sleep of the Master in his everlasting, dirty old cap. There are too many signs here of creature comfort, of daily routine, of earthly life spurned and abandoned yet held dear: something like the little basement left behind, but better, more beautiful, more desirable.

I trust this will not sound grandiloquent, for it is pure, unadulterated truth: here is a triumph of art over dust, over fear of inescapable death, over transience and brevity of human existence. A victory that might be illusory but is endlessly important and soothing to the soul.

No less precious, however, is another reward—the fate of the novel predicted in the book. "Your novel has some more surprises in store for you," Woland promises the Master, parting with him after the magic ball. We read these words as if they were addressed to *The Master and Margarita*.

The poetic impact of Bulgakov's book on today's reader bears out the prophecy made a quarter of a century ago: life itself has completed the novel in a novel, it has given the book a new fate and thus has made still more irresistible in its triumph the ideal of justice in which the author of *The Master and Margarita* believed so fervently.

The Poetics of Osip Mandelstam

LIDIJA GINZBURG

Mandelstam began as an heir to the Russian symbolists. Yet he did so at the moment when the disintegration of the symbolist movement was obvious to everyone, when Blok, its erstwhile standard-bearer, was seeking different answers to the disquieting questions of the era. The poems in Mandelstam's first collection *Stone* (1913) are free from symbolism's "other-worldliness," from its positive ideology and philosophy.

In 1912 Mandelstam joined the acmeists. These widely differing disciples of the symbolists were united by a common aspiration—the desire to return to an earthly source of poetic values, to a portrayal of the tridimensional world. The principal acmeist poets differed in their interpretation of this *tridimensionality.* Gumilëv's neoromanticism and exoticism[1] are a far cry from the concrete, everyday world of Akhmatova's early verse. As for Mandelstam, he was attracted to various facets of "tridimensionality," including the literal sense of the word—architectural proportions and building materials.

> Be lace, stone
> and a spiderweb.
> Stab the sky's empty breast
> With a fine needle.[2]

"Gothic dynamics" are important to Mandelstam not because they symbolize a striving toward the infinite—this is the romantic interpretation of the Gothic—but because they mark the triumph of construction over material, the transformation of stone into needle and lace.

This essay, translated here by Sona Hoisington, first appeared in *Izvestija Akademii Nauk SSSR, Serija literatury i jazyka* [News of the Soviet Academy of Sciences, literature and language series] (July-August 1972): 310-27. Excerpts from Clarence Brown's *Mandelstam* (New York: Cambridge University Press, 1973) are reprinted by permission of the publisher. Excerpts from *Osip Mandelstam: Selected Poems*, translated by Clarence Brown and W. S. Merwin, copyright © 1973 by Clarence Brown and W. S. Merwin, are reprinted by permission of Atheneum Publishers and Oxford University Press.

1. See "On a Generation that Squandered Its Poets" above, n.3.
2. Osip Mandelstam, *Kamen'* [*Stone*], *Sobranie sochinenij* [Collected works], Inter-Language Literary Associates (Washington, D.C., 1967), 1:17.

The architectural emphasis of Mandelstam's early poems should be broadly interpreted. In general, Mandelstam tended to conceive reality—from everyday occurrences to major cultural developments—in architectural terms, that is, as completed structures. Viktor Zhirmunskij was the first to draw attention to this salient characteristic of Mandelstam's poetry in a 1916 article entitled "Those Who Have Overcome Symbolism." Observing that Mandelstam finds inspiration in "the images . . . of life in the cultural and artistic creations of the past ages," Zhirmunskij examines a series of such "synthetic images" in Mandelstam's poetry: aging Venice, the musical élan of German romanticism, the Kremlin cathedrals, Homer.[3]

Making his debut in the 1910s when stylization reigned supreme —and stylization is always unhistorical—Mandelstam was struggling toward a historical grasp of cultures and styles.

The personality of the poet is not the focal point of the early Mandelstam's poetic world. Later, in *The Noise of Time* Mandelstam wrote: "My desire is to speak not about myself, but to track down the age, the noise, and the germination of time. My memory is inimical to all that is personal."[4] Yet, while constructing in *Stone* a world of objectified cultural phenomena Mandelstam did not doubt that in fact he was creating *lyric* poetry.

An epic work not only unfolds in time, but also constructs an objective space, apprehended by the reader, within which objects are located and events occur. A lyric event is quite a different matter. Whether the poem deals with personal emotions or with the outside world, it is the poet's consciousness, his inner experience that provides here the encompassing framework.[5] Within the lyric space concepts circulate freely, remote semantic categories crisscross as the abstract encounters the concrete, as subjectivity mingles with actuality, the literal meaning with the symbolic. This is clearly the case with the poems of *Stone* where inner experience is conveyed in mediated fashion and the personal is rarely mentioned.

To the young Mandelstam "overcoming of Symbolism" meant

3. See Zhirmunskij, *Voprosy teorii literatury* [Problems of literary theory] (Leningrad, 1928), pp. 328–30. —L.G.

4. *Shum vremeni* [The noise of time], Mandelstam's richly evocative autobiography, has been brilliantly rendered into English by Clarence Brown. (*The Prose of Osip Mandelstam*, trans. and with a critical essay by Clarence Brown, [Princeton, N. J., 1965], p. 122.)

5. There are, however, remarkable instances where a lyric poet constructs space along lines akin to prose. Many of Akhmatova's early poems are cases in point. —L.G.

a repudiation not merely of "other-worldliness," but also of flimsy subjectivism. Hence the author hidden behind the world both historical and concrete, hence the structural firmness of his poetic universe. Art itself is conceived here as an architectural principle superimposed by the artist upon life's natural disorder.

The chief among the historical and artistic cultures reflected in the early Mandelstam is the synthetic, Greco-Roman culture. Mandelstam perceives it through the prism of the Russian tradition, of eighteenth-century classicism, of Batjushkov, Pushkin, and Russian architecture. "And the architect was no Italian, / but a Russian in Rome."[6] This reference is to Voronikhin, architect of Kazan Cathedral.

It was not propensity for stylization that led Mandelstam to travel down the paths of world culture. It was rather the need to understand these cultures historically and to locate them in the context of Russia's cultural consciousness. This urge may well be traced back to Dostoevsky's notion of *universality* or *all-embracing humanity* as an inherent characteristic of Russian national consciousness. In Mandelstam, however, the problem is transposed to the linguistic plane, the most essential one, he feels, for a poet.

In his 1922 essay, "On the Nature of the Word," Mandelstam writes: "Russian is a Hellenistic language. Thanks to historical circumstances, the vital forces of Hellenic culture, having yielded to Latin influences and, having tarried for a while in childless Byzantium, rushed to the bosom of Russian speech, imparting to it the original secret of the Hellenistic world view, the secret of free incarnation. *That is why Russian became a sounding and speaking flesh.*"[7] The point here is not how well Mandelstam's linguistic notions correspond to scientific fact, but rather the role they play in his understanding of historical cultures and cultural styles.

In *Tristia* as in *Stone* Mandelstam steers clear of the poetic language of early nineteenth-century Russian classicism with its mythological bent and its conventional formulas.[8] His aim is to

6. *Sobranie sochinenij*, 1:38.
7. O. Mandelstam, *O poezii* [On poetry] (Leningrad, 1928), p. 31. —L.G.
8. Nor are the two basic meters of classicism, the ancient hexameter and the neoclassical alexandrine, characteristic of Mandelstam. Where long meters are required he resorts to the five-foot anapest or amfibrach. This is no accident. The "canonical" meters were closely associated with a certain semantic aura. Mandelstam had too keen a sense of style not to realize that the classical prosodic patterns would restrict his freedom, limit his "metaphorical flights" (Zhirmunskij). —L.G.

create a Hellenic poetic "dialect" of his own. Mandelstam's poetic language is synthetic and broad; it ranges from the solemn archaisms to the most ordinary words, from learned allusions to plain colloquialisms. What is at issue here is merely the classical "coloring" of Mandelstam's vocabulary, the impact of some particularly dynamic words, capable of "infecting" the entire context. Mandelstam and his contemporaries learned the use of such words from the poets of the Pushkin era: "I have studied the science of saying goodbye / in bareheaded laments at night."[9]

In a 1924 essay, "The Interlude," Jurij Tynjanov[10] commented: "In so receptive a poetic culture the grafting of a simple foreign word is enough to make 'saying goodbye,' 'bareheaded,' and 'waiting' as Latin-sounding as the 'vigils' [*vigilij*] and to assimilate 'sciences' and 'a pair of pants' to 'chebureki' [the latter observation is a reference to the poem "Feodosija"].[11]

For Mandelstam Hellenism is not only a source that fed Russian culture. In his poetic system of the 1910s and 1920s it is also the fountainhead of beauty. During those two decades Mandelstam, it seems, could not tear himself away from the beautiful.

Classicist aesthetics of the eighteenth and the nineteenth centuries frequently equated the beautiful with the artistic. At times, however, the former was interpreted more narrowly and distinguished from the merely characteristic or expressive in art. Since there is no room here for an extended discussion of the nature of the beautiful, this must remain a moot point. Suffice it to say that the experience of beauty is, indubitably, a distinctive psychological and aesthetic fact. The artistic systems of various ages invariably lay claim to this marvelous quality. Both classicism in all its variants and romanticism, in quite a different way, were such systems, even though the latter also provided a rationale for an aesthetic of the ugly.

9. The first two lines of the poem "Tristia" (1918), which gave its name to the 1922 collection. Quoted from Clarence Brown, *Mandelstam* (Cambridge University Press, 1973), p. 271. All Clarence Brown's translations are reprinted here *with* permission of the publisher.

10. Tynjanov, *Arkhaisty i novatory* [Archaists and innovators] (Leningrad, 1929), p. 573. —L.G.

11. Specifically to the passage from this 1920 poem that in a recent English rendition reads: "Let's go where they've a collection of sciences / and the art of making *shashlyk* and *chebureki*. / Where the sign shows a pair of pants / to tell us what a man is" (Osip Mandelstam, *Selected Poems*, trans. Clarence Brown and William Merwin [New York, 1974], p. 26.) *Chebureki* means roughly "meat pies" in Turkish. *Shashlyk* is shishkebab.

Symbolist aesthetics was heavily indebted to the romantic tradition, and more specifically, to the romantic concept of the beautiful. The futurists tried to refute the very principle of beauty in art, though, in actual fact the beautiful is present in the works of both Khlebnikov and Majakovskij. Among the other poets who followed in the wake of the symbolists, there was no agreement on this issue. Each in his own way sought to discover the source of beauty and of the poetic. The Roman–Italian motifs of *Stone*, the Hellenism of *Tristia* are Mandelstam's appeal to the sphere of the beautiful, consecrated by tradition, to be exact, by the Russian poetic tradition. No wonder Mandelstam loved Batjushkov so much. In Batjushkov's poetry he found the continuity of beautiful formulas rooted in tradition but transformed by a great poet's genius.

To Mandelstam of the 1910s beauty bequeathed by classical antiquity leaves its imprint on every mode of experience, be it the lofty civic-mindedness ("Let us celebrate, brothers, the twilight of freedom"), or everyday life. Thus, the tennis player plays against the girl "like Attica's soldier in love with his enemy." Thus, the street urchin staring at the ice-cream peddler's "itinerate icebox" partakes of classical splendor.

> But even the Gods do not know what he'll take—
> A diamond cream? A wafer filled with jam?
> But glittering under the sun's thin ray
> The divine ice will quickly melt.[12]

In his programmatic essay "On the Nature of the Word," Mandelstam contends that the Russian literary tradition knew *heroic* Hellenism and *domestic* Hellenism. He elaborates: "Hellenism —that is a cooking pot, an oven fork, a milk jug. It is household utensils, dishes, everything that surrounds the body. Hellenism is the conscious encirclement of man with the utensils instead of impersonal objects, the transformation of these objects into the utensils, the humanization of the surrounding world, heating it with the most delicate teleological warmth."[13]

These reflections are closely related to Mandelstam's own poetics as well as to that Russian literary tradition in which Mandelstam, as a zealous reader of *The Iliad* in Gnedich's translation,

12. *Sobranie sochinenij*, 1:39.
13. Ibid., 2:295.

was well versed. In the period of 1810–30 Gnedich elaborated what has been called the Russian "Homeric style."[14] This style departs from the French neoclassical concept of antiquity, combining solemn archaisms with vernacular expressions, workaday concreteness, and at times, elements of folklore. The Russian version of *The Iliad* is a good example of what Mandelstam meant by the domestic Hellenistic tradition. Among Mandelstam's more recent models were the translations of ancient authors done by Vjacheslav Ivanov.[15]

In her reminiscences about Mandelstam, Marina Tsvetaeva calls him a "Petersburgite and a Crimean."[16] Mandelstam passionately loved the Crimea and the sea. The Crimea became for him a *sui generis* native variant of antiquity. Crimean motifs permeate the Hellenism of *Tristia* and lend the cycle a certain intimacy. "In rock-strewn Taurida Hellenic science lives," writes Mandelstam.

> And in the white room silence stands like
> a spinning wheel,
> It smells of vinegar, paint, and new wine
> from the cellar.
> Do you remember, in the Greek house, the
> wife everyone loved?
> Not Helen. The other one—how long she
> could work at embroidering?[17]

Thus Mandelstam's "household-utensil" concept of Hellenism is brought forth and the boundaries between the Crimean and classical motifs obliterated.

In Mandelstam flocks of sheep are emblematic of the Crimea.

14. See A. Kukulevich, "N. I. Gnedich's Russian Idyll 'Fishermen,'" *Uchenye zapiski LGU* [Scholarly transactions of Leningrad State University], no. 3 (1939). On Gnedich as a Russian translator of Homer see also I. Medvedeva's introductory essay in *N. I. Gnedich: Poems* (Leningrad, 1956), and A. Egunov, *Homer in Russian Translations of the 18th–19th Centuries* (Moscow–Leningrad, 1964). —L.G.

15. The Polish scholar Ryszard Przybylski discusses classical motifs in Mandelstam's poetry in "Mandelstam's Arcadia" *Slavia Orientalis*, no. 3, (Warsaw, 1964): 243–62. Przybylski searches for Mandelstam's sources in the original works themselves; no attention is paid here to their Russian translations. —L.G.

16. Marina Tsvetaeva (1892–1941), one of this century's most remarkable Russian poets, was much involved with Mandelstam in 1916. The memoir that was to appear in the Soviet Union in 1966 was written in 1931, in France. —Ed. See "The Story of One Dedication," *Literaturnaja Armenija*, (1966): 59. —L.G.

17. Brown, *Mandelstam*, p. 265.

A system of images that keeps recurring in his verse of the 1910s includes flocks, shepherds, dogs, wool, sheeps' warmth. This cluster, grounded in a domestic locale, can be propelled into a Roman theme of a broad historical scope:

> The old ewes, the black Chaldeans,
> The spawn of night, cowled in darkness,
> Go off grumbling to the hills
> Like plebs annoyed at Rome.[18]

In *Tristia* Mandelstam uses Hellenism as a mode of the beautiful to talk of the lyric poet's enduring subjects—the creative process ("I have forgotten the word I wanted to say"), the passage of time, death, and love. There are many poems about love in *Tristia*. But for the most part the direct, traditionally lyrical expression of the love theme is absent here. It enters the collection in a covert, to be exact, semicovert fashion.

"Because I Was not Able to Restrain Your Hands" is one of the finest love lyrics in twentieth-century Russian poetry. The poet finds himself a participant in an ancient *agon*; the besieged Troy, the Achaian warriors, and Helen, not named but alluded to, are all "objective correlatives" for a throbbing, pent-up lyricism. But Mandelstam's semantics are so sensitive to lexical coloring that at times one name suffices to bring this lyricism to the fore. Why for instance, "Not Helen. The other?" Why is Penelope not named, but introduced in a roundabout, periphrastic manner? Because the beautiful Helen's name brings to the surface the personal theme, reinforced by "do you remember?" Though never fully articulated, it sends a current of lyrical uneasiness across the poem.

In the collection *Tristia* (1922) the function of the Hellenist style has changed. No longer employed to project the image of a historical culture, it now becomes authorial style, the language that encompasses Mandelstam's poetic universe, an embodiment of the beauty he seeks.

The reviewers of the 1920s contrasted the precision and concreteness of *Stone* with *Tristia*'s associative poetics. The shift from *Stone* to *Tristia* shows how substantial was the evolution Mandelstam had undergone. It is, however, the evolution of a single creative personality whose continuity is evident at all stages. The two collections are held together by a certain struc-

18. Mandelstam, *Selected Poems*, p. 8.

turing thrust that characterizes Mandelstam's perception of the world. Therefore, his associative semantics [*assotsiativnost'*], though dynamic, is not at all diffuse.

The artistic context that determines the meaning of a word may well extend far beyond the limits of a given work. Such a context can be provided by an entire literary movement or an individual poetic system. Blok's poetry, for example, cannot be understood apart from his large cycles, which ultimately merge into a single context, a "trilogy of incarnation [literally "humanization"], to use Blok's own phrase. In Pasternak's early poems, the verses rush along impetuously, breaking out of their boundaries to form a single lyrical torrent. Mandelstam, on the other hand, is a poet of delimited, though interrelated, contexts.

In a much quoted letter to Strakhov [23 April 1876], Tolstoy said that "art is a huge labyrinth of linkages" and that, as a writer, "[I am] guided by a need to gather thoughts that were linked together in order to express myself. Each thought, however, expressed separately loses its meaning and suffers terribly when it is taken out of the linkage to which it belongs." The decisive aesthetic role of the context and intensity of semantic interaction are inherent in all verbal art, not to mention lyric poetry, where interaction is especially dynamic. I keep referring to Mandelstam's associativeness, to poetics of linkages, since these characteristics acquire maximum intensity in his poetic system. There are historical reasons for this. The pupils of the symbolists repudiated their predecessors' "other-worldliness" but held firm to their discovery that in poetry the word has a heightened capacity for evoking unnamed notions, for filling the gaps with associations. This widened range of association is, perhaps, the most vital element of the symbolist legacy.

Mandelstam's taut contexts permit remote meanings to meet, crisscross, or come into conflict with one another. In his poems an epithet often refers to the context rather than to the object with which it is formally, or grammatically, linked. "I have studied the science of saying goodbye / In bare-headed laments at night."

Why are these laments "bare-headed?" The explanation is found in the last three lines of the same eight-line stanza:

When, lifting their load of sorrow for the journey,
Eyes red from weeping have peered into the distance
And the crying of women mingled with the Muses' singing.[19]

19. Brown, *Mandelstam*, p. 271.

These are tears and laments of bare-headed women (that is, women with uncovered heads), seeing their men off to battle.

The last collection of Mandelstam's poetry published in his lifetime (1928) includes *Stone, Tristia,* and a section labeled "1921–1925." The poems of these latter years, although akin in many ways to the *Tristia* collection, for the most part lack the stylistic coloring suggestive of classical antiquity. Hence, the principle that underlies the Mandelstam imagery emerges even more clearly. The section opens with the 1921 poem, "Concert at the Railway Station" (later in *The Noise of Time*[20] Mandelstam transferred the salient images of this poem from a poetic plane to the plane of everyday life). The architectonics of the poem are complex. The present mingles with childhood recollections of famous symphonic concerts held at the Pavlovsk train station. Within this all-embracing antithesis, three worlds collide: the *world of music* (like Blok, Mandelstam considers music not only an art form, but also a higher symbol both of the historical life of peoples and of the spiritual life of individual man), the *glass world* of the station's concert hall, and the *iron world* of the nearby railroad—a harsh, antimusical world. One should not, however, interpret such images ·allegorically and assign to them a single meaning; to do so would be to violate Mandelstam's poetic system.

> The Aeonian maids, at whose song the station trembles,
> And again the violin-laden air is sundered
> And fused together by the whistles of trains.
>
> Immense park. The station in a glass sphere.
> A spell cast again on the iron world.
> The train carriage is borne away in state
> to the echoing feast in misty Elysium.[21]

The three worlds are tightly interwoven into a single whole: the railway station with the "Aeonian maids" [muses], the whistles of trains with the violin-laden air. The iron world is drawn into the world of music. The very word *torzhestvenno* [in state] with its classical ambiance and stately sound does much to lend the train carriage a semblance of a musical "Elysium." The station trembles with music ("at the song of the Aeonian maids")—this tradi-

20. See n. 4 above.
21. *Selected Poems,* p. 39.

tional metaphor reappears in the last stanza in a new and complex guise: "And I think, how like a beggar the iron world / shivers, covered with music and lather."[22]

The iron world shivers. It is now bewitched, overcome by music. Therefore, it is covered with music, but also with lather, because the shiver has drawn into the semantic circle the notion of a winded, lathery horse. The unusual combination of music and lather lends a material quality to music and symbolic significance to the lather.

On no account should Mandelstam's associative resonance be confused with the "trans-sense," undifferentiated semantics and kindred phenomena that Mandelstam opposed vigorously. He pitted against the symbolist verbal music the poetically trans-formed meaning of the word, against the signs of the "unknow-able" the image as an expression of the sometimes elusive, but essentially knowable, intellectual connection between phe-nomena.

In the essay "The Morning of Acmeism," written about 1913, Mandelstam protests the "trans-sense" [*zaumnyj*] language of the futurists, arguing that logos, "the conscious sense of the word," is the very cornerstone of poetry: "For us a logical relationship is not some ditty about a siskin, but a choral symphony with organ, so difficult and inspired that the director must exert all his powers to keep the performers under his control."[23] That is how Mandel-stam viewed the semantic instrumentation in verse. A younger contemporary of Andrej Belyj and Khlebnikov, a peer of Tsvetaeva, Mandelstam is fully alive to phonic affinities between words, but he cherishes the auditory image chiefly as a generator of a new meaning.

Many years later Mandelstam returns to the problem of poetic logos in "Talking about Dante." In this essay he not only talks about the Italian poet, but also discusses at length both poetry in general and his own poetics in particular. "When, for example, we pronounce the word 'sun,' we do not expel a ready-made meaning—this would be a form of semantic abortion—but rather experience a *sui generis* cycle. Every word is a bundle from which meaning radiates in different directions, rather than converging

---

22. Ibid. I have substituted "lather" for "froth" of the Brown–Merwin ver-sion.
23. See Brown, *Mandelstam*, pp. 145–46.

on one official point. When we say 'sun,' we embark upon an enormous journey, one to which we have become so accustomed that we 'sleepwalk.' What distinguishes poetry from automatic speech is that it rouses us and shakes us awake in the middle of a word."[24]

In his memoirs Vsevolod Rozhdestvenskij recalls Mandelstam's early pronouncement: "Ideas should blaze up now here, now there like little marsh lights. They only appear to be disconnected. Everything is subject to reason, to sound rules of logic, yet they are buried deep down and are not readily accessible."[25]

Although the reader does not actually reconstruct the omitted semantic links, he nonetheless is aware of this "difficult and inspired" inner logic. With few exceptions, Mandelstam's poems can be explained; their author is not a poet who strings together "blissful and senseless" words. One should not misconstrue this formula as Mandelstam's poetic creed; it occurs in "We Shall Gather Again in Petersburg" (1920) and refers to the words of love. Many Mandelstam poems are effective because of their euphony or their lexical coloring. For him, however, this is always an auxiliary, secondary factor. It has been assumed that the poem "I Have Forgotten the Word I Wanted to Say" lacked a definable subject. Actually it has a theme—notably, creativity, the fear of muteness that haunts the poet. The young Mandelstam wrote about the delights of silence, beseeching the word to return to music. The mature Mandelstam knows that thought embodied in words is a necessity, that it is the poet's highest obligation. "More than anything else," Akhmatova recalls, "he feared his own muteness, calling it asphyxia. When it gripped him, he rushed about in terror":[26]

> I have forgotten the word I wanted to say.
> A blind Swallow returns to the palace of shadows
> on clipped wings to flicker among the Transparent
>   Ones.
> In oblivion they are singing the night song.

---

24. "Talking about Dante (1933)," trans. Clarence Brown and Robert Hughes, *Delos*, no. 6, p. 75.

25. Rozhdestvenskij, *Pages from Life*. Excerpts from *Literary Memoirs* (Moscow–Leningrad, 1965), pp. 129–30. —L.G.

26. Anna Akhmatova once let me read the manuscript of her memoirs about Mandelstam. —L.G. The following excerpts are taken from Mandelstam, *Selected Poems*, pp. 28. —Ed.

The blind swallow with clipped wings stands for the unspoken word. It returns to the kingdom of the dead, to the palace of shadows where everything is incorporeal and thus transparent, mute, and arid:

> No sounds from the birds. No flowers on the
>   immortelles.
> The horses of night have transparent manes.
> A little boat drifts on the dry river.
> Among the crickets the word fades into oblivion.

Unembodied, the poetic word loses its bearings. Tormented, like the poet himself, it fights for life:

> And it rises slowly, like a pavilion or a temple,
> performs the madness of Antigone,
> or falls at one's feet, a dead swallow,
> with Stygian tenderness and a green branch.

The word grows, bearing a green branch like the dove released from Noah's ark. Further on there is a fear of the opening void, and the muses (Aeonian maids) weep over the poet who has lapsed into silence.

> But I have forgotten what I wanted to say
> and a bodiless thought returns to the palace
>   of shadows.

Another poem also dated 1920 deals, on the other hand, with the realization of a poetic vision. The same Hellenic imagery is used simultaneously with the themes of poetry and love, death and creative immortality, and thus of time.

> Take from my palms, to soothe your heart,
> a little honey, a little sun,
> in obedience to Persephone's bees.

> You can't untie a boat that was never moored,
> nor hear a shadow in its furs,
> nor move through thick life without fear.

> For us, all that's left is kisses
> tattered as the little bees
> that die when they leave the hive.

> Deep in the transparent night they're still humming,
> at home in the dark wood on the mountain,

in the mint and lungwort and the past.

But lay to your heart my rough gift,
this unlovely dry necklace of dead bees
that once made a sun out of honey.[27]

The poem is constructed around two fundamental—and inter-related—symbols: bees and kisses. Kisses are the symbol of love; bees traditionally have been associated with poetry. The poets of classical antiquity (Horace, in particular) compared themselves to bees. Mandelstam had employed the images of the bee as poet and honey as poetry in one of his early poems, "On a Rocky Spur of Peoria." In "Take from My Palms" the image of the bee is more polysemous. Bees are an attribute of Persephone, queen of the underground kingdom of the dead, and goddess of fertil-ity and germination. Persephone is a symbol of the eternal cycle of death and rebirth in nature, of sprouting grain that has been dropped into the earth's womb. In the second tercet Mandelstam speaks of the subterranean, shadowy kingdom of Persephone, the ruler of the bees, and of the fear this kingdom inspires in mortals. In the third tercet kisses appear and immediately are identified with bees through the medium of Mandelstam's favorite device— the transfer of an attribute from one object to another. The kisses are "tattered [furry] as the little bees." These are the bees of poetry and love, and at the same time of the eternal cycle of death and renewal in nature. It is thus that they feed on the past as well as on lungwort. The bees, the kisses, and the feelings of the poet die. But the honey of creation and love is immortal, like the sun.

To understand this poem one need not have an extensive knowl-edge of mythology, but simply a general idea of the Persephone myth (much less than a reading of Pushkin's early poems and of other Russian poets of the period frequently requires). But one also needs to grasp the basic principle of Mandelstam semantics.

Poetry is a special mode of artistic cognition, of knowing things in their uniqueness, in their aspect at once generalized and in-dividual, thus inaccessible to scientific logical cognition. This uniqueness or individuality of the percept is more essential to the modern lyric poet than the sense of the author's or the hero's individuality. That is why poetic word is always a word trans-formed by the context, and qualitatively different from its prose equivalent.

27. Ibid., p. 30.

In "Talking about Dante," Mandelstam speaks at length about the poetic transformation of the world "with the aid of instruments commonly labeled images." Mandelstam expresses himself metaphorically: this is an organic trait of his thinking. In 1933 Mandelstam came to Leningrad. Several people, among them myself, gathered at Anna Akhmatov's to listen to him read his just completed "Talking about Dante." Mandelstam read the essay, read his poems, and talked copiously about poetry and about painting. We were struck by the remarkable affinities between the essay, the poems, and the table talk. Here was a single semantic system, a single stream of similes and juxtapositions. The image-bearing matrix from which Mandelstam's poems emerged became strangely tangible.

The same semantic principles are operative in Mandelstam's prose, including his essays. Paradoxical though it may seem, Mandelstam's prose is often more metaphorical than his poetry. This is true, at any rate, of *The Egyptian Stamp.* A metaphor brings together notions so as to form a completely new and indivisible semantic whole. This is not always the case with Mandelstam's "linkages." What matters most here are changes in meaning occasioned by the words' presence in the total context of the work where they can interact at a distance, often without a syntactic contiguity.

Within this overall pattern pivotal or key words acquire special impact. Mandelstam's insight into the nature of these words owes a great deal to Annenskij's poetry with its psychological symbolism. Mandelstam accepts the notion of life refracted through poetic symbols, but he cannot accept the abstractness of "professional symbolism." In the essay "On the Nature of the Word," (1922) Mandelstam writes:

> Images are disemboweled like stuffed animals and packed with foreign content. . . . That's what happens with professional symbolism. The result is a terrible quadrille of "correspondences" nodding to one another. Eternal winking. . . . Rose motions to girl, girl to rose. No one wants to be himself. . . . The Russian symbolists . . . sealed every word and every image, having earmarked them in advance for liturgical use alone. Something extremely awkward resulted; one could neither move, stand up, nor sit down. . . . All the utensils had risen in rebellion, the broom requested a day off, the pot no longer wanted to cook, but demanded instead absolute significance

(as if cooking were not an absolute significance).[28]

In an early essay on Villon, Mandelstam says approvingly that medieval allegories are "not disembodied." The same idea is also found in the essay "Remarks on Chénier:" "Very broad allegories, including such concepts as 'Liberty, Equality, and Fraternity,' are not at all incorporeal. For a poet and his epoch they are almost living persons, interlocutors. He discerns their features, feels their warm breath."[29] In an allegory or a simile Mandelstam wanted to preserve the sensual warmth of objects.

Mandelstam's key words are inherently symbolic: they were not drawn, however, from any symbolist stockpile. His symbols are original, the system his own. It is not surprising that his system took shape in the 1910s, when poets nurtured by symbolism were repudiating its philosophy. In the 1924 essay "Thrust" Mandelstam calls symbolism "generic [rodovoja] poetry," contending that after its collapse "the kingdom . . . of the poetic individual came into being," a kingdom in which "every individual stood separately, with his head bared."[30]

In *Tristia* and in the poems written during the first half of the 1920s emphasis on the objective and the narrative tenor of *Stone* recedes; to a large degree, the poet's experience is now an inner one. It is the experience of a man who loves life in all its beauty and significance, but finds it an inordinate burden because its harsh laws bear down on him and because he carries within himself elements of weakness and inadequacy that sap his creative powers and that creativity alone might be able to overcome.

This is also true of the later period. In Mandelstam's poems written in the 1930s there is fear, confusion, and despair, and at the same time an amazing, indestructible love of life. Tragedy coexists here with an ever-increasing delight in the phenomena of existence. The poet is in love with history, art, and life. Such is the cycle "Armenia" (1930), which marks the beginning of Mandelstam's final creative period.

> Oh, Erivan, Erivan! Did a bird draw you,
> or, like a child, a lion paint you out of a
> colored pencilcase?[31]

---

28. Mandelstam, *Sobranie sochinenij*, 2:296–97.
29. "Zametki o Shenie," ibid., p. 340.
30. Ibid., p. 272.
31. *Sobranie sochinenij*, 1:138.

The bird and lion are heraldic animals protrayed as a rule color-
fully and archetypally. The lion suggests beauty and strength,
but here the lion also has a childlike quality—a marvelous school-
boy with a pencilcase in its paw.

"Batjushkov" (1932) is a poem about the triumph of poetry.

> He brought us, tongue-tied,
> Our anguish, and our wealth,
> the noise of poetry-making, the bell of
> brotherhood
> and the soft downpour of tears.[32]

"Impressionism" is about our response to painting. Sensual
concreteness of perception approaches here a visual illusion.

> But the shadow, the shadow's getting ever
> more violet—
> A bow or a whip, it goes out like a match
> You may say: in the kitchen
> The cooks are cooking fat pigeons.[33]

Mandelstam's poetry always has its origin at the point where
fear of life and love of life meet. And so it is until the very end.
In one of the last Voronezh poems,[34] Mandelstam with unprecedented directness writes about his desire to possess the earth's
vital force, "to hear the axis of the earth."

> I do not draw or sing
> or ply the dark-varied bow.
> I simply drink life in and love to envy
> The strength and cunning of the wasps!
>
> Oh if only once the sting of the air and
> the heat
> of summer could make me hear
> beyond sleep and death
> the earth's axis, the earth's axis.[35]

---

32. Ibid., p. 174.
33. Ibid., p. 172.
34. In 1934 Mandelstam was arrested and he and his wife were sentenced
to three years of exile. Owing to the intervention of influential friends, the
Mandelstams were allowed to choose residence in a provincial town in European
Russia. They selected Voronezh.
35. *Selected Poems*, p. 93.

If in *Stone* problems of the world's cultures and of poetic styles
are predominant, in *Tristia* and the poems "1921–1925" adjoin-
ing it "eternal themes" of life and death, creation and love are
paramount. Here the love theme is partially concealed by imagery,
now classical, now old-Russian. The poet has moved into a different dimension; in *Tristia* structural ties appear to lose their external objective and narrative outlines, becoming instead an inner
logic of assocaitions.

The cluster of symbols that originally embodied Mandelstam's
concept of man, of his strengths and weaknesses, gave rise to a
number of secondary images. In 1915 he announced a change in
his materials. He wrote:

> Fire destroys
> My *dry* life
> and I sing now
> not stones, but *tree*.[36]

But at that time he was still speaking about "the wooden paradise
where things are so light." Eventually the theme of dryness and
the correlative one of wood becomes increasingly important to
Mandelstam. Dryness acquires the connotation of sapped vitality,
of inadequacy. In the poem "Because I Was not Able to Restrain
Your Hands" man is imprisoned in a wooden world peopled by
timbers, saws, wood, an ax, resin-oozing walls, the wooden ribs of
a city, a wooden rain of arrows like a grove of nut trees, and all
this is a retribution for man's powerlessness, for dryness.

> Because I was not able to restrain your hands,
> Because I betrayed your salty, tender lips,
> I must wait for dawn in this dense acropolis.
> How I despise these ancient reeking timbers.[37]

Another key word here is *blood*. Blood is a vital force: "But
blood has rushed to the stairs and started climbing . . ." Yet blood
too is threatened by dryness: "Nothing quiets the blood's dry
fever." The extraordinary coupling of dryness with blood is thus
justified.

The meaning of Mandelstam's images is determined by the context. Sometimes, however, their meaning is quite stable and is

36. *Sobranie sochinenij*, 1:45.
37. Brown, *Mandelstam*, p. 246.

transmitted from one poem to another. Dryness is failure—an "exchanged blood." This is fully explained by another poem of 1920 in which the love theme appears without any classical coloring:

> I want to serve you
> equally with others,
> to mumble fortunes
> with lips dry from jealousy.
> The word does not slake
> my parched mouth,
> and without you the dense air
> is empty again for me.
> I do not call you
> either joy or love,
> my blood has been exchanged
> for another, savage blood.[38]

In two poems of 1922, "No Way of Knowing When This Song Began," and "I Climbed into the Tousled Hayloft," both variations on the same theme, we are no longer confronted by the dryness of wood, but rather by the stifling dryness of hay and the hayloft. Hence, a whole series of secondary images *smothering hayrick, rustling, sack of caraway seeds, dry grass, hay-dust, matted scurf,* and finally *squabble.* Significantly, the image of blood is present here also. The poet must free it from dryness: "So that the pink link of blood / and the one-armed ringing of the grass may pronounce / their last goodbyes." As one can see, these poems share a single semantic key. Each of them is a whole; at the same time they are linked by the symbolism that runs through Mandelstam's poetry.

Critics have noted the presence of recurrent images in Mandelstam's poetry such as *salt* and *star.* Such images, however, occur not by themselves but in specific contexts. In "Talking about Dante," salt and blood are tied in one semantic "bundle:" "This is a song about the composition of human blood, which contains oceanic salt. The origin of the journey lies in the system of blood vessels. Blood is planetary, solar, salty." If blood is always perceived as a vital force, the image of salt in Mandelstam's poetry acquires various meanings. Sometimes salt means hurt, sometimes it too is a vital force—the salt of the earth.

38. Ibid., pp. 249–50.

In the poems of the 1920s, as in *Stone,* stars inspire in the poet feelings of distrust, hostility, and fear. As in the earlier verse, they represent the inscrutable and overwhelmingly vast universe from which one must seek protection in domesticity, in utensils, in the warmth of the earth: "There are seven stars in the Great Bear's dipper, / five good senses on the earth."[39]

In the 1925 poem "I'll Run Wild in the Dark Streets Gypsy Camp" the image of "prickly starry untruth" arises. Why are the stars "prickly?" Because they are cold, indifferent to man. Of course, the star's form, its slender rays, and sharp facets are also significant. Because of their sharp planes, stars resemble salt crystals. Thus salt, associated with stars through form, glitter, and milky dispersion, becomes a hostile force. And here something else comes into play—the corrosive power of salt.

> I was washing outside in the darkness,
> the sky burning with rough stars,
> and the starlight, salt on an ax-blade.
> The cold overflows the barrel.
>
> The gate's locked,
> The land's grim—as its conscience—
> I don't think there is a finer warp
> than the truth of a fresh canvas.
>
> Star, like salt, is melting the barrel
> Icy water is turning blacker,
> Death's growing purer, misfortune saltier
> The earth more truthful and dreadful.[40]

Rough stars, salt, an ax, icy water, the stern earth, unbleached canvas are all merciless to man, demanding from him an ultimate sobriety and truth and requiring him to look death and salty misfortune in the face.

The following poem also dates from the first half of the 1920s:

> To some winter is nut-stains and blue-eyed punch
> to some, wine fragrant with cinnamon, and to some
> it's a salt of commands from the cruel stars
> to carry into a smoky hut.

39. Ibid., p. 278.
40. *Selected Poems,* p. 40.

> The warm droppings of a few hens
> and a tepid muddle of sheep.
> For life, for life and care, I'll give up
>   everything
> A kitchen match could keep me
>   warm.[41]

Here Mandelstam's key symbols combine with a terribly direct, unvarnished conversation about the agonizing desire to live, to find warmth. And "A salt of command from cruel stars" is a new variant on the 1912 theme:

> And
>   in the sky gold is dancing
> And bids me to sing.[42]

The cold abstractness, the "cruelty" of vast spaces is juxtaposed with the warmth of sheep, chicken manure, smoke, wool, utensils; all these help sustain life, however frail.

> Look, all I have with me is a clay pot
> To smoothe out fur and turn straw in silence.[43]

In the final stanzas, cruel stars once again are coupled with the acidity of salt, with the bitter taste of smoke and wormwood.

Since persistently recurring images wander through Mandelstam's poems, they may be said to explain one another. But sometimes the key to the poem's interpretation is found outside the confines of Mandelstam's poetry. Thus, on occasions, the meaning of an entire poem or of individual images can be fully grasped only by consulting the memoirs of a contemporary.

In her reminiscences about Mandelstam,[44] Marina Tsvetaeva recalls that three of his 1916 poems were addressed to her, though there were no formal dedications. In 1916 Tsvetaeva in her own words, "made Mandelstam a present of Moscow," that is, showed him the city. It was her "tiger fur coat," we learn, that got intertwined with the Russo–Italian motif of Kremlin cathedrals:

> And Moscow's five-domed cathedrals
> With their Italian and Russian souls

41. Ibid., p. 40.
42. *Sobranie sochinenij*, 1:16.
43. *Selected Poems*, p. 40.
44. See n. 16 above.

> Remind me of Aurora, Goddess of dawn
> but with a Russian name, and in a fur coat.[45]

The following poem in the cycle is "On a Sledge, Overlaid with Straw." In this multilevel poem Tsarevich Dmitrij, murdered in Uglich, blends with the False Dmitrij, who, in turn, merges with the author and assumes independent existence: "I am conveyed about the streets bare-headed," but later "They are bringing the Tsarevich, the body's numb with terror."[46]

Let us imagine that this poem is preceded by a dedication to Marina Tsvetaeva: immediately it ceases to be enigmatic. The name Marina, bringing to mind Pushkin's *Boris Godunov*, is the key to the latent love theme in the poem. She is Marina, and he, therefore, is Dmitrij; at the same time he is the poet who is writing about Dmitrij and Marina.[47]

At times the poem's plot overlaps with history. For example, the line "And in Uglich the children play at knucklebones" alludes to an actual historical fact. The boyars, sent to Uglich by Godunov, declared that the Tsarevich was not murdered, but had accidentally stabbed himself with a knife while playing *svajka* (a game similar to knucklebones) with other children. The Pretender's ties with Rome and the Pope's futile attempt to use him as a means of introducing Catholicism into Russia are also historical facts. At times the poet moves away from history. The Pretender was not bound and carried around the city. He was murdered near the palace, and later his body was burned. This, perhaps, accounts for the line "And now the amber straw was set on fire." The False Dmitrij was red-haired. The chain of associations thus grows longer. Missing, however, is the final link, the name Marina Tsvetaeva, which would elucidate the poem once and for all. To find the link we must have recourse to material outside the text.

Recounting the story of the third poem dedicated to her, "No Believers in the Resurrection," Tsvetaeva observes: "I do not know whether it is necessary to footnote the everyday material used in poems. Poems grind up life and then discard it." This is true, but not entirely true. One should not confuse the origin

---

45. *Sobranie sochinenij*, 1:58.
46. Brown, *Mandelstam*, p. 222.
·47. In her poems Tsvetaeva sometimes identified herself with Marina Mniszek. [The Polish princess who is wooed by the Pretender. —*Ed.*] See, for example, the 1921 poem "Marina." —*L.G.*

of lyric material with its artistic function. A "real-life" source sometimes is incorporated into a poem's artistic structure in the form of its principal theme or semantic key or serves as a basis for associations essential to a total response. At times, however, the realia that set the poet's thought in motion prove to be aesthetically neutral. They have indeed been milled by the verses and then discarded.

Mandelstam was clearly the kind of poet who reacted strongly to the most diverse stimuli, including the mundane, the everyday. It is this concreteness of impulse, whenever the latter is unknown to the reader, that sometimes renders a poem unintelligible.

> The clock-cricket singing,
> that's the fever rustling,
> the dry stove hissing
> that's the fire in red silk.[48]

Speaking about this poem Akhmatova observed: "This is about how we heated the stove together. I have a fever and I take my temperature."

Most likely Mandelstam really "was washing outside in the darkness" (the opening line of a poem written in Tbilisi in 1921), or climbed the ladder ("I climbed into the tousled hayloft"). A locked gate, a barrel with icy water, the tousled hay, all these are real objects, transformed into elements of a poetic conversation about truth, death, and misfortune or about the universe and creativity. In instances such as these information about the actual sources of a poetic experience is pertinent only to the psychology of creation, remaining beyond the threshold of the work's aesthetic structure.

A similar fate befalls sometimes even the aesthetically effective realia that are essential to the interpretation of a given context. More exactly, their meaning is revealed elsewhere, notably in Mandelstam's prose or essays. One of his favorite images is the swallow. Its significance differs from one context to another. Swallows are bonded together into legions in one place and serve as a symbol of poetic language in another.[49] The swallow is an image

---

48. *Selected Poems*, p. 21.
49. Reference is respectively to the famous 1917 poem "The Twilight of Freedom," which contains the lines "We have bonded the swallows together / into legions for battle," and the already mentioned 1920 poem, "I Have Forgotten the Word I wanted to Say" (see nn. 26, 27).

found in ancient Greek folksongs. But this is not all. The meaning of bird imagery is elucidated in "Talking about Dante:"
"The quill is a tiny piece of bird flesh. Certainly Dante, who
never forgets the origin of things, keeps this in mind. The technique of writing with all its twists and flourishes develops into a
figured flight of birds in flock. . . . Old Italian grammar, not unlike
our Russian grammar, is the same agitated flock of birds."[50] Thus,
for Mandelstam bird symbolism is associated with writing, with
language (in *The Egyptian Stamp* there is an expression, "the
swallow's flourish"). Later, while in Voronezh, Mandelstam
wrote a radio essay on Goethe. In it the "technique of writing,"
to be exact, the handwriting of a great poet, is associated with the
swallow. Goethe's "handwriting is characterized at once by the
wildest swings and by harmony. His letters resemble fishermen's
hooks that slant diagonally as though a whole flock of swallows
were skimming smoothly and powerfully slantwise across the
page." The swallow's flight is the poet's handwriting; it is letters
and letters are a word. The chain of associations extend thus to
blind swallow, symbol of the unembodied poetic word. But the
links of these chains are buried in later essays.

For Mandelstam this was a natural process. So absorbed was he
in the single thrust of his poetic thought which he realized in
his verse, artistic prose, essays, and conversation, moving freely
from genre to genre, that he himself did not fully appreciate its
range.

The problem of the reader, the social existence of the work of art,
was a matter of major concern to Mandelstam. He advocated intellectuality in poetry and inner logic in poetic thought. In "Talking about Dante" he labeled the expectation that the reader would
grasp the cultural, historical, political, and technical notions introduced by the poet the poem's "reference keyboard." We have
seen, nonetheless, that he himself more than once pressed a key
that could not evoke the requisite response even in an experienced
reader. This was so not because his verse defied sense or lacked
a subject, but because in those instances the key to his poetic
logic was misplaced.

Mandelstam had great faith in the power of poetic linkages, so
characteristic of this system, in the dynamics of the context. (Whenever this faith was not justified, failure would ensue.) Mandelstam

---

50. *Sobranie sochinenij,* 2:446–47.

was confident that even where crucial poetic associations were not available to the reader, because he was not familiar with some aspect of the realia, the context would compensate by suggesting some other kindred associations. This held true for individual poetic images and occasionally also for poems constructed entirely around plots concealed from the reader.

An example of such a poem is "On the Stage of Ghosts a Pale Gleaming." In the last stanza we are confronted by Petrograd at night in the year 1920. "Smoke hangs in the ragged sheepskins. The street's black with drifted snow," while at the theater magnificent opera performances are taking place. We find the same theme in "We Shall Gather Again in Petersburg." The first two stanzas are a recollection of old Petersburg, with its grand theater exits, an illusory image of the nineteenth-century opera stage. The third stanza seems to stand at the juncture of these two planes. The name of Eurydice and the legend of Orpheus, who found Eurydice in the kingdom of shadows and lost her again thanks to a blunder, introduces a personal, lyric theme.[51] The poem's two motifs—love and music—have been brought together.

But how is one to understand the last two lines: "The living swallow fell / On hot snow."?

What is this? A diffuse, irrational motif? No, once again the factual link is missing, and we find it in Mandelstam's prose. In *The Egyptian Stamp* Mandelstam twice talks about the circumstances surrounding the death of the Italian singer, Angiolina Bosio.[52] Bosio sang in St. Petersburg during the years 1856–59; in 1859, at the age of thirty-five, she caught a cold and died of pneumonia. Her death made an extraordinary impression on St. Petersburg society. In the poem "On the Weather" (1865) Nekrasov recalls the event:

> Let us recall Bosio. Arrogant Petropolis
> Went all out for her.

---

51. Gluck's *Orpheus and Eurydice* was Mandelstam's favorite opera. Staged in 1911 by Meyerhold with sets by Golovin it was revived after the Revolution and performed a number of times in 1919 and 1920. —L.G.

52. *The Egyptian Stamp* [*The Prose of Osip Mandelstam*], p. 182. Mandelstam was so interested in the subject that he intended subsequently to return to it. Among the works announced for publication the [Leningrad] journal *Zvezda* [Star] mentions Mandelstam's "Death of Bosio: A Story." (Apparently the story was never written.) —L.G.

> But in vain did you wrap up in sable
> Your nightingale throat,
> Italy's daughter! Southern roses
> Cannot cope with Russian frost.[53]

"The stage of ghosts" of the first stanzas is the stage of the 1850s. Mandelstam's line "There's a rose under the furs," offers a variation on the above. In the next stanza he appears to take notice of Nekrasov: 'Ours is a cold winter, dear Eurydice. / Never mind . . ."[59]

The narrative core of the poem is thus encoded in the same way as the love theme. The reader's perception nevertheless moves along the track laid out, though not visible to him. What he perceives is the collision of two planes, one temporal, Petrograd of the 1920s and St. Petersburg of the nineteenth century, the other national, the Russo–Italian motif, crowned by the image of the singer–swallow lying in the St. Petersburg snows.[55]

In Mandelstam's poetry of 1921–25 Hellenism has been cast aside along with other stylistic conventions. It is a major step toward his works of the 1930s where the poet was to confront reality in a different, new way. A group of poems of 1923 and early 1924 help define this transition. One of the themes in *Tristia*, that of time, of alternating death and rebirth, is transferred from a philosophical domain, from the sphere of "eternal" lyric themes, to a historical one, becoming the theme of the age. This shift occurs in the poems "The Age," "He Who Finds a Horseshoe," "The Slate Ode," and "1 January 1924."

To seek a clear political program in Mandelstam's works of the 1920s would be futile. Mandelstam did accept the October Revolution, though not without hesitation and contradictions that characterized the initial response of many intellectuals formed before the Revolution. The burden of history, however, is heavy:

> Could I ever betray to gossip-mongers
> the great vow to the Fourth Estate
> and oaths solemn enough for tears?[56]

53. Nikolaj Nekrasov, *Polnoe sobranie sochinenij* [Complete works] (Moscow, 1968), 2:211.

54. *Selected Poems*, p. 29.

55. See *The Egyptian Stamp:* "And the Cavalier Guards will flock to the Church of Guarenzhi for the singing of the requiem. The golden vultures will render to pieces the Roman Catholic songstress" *(The Prose of Osip Mandelstam,* p. 154).

56. *Selected Poems*, p. 53.

Dry blood of *Tristia* gives way to blood mixed with lime. The persona now experiences directly the pressure of history. He still very much wants to live. Once again the imagery moves from impoverishment and extinction ("Breath growing weaker by the day"), to bursts of indestructible vitality.

> And in the sick son's blood the deposit
> of lime
> Will melt, and there'll be sudden blessed laughter.[57]

But the age itself seems to be the speaker's double; it too is frightened and hungry for life. At times it becomes difficult to distinguish the age from the lyrical "I" of this cycle. The latter is about the atrophy of the past, in particular, of the nineteenth century and "its survivors, those emigrants shipwrecked and cast by the will of fate onto a new historical continent," to use the words of Mandelstam's essay "The nineteenth century."[58] Mandelstam is speaking of the essence of the nineteenth century, an age of reflection and "relativism" ("my splendid derelict, my age") that continues to live in the consciousness of the old intelligentsia hesitatingly accepting the Revolution. All this emerges clearly from the poetic texts themselves. In addition, we can find theoretical corroboration of such a reading in Mandelstam's essays "The Word and Culture," "The Badger's Burrow," and, especially the 1922 one entitled "The Nineteenth Century."

"On the threshold of the nineteenth century Derzhavin scratched on slate several lines of poetry that may serve as a leitmotif for the entire coming century.

> The river of time in its onrush
> Carries away the affairs of men
> And drowns in the abyss of oblivion
> Peoples, kingdoms, and kings.
> And if anything survives
> In the sounds of the lyre and the trumpet,
> It shall be swallowed by the crater of
> eternity
> And shall not escape the common fate.

The rusty tongue of an aged century serves here to express with power and penetration the latent thought of the century yet to

---

57. Ibid., p. 52.
58. *Sobranie sochinenij*, vol. 2.

come. A moral is drawn, a keynote is sounded. This moral is relativism or relativity, "and if anything survives" . . .[59]

The above passage provides a clue to "The Slate Ode," seemingly one of Mandelstam's most difficult works. What Mandelstam cites is the first and only stanza of Derzhavin's ode "On Mortality," written down on slate several days before the poet's death (the slate is preserved in the Leningrad Public Library). "The Slate Ode" is also about the "river of time." It is, however, about a real river as well that cascades down, carrying an inverted reflection of its green banks.

> Like rubble from icy heights,
> from the backs of green icons,
> the famished water flows, eddying,
> playing like the young of an animal.[60]

Mountain villages envelop the river, and Mandelstam's Caucasian and Crimean motifs again appear:

> Steep goat cities
> The massive layering of flint . . .
> In the water their lesson, time
> wears them fine.[61]

The theme of flint, "a student of running water," represents a new bundle of meanings. It is also, however, Mandelstam's initial theme of stone, the medium of architects and poets.

Derzhavin, one of Mandelstam's favorite poets, is the hidden motivating force of the poem, written in imitation of Derzhavin's eight-line stanza, and celebrating a singularly significant creative act. Slate, the "lead stick" becomes its symbol.

> Terror and Split write with the same little
>   stick of milk.
> Here, taking form, is the first draft
> of the students of running water
> . . . .
> I hear the slate screech
> On the startled
>   crag.[62]

59. Ibid.
60. *Selected Poems*, p. 50.
61. Ibid., p. 49.
62. Ibid.

In the complex semantic instrumentation of "The Slate Ode" *water* is an emblem of time. Water-time erodes *flint*, which resists time, while *slate* is the vehicle of creativity that interprets time.

Unless the reader has read "The Slate Ode" with "The Nineteenth Century" in mind, he will not recognize the Derzhavin theme—that of the dying poet's writing on slate a poem about the river of time. However, the semantic current that emanates from this hidden source runs through all the poem's links. The reader is aware that the poem is about the lofty and the magnificent, about a rough draft written by a genius. In Mandelstam's poem, however, the river of time is, also, a mountain river. Mandelstam does not want his metaphors to be "incorporeal." Most likely, "The Slate Ode" originated at the confluence of two sets of impressions: the sight of a slate in the Public Library with the half-effaced Derzhavin autograph and the roar of a mountain river, rushing down a siliceous bed.

The 1923–24 cycle of poems about the age and time signals the appearance in Mandelstam of new tendencies. The hayloft in the poem "I Climbed into the Tousled Hayloft," the ax and the icy water in the poem, "I Was Washing Outside in the Darkness" are actualities that set the poet's thought in motion. Within the system of these poems, however, such objects have symbolic meaning, not at all "other-worldly," but expressive of the poet's inner experience.

In 1931 Mandelstam wrote a cycle of poems associated with Moscow ("Midnight in Moscow," "I'm Still not Patriarch") in which the themes of the age and of time, sounded in the 1923–24 poems, are again taken up. Yet we find ourselves now in a different world. Objects remain objects here, even if they acquire a new, vastly expanded meaning. The 1931 cycle is an attempt to define the relationship between the author and his era; its language is contemporary and workaday.

This is how Mandelstam now writes about the "great vow" to the revolutionary tradition and about the passage of time. Instead of searching for domesticity in the cold expanses of the age, the poet wanders along the streets and the embankments of Moscow.

> I love the starling streetcars starting off,
> And the asphalt's Astrakhan caviar,
> Covered with straw matting,
> Reminding me of a basket of Asti
> And steel ostrich-feathers

On the scaffolding of the Lenin Housing
Project.[63]

The young Mandelstam maintained that the poet ought to grasp
the tridimensional. *Stone* abounds in objects, but these are objects of a special sort. First and foremost, they are indicators of
cultural structures, of historical styles, be they the exedrae
of a temple or the checkered trousers of a Dickens character, the
lawyer's overcoat or the "sesquipedalian parts" of a musical composition by Bach.[64] In *Tristia* and in those poems of the early
1920s that followed in its wake, Mandelstam's is still a tridimensional world, both accessible to the senses ("five good senses on
the earth") and intelligible. But the predominance of the "Hellenic" stylistic pattern dematerializes this world. For the late Mandelstam history is the immediate present. The conventional styles
had to recede; they were ill equipped to tackle contemporary
life, to deal the the fluid, the incomplete, the as yet unnamed.
By now the very themes of poems emerge from unexpected impressions, thoughts, recollections, from any inner experience.
They bring in tow everyday, prosaic words, signifying the diversity
of contemporary reality and essential to the poet because they
provide direct contact with it.

Mandelstam's late works point toward a new relationship between poetic symbolism and reality.

63. *Sobranie sochinenij*, 1:175.
64. Reference is to several poems in *Stone*, "Hagia Sophia" ("the exedrae
of a temple"), "Dombey and Son," and "Bach."

Index